Judicial Dialogue on Human Rights

International Studies in Human Rights

VOLUME 120

The titles published in this series are listed at *brill.com/ishr*

Judicial Dialogue on Human Rights

The Practice of International Criminal Tribunals

Edited by

Paolo Lobba
Triestino Mariniello

BRILL
NIJHOFF

LEIDEN | BOSTON

Library of Congress Cataloging-in-Publication Data

Names: Lobba, Paolo. | Mariniello, Triestino.
Title: Judicial dialogue on human rights : the practice of international criminal tribunals / edited by Paolo Lobba, Triestino Mariniello.
Description: Leiden ; Boston : Brill, 2017. | Series: International studies in human rights ; volume 120 | Includes bibliographical references and index.
Identifiers: LCCN 2017029167 (print) | LCCN 2017031402 (ebook) | ISBN 9789004313750 (e-book) | ISBN 9789004313743 (hardback : alk. paper)
Subjects: LCSH: International law and human rights. | International criminal courts. | International Criminal Court. | European Court of Human Rights | International Tribunal for the Prosecution of Persons Responsible for Serious Violations of International Humanitarian Law Committed in the Territory of the Former Yugoslavia since 1991. | Human rights. | Judicial opinions.
Classification: LCC KZ1266 (ebook) | LCC KZ1266 .J83 2017 (print) | DDC 345/.02322–dc23
LC record available at https://lccn.loc.gov/2017029167

Typeface for the Latin, Greek, and Cyrillic scripts: "Brill". See and download: brill.com/brill-typeface.

ISSN 0924-4751
ISBN 978-90-04-31374-3 (hardback)
ISBN 978-90-04-31375-0 (e-book)

To Antonio, Maria Elena, Gael, Lavi and Max Robert who were born during the completion of this book and to those who are yet to be born.

Contents

PART 4
Fairness of International Criminal Proceedings: The (Side) Effects of Cross-fertilization

Foreword

As a judge of the European Court of Human Rights and previously a judge in my own jurisdiction in criminal cases, the sheer volume of criminal cases in the Court's docket did not surprise me. Without exaggeration, two thirds of the Court's work is about criminal law *latu sensu*, including criminal proceedings and other proceedings of a punitive nature such as administrative offences proceedings (*Ordnungswidrigkeiten, Verwaltungsstrafrecht*) and disciplinary proceedings. The weekly agenda of judges is invariably full of cases where issues like the fairness of the criminal proceedings, the guarantees of the right to liberty, the scope and breadth of the applicable penal law or the strictness of the prison policy of a Contracting Party to the European Convention on Human Rights are at stake.

It has always been like this. The preponderance of criminal law, criminal procedure and prison law in the Court's case law is even more patent when one goes back in time and recalls the leading cases of the Court's history. This started with its first judgment on the merits, *Lawless v. Ireland*, on the detention without trial of G.R. Lawless from 13th July to 11th December 1957, by virtue of Article 4 of the Offences against the State (Amendment) Act, 1940. Or the groundbreaking *Golder v. the United Kingdom*, on the right of access to justice and legal defence of a prisoner, which was the occasion for the Court to establish the sacrosanct principle that the Convention cannot be interpreted in a vacuum, but must be interpreted in harmony with other international law. Or with the seminal case *Tyrer v. the United Kingdom*, on the punitive practice of "birching" students, in which the Court for the very first time used the *leitmotiv* of "the Convention as a living instrument", which must be interpreted in the light of present-day conditions. Many other examples of criminal law-related cases, which stand out in the Court's history, could be added.

These cases have set out principles of public international law and particularly of human rights law, which cannot be ignored by international criminal tribunals, and this for a couple of reasons that immediately come to mind. Firstly, the now 60 year-old Court's case law has impacted all over the world, even far away from the geographical confines of Europe, both through the remarkable work of the Inter-American Court and Commission on Human Rights and, more recently, of the African Court on Human and Peoples' Rights, and the attentive reading of Constitutional and Supreme Courts of such countries as Brazil, Canada, India, Japan and South Africa. Such worldwide repercussion shows that, in some respects, these are no longer strictly "European" standards, but global standards. Likewise, the Strasbourg Court has been open to valuable contributions from international and domestic jurisdictions for the development of its own case law, of which the contribution of the Inter-American Court's case law on forced disappearances is perhaps the most eloquent. This judicial cross-fertilisation has enriched human rights case law enormously.

Secondly, some of the most significant standards of the European Court's case law have also been consolidated into treaty law, like in the recent Council of Europe conventions on the fight against terrorism, cybercrime or violence against women. Such consolidation reflects the wide State support that the European standards on human rights protection have won over time, including among States that do not belong to the Council of Europe. The proliferation both nationally and internationally of hard and soft law instruments inspired by the Court's case law speaks strongly in favour of a widespread recognition of its force as *res judicata*.

Thirdly, the Strasbourg Court has explicitly dealt on various occasions with situations related to international and transnational crime, which sometimes occurred long ago. Cases of such magnitude as *Kunonov v. Latvia* and *Vasiliauskas v. Lithuania* have given the Court the opportunity to deal with the intricacies of human rights protection in the context of prosecution of alleged crimes of genocide, war crimes and crimes against humanity. Recent international and non-international armed conflicts have also been brought to the attention of the Court, namely in extremely sensitive inter-state cases. In some of these cases the Court was explicitly called to confront the question of the relationship between international humanitarian law and human rights law, which it did.

International courts are not isolated "little empires", as Judges Pellonpää and Bratza put it in their concurring opinion appended to *Al-Adsani v. the United Kingdom*. This is also true for international criminal tribunals. They are not supposed to function as self-sufficient systems that ignore the work previously done by other international institutions, especially those of a judicial or quasi-judicial nature, and even more those specialised in human rights law. International criminal tribunals should not be tempted to elaborate from scratch their own system of principles, substantive criteria and interpretative tools without giving proper consideration to the internationally recognised standards in human rights law, or to use these as mere rhetorical instruments. Otherwise, they would miss the full picture of international law, and perhaps the incentive to make significant progress in the specific area of their competence. Some very concrete examples of this potential progress of international criminal law come to my mind. Regarding victims and witnesses of international crimes, major decisions of the European Court could provide better protection and an accrued procedural intervention in proceedings before international criminal tribunals. Furthermore, remedies for crimes within the remit of international criminal tribunals could eventually be shaped in accordance with the well-established and immensely rich case law of the Inter-American Court of Human Rights on this issue. Regarding convicted offenders, sentencing and enforcement of sentence are also an area where international criminal law could profit from the advancement of human rights law, which requires that resocialisation be the guiding principle for those purposes. Moreover, convicted offenders should know from the outset of the service of the sentence when, how and by what procedure early release may be considered. Cross-fertilisation of jurisprudence in these aspects, as in many others, would certainly benefit defendants, victims and their relatives: in short, the justice delivered by international criminal courts.

In the words of von Liszt, in the famous *Die deterministischen Gegner der Zweckstrafe* of 1893, "However paradoxical it may sound, the Criminal Code is the offender's *magna charta*. It guarantees his right to be punished only in accordance with the requirements set out by the law and only within the limits laid down in the law". Today, von Liszt, who was himself an internationalist too, would agree that human rights law is also a crucial limit to criminal justice, and there can be no correct construction of penal law, no fair criminal procedure, no just sentencing and no human enforcement of punishment without proper consideration of human rights law.

Paulo Pinto de Albuquerque
Judge at the European Court in Strasbourg
Ordinary Professor at the Catholic University in Lisbon
Strasbourg, January 2017

List of Abbreviations

ACHR	American Convention on Human Rights
ASP	Assembly of States Parties to the Statute of the ICC
ECCC	Extraordinary Chambers in the Courts of Cambodia
ECHR	European Convention on Human Rights
ECtHR	European Court of Human Rights
HRC	Human Rights Court
IACtHR	Inter-American Court of Human Rights
ICC	International Criminal Court
ICCPR	International Covenant on Civil and Political Rights
ICJ	International Court of Justice
ICT(s)	International Criminal Tribunal(s)
ICTR	International Criminal Tribunal for Rwanda
ICTY	International Criminal Tribunal for the former Yugoslavia
ILC	International Law Commission
MICT	Mechanism for International Criminal Tribunals
PCIJ	Permanent Court of International Justice
RPE	Rules of Procedure and Evidence of the International Criminal Court
SCSL	Special Court for Sierra Leone
STL	Special Tribunal for Lebanon
UN	United Nations

Contributors

Paulo Sérgio Pinto de Albuquerque
is a Judge of the European Court of Human Rights. His nine-year term of office began on 5 February 2011. A distinguished jurist and legal academic, Judge de Albuquerque is an Ordinary Professor at the Faculty of Law of the Catholic University of Lisbon. He has served as a judge in various civil and criminal courts in Lisbon, an expert with the Council of Europe's GRECO (Group of States against Corruption), an advisor to the Portuguese Ministry of Internal Affairs, and a Member of the Portuguese Ministry of Justice Taskforce for the Penal Reform.

Kerstin Braun
is a lecturer in the School of Law and Justice at the University of Southern Queensland, Australia, where she teaches criminal law and procedure as well as legal research and writing in the Bachelor of Laws and Juris Doctor Programs. Kerstin has guest lectured at the University of Bonn, Germany and the University of Reggio Calabria, Italy. She holds a Doctorate of Philosophy in law from the University of Queensland.

Her research interests lie in the area of criminal law and procedure as well as comparative and international law. A key focus of her research is the treatment of crime victims in different criminal justice systems. She has published widely in leading Australian and international journals on issues relating to human rights law as well as German and Australian criminal law.

Christoph Burchard
holds the chair for German, European and International Criminal Law and Procedure as well as for Comparative Law and Legal Theory at the Goethe University Frankfurt am Main, Germany, where he is also Principal Investigator at the Cluster of Excellence 'The Formation of Normative Orders'. He is, inter alia, in the editorial committee of the Journal of International Criminal Justice and of the (German) Journal for Supreme Court Jurisprudence (HRRS). In his research, he focuses on the foundations of criminal law and justice, be it meted out within, between or beyond the nation state. His latest, soon to be published book is about the "Constitutionalization of Mutual Recognition in the Cooperation in Criminal Matters between the EU Member States". He also headed the Research Network on the "Role of Comparative Law in the Europeanization of Criminal Law and Justice".

Paolo Caroli
obtained his PhD in criminal law at the University of Trento in 2017, with a dissertation on the Italian experience of transitional justice after World War II. He also practises as attorney and works as a journalist. In 2012 he worked as intern in the *International Crimes and Accountability* team of the *European Center for Constitutional and Human Rights* (ECCHR) in Berlin.

Christophe Deprez
holds a Master's degree in law from the University of Liège (2010), an LL.M. in public international law from the University of Amsterdam (2011), and a Ph.D. in international criminal law from the University of Liège (2016). He was from October 2011 to September 2015 a research fellow of the Belgian Fund for Scientific Research (F.R.S.-FNRS), devoting his doctoral thesis to the rights of suspects deprived of their liberty before the International Criminal Court. Christophe is now a postdoctoral researcher and an assistant lecturer at the University of Liège Law School. From January to July 2016, he was also a visiting scholar at Columbia Law School, New York.

Julia Geneuss
is a Senior Researcher and Lecturer in Criminal Law at the University of Hamburg (Germany). She graduated in Freiburg. She holds a Dr. iur. from Humboldt-University Berlin and a LL.M. from NYU School of Law (USA). For her doctoral thesis on the prosecution of international crimes in Germany, in particular under the principle of universal jurisdiction, she was awarded the Humboldt-University Law Faculty's prize for the best dissertation in criminal law as well as a second prize of the Deutscher Studienpreis 2014 awarded by the Körber Foundation for outstanding dissertations. She is a member of the Editorial Committee of OUP's Journal of International Criminal Justice and was a Graduate Editor of NYU's Journal of International Law and Politics. Her teaching and research interests include German and international criminal law. She is the author or editor of a number of books and has published a number of journal articles, book chapters, essays and reviews in German, English and Spanish.

Yael Vias Gvirsman
is a lawyer and academic specialising in International Criminal Law. Yael is the Director and founder of the International Criminal and Humanitarian Law Clinic in Israel, based at the Radzyner Law School, Interdisciplinary Center, Herzliya. She is a member of the Committee on Complementarity at the International Law Association and is completing her Ph.D. on the ICC as a

form of intervention in conflicts and conflict resolution at the Hebrew University of Jerusalem. Having completed her legal education in France and The Netherlands, Yael holds a 'Maitrise' in law and a Masters in International Relations (DESS). She worked with the Defence at the ICTR (2008), ICC (2011 onward) and SCSL (2012) and is a member of the Israeli Bar Association since 2006. Yael worked at the International Law Department of the Israeli Ministry of Foreign Affairs; was a prosecutor with the State Attorney's office; and, as an Eligibility/Legal Officer with the UNHCR office in Tel Aviv. Between 2008–2011, she participated in the DOMAC research, the Effectiveness of International Adjudication research and with the Institute for National Security Studies.

Paolo Lobba
combines advanced academic knowledge of domestic, European and international criminal law with practical experience in the field. After having obtained a double Ph.D. at the University of Bologna and Humboldt University of Berlin, he has worked in both Bologna and Berlin as post-doctoral research fellow while practising as a lawyer. In this capacity he has published a number of peer-reviewed articles in well-renowned law journals such as the *European Journal of International Law, the European Criminal Law Review*, and the *New Journal of European Criminal Law*. Dr. Lobba is currently employed as Legal Officer by the United Nations, serving the Extraordinary Chambers in the Courts of Cambodia, where he has already been working for over two years. His research interests have frequently involved topics concerning the interpretation and application of human rights by international criminal courts. For instance, his studies tackled the issues of reparation for victims of grave violations of human rights, contempt of court before international criminal courts and the jurisprudence of the European Court of Human Rights on the denial of the Holocaust and other international crimes.

Elena Maculan
holds a PhD in 'Comparative and European Legal Studies' by the University of Trento (Italy) and in "Peace and International Security" by the UNED of Madrid (Spain), under a co-tutelage regime. She also holds the Label of "Doctor Europaeus".

She is currently a post-doc research fellow at the Instituto Universitario Gutiérrez Mellado (UNED) in Madrid. At the Institute she is also lecturer in the Doctoral Program and in the Master's Degree in International Security and she is member of an international Research Project directed by Prof. Alicia Gil, about "Victims' influence on dealing with collective violence". She has also been working at the University of Trento (Italy) as a lecturer in International Criminal Law and Promotion and Protection of Human Rights and she currently teaches Transitional Justice there.

Her main research fields are International Criminal Law, Transitional Justice and Comparative Criminal Law, with a special focus on Latin-American systems, on the judicial cross-fertilization dynamics and on transitional experiences and terrorism.

Triestino Mariniello
is a Senior Lecturer in Law at Edge Hill University (UK). He has published a considerable number of peer-reviewed articles and chapters in edited collections on the interpenetration between (international) criminal justice and human rights. His academic writing has appeared in a variety of journals, including the *Journal of International Criminal Justice*, *American Journal of International Law*, *Diritti umani e diritto internazionale*, and *Nordic Journal of International Law*. He is also the editor of the book titled 'The *International Criminal Court in Search of its Purpose and Identity*' (Routledge 2015). On account of the reputation he is progressively building, he has been consulted as an expert in international criminal justice and human rights by governmental and non-governmental organisations, such as the European Commission, Italian Ministry of Defence, Italian Ministry of Justice, Tunisian Ministry of Justice, Montenegrin Ministry of Justice, International Bar Association, International Observatory of Human Rights, and Italian Training School for Judges and Prosecutors. He has also served as a Visiting Professional and Associate Legal Officer at the Pre-Trial Division of the International Criminal Court, working on Situations in Sudan, Democratic Republic of Congo and Republic of Kenya.

Alice Riccardi
is research fellow in International Law at the University Roma Tre of Rome, adjunct professor of International Criminal Law at LUMSA University of Rome and King's College of London Transnational Law Institute fellow. She is the author of the book *Sentencing in International Criminal Law: From Nuremberg to the Hague* (Eleven International Publishing-Giappichelli Editore 2016). She is also a member of the Transnational Listing Project, working on UNSC 1267 sanctions. Previously, she was a research fellow in International Law within the International Disaster Law Project and a visiting scholar at the Max Plank Institute for International and Comparative Criminal Law. She holds a PhD in International Law *cum laude* from the Sant'Anna School of Advanced Studies (Pisa, Italy).

Frauke Sauerwein
was, at the time of writing, working as a research fellow at the Max Planck Institute for Comparative Public Law and International Law in Heidelberg, Germany. She studied law in Heidelberg and Strasbourg. She was a scholarship holder of the "Cusanuswerk". Her PhD project, elaborated under the supervision of Prof. Dr. Armin von Bogdandy, investigates the interactions between the International Criminal Tribunal for the former Yugoslavia and the European Court of Human Rights.

Damien Scalia
is Professor at the Faculty of Law at the Université Libre de Bruxelles (ULB) and invited Professor at the Universities of Lausanne and at the CERAH (Geneva). He was Visiting Scholar at the Columbia Law School (New-York) and the Oxford Institute for Ethics, Law and Armed Conflict (UK).

After completing his PhD in international criminal law (Geneva University and University Paris-Nanterre) and conducting post-doctoral research on sentences pronounced by the international criminal tribunals with the Irish Centre for Human Rights and the Oxford Institute for Ethics, Law and Armed Conflict, Damien Scalia conducted research on international prison law. His current research is about the perception of international criminal justice from the viewpoint of persons accused (acquitted and condemned) by the International Criminal Tribunal for the former-Yugoslavia and by persons tried by the International Criminal Tribunal for Rwanda.

Elizabeth Santalla Vargas
is a Bolivian lawyer and academic specialising in international law, particularly in international criminal law, international humanitarian law and human rights law. She is currently a *Rapporteur* for Oxford University Press database projects on International Criminal Law and the Law of International Organisations, coordinated by Middlesex University and the Manchester Centre of International Law, respectively. She has taught and lectured at various academic programmes at the graduate and post-graduate level. She has been, inter alia, an associate legal officer at the ICTY, a visiting professional at the Pre-Trial Division of the ICC, a legal adviser at the Implementing Agency in Bolivia of the UNHCR. She has also consulted for various projects, inter alia, of the ICRC, the Peace and Justice Initiative, Bolivia's Ombudsman and the UNHCHR—Bolivia's Office. Her publications encompass a wide range of topics in both substantive and procedural issues on international criminal law, including international humanitarian law.

Dr Sergey Vasiliev

is Assistant Professor at the Grotius Centre for International Legal Studies, Leiden University.

Giulio Vanacore

is a magistrate in the Italian judiciary. In 2011 he obtained a Ph.D from the University of Urbino, presenting a thesis titled "*The Admissibility Assessment Before the International Criminal Court and the First Case Law: A Model of Complementarity*".

He was a post-doc researcher in Criminal Law at the University of Urbino, and has been collaborating with the Department Chairs of International, Comparative and Italian Criminal Law at the Second University of Naples and at the University of Urbino, as well as with the Department Chair of International Law at the Federico II University of Naples.

In 2012, he worked as an intern with trial chambers of the United Nations International Criminal Tribunal for the former Yugoslavia. In 2013, he participated in an Italian Government Commission of Experts, appointed with the aim of studying and amending several criminal provisions on organized crime, mafia and economy crimes. In 2015 he was research fellow at the Department of International and Comparative Criminal Law, University of Cologne.

Yvonne McDermott

is a Senior Lecturer in Law at Bangor University, Wales, where she is the Director of the Bangor Centre for International Law and Director of Teaching and Learning for the School. Her PhD thesis, 'The Right to a Fair Trial in International Criminal Law' was awarded the special mention by the International Institute of Human Rights in their René Cassin Thesis Prize 2013. Her first monograph, Fairness in International Criminal Trials, has been published by OUP in 2015.

The Grammar of the Judicial Dialogue between International Criminal Tribunals and the European Court: Introductory Remarks

Paolo Lobba and Triestino Mariniello

The issue of the interplay between international criminal tribunals and human rights bodies has frequently emerged in academia as well as in the case law. The present study relies on the idea that the various fields of international law have become increasingly intertwined, and this process has manifested itself in the 'gradual interpenetration and cross-fertilization of previously somewhat compartmentalised areas of international law'.[1] This wider phenomenon is especially reflected in the field of international criminal law, which appears as a vivid demonstration of the cross-fertilization practice, since its normative content is often drawn from other fields of law, including international human rights law, international humanitarian law, as well as domestic criminal law and procedure. Particularly in the area of the implementation of human rights standards, there are strong connections between ICTs and human rights bodies.

This interaction has been particularly apparent in the progressive emergence of a practice of cross-referencing between ICTs and the ECtHR. Whereas the ECtHR has (sporadically) made use of the jurisprudence of ICTs, most of the references originate from the ICTs, which have frequently resorted to the European Court's *dicta* in order to elucidate the definition, scope and application of human rights. The areas of law where these human rights norms have been invoked, re-interpreted and applied include, *inter alia*, the right to freedom of expression, *nullum crimen sine lege*, the right not to be subject to inhumane or degrading treatment, fair trial rights, the right to an effective remedy, sentencing and pre-trial detention, the right to remain silent, self-representation, and *ne bis in idem*.

The common argument that this work seeks to challenge is that cross-fertilization between ICTs and the ECtHR is bound (or at least likely) to produce positive effects. A part of scholarship has argued, for example, that reliance by ICTs on the interpretation of human rights principles articulated by regional human rights courts prevents fragmentation, and thus facilitates the advent of a common understanding of fundamental rights. Observance of the authori-

1 Antonio Cassese, *International Law* (OUP 2005) 45.

 | DOI: 10.1163/9789004313750_002

tative interpretations of human rights norms is believed to ensure that such rights are not curtailed in international criminal proceedings. The recognition of such norms by ICTs is also seen as fostering the rule of law and due process in post-conflict societies. Finally, given the cosmopolitan character of the ECHR system, the use of the principles developed therein is alleged to help fashion a fair procedural scheme without making any of the domestic models dominant in international criminal law.

Nonetheless, scholarly research has thus far fallen short of developing a systematic approach to the appraisal of the interactions between human rights bodies and international criminal tribunals. Hence our submission that the said positive discourse about cross-referencing by ICTs is yet to be grounded on solid research and risks being rhetorical. Indeed, a number of crucial questions concerning the use of human rights jurisprudence by ICTs remain mostly unaddressed in the literature. For example, are there discrepancies in the interpretation of the same right by the ECtHR and ICTs? If so, can such discrepancies be justified by institutional differences or other legitimate circumstances? What methodologies can be used to enable a more accurate, and potentially justiciable, appraisal of the process of transplantation of external legal notions? What are the parameters that may legitimise a re-interpretation (or 'translation') of ECHR standards in relation to the 'unique' context of international(ised) courts adjudicating serious international crimes? Is there a 'common grammar' of inter-systemic referencing emerging in international criminal justice which could be used to assess practices of (non-)cross-referencing, (non-)engagement, dismissal or endorsement, with respect to human rights courts' jurisprudence?

Therefore, the effective import of this inter-systemic communication between the ECtHR and ICTs has been rarely called into question. This is in sharp contrast to other legal fields, where there has been extensive academic debate providing a critical reading of transjudicial dialogues. As a consequence, methodologies and parameters to assess the reliance of ICTs on human rights courts' jurisprudence are still uncertain. The very notion of 'fertilising' a different field, rather than a neutral designation, ascribes an immediately positive connotation to the process of transplantation. Still, this optimistic understanding seems to be grounded in *prima facie* sensible, though as yet unsupported and unverified, premises.

This book shows how a critical reading of the interactions between human rights law and ICTs' jurisprudence cannot continue to support a purely positive understanding of transjudicial 'dialogue'. Given the breadth of potentially relevant case law, the study is restrained to the most frequent direction in which the cross-referencing has taken place: the use that ICTs have made of the ECtHR's jurisprudence. The chapters contained in this volume aim to determine whether and to what degree ICTs have correctly applied the imported human rights principles and to identify the areas of discrepancy.

Existing literature primarily focuses on evaluating the products of judicial dialogue, ie the outcome of the interpretation of human rights norms by ICTs. Expanding the scope of the purview, the chapters collected in this book also seek to develop a coherent methodology of cross-referencing. Such a methodology can be used to objectively scrutinise ICTs' practice of importation of human rights concepts from external sources and will help strengthen judicial reasoning and make it more transparent, accessible, and foreseeable.

In light of this ambition, the analysis begins with a first Part containing three essays devoted to carving out the rules of a proper methodology for judicial cross-referencing. These three Authors note that such dynamic is often selective and shaped by pragmatic rather than scientific goals. They also concur that comparative law epistemology is useful guidance for ICTs' practice. However, whereas rules of comparison require the borrowing system (ICTs) to read the 'imported' legal concepts through the lenses of the parent system (human rights litigation), some room for adaptation of external rules to the new context should be allowed. This would lead to the development of a sub-set of human rights principles applicable to the special context of international criminal justice. All Authors recognise that demanding ICTs to put in more effort in their comparative practices may set expectations too high, but this is seen as necessary in order to counterbalance the absence of a system of checks and balances, and is ultimately believed to foster greater legitimacy.

In particular, Sergey Vasiliev's chapter addresses the following central questions: What rules of transjudicial communication govern ICTs' invocation of the ECtHR's jurisprudence? What parameters should guide the assessment of inter-curial cross-referencing—and on what basis can the specific instances thereof be deemed appropriate or otherwise? The Author identifies, and demonstrates with examples from jurisprudence, four basic rules of 'transjudicial grammar' that international criminal judges should respect when relying on Strasbourg human rights principles: (i) avoiding misleading parallels and false analogies; (ii) restating and applying legal tests accurately; (iii) appreciating the context of jurisprudence; and (iv) re-adjusting the borrowed legal tests or concepts only if and as appropriate. The piece also reflects on the potential consequences that could follow from failure to abide by those rules, including the diminished analytical rigour, persuasiveness, and quality of judicial reasoning. According to the Author, an indirect yet no less important consequence is the reputational cost incurred by individual judges and institutions.

Julia Geneuss posits that, in order to authentically transmit the meaning of a legal concept or norm from the context of the ECtHR to the context of the ICC, such notions must in the first place be subject to a process of 'translation'. She notes that, in being translated, the legal concept or norm should not lose its normative meaning and that the approach to the translation process must be transparent, principled, and methodologically coherent in order to prevent curbing the rights of the accused as a result of arbitrary decision making. As a starting point, she suggests that the jurisprudence of the ECtHR should be regarded as 'directory authority' rather than mandatory or persuasive authority; this means that the authority should be followed, but can be outweighed if appropriate justifications exist, as this counterbalances the lack of a real communicative process between ICTs and the ECtHR. Whereas ICTs are not bound by the Strasbourg case law, they have to thoroughly engage with it before proceeding to deviate from or re-interpret the relevant human rights standards to which such jurisprudence refers. While Geneuss acknowledges that this method of translation sets high expectations for ICTs' judges, as there is no formalised communication structure for dialogue with the ECtHR, she argues that the effort is justified and necessary in order to create a coherent context-based set of human rights standards.

In his piece, Christoph Burchard suggests that comparative criminal law and justice can provide valuable insights into how and why ICTs may or may not, should or should not, refer to human rights sources. To make his argument, he relies on two distinct methodological approaches: a realistic approach, aimed at understanding why and how specific actors in fact engage in cross-referencing; and a normative approach, whereby the focus is on whether and to what extent reference to extra-systemic reasoning should occur. Addressing his research question from the viewpoint of legal realism, Burchard points to a selective and result-driven use of the human rights jurisprudence by ICTs. Addressing the question from a 'realistic' standpoint, he takes issue with the assumption that only neutral and all-encompassing comparison is acceptable in legal reasoning. Rather, comparative law arguments, like others, tend to be cherry-picked, as they are 'teleologically framed'. Although instrumentality and selectivity certainly affect the legitimacy that ICTs may draw from comparative reasoning, Burchard posits that the compelling nature of ICTs' decisions ultimately depends on the quality of the argument and the reputation of the 'giving' legal order. That said, ICTs should indeed engage with human rights courts' jurisprudence, since this judicial dialogue, when carried out correctly, is a chance to 'tame power', that is, to ensure that ICTs—which operate in a legal context devoid of effective checks and balances—comply with human rights. Hence, the judicial dialogue can serve as checks and balances both 'within' and 'without'; 'within' since ICTs referencing to human rights courts' case law leads them to review their own jurisprudence, and 'without' since the comparison can serve as checks and balances on the legal finding being compared.

Part 2 shifts the focus of the book from general methodological questions to the law and practice of ICTs. Two chapters tackle the issues raised by Article 21(3) of the ICC Statute, offering distinct perspectives on the scope and character of the provision as well as on the sources of law from which 'internationally recognized' human rights may be deduced. Although both Authors aver that Article 21(3) may produce significant normative consequences, they proceed from different premises as to the compulsory nature of judicial dialogue at the ICC and the role that human rights regional bodies' jurisprudence should assume.

Volker Nerlich, notably, examines the requirement under Article 21(3) of the ICC Statute that the application and interpretation of the ICC's legal instruments must be consistent with internationally recognised human rights. He notes that this norm could have far-reaching consequences, resulting, as the case law he refers to illustrates, in the non-application of express provisions of the ICC Statute or the application of extra-systemic rules. Nerlich argues that the following sources may constitute internationally recognised human rights: (1) binding international human rights instruments; (2) jurisprudence of human rights treaty bodies; (3) regional treaties and jurisprudence of attendant treaty bodies, especially the ECtHR; and (4) 'soft' human rights law, such as declarations and resolutions of organs of international institutions. In contrast, he does not believe that the jurisprudence and legislation of domestic and international jurisdictions fall within the scope of Article 21(3). When deriving internationally recognised human rights from these sources, Nerlich concludes that a 'differentiated approach' should be adopted. The human rights precepts that qualify as *jus cogens* within the meaning of Article 53 of the Vienna Convention should override the ICC Statute in the event of conflict. In contrast, norms that do not fall under that ambit, in particular human rights 'soft law', should only be resorted to as a source of guidance, but should not prevail over the ICC Statute. It appears, therefore, that Nerlich advances an interpretation of Article 21(3) that puts its real effect into perspective. To the extent that Article 21(3) mandates the non-application of express provisions of the ICC legal framework, it does not add anything to Article 53 of the Vienna Convention; to the extent it dictates to seek guidance from human rights principles, it does not demand a change from the situation already in place at other ICTs, where resort to external principles is one that has often been criticised as non-binding, erratic and unsystematic.

In 'Article 21(3) of the ICC Statute and "Internationally Recognised Human Rights" as a Source of Mandatory Judicial Dialogue', Christophe Deprez considers that due to Article 21(3) of the ICC Statute calling upon the ICC to adhere to internationally recognised human rights, judicial cross-fertilisation between the ICC and human rights bodies has often become a mandatory process. He emphasises that this departure from the traditional divide between human rights law proper and human rights bodies' case law should be welcomed since the ICC is not a party to the relevant international human rights instruments. Deprez explains how under Article 21(3) the ICC has justified upholding human rights through the interpretation of case law, by disregarding parts of the ICC Statute that do not entirely comply with internationally recognised human rights standards or by assuming extra-statutory powers. Deprez argues that the ICC's use of human rights case law to conclude that a certain right is protected illustrates the ICC's acknowledgment of its obligation to abide by judge-made human rights standards. Thus, in partial contrast with the views of Braun and Caroli that cross-fertilisation has been used as a rhetorical and discretionary tool, Deprez views judicial dialogue as being mandatory for the ICC when it comes to upholding (judge-made) internationally recognised human rights as required by Article 21(3).

In the last chapter of this Part, Frauke Sauerwein offers a comprehensive assessment of the references made by the ICTY to the ECtHR's jurisprudence, analysing all non-confidential judgments and decisions issued by the *ad hoc* tribunal at the time of writing. The Author provides a quantitative examination of ICTY cases referring to the ECtHR and of the development of its citation practice since its establishment. The chapter unveils the width and the depth—and on occasion the superficiality—of the references to the Strasbourg jurisprudence. The Author emphasises how some cases are particularly problematic, since crucial aspects of European jurisprudence are misconstrued and end up being used to support positions that are discordant with those of the ECtHR. According to Sauerwein, this is evident in references justifying a long pre-trial detention by using exceptional cases in the ECtHR jurisprudence as the norm. The paper ultimately reveals that the citation of the European jurisprudence is not critically assessed by the ICTY and considers that clear rules concerning cross-referencing should be devised.

Moving to Part 3, titled 'Cross-Fertilisation and Substantive Issues: Crimes and Punishment', both Damien Scalia's and Giulio Vanacore's papers address the interpretation of the legality principle put forward by the ECtHR. Scalia, in particular, explores judicial dialogue between ICTs and the ECtHR in relation to the legality principle of penalties. The Author assesses how the qualitative criteria identified by the ECtHR are not fulfilled by the ICTY and ICTR law and practice. Although the Rome Statute explicitly establishes the *nulla poena sine lege* principle, the meaningful protection of such a principle is extremely limited. According to Scalia, this is due to the vagueness of the ICC founding instruments and the broad discretion bestowed to the judges in sentencing. The final part of this chapter explores the *Galić* case in order to show how the misuse of the European jurisprudence by ICTs occurs also at the stage of the execution of sentences.

Vanacore interestingly proposes that the concepts of accessibility and foreseeability should be applied, in the context of the ICC, not only to the definition of crimes, but also to the modes of liability (Article 25 of the ICC Statute), *mens rea* (Article 30), and mistake (Article 32). With regard to the modes of liability, Vanacore analyses the theory of 'control over the crime' and its variant of 'control over an organisation' developed by the ICC for the interpretation of indirect (co-)perpetration. He questions whether such a theory, which is borrowed exclusively from a single national theory falling outside the boundaries of the legal system of the accused, is consistent with the criteria of accessibility and foreseeability. The Author posits that theories used for the interpretation of modes of liability must be widely accepted by a number of legal systems in order to be deemed accessible and, consequently, foreseeable. For this reason, he proposes to create an international criminal law *Dogmatik*, which could constitute an acceptable compromise between filling statutory gaps and enforcing the ECtHR's ideas of accessibility and foreseeability, in order to safeguard accused persons from any legal abuse.

Alice Riccardi examines cross-fertilisation between ICTs and the ECtHR with regard to the right to rehabilitation of offenders. She focuses on the *Vinter and Others v United Kingdom* before the ECtHR and the *Galić* decision adopted by the President of the Mechanism for ICTs. She argues that, at first sight, the recent recognition of life sentence prisoners' right to rehabilitation by both the ECtHR and *ad hoc* Tribunals might be seen as a form of transjudicial communication. However, at a closer look, she states that these cases constitute the final part of a longer story of misuse of external precedents. Following such analysis, the Author interestingly examines three examples of transjudicial communication, with a view to determining whether ICTs and the ECtHR used appropriate methods of importation of external precedents. On the basis of the selected case studies, she argues that a normative convergence on rehabilitation occurs between ICTs and the ECtHR. Nonetheless, she claims that such convergence does not expose an 'emerging global jurisprudence', but simply the existence of context-specific trajectories.

The next two papers address a much-debated issue, ie how human rights law had an impact on the definition of torture eventually adopted by ICTs. Elena

Maculan's chapter shows that international judges have systematically used human rights bodies' jurisprudence to establish the constitutive elements of this offence. The Author investigates how the reliance on European jurisprudence by ICTs has caused a twofold evolution in the concept of torture. On one hand, the use of the Strasbourg case law has fostered harmonisation of the definition of torture in international criminal justice. On the other, the reference to the European jurisprudence has also had the effect of broadening of the scope of the definition of this office, which can result in the infringement of fundamental rights of the suspect. As stated by Maculan, the reliance on the definition of torture provided by the ECtHR offers a significant case study in order to assess the 'shadowy sides' of judicial cross-fertilisation. At the same time, the Author analyses how the judicial interpretation of torture provides some relevant suggestions that could both enhance the potentialities of cross-fertilisation and overcome its dangers.

The chapter by Elizabeth Santalla looks at the same issue from a different perspective. In particular, the Author investigates the divergent criminalisation of torture as a war crime and as a crime against humanity before the ICC. She notices how incongruent features of torture under the Rome Statute go beyond the divergence inherent in the contextual elements of the two international crimes it may make out. She explores the consequences and implications of this divergent criminalisation for *ne bis in idem* in the context of cumulative charges and convictions. In sum, this chapter explores the way in which such divergent criminalisation between war crimes and crimes against humanity fosters a further discussion on the interpretation and application of the principle of *ne bis in idem* in relation to torture and other ill-treatment. The Author explains why the ECtHR's case law approach to *ne bis in idem* may not prove suitable for the jurisprudence of ICTs.

All four chapters contained in Part 4 put forward quite dark pictures of how cross-referencing worked out in relation to different aspects linked to the fairness of criminal proceedings. They point to instances of alleged instrumental use of ECtHR precedents resulting in unfairness to the accused. This scenario confirms that it is often difficult to extrapolate general principles from human rights cases, given that the ECtHR approach is perforce casuistic and highly context-sensitive. It is also testament, however, to the need to elaborate an agreeable set of 'grammar rules' to govern the practice of cross-fertilisation, lest the legitimacy of ICTs be compromised.

Yvonne McDermott's study addresses the right of the accused persons to challenge the witnesses and evidence presented against them. It explores the ECtHR jurisprudence on the compatibility of convictions that were largely based on the accounts of unavailable witnesses with the right to a fair trial.

Following the analysis of the Strasbourg case law, the Author examines how ICTs have used and misused European decisions on the interplay between the rights of witnesses and the rights of accused persons surrounding absent witnesses in international criminal trials. According to the Author, the use of ECtHR case law by ICTs is characterised by 'exceptionalism' and 'selectivity'. She notices that ICTs have rarely implicitly recognised the value of human rights bodies' case law and its potential applicability before ICTs, but have been highly selective in the use of those standards. The Author emphasises how an ECtHR decision has also been used as justification for reaching the precise opposite conclusion than the ECtHR had reached in that decision.

Yael Vias Gvirsman also conducts an illuminating exploration on the use of witness testimony. Her chapter takes issue with the way in which the Special Court for Sierra Leone (SCSL) in the *Taylor* case applied the yardstick set out by the ECtHR in respect of hearsay evidence. She argues that internationally-recognised principles of evidence rely on the 'sole or decisive' rule, which stipulates that a conviction is (normally) unfair where it is based solely or to a decisive extent on the testimony of a witness whom the accused could not examine at any stage of the proceedings, since this would unduly restrict the right of the defence to challenge incriminating evidence. Vias Gvirsman examines the ECtHR case of *Al Khawaja and Tahery v United Kingdom* to demonstrate that the exception to the 'sole or decisive' rule that the Grand Chamber articulated therein only applied to the legal system under scrutiny, ie the United Kingdom, which contains adequate safeguards against improper use of hearsay evidence. These safeguards, she submits, are absent in the procedural law of the SCSL, which follows a more liberal approach in the admissibility and evaluation of evidence. Hence the 'sole or decisive' rule should in her view have been applied in its stricter formulation, preventing a conviction being based solely or substantially on hearsay evidence, unless strong corroboration was provided. This not being the case in *Taylor*, Vias Gvirsman concludes that the SCSL misapplied the ECtHR jurisprudence.

Paolo Caroli addresses cross-fertilisation by focusing on a decision rendered by Judge Steiner at the ICC, which touched upon the issue of victims' right to the truth. He posits that the logic underlying the decision could potentially pose a danger to the rights of the accused. Caroli notes that although Judge Steiner refers to cases from the ECtHR and the IACtHR relating to victims' right to the truth, there is no direct link between this topic and the legal question before Judge Steiner. Hence, the reference to the human rights jurisprudence was purely rhetorical and instrumental, with a view to reinforcing or even legitimising her decision. Thus, Caroli argues that cross-fertilisation without limits can lead to manipulations or mistakes in its application, as judges can use cross-fertilisation as a convenient tool to achieve a desired outcome, without actually resorting to the legal reasoning for the referenced decision. Like Braun (see below), Caroli warns that ICTs should be wary of cross-fertilisation, especially when the reference to the other court's decision does not engage with that court's reasoning, as this can have a negative effect on international human rights law, specifically, as Geneuss also notes, by potentially modifying and adversely impacting the rights of the accused.

Kerstin Braun's chapter, titled 'Self- or Cross-Fertilisation? Referencing ECtHR Jurisprudence to Justify Victim Participation at the ICC', analyses a decision by the Pre-Trial Chamber of the ICC within the context of the Situation in the Democratic Republic of Congo, to help clarify what cross-fertilisation should entail. Braun argues that since the right established in the decision has not been established by the referenced ECtHR jurisprudence, the Pre-Trial Chamber relied on the ECtHR to add validity and authority to its decision and avoid subsequent criticism, rather than to endorse the legal reasoning of the ECtHR. Additionally, Braun notes that even if such a right could be deduced from the referenced ECtHR jurisprudence, the significant differences between the ICC and domestic criminal justice systems would require that the right is 'translatable', ie that it can be placed into the ICC context without modification. While recognising that cross-fertilisation on the international level can be a positive development by creating widely applicable human rights standards across national, regional, and international levels, Braun argues that the Pre-Trial Chamber's decision is instead an instance of self-fertilisation. Ultimately, Braun suggests that self-fertilisation under the guise of cross-fertilisation can do more harm than good to international human rights law by undermining transjudicial dialogue.

It is hoped that the vast array of thematic areas, controversial issues and case studies covered in this volume contributes to instil a greater awareness into doctrinal and judicial disputes around the phenomenon of transjudicial communication in the field of international criminal justice. Various chapters revealed that, as observed in several preexisting commentaries, ICTs did in fact engage, at times, in a well-documented misuse of the ECtHR case law. Nevertheless, the overall practice is multifaceted and cannot be simplistically decried as instrumental and opportunistic. Many critiques found in the literature appeared to be more unsatisfied with the outcome of a judicial decision than its rules of interpretation of a foreign notion. Conversely, judges did not have the resources to embark on lengthy theoretical disquisitions, their aim being pragmatic, ie finding a workable solution to a contingent legal issue. This volume offers a first set of 'grammar rules' that, if adopted as common protocols of communication, may allow the different actors to speak the same language.

PART 1

Dynamics of Judicial Dialogue: Methods and Rationales

CHAPTER 1

Cross-fertilisation under the Looking Glass: Transjudicial Grammar and Reception of Strasbourg Jurisprudence by International Criminal Tribunals

*Sergey Vasiliev**

1 Introduction

The recent upsurge of interest in the phenomenon of transjudicial communication shed a new light on various aspects of migration of legal rationales among international courts: the nature and import of judicial cross-fertilisation; the uses made of external precedents in international adjudication; and patterns of cross-referencing.[1] The renewed attention for inter-curial interactions is consistent with recognition of an ever-growing importance of judicial institutions in the international society, as attested by the continued proliferation of specialised courts and increased resort to adjudication. But States' intermittent compliance with judicial rulings and political backlashes against international courts, fuel preoccupations about their role and authority.[2] This may raise questions about the judicial arm's potency as an agent of international governance. Against this mixed backdrop, the incidence and tone of inter-judicial conversation is not only taken as proof of the existing 'international judicial community' but also a measure of courts' collective capacity to promote common goals in a more or less coordinate, yet complementary,

* [s.vasiliev@law.leidenuniv.nl]. I am grateful to the editors of the volume for fostering the academic debate on this topic, and for their unparalleled patience.

1 See special issue 84 of the Nordic Journal of International Law (2015); Stewart Manley, 'Referencing Patterns at the International Criminal Court' (2016) 27(1) European Journal of International Law 191; Aldo Zammit-Borda, 'Appraisal-Based and Flexible Approaches to External Precedent in International Criminal Law' (2015) 28(3) Leiden Journal of International Law 643.

2 Karen J. Alter and others, 'Backlash against International Courts in West, East and Southern Africa: Causes and Consequences' (2016) 27(2) European Journal of International Law 293.

 | DOI: 10.1163/9789004313750_003

fashion—despite their functional specialisation and the fragmented state of international law.[3]

Human rights is one area in which international judicial dialogue has been deemed important for the above reasons. Transjudicial communication, it is argued, could preserve the unity and integrity of international human rights law (IHRL) and safeguard an adequate level of protection across the board.[4] The systemic effects of this kind are often expected of the 'dialogues' conducted by international criminal tribunals and the European Court of Human Rights,[5] which, in reality, are mostly parallel, and only episodically interlocking, monologues.[6] The debates on transjudicial interactions along this axis often proceed on the tacit premise that, when dealing with human rights issues, ICTs ought generally to defer to Strasbourg.[7] Under this view, ICTs should treat ECtHR case law as more than a mere source of inspiration and persuasive authority, and place themselves on the receiving end of cross-fertilisation. Commentators see this relationship as a solution to the unremitting concerns

3 António A. Cançado Trindade, 'Contemporary International Tribunals: Their Continuing Jurisprudential Cross-Fertilization, in Their Common Mission of Imparting Justice' (2013) 1 The Global Community: Yearbook of International Law and Jurisprudence 155, 160; id, 'Contemporary International Tribunals: Their Continuing Jurisprudential Cross-Fertilization Pertaining to Human Rights Protection' (2014) 1 The Global Community: Yearbook of International Law and Jurisprudence 215, 215 and 219.

4 id, 'Contemporary International Tribunals: Their Continuing Jurisprudential Cross-Fertilization, with Special Attention to the International Safeguard of Human Rights' (2012) 1 The Global Community: Yearbook of International Law and Jurisprudence 181, 181 and 188.

5 eg Annika Jones, 'Insights into an Emerging Relationship: Use of Human Rights Jurisprudence at the International Criminal Court' (2016) 16(4) Human Rights Law Review 701, 704–705.

6 On cross-referencing asymmetries between ICTs and the ECtHR, see Sergey Vasiliev, 'International Criminal Tribunals in the Shadow of Strasbourg and the Politics of Cross-Fertilization' (2015) 84 Nordic Journal of International Law 371, 374–378; Nicolas A.J. Croquet, 'The International Criminal Court and the Treatment of Defence Rights: A Mirror of the European Court of Human Rights' Jurisprudence?' (2011) 11(1) Human Rights Law Review 91, 92 and 111–112 (characterising ICC—ECtHR cross-fertilisation on procedure as 'uni-directional'); Julia Geneuss, 'Obstacles to Cross-fertilisation: The International Criminal Tribunals' "Unique Context" and the Flexibility of the European Court of Human Rights' Case Law' (2015) 84 Nordic Journal of International Law 371, 423. See also Antonios Tzanakopoulos, 'Judicial Dialogue as a Means of Interpretation' in Helmut P. Aust and Georg Nolte (eds), The Interpretation of International Law by Domestic Courts: Uniformity, Diversity, Convergence (OUP 2016) 75.

7 See further Vasiliev (n 6) 378–383.

about ICTs' human rights performance,[8] and a means to consolidate a 'common understanding' of human rights.[9] And indeed, some ICTs have shown great—arguably, 'excessive'—deference to ECtHR in specific areas.[10]

In a previous contribution to the debate, this author challenged the normative expectation of an almost mandatory deference to ECtHR *rationes* by ICTs. Not only is it inconsonant with the language of transjudicial dialogue, but it is also an ineffective stratagem to compel a better performance by ICTs; treating external jurisprudence as quasi-binding is not guaranteed to enhance human rights protection. Were ICT judges simply to re-use rationales from an adjudicatory context different from their own, and subject to unique objectives and constraints, they would risk abdicating responsibility for ensuring genuine (ie not merely *pro forma*) fairness. Courts must weigh the entirety of relevant circumstances and rekindle standards and tests accordingly before putting them to use. Building and following up on this argument, this chapter takes up the methodological question posed earlier: 'when and how [may] the tribunals invoke the ECtHR's jurisprudence and which usages are proper or otherwise'?[11]

This chapter responds to the call for research into the 'methodologies and parameters to assess the reliance of ICTs on human rights courts' jurisprudence', in order to develop 'a coherent set of principles, which may guide the transit of human rights standards into the practice of international criminal tribunals'.[12] The informal and discretionary character of judicial dialogue does not—and should not—mean that 'anything goes'. However, this raises methodological questions: What 'grammar' governs the invocation of ECtHR *rationes* by ICTs and what parameters should guide the appraisal of judicial cross-referencing and borrowing? Does it matter, for the purpose of seeing 'use' from 'abuse' of Strasbourg jurisprudence, *how* an ICT engages with ECtHR rationales before deploying them, or should one rather consider the objectives and the ultimate result of this exercise?

---

8 eg Julian Nicholls, 'Evidence: Hearsay and Anonymous Witnesses' in Roelof Haveman and others (eds), *Supranational Criminal Law: A System Sui Generis* (Intersentia 2003) 287 (ECtHR jurisprudence should 'guide, and to an extent bind, the decisions of the ICTY').

9 Reporting a common belief to this effect, Triestino Mariniello and Paolo Lobba, 'Editorial. The Cross-fertilisation Rhetoric in Question: Use and Abuse of the European Court's Jurisprudence by International Criminal Tribunals' (2015) 84 Nordic Journal of International Law 363, 364. See eg Jones (n 5) 723.

10 Croquet (n 6) 92 and 122 (as regards the external limitations on the defence rights, the ICC jurisprudence has (unnecessarily) mirrored that of the ECtHR).

11 Vasiliev (n 6) 373. See also Mariniello and Lobba (n 9) 364.

12 Mariniello and Lobba (n 9) 364.

In tackling these issues, the chapter first argues that objectives and implications of the import of another court's *rationes* are irrelevant for categorising it either as 'use' or 'abuse'. In evaluating judicial cross-fertilisation, the valid questions are 'what' and 'how', not 'whether' and 'why'; it is only the method that matters. The chapter then highlights, with the aid of examples from ICTs' case law, four 'grammar rules' that (should) govern their use of ECtHR jurisprudence. Lastly, it ponders the costs of 'grammar errors' for the court in question, as a way to gauge said rules' deterrent potential.

2 How to Appraise Cross-fertilisation? Moving Away from Outcomes …

2.1 *Outcome-Driven Approaches and Their Discontents*

As a variety of criteria can be used to appraise judicial cross-fertilisation, cardinally diverging evaluations of the same episodes of borrowing and recycling of tests and rationales from another court are not precluded. Notably, the choice of benchmarks is shaped by one's conceptualisation of the cross-fertilisation phenomenon and its *raisons d'être*. In this sense, it is worthwhile identifying 'progressive', 'unitary', and 'systemic' accounts, as these are most prominent in the debates on transjudicialism.

If one were to adopt the 'progressive' view, strengthening due process in ICTs would be posited as the principal rationale for transplanting ECtHR legal tests. Only those uses of Strasbourg precedents which promote that goal would be deemed legitimate. Occasionally, ICTs reference human rights jurisprudence to justify their refusal to apply a higher standard of protection or to adopt an interpretation favorable to the accused. Insofar as such maneuvres would be at odds with the putative objective of enhancing protection, the proponents of a more progressive human rights approach are likely to criticise them as an 'abuse' of established jurisprudence perverting its core purpose. In turn, if the perceived rationale of the ECtHR—ICT communication is to consolidate international jurisprudence on human rights or achieve a uniform understanding of their scope and content, it is only when the ICT tracks the ECtHR consistently and without deviation that its invocation of Strasbourg precedents might qualify as appropriate. According to the 'unitary' view, ICTs should steer clear of re-using ECtHR tests and interpretations in the way that risks fragmenting IHRL, with the degree of enjoyment of rights before the ICT being a secondary issue. And yet, to the adherents of the 'systemic account', who view cross-fertilisation as the function of fortifying the emergent 'international judicial system', the key parameter is the very fact of a judicial dialogue being conducted and possibly its tone. A constructive and cordial conversation in the spirit of mutual respect, on the basis of parity and recognition of each other's specialised expertise, promotes the image of a cohesive community of international courts. This image would be undermined by mutual neglect or by confrontational interactions which betray the lack of comity: eg inter-tribunal bickering about the content of IHRL, 'turf wars' over competence, and dismissive references to fellow judges' analyses and constructions.

Each of these paradigms of cross-fertilisation entails an outcome-based evaluative approach. Under this approach, any inter-curial transfer of normative structures, concepts or rationales is characterised either as 'proper' or otherwise, primarily in view of its presumed ability to promote certain objectives: increasing the level of human rights protection, enhancing the unity of the law, strengthening international judiciary or, for that matter, any other equivalent normative or policy goal.[13] While it is not suggested that such conceptions are necessarily wrong and could not serve as a lens to assess transjudicial dialogue, none of them is helpful in distinguishing 'use' from 'abuse' of external human rights precedents for at least two reasons.

First, no uniform, clear and objective criteria for the appraisal of judicial dialogue can be derived from these competing outcome-based frameworks, the choice of which is inherently ideological and subjective. The attributed goals of judicial cross-fertilisation as outlined above, are at cross-purposes, incommensurable, and ranking them is anything but a straightforward task. Each of the guiding paradigms imposes a unidimensional metric incompatible with its alternatives. As noted, in many cases, this can lead to opposite, equally contestable conclusions with regard to the same episodes of judicial borrowing. Thus, an ICT's invocation of ECtHR precedents that appears legitimate to proponents of the 'progressive' concept because it maximises the protection of rights, might be found objectionable by champions of the unity of IHRL in case the ICTs has deviated from such precedents, and vice versa.

Second, the outcome-driven evaluative approaches presuppose that, whenever engaging with another court's jurisprudence, judges are guided, exclusively or primarily, by ulterior considerations extraneous to the immediate sphere of adjudication. However, it is questionable whether ideological goals, meritorious or otherwise, such as achieving a higher level of protection of spe-

13 Thus, self-legitimisation and lending legitimacy to the counterpart court may be another leitmotif of cross-referencing: eg Shai Dothan, 'How International Courts Enhance Their Legitimacy' (2013) 14 Theoretical Inquiries in Law 455, 571; Marlene Wind, 'Do Scandinavians Care about International Law? Study of Scandinavian Judges Citation Practice to International Law and Courts' (2016) 85 Nordic Journal of International Law 281, 289.

cific rights, guarding IHRL against fragmentation, or writing an 'international judicial system' into existence, can in earnest be attributed to adjudicators. Doing so appears counterfactual: Even if individual judges may share any of those goals, it is not granted they will seek to promote them through the practice of jurisprudential cross-referencing. On the contrary, this is arguably a much more down-to-earth affair: The use of external jurisprudence is guided not by any extrinsic objectives, but by the rationales intrinsic to adjudication itself.

The practice of international criminal adjudication reveals that judges hardly ever rely on external authorities, including human rights jurisprudence, for extrajudicial purposes. Rather, they refer to ECtHR judgments for concrete and practical reasons: ie if and when this assists them in producing well-reasoned decisions. In particular, judges will engage with ECtHR legal rationales and tests in order to: establish the content of IHRL regarding a specific issue, as a way to interpret a provision or identify a gap in the ICT's legal framework; fill a perceived lacuna through creative interpretation or analogical inference; and bolster an innovative line of argument or a legal construction. This approach to the use of external case law may appear instrumental and selective—or even unprincipled and opportunistic.[14] But, aside from reflecting what courts actually do, it could also be characterised—less suggestively—as a quintessentially judicial and pragmatic one.

The jurisprudence of ICTs contains copious evidence of judicial recourse to external case law for one or more of the above rationales. To take a notable example, in the *Rwamakuba* case the ICTR relied extensively upon external human rights precedents, including Strasbourg jurisprudence, to fill a legal gap in its human rights regime. The Trial Chamber accorded the right to an effective remedy in the form of financial compensation, to the acquitted person whose right to legal assistance had been violated. It did so in the absence of a respective provision in the Statute by means of exercising an inherent power. The court drew heavily upon Strasbourg case law regarding the right to an effective remedy.[15] In particular, it made use of the test from ECtHR case

14 Antonio Cassese, 'The Influence of the Eropean Court of Human Rights on International Criminal Tribunals—Some Methodological Remarks' in Morten Bergsmo (ed), *Human Rights and Criminal Justice for the Downtrodden: Essays in Honour of Asbjørn Eide* (Martinus Nijhoff 2003) 21–24 and 50 (critical of ICTs' 'wild approach' to external precedents, when used not 'to establish the existence of a rule of customary international law or general principles of law, but rather directly to resolve the legal problem'); Mariniello and Lobba (n 12) 364 (ICTs' transplanting of human rights standards is landmarked by 'uncertainty, selectivity and instrumentalisation'; 'ambiguity and arbitrariness').

15 *Prosecutor v Rwamakuba*, ICTR-98-44C-T, Decision on Appropriate Remedy, Trial Chamber III, 31 January 2007 ('*Rwamakuba* remedy decision'), paras 39, 52, 68, 47, 49, 58, and 99.

law—which it characterised as 'significant' and 'persuasive'[16]—when deciding whether to award pecuniary and non-pecuniary damages for the violation of the right to legal assistance.[17] In the same decision, it drew upon ECtHR jurisprudence to affirm the importance of the right to counsel under IHRL, and to extend its application to the investigation and pre-trial stages of the proceedings.[18]

One finds comparable usages of Strasbourg jurisprudence in other ICTs. A survey of the ICC case law reveals that this Court has regularly and systematically engaged with ECtHR jurisprudence, in particular on issues of criminal procedure:[19]

- the right to disclosure of (exculpatory) material;[20]
- the right of the accused to be informed of the nature, cause and content of the charges;[21]
- the right of effective participation in a criminal trial;[22]
- the judicial duty to provide sufficient reasoning;[23]
- the primary authority and ultimate responsibility of the judges for safeguarding a fair trial;[24]

---

16 *Rwamakuba* remedy decision (n 15) paras 69 and 70.

17 ibid, paras 68–70 fns 120–123, 126, citing over a dozen ECtHR judgments and applying a Strasbourg test for the award of damages (at paras 69–73).

18 *Rwamakuba* remedy decision (n 15) para. 17 fns 26–27, holding that it was in the interests of justice to provide the right to legal assistance to international defendants 'from the earliest stages of the proceedings', due to the complexity of cases, seriousness of the offences, and potentially significant sentences, with reference to criteria established in ECtHR case law.

19 Croquet (n 6) 92, 108 (on the ICC's referencing of Strasbourg jurisprudence as being most consistent and systematic among ICTs).

20 *Prosecutor v Lubanga*, ICC-01/04-01/06-1401, Decision on the consequences of non-disclosure of exculpatory materials covered by Article 54(3)(e) agreements, Trial Chamber I, 13 June 2008 ('*Lubanga* non-disclosure decision'), paras 77 fn 130, 80 fns 134–135, and 79.

21 *Prosecutor v Bemba*, ICC-01/05-01/08-3343, Judgment pursuant to Article 74 of the Statute, Trial Chamber III, 21 March 2016 ('*Bemba* trial judgment'), paras 31 fns 90–91, 33 fn 100.

22 *Prosecutor v Gbagbo*, ICC-02/11-01/11-286-Red, Decision on the fitness of Laurent Gbagbo to take part in the proceedings before this Court, Pre-Trial Chamber II, 2 November 2012, paras 46–48 fns 57–60, 51–52 fns 66–69.

23 *Prosecutor v Lubanga*, ICC-01/04-01/06-773, Judgment on the appeal of Mr. Thomas Lubanga Dyilo against the decision of Pre-Trial Chamber I entitled "First Decision on the Prosecution Requests and Amended Requests for Redactions under Rule 81", Appeals Chamber, 14 December 2006, para. 20.

24 *Lubanga* non-disclosure decision (n 20) paras 82–88.

- the right to privacy;[25]
- the doctrine of abuse of process and the character of breaches making a fair trial impossible;[26]
- the right to compensation for unlawful deprivation of liberty and for grave and manifest miscarriages of justice;[27]
- cumulative convictions;[28] and so on.[29]

The ICC's cross-referencing patterns demonstrate that this practice is driven by discretion and pragmatism. Judges have recourse to external authorities as a way to fortify their own *rationes decidendi*. It is striking, but also unsurprising then, that such recourse is episodic: some decisions on the same issues dealt with in the previous rulings that did refer to ECtHR case law, do not even mention it, although it was invoked in the submissions.[30] On occasion, ICTs have expressly refused to be 'fertilised' with ECtHR rationales: for instance when judges did not regard its specific judgments or a strand of jurisprudence useful for the determination of matters before them, or the proposed analogy an appropriate basis for cross-judicial borrowing.[31] Such reticence says as much as—if not more than—express engagement does: It underscores the informal and situational character of transjudicial loans. Sporadic attempts by ICTs to constrain and introduce preconditions for recourse to external precedents, such as perceived deficiencies in the Tribunal's own instruments and jurisprudence, cannot but appear opportunistic, given the lack of methodological grounding and pervasive inconsistencies.[32]

---

25 *Prosecutor v Lubanga*, ICC-01/04-01/06-1981, Decision on the admission of material from the "bar table", Trial Chamber I, 24 June 2009, paras 22–24, 26.

26 *Prosecutor v Lubanga*, ICC-01/04-01/06-772, Judgment on the Appeal of Mr. Thomas Lubanga Dyilo against the Decision on the Defence Challenge to the Jurisdiction of the Court, Appeals Chamber, 14 December 2006, paras 37–38.

27 *Prosecutor v Ngudjolo*, ICC-01/04-02/12-301-tENG, Decision on the "*Requête en indemnisation en application des dispositions de l'article 85(1) et (3) du Statut de Rome*", Trial Chamber II, 16 December 2015, paras 15 fn 22, 18 fn 30, and 43 fn 71.

28 *Bemba* trial judgment (n 21) para. 747 fn 2222.

29 Providing further examples, Croquet (n 6) 109–110; Jones (n 5) 716, 718.

30 *Prosecutor v Lubanga*, ICC-01/04-01/06-2690-Red2, Redacted Decision on the Public "Defence Application Proceedings", Trial Chamber I, 7 March 2011 (*not* engaging with ECtHR jurisprudence despite LRV's reliance thereon; see para. 16); *Prosecutor v Bemba*, ICC-01/05-01/08-802, Decision on the Admissibility and Abuse of Process Challenges, Trial Chamber III, 24 June 2010.

31 See further 3.2.1.

32 Vasiliev (n 6) 386–387.

2.2 *Quality of Reasoning as Defining Parameter*

ICTs utilise external jurisprudence not in a theoretically-informed but instrumental fashion where the main goal is enhancing the quality of judicial reasoning and decision-making. Accordingly, it is logical and justified for the appraisal of cases of cross-fertilisation to be guided by the same parameter: whether the engagement with, and transposition of, another court's legal tests or concepts effectively serves that purpose. Does the import of a foreign rationale make judicial analysis and decision stronger and more persuasive or, on the contrary, more vulnerable? The perusal of ECtHR case law by ICTs would normally add strength to the legal underpinning of the decision and improve the quality of judicial analysis. But this effect will be diminished or precluded where the ICT's use of external case law is objectionable for the reason of substance and method, *ie* if it is at odds with the 'grammar' of inter-judicial communication.[33]

Therefore, for the purpose of devising a methodology to distinguish the 'use' from 'abuse' of human rights jurisprudence by ICTs, judicial cross-fertilisation should be recognised to have no *intrinsic* value other than what it can add to the process and quality of judicial motivation. The 'immediately positive connotation'[34] carried by the notion of 'cross-*fertilisation*' is but a function of imperfect language. Its merit hinges neither on the mere fact of one international court consulting the other's case law (cross-fertilisation for its own sake), nor on such gesture's potential to promote extra-judicial agendas.[35] Indeed, why assess the work of the judges on what they do not mean and, arguably, are not meant to be doing?

Under this view, judicial cross-fertilisation practice must be appraised neutrally and objectively. The use of external jurisprudence should not be assessed positively if it undermines rather than strengthens the recipient court's *rationes decidendi*. The necessary implication of this point is the shift away from *outcome-based* evaluative approaches to the *method-based* approach.[36] The lat-

33 Similarly, Mariniello and Lobba (n 12) 364 ('the use of external precedents as guidance is desirable, as far as it follows a proper "grammar", which ensures that the process may be objectively assessed as sound or erroneous.').

34 Mariniello and Lobba (n 12) 364.

35 cf Jones (n 5) 706 (not distinguishing between intrinsic and extrinsic rationales of cross-fertilisation but stating nonetheless that insofar as interaction between the ICC and human rights courts serves 'to enrich judicial debate and prompt stronger justifications for the approaches that are ultimately adopted', it 'can be viewed as beneficial *regardless of whether or not it contributes to the coherence of international law*.' Emphasis added.)

36 See also Geneuss (n 6) 424 (calling on ICTs to focus 'less on the "product" or "outcome" of the translation than on the method of incorporation, that is on the translation process').

ter sees the worth of transjudicial dialogue in the *method* of engagement with foreign judicial rationales, including steps such as the identification, analysis, readjustment and importation. These are the aspects on which the validity and persuasiveness of judicial reasoning is usually probed and challenged. Hence, when assessing cross-systemic migration of judicial rationales, 'what?' and 'how?' are the right questions that help discern sound engagement from flawed invocations of external case law; not 'whether?' and 'why?' cross-fertilisation is taking place. But what does one mean by 'method', and what do the 'what?' and the 'how?' of cross-fertilisation encompass?

3 … to Methods: Towards Transjudicial Grammar

3.1 *Use v Abuse: Aspects of Method*

The recognition of the centrality of method to any valid importation of foreign legal rationales and techniques into international criminal adjudication is not new. Notably, the discussion and critique have so far been focused on whether the use of ECtHR jurisprudence comports with the framework of legal positivism: the system of sources of law and rules of interpretation applied by ICTs. The tribunals have often been excoriated for their chronic failure to theorise and explain the legal bases for introducing rationales of regional human rights courts into their decision-making (the so-called 'wild approach').[37] Thus, it is expected that ICTs present this exercise as the ascertainment of customary international human rights law, or an exegesis of the provisions in the Statutes and Rules, including through the interpretive vehicle of the widely-debated Article 21(3) of the ICC Statute.

There is no doubt about the importance of this formal aspect of methodology: It directs judges to always provide a solid justification for their recourse to ECtHR case law. In turn, this enhances the transparency of judicial treatment of authorities and reliance on interpretive techniques, and, hence, lays down a stronger legal foundation for the rulings. However, the insistence that judges systematically anchor their resort to external jurisprudence to legal formalism is not all that there is to method. The quality of judicial reasoning must be scrutinised not only on its formalist grounding but, crucially, also on the aspects of *substantive* engagement with human rights precedents—ie the accuracy of the identification, restatement, analysis and transposition; being the very purposes of invoking foreign judicial rationales in the first place.

---

37 eg Cassese (n 14) 20–24; Croquet (n 6) 109; Jones (n 5) 722–727.

Despite their evident significance as part of 'method', there has been virtually no debate on what rules or 'good practices' the courts must follow in the process of transposing externally-sourced judicial techniques and *rationes*.[38] Accordingly, the following section highlights a number of basic rules of 'trans-judicial grammar' and demonstrates them through examples of (non-)compliance drawn from ICTs' practice. These rules should guide ICT judges in their use of human rights jurisprudence and will help commentators assess whether such jurisprudence has been 'used' or 'abused'. For the present purposes, 'abuse' stands for an erroneous, misleading or manipulative, or otherwise methodologically inappropriate invocation of external jurisprudence. The following four rules, along with their representative breaches, do not necessarily exhaust the 'transjudicial grammar book'. But they are indeed most elementary and fundamental to valid inter-systemic transfer of judicial rationales.

3.2 *Basic Grammar Rules*

3.2.1 Avoid False Analogies

The first rule of transjudicial borrowing is for the recipient court to avoid misleading parallels and false analogies. Judges should justify their choices of the legal order or area of law from which they source a standard, concept or test, and they should explain what makes that specific legal unit eligible for transfer. The power of judicial reasoning weakens or dissipates where the court fails to show the relevance of any juridical loans. It is therefore good practice to specify what makes the donor court's solution useful in the matter before the recipient court, and the transposition of that solution logical. This substantive aspect is distinct from concerns rooted in legal formalism, ie the question of the legal basis for invoking an external precedent.

The ICTs' jurisprudence offers a score of examples of demonstrated respect for this rule, both where ICTs asserted and rejected the analogy. The example of the former is the ICC Trial Chamber's decision on reparations in *Lubanga*. The ICC drew heavily upon regional human rights jurisprudence, including ECtHR judgments, to clarify the types of harm subject to compensation.[39] The Trial Chamber acknowledged those courts' 'substantial contribution' to

---

38 but see Geneuss (n 6) 406 (underlining the importance of method for 'translating' norms and concepts into ICTs' context) and 425–426 (proposing the 'persuasive authority'-based approach, which, in the present author's view, still goes to the substance rather than the process of translation *stricto sensu*).

39 *Prosecutor v Lubanga*, ICC-01/04-01/06-2904, Decision establishing the principles and procedures to be applied to reparation, Trial Chamber I, 7 August 2012, paras 230 fns 414–419.

promoting the right to an effective remedy and reparation, and the relevance of their jurisprudence in the context of ICC reparation proceedings.[40] Although those courts award reparations against states rather than individuals, the general concepts elucidated in their case law were a 'useful guidance'. This reflective approach to the utilisation of external precedents compares favourably to the earlier jurisprudence seeking to interpret the notion of 'harm' under Rule 85 of the ICC RPE with reference to some of the same ECtHR decisions, but without clarifying their pertinence.[41]

Likewise, in the part of the *Al-Senussi* admissibility judgment dealing with the issue of the burden of proof, the ICC Appeals Chamber deemed regional human rights jurisprudence and decisions of the UN Human Rights Committee referred to by the defence, to be of 'only very limited relevance'.[42] That case law related to the determination of individual complaints against states whereas the ICC admissibility proceedings are primarily meant to determine which forum—the ICC or a domestic court—would exercise jurisdiction. In the Appeals Chamber's view, while in limited circumstances human rights violations may have a bearing on admissibility determinations, the respective proceedings are not a vehicle to address them. As a result, it refused to be guided by human rights jurisprudence cited in support of the defence claim that the PTC reversed the burden of proof when requiring the defence to raise substantiated allegations regarding the treatment of Mr. Al-Senussi in detention before Libya had to disprove them.[43]

Notably, the Appeals Chamber's statement about the irrelevance of external jurisprudence is not a blanket dismissal: It concerns a limited issue of the burden of proof in the specific context of case admissibility proceedings, which are distinct from the proceedings for determining state responsibility for alleged violations of individual rights. Hence its refusal to 'fertilise' its analysis with imported rationales in this instance can be deemed as both reasoned and balanced. Unlike the ICTY's sweeping and unnecessary rhetoric about the limited relevance of human rights jurisprudence in the matter of admissibility of

40 ibid, para. 186 fn 377.

41 *Situation in the DRC*, Decision on the Applications for Participation in the Proceedings of VPRS 1, VPRS 2, VPRS 3, VPRS 4, VPRS 5 and VPRS 6, ICC-01/04-101-tEN-Corr, Pre-Trial Chamber I, 17 January 2006 ('*DRC* victim participation decision'), paras 116 fn 87–89, 146 fn 102, 172 fn 125.

42 *Prosecutor v Gaddafi*, ICC-01/11-01/11-565, Judgment on the appeal of Mr Abdullah Al-Senussi against the decision of Pre-Trial Chamber I of 11 October 2013, Appeals Chamber, 24 July 2014, para. 169.

43 ibid, para. 162.

anonymous witness testimony in *Tadić*,[44] the ICC Appeals Chamber's approach comports with the need to avoid false analogies without unnecessarily discarding the entire corpus of ECtHR *rationes* in one fell swoop.

By contrast, the earlier ICC case law holding that victims have general participatory rights during the investigation of a situation arguably is an example of a flawed transposition. In its first decision on this matter, Pre-Trial Chamber I drew upon regional human rights case law in determining, in light of the object and purpose of the Statute, that Article 68(3) applies during that stage.[45] The Chamber pointed out that in its review of domestic systems allowing victims to participate in criminal proceedings, the ECtHR deemed Article 6(1) of the Convention applicable from the investigation stage, particularly where the outcome was of decisive importance to victims in terms of obtaining reparations.[46] The Chamber used ECtHR jurisprudence to bolster a conclusion it had reached by other means, without having satisfied itself that the analogy with the domestic systems examined by the ECtHR was meaningful and appropriate. Arguably, the extrapolation of ECtHR rationales to the exercise of interpreting the ICC Statute, overlooked the distinct character of ICC procedure, and was not conducive to stronger reasoning.[47]

---

44 *Prosecutor v Tadić*, IT-94-1-T, Decision on the Prosecutor's Motion Requesting Protective Measures for Victims and Witnesses, Trial Chamber, 10 August 1995 ('*Tadić* protective measures decision'), paras 27–28 ('The fact that [ICTY] must interpret its provisions within its own legal context and not rely in its application on interpretations made by other judicial bodies is evident in the different circumstances in which the provisions apply … [It] is adjudicating crimes which are considered so horrific as to warrant universal jurisdiction. The [ICTY] is, in certain respects, comparable to a military tribunal, which often has limited rights of due process and more lenient rules of evidence.'). But cf ibid, paras 54–75 (seeking guidance from *Kostovski v the Netherlands*, App 11454/85 (ECtHR, 20 November 1989)). For critical notes, see eg Masha Fedorova and Göran Sluiter, 'Human Rights as *Minimum* Standards in International Criminal Proceedings' (2009) 3 *Human Rights & International Legal Discourse* 9, 39–40; Vasiliev (n 6) 382–383.

45 *DRC* victim participation decision (n 41) para. 54.

46 ibid, para. 52.

47 The Appeals Chamber subsequently abolished the 'general participatory right' of victims during investigation, although without specifically addressing the PTC's reliance on external case law: *Situation in the DRC*, ICC-01/04-556, Judgment on victim participation in the investigation stage of the proceedings in the appeal of the OPCD, 19 December 2008; *Situation in Darfur*, ICC-02/05-177, Judgment on victim participation in the investigation stage of the proceedings in the appeal of the OPCD against the decision of Pre-Trial Chamber I of 3 December 2007, 2 February 2009.

3.2.2 Restate and Apply Legal Tests Accurately

The second rule governing ICTs' recourse to external precedents is self-evident, but no less important for that. Whenever engaging with, and relying on, such precedents, a recipient court develops its own 'interpretations of interpretations' of human rights standards by a donor court. It is important to get the gist and implications of the latter court's *ratione* right. At a minimum, the judges must care to restate the relevant legal formula faithfully and beware distorting it. In case they decide to integrate the borrowed test or concept into their own *rationes decidendi*, they must apply it correctly to the situation at hand rather than miscalculating its practical effects. An invocation of external jurisprudence that falls short in this regard, whether deliberately or not, would amount to a methodological 'abuse'. While the two types of breaches—misstatement and misapplication—are distinct, they may be examined jointly. It is sometimes difficult to establish at what point the error crept in: whether the court misconstrued the test or whether it lost its footing when matching it to facts.

The ICC practice provides some examples of erroneous restatement and/or application of external human rights tests. In interpreting the standard of proof for the issuance of arrest warrant or summons to appear,[48] PTCs have relied on the requirement of 'reasonable suspicion' under Article 5(1)(c) of the ECHR and its interpretation by the ECtHR.[49] In *Al Bashir*, the PTC majority denied the prosecution application for an arrest warrant against the Sudanese President with regard to the charge of genocide because the standard of 'reasonable grounds' had not been met.[50] The PTC construed the Article 58 standard as requiring that the existence of the Government of Sudan's genocidal intent be the only reasonable conclusion available on the materials provided by the prosecution. Judge Ušacka distanced herself from this finding, opining that the threshold for the issuance of arrest warrant was thus set too high. According to her, under the 'reasonable grounds to believe' test, the prosecution had to show that a reasonable inference that the person has committed the crime,

48 Art 58(1)(a) and (7) ICC Statute ('reasonable grounds to believe that the person has committed a crime').

49 *Prosecutor v Harun*, ICC-02/05-01/07-1, Decision on the Prosecution Application under Article 58(7) of the Statute, Pre-Trial Chamber I, 27 April 2007, para. 28; *Prosecutor v Al Bashir*, ICC-02/05-01/09-3, Decision on the Prosecution's Application for a Warrant of Arrest against Omar Hassan Ahmad Al Bashir, Pre-Trial Chamber I, 4 March 2009 ('*Al Bashir* I pre-trial arrest warrant decision'), paras 32 fn 33 and 160 fn 180 (referring to five ECtHR judgments).

50 *Al Bashir* I pre-trial arrest warrant decision (n 49) paras 158–161, 205.

could be made on the materials presented, not that this was the *only* reasonable inference.[51]

The Appeals Chamber sided with the dissenting judge and reversed the PTC decision on the ground that the construction and application of the Article 58 standard by the PTC majority was erroneous; the standard adopted was more exacting than necessary at the stage of issuance of arrest warrant.[52] The appeal judges specifically pointed out its inconsistency with ECtHR interpretation of the analogical standard of 'reasonable suspicion' in *Fox et al v the United Kingdom*—the case also referenced by the PTC—, 'presuppos[ing] the existence of facts or information which would satisfy an objective observer that the person concerned may have committed the offence' and, therefore, not requiring certainty.[53] Hence, although the PTC drew upon and referenced relevant ECtHR jurisprudence for interpretive ends, it misconstrued the standard and, as a result, applied it incorrectly. By implicating Strasbourg case law in this error and by failing to benefit from it in a way bolstering its reasoning, it arguably breached the rule governing the transfer of judicial rationales, making itself liable to reversal.

To give another example, it is worth considering the controversial decision to issue a notice to participants about the possible change of the legal characterisation of facts pursuant to Regulation 55 of the Regulations of the Court during the deliberations phase in *Katanga and Ngudjolo*. This ultimately resulted in the substitution of Mr. Katanga's mode of liability for the one not charged by the prosecution and his conviction under Article 25(1)(d) of the Statute.[54] Among others, the Regulation 55 ruling is remarkable for an extensive—and not entirely judicious—use of external human rights precedents. The majority of Trial Chamber II drew heavily on ECtHR case law as a means to shield itself from the critique that triggering Regulation 55 at so late a stage did not violate the rights of the accused.

The majority referred to Strasbourg judgments in support of the position that legal recharacterisation of facts notified at a late stage in the trial or after conviction at trial, is unproblematic, provided that the accused was informed

51 Separate and Partly Dissenting Opinion of Judge Anita Ušacka, *Al Bashir* I pre-trial arrest warrant decision (n 49) paras 31–34.

52 *Prosecutor v Al Bashir*, ICC-02/05-01/09-73, Judgment on the appeal of the Prosecutor against the "Decision on the Prosecution's Application for a Warrant of Arrest against Omar Hassan Ahmad Al Bashir", Appeals Chamber, 3 February 2010, paras 1, 31–33, 39, 41.

53 Ibid, para. 31 fn 89.

54 *Prosecutor v Katanga*, ICC-01/04-01/07-3436-AnxI, Judgment pursuant to Article 74 of the Statute, Trial Chamber II, 7 March 2014 ('*Katanga* judgment').

and had an opportunity to contest the modification.[55] The majority qualified its reliance on ECtHR judgments by pointing out that those 'were handed down in cases distinct in nature from the cases before the Court', but fell short of addressing the implications of this concession. The judges nevertheless proceeded to saying, with reference to ECtHR case law, that in domestic jurisdictions, the modification of a charge is typically decided during deliberations, and that 'late recharacterisation does not, per se, oppugn the right to a fair trial, or indeed the impartiality of the judges'.[56] Nor did the recharacterisation, in the opinion of the majority, violate other rights of Mr. Katanga, for the elucidation of which it, again, provided copious cites to ECtHR interpretations, including: the right to be informed of the nature, cause, and content of the charges;[57] the right to have adequate time and facilities for the preparation of the defence;[58] the right to be tried without undue delay;[59] and the right not to be compelled to testify against oneself.[60]

In challenging the majority's portrayal of the measure taken under Regulation 55 as fair, Judge Van den Wyngaert also relied upon ECtHR jurisprudence—both in her dissents to the notice decision and to the judgment convicting Mr. Katanga. Judge Van den Wyngaert employed Strasbourg case law in her pointed attack on the Chamber's reasoning, wielding it as a sword to batter the majority's defences and counter its findings of non-violation of Mr. Katanga's rights. Citing to ECtHR judgments, the judge dispelled the notion that the Regulation 55 notice did not violate the right to a fair and impartial proceeding;[61] the right

55 *Prosecutor v Katanga*, ICC-01/04-01/07-3319-tENG/FRA, Decision on the implementation of regulation 55 of the Regulations of the Court, Trial Chamber II, 21 November 2012 ('*Katanga and Ngudjolo* Regulation 55 decision'), para. 16 fn 29. Upholding these findings and citing to ECtHR judgments, see *Prosecutor v Katanga*, ICC-01/04-01/07-3363, Judgment on the appeal of Mr Germain Katanga against the decision of Trial Chamber II of 21 November 2012, Appeals Chamber, 27 March 2013 ('*Katanga* Regulation 55 appeal judgment'), paras 93–94 fns 200–201.

56 *Katanga and Ngudjolo* Regulation 55 decision (n 55) para. 18 fn 31.

57 ibid, para. 22 fn 35–36. See also *Katanga* Regulation 55 appeal judgment (n 55) para. 100 fn 202.

58 ibid, para. 37 fn 56–58.

59 ibid, para. 43 fn 61 and 63.

60 ibid, paras 48–49 fns 64–67.

61 Dissenting Opinion of Judge Christine Van den Wyngaert, *Katanga and Ngudjolo* Regulation 55 decision (n 55) para. 32 fn 50 (arguing that 'triggering Regulation 55 at the very end of the deliberations ... risks creating a perception of partiality' which, according to ECtHR jurisprudence violates the court's obligation of impartiality).

to be informed about the nature, scope and content of the charges;[62] and the right to be tried without undue delay.[63] The dissenting judge's verdict on the majority's use of ECtHR judgments and its outcome was stern:

> An analysis of whether a given invocation of Regulation 55 is fair must thus be done on a case by case assessment in light of the Court's procedural structure and must be mindful of how the trial has been conducted when a recharacterisation is proposed. The Majority's reference to cases from the European Court of Human Rights, concerning late recharacterisations in particular domestic contexts, which were found not to be rights violations, is therefore of limited interest. In the end, all that matters is whether this proposed recharacterisation is fair in light of the way in which this trial has been conducted.[64]

In so far as Judge Van den Wyngaert's critique goes, the implication is that the majority effectively misapplied ECtHR jurisprudence by drawing wrong inferences from respective tests, and letting the analytical fallacy control the outcome. The judges downplayed the aspects of ECtHR's *rationes* that posed obstacles *en route* to the finding of non-violation of rights, or failed to carefully match the relevant legal tests to the factual circumstances relating to the conduct of the case proceedings. These 'grammar errors' arguably zeroed out the corroborative value of the Chamber's cross-references to ECtHR jurisprudence.

3.2.3 Appreciate the Context of Jurisprudence

Yet another type of common mistake in drawing upon another court's jurisprudence, is 'missing the forest for the trees', ie failing to appreciate the meaning of a legal rationale or its elements within a broader context of the donor court's case law, or disregarding judgments relevant to the issue at hand and, possibly,

---

62 ibid, para. 47 fn 67 (disagreeing that the mere existence of Regulation 55 constitutes a sufficient notice of a possible legal recharacterisation of facts and directly countering this notion by a lengthy quote from *IH et al v Austria*, App 42780/98 (ECtHR, 20 April 2006) paras 32–34).

63 ibid, para. 51 fn 70 (opining that the Regulation 55 notice risks causing an undue delay attributable to the Chamber, with reference to ECtHR judgments). See also Minority Opinion of Judge Christine Van den Wyngaert, ICC-01/04-01/07-3436-AnxI, *Katanga* judgment (n 54) paras 120 fn 152 and 121 fn 157 (referring to further ECtHR judgments).

64 Dissenting Opinion of Judge Christine Van den Wyngaert, *Katanga and Ngudjolo* Regulation 55 decision (n 55) para. 57. See also Minority Opinion of Judge Christine Van den Wyngaert (n 63) para. 96.

(more) representative of the status of jurisprudence. This fault is contiguous to a failure to identify or restate the relevant foreign test correctly and may be caused by the recipient court's incomplete knowledge or deficient understanding of the donor court's jurisprudence. It could also result from a deliberately selective, goal-driven approach to transjudicial importation whereby the donor court's jurisprudence not supporting the recipient court's reasoning, is significantly downplayed or simply ignored. Blunders or manipulations of this kind are difficult to detect due to their relative subtlety, and hard to come by. Fortunately, ICT judges and legal staff typically demonstrate a solid knowledge of ECtHR jurisprudence and extend research far enough to be able to 'see the forest for the trees'. However, aberrations are not precluded and ICTs should care to avoid them, if only to avoid giving an impression of manipulative use of authorities. Additionally, commentators ought to take ICTs' restatements and summaries of positions of other courts, which usually precede declarations of adherence or deviation, with a grain of salt.

Some of the examples already provided might indicate that the judges' case-law research is not always comprehensive enough, which occasionally results in a failure to mention and appreciate ECtHR judgments of considerable relevance, next to others courts choose to discuss.[65] Deficient knowledge or less than holistic understanding of the context of the counterpart court's jurisprudence can become apparent from ICTs' partial engagement with foreign *rationes*. In *Tadić*, the Appeals Chamber decided to give the principle of equality of arms 'a more liberal interpretation than that normally upheld with regard to proceedings before domestic courts', the one making the prosecution a beneficiary, to the disadvantage of the accused.[66] It ruled that 'the Prosecution and the Defence must be equal before the Trial Chamber', considering that both parties are facing comparable difficulties related to the dependence on (the often unavailable) state cooperation, which is a factor outside the Tribunal's control.

Aside from the problem that the Appeals Chamber did arguably not readjust the content of the principle to factor in the structural constraints on the defence (which is potentially caught by the 'grammar rule' to be discussed next),[67] it also appears to have assumed that its reliance on the argument

65 eg Dissenting Opinion of Judge Christine Van den Wyngaert, *Katanga and Ngudjolo* Regulation 55 decision (n 55) para. 47 fn 67; *Katanga and Ngudjolo* Regulation 55 decision (n 55) para. 52.

66 *Prosecutor v Tadić*, IT-94-1-A, Judgement, 15 July 1999 ('*Tadić* appeal judgment') paras 51–52.

67 Gabrielle McIntyre, 'Equality of Arms—Defining Human Rights in the Jurisprudence of

about the unavailability of state cooperation is censured under the standard upheld under ECtHR jurisprudence. However, this is not the case; its demonstrative departure from the established interpretation was superfluous and the thus inaugurated 'more liberal interpretation' a misnomer.[68] Under the Strasbourg legal test, the respondent state will not automatically be found in violation of the right to obtain the attendance and examination of witnesses under Article 6(3)(d) of the Convention where the required cooperation from a foreign state could not be obtained, as long as the party concerned was not placed at a substantial disadvantage vis-à-vis the opponent in presenting its case.[69] It is another matter that unequal access by the defence to evidence due to ineffective or absent state cooperation and inability of the court to assist, may be a chronic malaise for ICTs, calling for a more rigorous, as opposed to more liberal, interpretation.

Thus, an ICT's treatment of issues may deviate from the established human rights practice while it assures of its adherence thereto and, vice versa, its practice may in fact and on substance be in accord with the ECtHR's rationales despite 'centrifugal rhetoric'. The line between cases where human rights jurisprudence has been 'abused' and where an ICT has not used it enough, or as much as it should have, is thin and difficult to draw. But, whenever detected, a failure to appreciate a broader context of the donor court's jurisprudence gives rise to a perception that the recipient court does not engage with it in earnest, and that it rather manipulates—cherry-picks and neglects at will—the external authorities in promoting specific outcomes. Any invocation of human rights jurisprudence cast in this light would be self-defeating because it undermines rather than enhances the persuasiveness of judicial reasoning and the quality of the decisions.

3.2.4 Readjust Legal Tests If and as Appropriate

The fourth basic rule regarding the use of human rights jurisprudence by ICTs, concerns the duty of a recipient court to readjust or 'translate' the borrowed legal tests or concepts—if and as appropriate. The court should assess whether the transjudicial loan at issue can be utilised in its own decision-making with-

---

the International Criminal Tribunal for the former Yugoslavia' (2003) 16 Leiden Journal of International Law 269–320.

68 See also Fedorova and Sluiter (n 44) 50.

69 eg *PV v FRG*, Admissibility, App 11853/85 (ECommHR, 13 July 1987), para. 4(c) (Art. 6(3)(d) 'does not grant the accused an unlimited right to secure the appearance of witnesses in court. Its purpose is rather to ensure equality between the defence and the prosecution as regards the summoning and examining of witnesses.').

out modifications; and, conversely, whether changes it considers introducing, would be warranted by its unique (or not so unique) jurisdictional and legal setup of adjudication.[70] Any such parameters of legal import are situational, and will need to be factored in when determining the applicable 'thick' human rights standards. Therefore, any good-faith interpretation of human rights norms should aim at endowing them with requisite regulatory density within specific proceedings. It must be context-sensitive and reasonably casuistic, ie fact-driven. Because only then will it allow for a *principled and careful* rebalancing of established legal tests in light of the circumstances before the court.[71] Judges should remain alert to factual, institutional, and legal parameters of cases before them, and account, as part of the applicable rationales, for material parameters relating to the purpose, nature, and the institutional setting of adjudication.

In particular, ICT judges should be—and are—cognizant of the distinct nature and constraints of the supervisory mandates regional human rights courts exercise vis-à-vis domestic systems. The ECtHR interprets 'minimum standards' set forth in the Convention when reviewing the States' compliance. This supervisory role entails neither handing down 'thick' prescriptions (as opposed to open-ended principles) on what contracting parties should do, nor directly performing functions of criminal adjudication like ICTs do. In this sense, the ECtHR's mission is more akin to that of a constitutional court.[72] In order to avoid charges of 'abuse' of external precedents, judges are well-advised to resist the dual temptation: on the one hand, to unreflectively transfer ready-made tests developed in and for other contexts; and, on the other hand, to amend them in ways not warranted by peculiarities of their case docket, or distort the purport of the borrowed tests and their components.

One low-hanging-fruit example of neglecting this rule, is the *Government II* case before the ICTR. In that case, the Trial Chamber was faced with a string of defence motions alleging violations of the right to be tried without undue delay.[73] This complaint was ultimately tackled as part of the appeal from the

70 Questioning the 'uniqueness dogma' as the basis for ICTs' disregard of ECtHR jurisprudence: Geneuss (n 38) 407, 412–414.

71 Calling for caution when 're-orienting' standards, Fedorova and Sluiter (n 44) 33–34, 51.

72 Croquet (n 6) 92–93, 124–125; Geneuss (n 6) 415–420.

73 *Prosecutor v Bizimungu*, ICTR-99-50-T, Decision on Prosper Mugiraneza's Fourth Motion to Dismiss Indictment for Violation of Right to Trial without Undue Delay, Trial Chamber II, 23 June 2010 (*'Bizimungu et al* undue delay decision IV'); *Prosecutor v Bizimungu*, ICTR-99-50-T, Decision on Prosper Mugiraneza's Third Motion to Dismiss Indictment for Violation of His Right to a Trial without Undue Delay, Trial Chamber II, 10 February 2009

trial judgment.[74] The relevant time span related to the period when the trial judgment was being prepared: the deliberation took almost three years after the closing arguments, with the time the accused spent in detention totaling twelve years from their surrender to the ICTR in 1999. The legal test governing the determination of whether the right to an expeditious trial, which the Appeals Chamber pronounced and directed the Trial Chamber to apply, featured five elements: (1) the length of the delay; (2) the complexity of the proceedings, such as the number of charges, the number of accused, the number of witnesses, the volume of evidence, the complexity of facts and law; (3) the conduct of the parties; (4) the conduct of the relevant authorities; and (5) the prejudice to the accused, if any.[75] The appeal judges also ruled that it was erroneous for the Trial Chamber to take into consideration 'the fundamental purpose of the Tribunal' and the 'ends of justice' against which the right of the accused to an expeditious trial was to be balanced.[76]

While this test largely emulates that which was developed by the ECtHR and cited in earlier ICTR decisions,[77] there are also material differences. The ECtHR determines unreasonable delay considering in particular the complexity of the case, the conduct of the applicant and of the relevant authorities, as well as the

('*Bizimungu et al* undue delay decision III'); *Prosecutor v Bizimungu*, ICTR-99-50-T, Decision on Prosper Mugiraneza's Second Motion to Dismiss for Deprivation of his Right to Trial Without Undue Delay, Trial Chamber II, 29 May 2007 ('*Bizimungu et al* undue delay decision II'); *Prosecutor v Bizimungu*, ICTR-99-50-T, Decision on Prosper Mugiraneza's Motion to Dismiss the Indictment for Violation of Article 20(4)(C) of the Statute, Trial Chamber II, 2 October 2003 ('*Bizimungu et al* undue delay decision I'). See also *Prosecutor v Mugiraneza*, ICTR-99-50-T, Decision on Prosper Mugiraneza's Application for a Hearing or other Relief on his Motion for Dismissal for Violation of his Right to Trial without Undue Delay, Trial Chamber II, 3 November 2004; *Prosecutor v Mugenzi*, ICTR-99-50-I, Decision on Justin Mugenzi's Motion for Stay of Proceedings or in the Alternative Provisional Release (Rule 65) and in Addition Severance (Rule 82(B)), Trial Chamber II, 8 November 2002 ('*Mugenzi et al* stay decision').

74 *Prosecutor v Mugenzi*, ICTR-99-50-A, Judgement, Appeals Chamber, 4 February 2013.

75 *Prosecutor v Bizimungu*, ICTR-99-50-A73, Decision on Prosper Mugiraneza's Interlocutory Appeal from Trial Chamber II Decision of 2 October 2003 Denying the Motion to Dismiss the Indictment, Demand Speedy Trial and for Appropriate Relief, Appeals Chamber, 27 February 2004, at 2.

76 ibid; *Mugenzi et al* stay decision (n 73) para. 32; *Bizimungu et al* undue delay decision I (n 73) para. 11.

77 *Prosecutor v. Kanyabashi*, ICTR-96-15-I, Decision on the Extremely Urgent Motion on Habeas Corpus and for Stoppage of Proceedings, Trial Chamber II, 23 May 2000, para. 68.

importance of what is at stake for the applicant in the litigation.[78] Although the Appeals Chamber did not reference that jurisprudence—or any case law at all for that matter—, it most certainly drew upon it, as attested by the formulation of specific elements. The purport and validity of the modifications it introduced to the established human rights test can with reason be questioned. This concerns in particular the 'prejudice' element: would not any delay by definition be prejudicial to the accused? The addition of this prong is neither explained in light of the legally relevant circumstances of the case or the ICTR docket in general, nor corroborated by any authorities. Worse still, it elevates the bar for the accused as it makes the showing of a violation for a moving party more difficult. It is unsurprising then that, despite inordinate delays in the case, the defence complaints were consistently turned down by the Trial Chamber, who cited, among others, a failure to show prejudice.[79]

Furthermore, there are grounds to consider that the Trial Chamber's application of the individual elements of the test was skewed. Its reasoning did not adequately take into account the factual circumstances that were highly relevant for the determination of the scope of legal protection of the right to be tried without undue delay. First, as Judge Short stated in his dissenting opinions to the Trial Chamber's 4th undue delay decision and to the trial judgment, in assessing the reasonableness of the delay, the majority did not factor in the length of the deliberation phase in light of the totality of the proceedings.[80] Second, the majority's analyses of the 'conduct of authorities' element conveniently under-emphasised the highly relevant factor, namely the conduct of the court and of the relevant UN organs. This issue was flagged by Judge Short who was critical of the ICTR management's 'policy of pursuing new cases prior to reaching judgement in ongoing cases' and the practice of judges being involved in multiple cases at the same time which brought about administrative and scheduling problems. The fault for that was also attributable to the UN General Assembly and the Security Council which failed to organise the ICTR in such a way as to prevent or remedy those delays, as the ECtHR requires of

78 *Eckle v Germany*, App 8130/78 (ECtHR, 15 July 1982), para. 80; *Zimmerman and Steiner v Switzerland*, App 8737/79 (ECtHR, 13 July 1983) para. 24; *Pélissier and Sassi v France*, App 25444/94 (ECtHR, 25 March 1999) para. 67.

79 *Bizimungu et al* undue delay decision II (n 73) paras 38–39; *Bizimungu et al* undue delay decision III (n 73) paras 21–24; *Bizimungu et al* undue delay decision IV (n 73) paras 17–19.

80 Partially Dissenting Opinion of Judge Emile Francis Short, *Bizimungu et al* undue delay decision IV (n 73) para. 2; *Prosecutor v Bizimungu*, Partially Dissenting Opinion of Judge Emile Francis Short, Judgement, ICTR-99-50-T, Trial Chamber II, 30 September 2011 ('*Bizimungu et al* trial judgment dissent'), para. 3.

domestic authorities.[81] With respect to the defence of excessive case-load, the Tribunal arguably turned a blind eye to the requirement under ECtHR case law that the relevant authorities must show diligence and undertake, with requisite promptness, remedial action to address an 'exceptional situation' of a 'temporary backlog of business'.[82] In the event of inordinately lengthy delays, there is a presumption of violation and a burden on the authorities to rebut it.

Judge Short found that the right of the accused to be tried without undue delay was violated in view of the excessive duration of the judgment-drafting phase. This conclusion and the underlying reasoning resonated with Judge Robinson of the Appeals Chamber, the majority of which, however, also sided with the trial court's majority on this matter.[83] Judge Robinson opined that the exigencies of the ICTR's work provided no justification for the length of time taken by the Trial Chamber in preparing the judgment, and that the delay was unreasonable in the circumstances.[84]

The dissenting voices in *Government II* not only put a question mark over the position of the majority. They also shed a critical light on the method employed in (tacitly) importing and reforming an established test from human rights jurisprudence. The majority's examination of the standards from ECtHR jurisprudence should have been more robust and comprehensive. Any alterations to the legal test, if they had to be made at all, must have been thoroughly explained and justified. Overall, the ICTR should have accorded greater weight to the factual circumstances that the ECtHR considers material. There were no good reasons for it not to do so, at least none transpire from the majority's reasoning. Had the judges applied the elements of the test faithfully, their reasoning would have been more persuasive, and the outcome of the determination of the alleged violation of the right to be tried without undue delay, would have likely been different. The credibility of ICTR jurisprudence on this matter can with reason be questioned. It raises the spectre of an opportunistic and end-driven utilisation of the imported judicial rationales.

---

81 Partially Dissenting Opinion of Judge Emile Francis Short, *Bizimungu et al* undue delay decision IV (n 73) paras 3–5; *Bizimungu et al* trial judgment dissent (n 80) para. 5.

82 *Eckle v Germany* (n 78) para. 92; *Milasi v Italy*, App 10527/83 (ECtHR, 26 June 1987) para. 18. *Bizimungu et al* trial judgment (n 81) para. 74 (expressly recognising 'concerns that the conduct of the Tribunal, and the increased workload of the presiding judges more specifically, has contributed to this delay' and failing to show what measures of prompt remedial action were taken).

83 *Prosecutor v Bizimungu*, Judgement, ICTR-99-50-A, Appeals Chamber, 4 February 2013, paras 30–37.

84 ibid, Partially Dissenting Opinion of Judge Patrick Robinson, paras 2 and 8.

4 Costs of Abuse

What are the consequences of breaching the above transjudicial 'grammar rules', if any? Could they discourage judges from misusing external human rights precedents? One evident corollary is the diminished analytical rigour, persuasiveness, and quality of judicial reasoning. Unless spotted and rectified at appellate review, a methodologically deficient invocation and importation of a foreign legal rationale will remain a stain on the texture of the ruling, weakening its legal foundation and undermining the legitimacy of the outcome. The prospect of a reversal by the higher court is a significant disincentive, but it is no antidote where it is the Appeals Chamber itself that treats another court's *rationes* cavalierly, in the lack of external human rights supervision over ICTs.

The extra-systemic cost of 'abusing' external human rights precedents can be appreciated considering the discretionary and informal character of transjudicial communication, and the non-hierarchical relationship between international courts. In this view, an indirect but no less important consequence, is the reputational cost incurred by individual judges and institutions. Serious and pervasive 'grammar errors' inevitably affect their standing within the international judicial profession and the 'community of international courts'. International judicial cross-fertilisation hinges on courts' mutual recognition as equals possessing specialist legal expertise and interpretive and normative authority in their respective fields, and it is contingent on the perceived quality of their jurisprudence. The court which is careless in using a counterpart's jurisprudence, risks detracting from its own gravitas and compromising its position as an equal participant in a judicial dialogue. The precedential value of its rationales will suffer a blow, as will its ability to cross-fertilise back: other courts may become unwilling to invoke and rely on its *rationes* as a means to bolster their analyses. Cross-referencing asymmetries might take root as a result. The blundering court will increasingly be confined to the role of a passive consumer of external rationales, as opposed to donor. This would bar its contributions to the *acquis* of human rights and the construction of an authoritative sub-regime of IHRL tailored for ICTs. As such consequences are remote, it is questionable whether they constitute compelling disincentives, let alone deterrents, to the 'abuse' of external jurisprudence.

Finally, could the ICTs' inept engagement with human rights jurisprudence affect their standing vis-à-vis domestic courts? Coincidentally, some of the latter might be well familiar with the misused jurisprudence and able to spot flaws in the ICTs' methodology. One could think that in such scenarios domestic courts would be less likely to view ICTs as 'role models' in formulating and applying human rights norms.[85] However, it is questionable whether the 'role model' ambition is tenable at all to begin with. In several respects, ICTs have not been able to lead by example in the area of upholding human rights and are unimpressive competitors to the regional human rights courts' influence. Domestic courts will rather continue looking to Strasbourg and San José for guidance, and for the better. Likewise, the episodic role as trend-setters and originators of innovative solutions to the challenges of prosecuting international crimes ICTs may play vis-à-vis domestic courts, is not evidently contingent upon treatment of external human rights jurisprudence. Therefore, instances of erroneous utilisation thereof will hardly substantially affect that role.

5 Conclusion

This chapter has constructed a methodological framework for the evaluation of cross-pollination of judicial rationales between ICTs and the ECtHR that can hopefully assist scholars and practitioners in categorising specific instances of importation of external human rights rationales, either as use or abuse. A variety of extra-judicial objectives tend to be attributed to international courts in connection with judicial cross-fertilisation, depending on one's normative view of this phenomenon. Under several competing accounts, such putative goals are: the unity and coherence of international law, stronger protection of human rights across the board, and the consolidation of the influence of international judiciary as a branch of international governance. Each of these outcome-based conceptions entails an evaluative approach that employs different and incommensurable criteria for the appraisal of invocations of external jurisprudence. Such normative accounts are myopic and, hence, unequipped for the heuristic task of seeing use from abuse of foreign judicial rationales. Instead, the line between proper and improper engagement with foreign jurisprudence must be drawn considering the principal reason which motivates transjudicial cross-referencing: enhancing the quality of judicial reasoning and the depth of legal analysis.

Accordingly, this intrinsic rationale should be accepted as the only appropriate criterion for distinguishing between use and abuse of external jurisprudence. This approach requires focusing on the key indicator of the quality of ICTs' treatment of external jurisprudence: the *methodology* of trans-systemic

85 Fedorova and Sluiter (n 68) 40 (referring to ICTs' 'partial role as human rights tribunals' and their mandate 'to provide a "model of enlightened justice"').

import of judicial rationales, as opposed to its potential outcomes and effects for the unity of IHRL, authority of the international judiciary, and the level of rights protection. The question is whether ICT judges have correctly identified, construed, applied, and, if need be, readjusted an imported legal test; not whether the importation serves any extrinsic, quasi-ideological rationale. An equation of adherence or mere citation to ECtHR *rationes* to use, and of departure to abuse, is baseless, and an example of oversimplified rhetoric surrounding the cross-fertilisation debate. As part of the methodological assessment of the way any ICT has utilised ECtHR rationales, it is not sufficient to look at whether the ICT has embedded its invocations of Strasbourg jurisprudence within the framework of legal formalism. It is equally important to review exactly *how* the recipient court has engaged with foreign concepts, tests, or rationales on substance. When assessing the quality of judicial reasoning, it matters whether the recipient court has identified and restated the 'judicial loan' correctly, with knowledge of the donor court's case law; whether it has faithfully followed or aptly readjusted the test or concept subject to importation; and whether it drew reasonable inferences from said test while transposing it.

Therefore, the use of ECtHR jurisprudence is objectionable not only when an ICTs fails to offer an adequate reasoning for its invocation, but also when it utilises it injudiciously or abusively. The chapter has demonstrated this through examples from practice and identified four rules of 'transjudicial grammar'. These include: avoidance of false analogies with ECtHR case law or dismissal of its relevance without sound reasoning; prohibition on misstating or bending ECtHR rationales to fit the argument; holistic consideration of external jurisprudence, including rationales which may be less favourable to the outcome reached by the court by other means; and the obligation to refrain from unreflectively following ECtHR jurisprudence or altering relevant tests in ways not warranted by the circumstances material for the determination of the scope of protection. This inventory is not exhaustive and further rules could possibly be identified. However, it is argued that where an ICT steers clear of violating at least these basic prescriptions, its use of external human rights jurisprudence will be considerably more solid and unimpeachable from a methodological perspective.

Finally, the chapter has shown that the costs an ICT may incur as a result of its abuse of external jurisprudence are almost entirely reputational and, hence, relatively low. No adverse formal consequences attach to inept treatment of external precedents, save for potential reversal by a higher court, due to the absence of human rights supervision over ICTs. The costs for the blundering court are limited to a diminution of its informal authority vis-à-vis other international as well as national courts. Thus, chronic and serious errors might affect the ICT's standing as a member of the 'community of courts' and devalue its *rationes decidendi* on the marketplace of international judicial rationales, potentially deepening any cross-referencing asymmetries. Repercussions of the abuse of human rights jurisprudence for ICTs' reputation with national courts will hardly be felt. Unlike regional courts and treaty bodies exercising supervision over human rights compliance of domestic jurisdictions, ICTs are an unlikely and, arguably, unfit source of guidance on human rights matters to begin with. Even if one were to accept its initial tenability, the ICTs' attributed 'role model' ambition has never come to pass due to their mixed track record in this regard. In the absence of any real disincentives and deterrents for erratic engagement with external case law, one has little else to hold on to than legal competence, ethical integrity, and professionalism of international judges.

CHAPTER 2

'Directory Authority': Fertilising International Criminal Tribunals' Human Rights Standards with European Court of Human Rights' Case Law

*Julia Geneuss**

1 Introduction: Cross-referencing and Cross-fertilisation

When discussing human rights issues, in particular the rights of the accused, international criminal courts frequently refer to the European Convention on Human Rights and the jurisprudence of the European Court of Human Rights. This phenomenon occurs despite the fact that no formal relationship between ICTs and the European Court—or any other international human rights court—exists and, thus, the jurisprudence of the latter is not legally binding on the former.

With this practice of cross-referencing of legal norms and decisions, the tribunals engage in 'transjudicial communication' as an interactive process across the boundaries of two different legal systems, the international criminal justice system on the one hand and the European human rights system on the other.[1] This exercise of 'cross-jurisdictional referencing' is, first and foremost, social and legal practice.[2] Cross-referencing is flexible and pragmatic, but also selective and arbitrary. Its form and value can vary, so can the degree of reciprocity.[3]

* Revised and shortened version of 'Obstacles to Cross-Fertilisation: The International Criminal Tribunals' "Unique Context" and the Flexibility of the European Court of Human Rights' Case Law' (2015) 84 Nordic Journal of International Law 404.

1 On transjudicial communication see generally Anne-Marie Slaughter, 'A Typology of Transjudicial Communication' (1994) 29 University of Richmond Law Review 99.

2 Antje Wiener and Philip Liste, 'Lost Without Translation? Cross-Referencing and a New Global Community of Courts' (2014) 21 Indiana Journal of Global Legal Studies 263, 266 and 268.

3 Slaughter (n 1) 101. According to Slaughter's 'geometry of transjudicial communication', the cross-referencing of ICTs to the ECtHR case law would be horizontal (the ICTs are not bound to follow or even take account of the ECtHR's jurisprudence under a formal relationship) and as regards the degree of reciprocal engagement rather take the form of a monologue than a dialogue (the ECtHR is not an active participant in the communication process). On this last point, see *infra*.

 | DOI: 10.1163/9789004313750_004

Its main function can be normative with the intention to find an effective and acceptable solution for a specific legal problem within the borrowing court's own legal system.[4] Or cross-referencing can be done for more strategic reasons in order to enhance the legitimacy of the decision of the borrowing court.

According to Antje Wiener and Philip Liste, cross-fertilisation, on the other hand, is not a practice but an effect than can result from (normative) cross-referencing and refers to the 'transmission of meaning from one (legal) context to another'.[5] Understood in this narrower sense, cross-fertilisation requires not only a 'shared understanding of meaning', but also the willingness or readiness to change one's own normative structure.[6] Therefore, cross-fertilisation can be described as the 'integration of normative spheres'.[7] However, a direct 'cut and paste' transmission or transplant of legal norms or concepts between different legal systems is rarely possible. Rather, the legal norm or concept must be translated from the language of the original legal system into the language of the receiving one.[8] Inherent to any translation is the risk of misinterpretation of the original understanding of meaning. Thus, for a successful translation, a 'detailed hermeneutic understanding both of the context in which it was originally embedded and of the new context for which it is destined' is necessary.[9]

---

4 According to Michal Bobek, *Comparative Reasoning in European Supreme Courts* (OUP 2013) 245, the purpose of cross-referencing of domestic constitutional courts is to find inspiration for a workable and acceptable solution, which could be introduced into the own domestic normative environment; it implies a pragmatic, not a scientific process, that is selective and non-representative.

5 Wiener and Liste (n 2) 264; see also ibid 267. Wiener and Liste argue that only when such effective cross-fertilisation ensues one can speak of a 'global community of courts'. For a less demanding and rather loose definition of cross-fertilisation, see Slaughter (n 1) 117, who argues that cross-fertilisation is the dissemination of ideas from one legal system to another with the purpose to provide inspiration for the solution of a particular legal problem.

6 Wiener and Liste (n 2) 270 ('These enactive practices include, for example, translating other normative meanings into one's own normative structure to the effect that domestic structures of meaning are challenged and may—over the ensuing course of contestation—become subject to change').

7 Wiener and Liste (n 2) 286.

8 Wiener and Liste (n 2) 265. On the translation of international law by domestic judges, see Karen Knop, 'Here and There: International Law in Domestic Courts' (2000) 32 New York University Journal of International Law and Politics 501.

9 Neil Walker, 'Postnational Constitutionalism and the Problem of Translation' in Joseph H.H. Weiler and Marlene Wind (eds), *European Constitutionalism Beyond the State* (CUP 2003) 27, 37, cited according to Wiener and Liste (n 2) 265.

In order to evaluate the translation, two aspects can be distinguished:[10] First, the product or outcome of the translation, that is if the norm or concept was translated from its old to the new context without losing its normative meaning. Second, the method of the translation, that is the translation process itself. When translating legal norms or concepts into their own legal context, courts must follow a principled, methodologically coherent and consistent, as well as transparent approach.

It has often been observed that when ICTs refer to ECtHR jurisprudence they follow what Antonio Cassese has described as the 'wild approach':[11] An unprincipled and erratic use of ECtHR case law, for pragmatic and strategic reasons primarily when Strasbourg judgments contain an interpretation of an ECHR right that the ICT judges find convincing and that supports a conclusion they have already made. In general, there is no thorough discussion of the ECtHR human rights interpretation and thus this practice of cross-referencing says little about the value or significance that ICTs assign to ECtHR case law.[12] As a result, a cross-fertilisation effect will hardly ensue from this practice.

In this paper, an argument will be made that in order to minimise the risk of arbitrary decision making and to benefit from a fertilisation effect ICTs should focus more on the method of translating ECtHR case law into their own language, a process which should be less 'wild', but more principled, transparent and methodologically coherent. First, this paper will take a brief look at ICTs' view on ECtHR (and human rights courts) case law, the risks of contextual re-interpretation of human rights standards by ICTs and to what degree the common argument of the ICTs' 'uniqueness' justifies a deviation from the interpretation of human rights courts and bodies. After that the different ways in which the ECtHR and ECHR member States on the one hand as well as ICTs on the other develop their respective set of human rights standards will be analysed. It will be shown that domestic courts and the ECtHR are engaged in a

---

10 Walker (n 9) 37, cited according to Wiener and Liste (n 2) 265, 269 ('those who can claim membership of both linguistic communities must agree that the *method and product* of the translation is adequate to capture and convey a similar meaning in the two languages' (emphasis added)). See also Knop (n 8) 530 ('the idea of translation requires us to be faithful to the other language as well as to assert our own').

11 See Antonio Cassese, 'The Influence of the European Court of Human Rights on International Criminal Tribunals—Some Methodological Remarks' in Morten Bergsmo (ed), *Human Rights for the Downtrodden: Essays in Honour of Asbjørn Eide* (Martinus Nijhoff 2003) 19, 21 and 50.

12 See Cassese (n 11) 21.

fruitful dialogue whereas ICTs regularly interpret and apply human rights standards without any communicative process. Against this backdrop, an argument will be made that, in order to counterbalance the risks inherent in this communicative solitude, ICTs should regard the jurisprudence of the Strasbourg Court not as 'persuasive' but as 'directory authority'.

II International Criminal Justice and Human Rights

The relationship between international criminal justice and human rights law is complex and has been dealt with, from many different angles and legal standpoints, extensively in the academic literature. There seems to be consensus that ICTs are bound by human rights.[13] Less clear, but not the topic of this paper, are the sources of the obligation to respect human rights and how international human rights law enters the ICT's respective system.[14] And even more unclear, so it seems, is whether and to what degree ICTs are free to deviate from human rights standards developed by human rights courts or bodies or, to put it the other way round, if ICTs can in some (informal) way be 'bound' by the latters' interpretation.

1 *Re-interpretation of Human Rights*

As is well-known, a Trial Chamber of the ICTY in the 1995 *Tadić* Protective Measures decision found that it was not bound by human rights principles as

13 As regards the ICC, see Article 21(3) of the ICC Statute. Regarding the ad hoc tribunals, the UN Secretary General stated that 'the International Tribunal must fully respect internationally recognized standards regarding the rights of the accused at all stages of its proceedings', see UNSC, Report of the Secretary-General Pursuant to Para. 2 of the Security Council Resolution 808 (1993), para. 6. From the academic literature, see only Gerhard Werle and Florian Jeßberger, *Principles of International Criminal Law* (3rd edn, OUP 2014) marg. no. 146; Lorenzo Gradoni, 'International Criminal Courts and Tribunals: Bound by Human Rights Norms … or Tied Down?' (2006) 19 Leiden Journal of International Law 847, 850; Lorenzo Gradoni, 'The Human Rights Dimension of International Criminal Procedure' in Göran Sluiter and others (eds), *International Criminal Procedure: Principles and Rules* (OUP 2013) 74, 81, both with further references; Masha Fedorova and Göran Sluiter, 'Human Rights as *Minimum* Standards in International Criminal Proceedings' (2009) 3 Human Rights and International Legal Discourse 9, 18. But see Salvatore Zappalà, *Human Rights in International Criminal Proceedings* (OUP 2003) 7 (who argues that the adherence of ICTs to international human rights is a policy issue, not a legal question).

14 See Gradoni, 'Human Rights Dimension' (n 13) 74; Gradoni, 'International Criminal Courts and Tribunals' (n 13) 847; Fedorova and Sluiter (n 13) 9.

interpreted by the ECtHR or any other human rights court or body.[15] Instead it was free to (re-)interpret the fair trial guarantee and other human rights principles 'within its own legal context'.[16] The 'context of its unique legal framework' was determined by its mandate to adjudicate on an international level 'crimes which are considered so horrific as to warrant universal jurisdiction' and not merely 'ordinary' crimes like domestic courts subject to the review of human rights courts and bodies.[17] Due to the different circumstances in which the right to a fair trial is to be interpreted, the Tribunal argued, it was comparable to a 'military tribunal, which often has limited rights of due process and more lenient rules of evidence'.[18] Similarly, yet without the unfortunate comparison with a military tribunal, in 1999 the ICTR Appeals Chamber argued that the jurisprudence of the ECtHR and other human rights courts is not binding on the Tribunal, but is to be regarded as 'persuasive authority which may be of assistance in applying and interpreting the Tribunal's applicable law'.[19] This, so it seems, has been the predominant position of ICTs ever since.[20]

In the academic literature, while often criticising specific decisions of ICTs, it is acknowledged that human rights standards and related case law are not transposable, as such, to ICTs, but that a certain 're-interpretation' or 're-orientation' is necessary.[21] This, so it is argued, is because human rights are princi-

15 *Prosecutor v Tadić*, ICTY IT-94-1, Decision on the Prosecutor's Motion Requesting Protective Measures for Victims and Witnesses, Trial Chamber, 10 August 1995 ('*Tadić* Decision on Protective Measures'), paras 17–30.

16 ibid para. 28.

17 ibid paras 27–28.

18 ibid para. 28.

19 *Prosecutor v Barayagwiza*, ICTR-97-19, Decision, Appeals Chamber, 3 November 1999, para. 40.

20 See also *Prosecutor v Galić*, ICTY IT-98-29, Judgment, Appeals Chamber, Separate Opinion of Judge Shahabuddeen, 30 November 2006, paras 18–19 ('It is good jurisprudence that the particular provisions of internationally recognised human rights instruments do not apply to the Tribunal lock, stock and barrel; it is superfluous to cite authority'). For a thorough overview of the ad hoc Tribunals' approach towards a re-interpretation of human rights standards, see Cassese (n 11) 19. For more examples from ICTs' case law, see Gradoni, 'Human Rights Dimension' (n 13) 85; Sergey Vasiliev, 'Fairness and its Metric in International Criminal Procedure', http://papers.ssrn.com/sol3/papers.cfm?abstract_id=2253177 accessed on 1 August 2016.

21 Vasiliev (n 20) 49, with further references in ibid fn. 318; Gabrielle McIntyre, 'Defining Human Rights in the Arena of International Humanitarian Law: Human Rights in the Jurisprudence of the ICTY' in Gideon Boas and William A. Schabas (eds), *International Criminal Law Developments in the Case Law of the ICTY* (Martinus Nijhoff 2003) 193, 194;

ples that can only have meaning in context.[22] Since human rights were developed to bind States vis-à-vis their citizens and therefore also the rights of the accused only have meaning in context of a domestic criminal trial, ICTs are entitled to develop their own set of human rights standards.[23] Thereby, ICTs may deviate from human rights case law and determine a different scope of rights, because ICTs and national courts are not in comparable situations.[24] Other authors, however, argue for a more careful approach when it comes to the re-interpretation of human rights.[25] Those authors generally concede that a certain 're-orientation' concerning human rights might be necessary, but emphasise the significant risk that a contextual interpretation and application of human rights, if taken too far, can result in a reduced minimum protection of the accused.[26]

2 *The Risks of Contextual Re-interpretation*

The contextual (re-)interpretation and application of human rights by ICTs entail a significant risk of reducing the rights of the accused.[27] This is due to the

Cassese (n 11) 26–30, 49; Erik Møse, 'Impact of Human Rights Conventions on the Two Ad Hoc Tribunals' in Morten Bergsmo (ed), *Human Rights and Criminal Justice for the Downtrodden: Essays in Honour of Asbjørn Eide* (Martinus Nijhoff 2003) 179, 208; Christophe Deprez, 'Extent of Applicability of Human Rights Standards to Proceedings before the International Criminal Court: On Possible Reductive Factors' (2012) 12 International Criminal Law Review 721, 723; Fedorova and Sluiter (n 13) 30, 33, 51. But see Julian Nicholls, 'Evidence: Hearsay and Anonymous Witnesses' in Roelof Haveman and others (eds), *Supranational Criminal Law: A System Sui Generis* (Intersentia 2003) 239, 287 ('it is difficult to find reasons why the international norms embodied in the European Court's jurisprudence should not guide, *and to an extent bind*, the decisions of the ICTY').

22 McIntyre (n 21) 194.

23 ibid. Although McIntyre agrees that a bifurcation between human rights standards that bind domestic (criminal) legal systems and human rights standards that bind international (criminal) legal systems might be difficult to justify before the universalistic aspiration of human rights, to her the real issue of concern should not be whether ICTs adhere to existing interpretations of human rights, but whether the 'new' standards are proper international standards so that the ICTs adhere to the rule of law.

24 Møse (n 21) 189 (the principle of equality of arms must be given a more liberal interpretation than is normally upheld with regard to domestic proceedings).

25 Fedorova and Sluiter (n 13) 34, 46; Göran Sluiter, 'Human Rights Protection in the ICC Pre-Trial Phase' in Carsten Stahn and Göran Sluiter (eds), *The Emerging Practice of the International Criminal Court* (Brill 2009) 459, 461.

26 Fedorova and Sluiter (n 13) 33, 55.

27 Vasiliev (n 20) 50, argues that the re-interpretation of rights could also have an opposite effect and invite the application of higher standards of protection for the accused. How-

paradoxical shield/sword dichotomy of human rights within the criminal law context.[28] Criminal law, as such, severely infringes the rights of individuals.[29] Therefore, in criminal law human rights traditionally play a defensive role. Their function is to afford protection and to shield the individual from the boundlessness and the abuse of the (State's) coercive *ius puniendi*. However, a rather recent development additionally assigns human rights an offensive role, where criminal law is a mechanism to enforce and protect human rights. In their function as 'sword' human rights trigger the expansion and the increased application of criminal law.[30]

The tension between these two human rights functions—shield and sword —is particularly prevalent in international criminal law. International crimes are per definition massive violations of fundamental human rights that attack the interest of the international community as a whole. Therefore, international human rights law imposes an *erga omnes* obligation on States to investigate, prosecute, and punish the perpetrators.[31] Since States regularly fail to comply with these obligations ICTs were established to close the 'impunity gap' on the international level.[32] As a result, ICTs are often perceived as human rights enforcers and less as criminal courts.[33] The nature and gravity of the crimes, the 'end impunity' mantra that reflects the ultimate purpose of ICTs,

ever, as Sluiter (n 25) 461 observes, there does not seem to be a decision of a contemporary ICT in which the conclusion is reached that the circumstances surrounding the functioning of these tribunals should result in increased defence rights.

28 See only Françoise Tulkens, 'The Paradoxical Relationship between Criminal Law and Human Rights' (2011) 9 Journal of International Criminal Justice 577, 593 with further references in ibid fn. 5; the shield/sword metaphor is attributed to Christine Van den Wyngaert.

29 On the importance of human rights in criminal proceedings, see only Stefan Trechsel, *Human Rights in Criminal Proceedings* (OUP 2005) 6 ('An individual's reputation, financial position, personal liberty, even life … is at stake').

30 Tulkens (n 28) 593, quoting authors who describe this development as a 'turnaround in human rights', or 'Copernican revolution'.

31 On the duty to investigate, prosecute, and punish perpetrators of international crimes, see Christian Tomuschat, 'The Duty to Prosecute International Crimes Committed by Individuals' in Hans-Joachim Cremer and others (eds), *Tradition und Weltoffenheit des Rechts. Festschrift für Helmut Steinberger* (Springer 2002) 315; Werle and Jeßberger (n 13) marg. no. 228.

32 See Werle and Jeßberger (n 13) marg. nos. 94, 101.

33 This is also reflected in the somehow 'schizophrenic' attitude of human rights activists towards international criminal law: While often sceptical about the mechanisms of criminal justice in the national context, when it comes to international crimes NGOs promote a relentless 'fight against impunity'; on this, see William A. Schabas, 'Criminal Responsibil-

and international criminal justice's occasional attitude of moral superiority involve the risk of a pull towards the sword aspect of human rights.[34] In particular, it is a 'victim focused teleological reasoning',[35] which entails the risk that every balancing exercise is resolved to the detriment of the accused.[36]

3 *ICTs' 'Uniqueness'*

In the ICTs' jurisprudence and the academic literature it is frequently argued that the main reason for the need to re-interpret international human rights standards as developed by human rights courts and bodies is the 'uniqueness', 'specificity', 'distinctiveness', or 'contradistinction' of ICTs vis-à-vis domestic (criminal) courts.[37] Some of the features that are mentioned to prove the ICTs' 'uniqueness' and the unique context in which they operate include:[38] the establishment of international criminal tribunals by international law and their operation on the international level; the subject matter ICTs deal with, ie 'the most serious crimes of concern to the international community as a whole'[39]—these crimes constitute complex macrocriminality and are committed in a context of organised violence, often State-sponsored, which turns an ordinary crime into an international crime; the ICTs' dependency on State cooperation; in addition to the gravity and the complexity of international crimes *per se*,

ity for Violations of Human Rights' in Janusz Symonides (ed), *Human Rights: International Protection, Monitoring, Enforcement* (Ashgate 2003) 281, 297.

34 Patricia Pinto Soares, 'Tangling Human Rights and International Criminal Law: The Practice of International Tribunals and the Call for a Rationalized Legal Pluralism' (2012) 23 Criminal Law Forum 161, 171, arguing, with a focus on the effects of human rights law application on the criminal law principles of legality and individual culpability, that a teleological interpretation of international criminal law in human rights law rationales will necessarily lead to the result that ensues satisfaction to a larger number of human beings, ie victims.

35 Darryl Robinson, 'The Identity Crisis of International Criminal Law' (2008) 21 Leiden Journal of International Law 925, 933.

36 Sluiter (n 25) 461 (re-interpretation by definition results in reduced protection and always favours the interests of the prosecution and/or the victims over those of the accused). A number of authors noticed an erosion of the principles that traditionally ensured the protection of the rights of the accused; see only Tulkens (n 28) 593 with further references in ibid fn. 70.

37 See only Cassese (n 11).

38 In general, see Deprez (n 21), who argues that several of these specific features are capable of reducing the level of human rights protection. See also Colin Warbrick, 'International Criminal Court and Fair Trial' (1998) 3 Journal of Conflict and Security Law 45, 48.

39 McIntyre (n 21) 199 (unique subject matter with which the ICTY deals).

ICTs, in particular the ICC, often have to investigate in on-going conflict situations or fragile transitional societies; the importance of the protection of victims and witnesses; the nature of the international criminal procedure as a mixture between the Romano-Germanic and the Anglo-American law tradition; and, finally, the ICTs' specific goals that go beyond those of a domestic justice system, eg maintain and restore international peace and security, deter further violations, remove those guilty of the crime from future political life, assuage feelings of revenge and reduce the ascription of collective guilt, and provide an impartial historical record of the events.

It cannot be denied that ICTs display certain features that make them different compared to domestic criminal legal systems. However, despite all the 'uniqueness' of ICTs as regards their institutional, operational, and legal context, it seems necessary to emphasise the common features of international criminal courts and criminal courts operating on the national level. Most importantly, both are *criminal* courts, both exercise criminal jurisdiction. They are repressive mechanisms with the power to investigate crimes, prosecute and try, as well as punish and imprison individuals.[40] In both cases the actors within the criminal legal system—the prosecutors and judges—exert power over individuals. Looking at those similarities it is not immediately apparent why ICTs should not be bound by the same human rights standards as States when exercising their *ius puniendi*.[41] As such the defensive function of human rights law—the constraint of the use of coercive powers against individuals—is by no means less important than on the domestic level.

Second, an argument can be made that ICTs, in particular the ICC with the complementarity principle as cornerstone of its statute, were established to step in whenever the State where the crimes took place is unwilling or unable to

40 While in domestic legal systems the right to punish, the so-called *ius puniendi*, is part of the State's general authority, the ICTs derive their right to punish either from their (member) States or it flows directly from the *ius puniendi* of the international community as a whole. On the *ius puniendi* of the international community, see Kai Ambos, 'Punishment without a Sovereign? The *Ius Puniendi* Issue of International Criminal Law: A First Contribution towards a Consistent Theory of International Criminal Law' (2013) 33 Oxford Journal of Legal Studies 293; Julia Geneuss, *Völkerrechtsverbrechen und Verfolgungsermessen* (Nomos 2013) 67.

41 See also Deprez (n 21) 741. But see Cassese (n 11) 22 (underlining that 'international tribunals belong to a *totally distinct legal system from that of national courts*, a legal sphere with its own rules, time-frame and institutions' (emphasis in original)); similarly, Vasiliev (n 20) 62 ('The assumption to the effect that international and national judicial environments form parts of the same continuum is fraught with the risk of overlooking the material differences which (should) attract normative consequences').

take proper action. When ICTs investigate, prosecute, and punish those responsible for international crimes, they replace the domestic criminal justice system and fulfil the *erga omnes* obligations States owe to the international community.[42] However, if ICTs merely replace the domestic system their mandate and function cannot go beyond that of a domestic criminal court. The mere fact that the prosecution takes place on the international and not on the national level cannot justify cuts to the rights of the accused.

Third, the 'uniqueness dogma' should not be used to overcome the purely practical difficulties that—to be sure: highly complex—international criminal law investigations and trials entail.[43] In this regard, it might be useful to distinguish between the uniqueness of ICTs as *international* criminal tribunals, criminal tribunals operating on the international level, on the one hand and the fact that their subject-matter jurisdiction covers *international crimes* on the other. As regards the latter, ICTs are not so unique after all, because also domestic criminal courts deal with international crimes. It is not for nothing that domestic courts, in particular when acting on the basis of the principle of universal jurisdiction, are sometimes referred to as 'de facto international actors' or 'ad litem international courts'.[44]

III Development of Human Rights Standards

So far it has been argued that while ICTs need to re-interpret Strasbourg case law in order to adapt it to fit their respective legal system, this should be done carefully, with less emphasis on the (not so unique) 'uniqueness' of ITCs and without losing sight of the similarities between domestic and international criminal courts. In addition, due to the different ways in which ECHR member States on the one hand and ICTs on the other develop their respective set of

42 For this argument, see Geneuss (n 40) 87.

43 Similarly Vasiliev (n 20) 57.

44 It is often argued that third States, that is States exercising jurisdiction on the basis of the universality principle, act 'on behalf of' or as 'trustees' of the international community. Thus, their prosecution authorities and courts are sometimes regarded as the international community's functional organs—an idea that resembles George Scelle's theory of *dédoublement fonctionnel*. See eg Paola Gaeta, 'International Criminalization of Prohibited Conduct' in Antonio Cassese and others (eds), *Oxford Companion to International Criminal Justice* (OUP 2009) 63, 65; Yuval Shany, *Regulating Jurisdictional Relations* (OUP 2007) 97; Luc Reydams, 'In re Pinochet' (1999) 93 American Journal of International Law 700, 703.

human rights standards, it becomes apparent why a more principled approach of translating Strasbourg case law into is advisable.

1 *Dialogue: ECtHR and ECHR States Parties*

Decision making in Strasbourg is rather flexible.[45] Besides the specificities of human rights interpretation in general, which is contextual, fact dependant and casuistic,[46] the Strasbourg Court, which operates as a review court only, developed several 'doctrinal tools',[47] like the widely discussed margin of appreciation to allow for a certain 'manoeuvring room' or 'normative flexibility' regarding the accommodation of the States' legal, social, cultural and political context.[48] With these tools, the ECtHR recognises legal and cultural diversity among the member States and allows for a degree of local variety of the same values and principles.[49] Thus, the ECtHR judgments are tailored towards the legal system of the State party concerned, which set limits on the *erga omnes* effect (*res interpretata*) of ECtHR judgments, that is the legally binding effect on all States parties of the content that can be generalised beyond the individual case of a Court's judgment.[50]

---

45 For more on this see Julia Geneuss, 'Obstacles to Cross-Fertilisation: The International Criminal Tribunals' "Unique Context" and the Flexibility of the European Court of Human Rights' Case Law' (2015) 84 Nordic Journal of International Law 404.

46 Steven Greer, *The European Convention on Human Rights: Achievements, Problems and Prospects* (CUP 2006) 193; Catherine van de Heyning, 'No Place Like Home: Discretionary Space for the Domestic Protection of Fundamental Rights' in Patricia Popelier and others (eds), *Human Rights Protection in the European Legal Order: The Interaction between the European and the National Courts* (Intersentia 2011) 65, 68.

47 Nico Krisch, 'The Open Architecture of the European Human Rights Law' (2008) 71 *Modern Law Review* 183, 206.

48 Krisch (n 47) 206. See also Jan Kratochvíl, 'The Inflation of the Margin of Appreciation by the European Court of Human Rights' (2011) 29 Netherlands Quarterly of Human Rights 324, 327 ('notion of space in which States can legally move').

49 See van de Heyning (n 46) 68. See also Krisch (n 47) 206.

50 In contrast to the *inter partes* effect of ECtHR judgments, ie the decisional authority of the operative part of the judgment which binds the State Party concerned and which is explicitly foreseen in Article 46(1) of the Convention, the *erga omnes* effect is not explicitly recognised in the ECHR and is controversial. See Samantha Besson, 'The *Erga Omnes* Effect of Judgments of the European Court of Human Rights—"What's in a Name?"' in Samantha Besson (ed), *La Cour Européenne des Droits de l'Homme Après le Protocole 14: Premier Bilan et Perspectives* (Schulthess 2011) 125, 128; Adam Bodnar, 'Res Interpretata: Legal Effect of the European Court of Human Rights Judgments for Other States Than These Which Were Party to the Proceedings' in Yves Haeck and Eva Brems (eds), *Human Rights and Civil Liberties in the 21st Century* (Springer 2014) 223. Arguing in favour of

As a result according to a pluralist approach 'there is no such thing as one "ECHR law", but rather a Strasbourg and forty-seven other national versions'.[51] These 'national versions of ECHR law' are developed by way of a judicial dialogue between the ECtHR and domestic courts. Thus, the interpretation of ECHR rights evolve as a two way street.[52] Such a fruitful judicial dialogue between the Strasbourg Court and domestic courts can be regarded as the prime example of cross-fertilisation.

2 *Monologue: ICTs' Lonely Discursive Exercise*

In contrast to States ICTs are not part of the ECHR system and thus lack the formalised communication structures for a dialogue with the ECtHR. Instead each ICT develops and shapes its own set of human rights standards. While doing so ICTs are under no supervision by an external (human rights) court—in contrast to domestic criminal courts and (criminal) authorities, which are generally supervised by a domestic constitutional court *and* an international human rights court.[53]

Before this backdrop it becomes apparent why it is difficult to use the cross-fertilisation rhetoric—in the narrow sense outlined above—in the context of

---

redesigning the ECHR system to bolster the *erga omnes* effect in order to cope with the massive case overload, see Steven Greer and Luzius Wildhaber, 'Revisiting the Debate about "Constitutionalising" the European Court of Human Rights' (2012) 12 Human Rights Law Review 655.

51 Stéphanie Hennette-Vauchez, 'Constitutional v International: When Unified Reformatory Rationales Mismatch the Plural Paths of Legitimacy of ECHR Law' in Jonas Christoffersen and Mikael R. Madsen (eds), *The European Court of Human Rights between Law and Politics* (OUP 2011) 144, 145, cited according to Greer and Wildhaber (n 50) 681. Of course, these different versions of ECHR law do not differ in every aspect. In particular the scope of absolute rights and the interpretation of autonomous concepts leaves little room for local variations. See also Besson (n 50) 161; similarly Spano, 'Universality or Diversity of Human Rights? Strasbourg in the Age of Subsidiarity' (2014) 14 Human Rights Law Review 487, 493.

52 Besson (n 50) 152; see also Yutaka Arai-Takahashi, 'The Margin of Appreciation Doctrine: A Theoretical Analysis of Strasbourg's Variable Geometry' in Andreas Follesdal and others (eds), *Constituting Europe—The European Court of Human Rights in a National, European and Global Context* (CUP 2013) 62, 95 ('joint "ownership"').

53 In addition, in contrast to ICTs domestic criminal courts operate within their State's own—fully-fledged, deeply rooted and highly elaborate—fundamental rights framework. For them, the international human rights layer is just an additional frame of reference that establishes the outer limits of human rights protection. ICTs lack such a two-layered human rights frame of reference.

ICTs and the European Court. There is no judicial dialogue that would result in a 'Strasbourg and ICT' version of ECHR law. Rather the degree of reciprocal engagement is unilateral and can be characterised more as a 'monologue' on the part of the ICTs.[54] It is on the judges—whose primary function, however, is to decide (international) criminal law questions—to carve out the 'Strasbourg and ICT' version of ECHR law, that is to (re-)interpret the human rights standards and at the same time set limits to their own (re-)interpretation; a difficult internal discursive process. Against this backdrop the criticism of ICTs of being selective, messy, cherry-picking, and operating in a theoretical and methodological void—in short, the 'wild approach'—can entail the accusation of abuse.[55]

IV ECtHR Case Law as 'Directory Authority'

In order to reduce the risk of arbitrary decision-making and acknowledging the benefits of a true fertilising effect—and not only using ECtHR case law for practical and strategic reasons—ICTs should undertake a more principled effort to translate Strasbourg case law into their own context. Thereby their focus should be less on the 'product' or 'outcome' of the translation than on the translation process. So far, however, the method of translating human rights into the ICTs context has been rather under-developed. A starting point for the development of a methodology could be the frequent characterisation by ICTs of ECtHR jurisprudence as 'persuasive authority' (in contrast to 'binding' or 'mandatory' authority). According to the majority of scholars 'persuasive authority' means that judges and other decision-makers are not required to follow the result or reasoning, but have a choice whether to use the authority or not.[56] Thus, generally and also in the ICTs' vocabulary, 'persuasive authority' seems to be interchangeable with the terms 'inspiration', 'basis for discussion', 'assistance', 'orientation', or 'interpretive guidance'. However, as Frederick

---

54 On the different forms of transjudicial communication, see Slaughter (n 1) 113.

55 This criticism—arbitrariness, instrumentalisation, subjectivity, misunderstanding the original context, lack of methodology—can similarly be found as regards comparative constitutional reasoning in general, see Bobek (n 4) 240 (comparative reasoning 'is dominated by a laisser-faire mentality, which reminds one of a Nike commercial—"Just do it!"', ibid 241).

56 Thus, according to Frederick Schauer, 'Authority and Authorities' (2008) 94 Virginia Law Review 1931, 1946, the better term for 'persuasive authority' would be 'optional authority'.

Schauer points out, 'persuasive authority' is a term that seems to contradict itself:[57] On the one hand, the characteristic feature of authority is specifically its content-independency.[58] The force of authority comes from its source—who it is, rather than what it says—and generally authority implies an element of bindingness.[59] On the other hand, persuasion refers to the contents and substantive reasons of a decision or judgment.[60] Only when a judge or court finds the reasoning of a decision persuasive it will make a reference to this decision or judgment. However, if one is persuaded by the contents of a decision of judgment and the substance of an argument, then there is no room for—content-independent, but source-based—authority.

Taking advantage of the ambiguity of the term 'persuasive authority' it could be argued as follows: Whenever faced with a human rights issue ICTs are obligated to consult ECtHR jurisprudence. In contrast to what has been the approach so far, human rights jurisprudence not only '*may* be of assistance in applying and interpreting the Tribunal's applicable law',[61] but *shall* be taken into account. It is not at the discretion of ICT judges whether to consult human rights jurisprudence or not. Only after a thorough review can ICTs decide whether they are persuaded by the ECtHR's reasoning or whether they want to deviate from and re-interpret the human rights standard.[62]

As regards the first step, the focus is on the source-based *authority* of the Strasbourg Court.[63] The Court's jurisprudence is regarded as experts' exper-

57 See Schauer (n 56) 1940. On the notion of persuasive authority, see also Grant Lamond, 'Persuasive Authority in the Law' (2010) 17 The Harvard Review of Philosophy 16; Chad Flanders, 'Toward a Theory of Persuasive Authority' (2009) 62 Oklahoma Law Review 55.

58 Schauer (n 56) 1935.

59 See generally Flanders (n 57) 59.

60 Schauer (n 56) 1941.

61 See *Prosecutor v Barayagwiza* (n 19) (emphasis added).

62 This approach merges source-based and content-based considerations and oscillates between binding authority and mere inspiration; see also Bobek (n 4) 244.

63 As regards international human rights, the ECtHR, which is sometimes being referred to as the 'world court of human rights', is high on the 'scale of persuasive authorities'. On the authority of the ECtHR, see eg Anne-Marie Slaughter, 'Judicial Globalization' (2000) 40 Virginia Journal of International Law 1103, 1110, citing to John B. Attanasio (ECtHR as some sort of 'world court of human rights', whose judgments are increasingly quoted by national courts—also beyond Europe—and accepted by them; thus, the ECtHR can be regarded as a source of authoritative pronouncements on human rights law for national courts that are not directly subject to its authority). See also Cassese (n 11) 24 (in particular: ECtHR case law represents an extremely interesting 'sample of legal systems' from both the common law and civil law tradition).

tise that carries 'expertise-based legitimacy'.[64] In contrast to ICTs' judges, who are (or: should be), first and foremost, experts on international criminal law, ECtHR's judges are regarded as experts on international human rights issues. Their level of human rights knowledge gives their arguments more credibility. Their judgments are 'all-things-considered-judgments'[65] that *prima facie* strike the right balance between, for example, the right to a fair trial and public interests. As a consequence, the authority of their judgments is neither mandatory nor merely advisory, but 'directory', that is authority that should be followed, but can be outweighed.[66]

In a second step, the *persuasiveness* of the ECtHR jurisprudence becomes relevant. Here, ICTs look at the contents of ECtHR case law and can decide whether and how they want to translate the ECtHR standard into their own context and whether the balance between, for example, fair trial and public interest must be struck differently, because of the different context in which ICTs operate. However, since ECtHR case law carries the weight of 'directory authority' and any deviation and differences in meaning must carefully be explained and justified. Here, as a guideline, the re-interpretation of a straightforward (autonomous) interpretation of specific terms that determine the scope of applicability of a human rights norm by the ECtHR, like criminal charge, witness or penalty, seems to be possible only in very exceptional circumstances; the degree of persuasiveness is rather high. As regards a re-interpretation of generalisable juridical test, on the other hand, ICTs must identify the factors used by the ECtHR. Then ICTs can add additional factors that reflect the unique context in which they operate and might omit those factors that are not relevant because they only matter in the domestic context.[67]

That such thoroughly reasoned judgments carry greater weight can also be observed in the more recent jurisprudence of the Strasbourg Court. The ECtHR

64 George Letsas, 'The ECHR as a Living Instrument: Its Meaning and Legitimacy' in Andreas Føllesdal, and others (eds), *Constituting Europe—The European Court of Human Rights in a National, European and Global Context* (CUP 2013) 106, 129 (who, however, has doubts whether Strasbourg judges have greater human rights expertise than national institutions).

65 Lamond (n 57) 19.

66 On the distinction between mandatory, directory, and advisory authority, see Lamond (n 57) 24ff. The directory normative force of decisions of human rights courts counteracts fragmentation; similarly Flanders (n 57) 84 (persuasive authority seeks 'uniformity across space'), who also assumes a scale of bindingness below the threshold of 'binding authority'.

67 Similarly Vasiliev (n 20) 60.

takes a more restraint approach, that is, it grants a wider margin of appreciation, in cases where it is presented with a substantively reasoned opinion of one of the domestic highest courts that analyses in a thoughtful, comprehensive and convincing manner the State's obligations under the Convention and the relevant ECHR case law.[68] In sum, the quality of the decision-making is crucial.

V Conclusion

In particular from a practitioners point of view a sound argument can be made that the approach presented in this paper—obligation to take into account and review any relevant ECtHR (and other international human rights court's) jurisprudence and thorough and transparent justification of any deviation—lacks judicial practicability and sets (scholarly) expectations on ICTs judges far too high.[69] Yet, while the method of translation might be a demanding exercise for the ICTs' judges, it is necessary in order to build a coherent and theoretically well-founded and context-dependent set of own human rights standards.

In the end, the crucial question is by what standards we want to enforce international criminal law. What level of human rights protection do we want to accord alleged perpetrators of massive human rights violations? And how do we want the ICTs decisions in this regard to be perceived?

Of course, the comprehensive engagement with human rights courts' jurisprudence is time- and resource-intensive, and costly—issues that already at the time being are highly problematic and trigger a lot of criticism. However, if ICTs create the impression that in the course of developing their own set of human rights standards in general and 'defence rights' in particular they adopt a laissez-faire attitude, international criminal justice as a whole may lose legitimacy. Therefore, the considerable effort—which will diminish over time—is justified and worth it.

---

68 See van de Heyning (n 46) 92; Spano (n 51) 491, 498, both with reference to ECtHR case law.

69 On excessive demands regarding comparative reasoning by domestic constitutional courts, see Bobek (n 4) 242.

CHAPTER 3

Judicial Dialogue in Light of Comparative Criminal Law and Justice

Christoph Burchard[*]

The very idea of a judicial dialogue between International Criminal Tribunals (ICTs) and Human Rights Courts (HRCs) is a demanding and normatively charged concept. Just like the idea of mutual cross-fertilisation, it carries the expectation of a union or a community of international courts and judges; and this union or community then (allegedly) feeds into surpassing the fragmentation of international law in general and of international human rights law in particular.[1] In this short essay, I will not enter into the debate whether these liberal (and also somewhat elitist) visions carry water, that is, whether they are empirically sound or normatively appealing. Rather, I make the modest suggestion to explore the possible judicial dialogue between ICTs and HRCs, especially the one-sided conversation of ICTs with the European Court of Human Rights, in light of comparative criminal law and justice. My claim is that the theoretical and methodological discussions on comparative criminal law and justice provide helpful insights into why and how ICTs actually do (not) refer to HRCs and into why and how they should (not) do so.

I Framing My Lines of Thought

My proposal to draw on comparative criminal law and justice in order to explore the judicial dialogue between ICTs and HRCs is framed by four considerations:

---

* Many thanks to my assistant Dušan Bačkonja for his support in finalising this essay.

1 See the foundational reflections by Anne Marie Slaughter, *A new world order* (Princeton University Press 2004). As to recent analyses see Eric Bjorge, 'The International Court of Justice's Methodology of Law Ascertainment and Comparative Law' in Mads Andenas and Duncan Fairgrieve (eds), *Courts and Comparative Law* (OUP 2015) 213, 231. See also Triestino Mariniello and Paolo Lobba, 'The Cross-fertilisation Rhetoric in Question: Use and Abuse of the European Court's Jurisprudence by International Criminal Tribunals' (2015) 84 Nordic Journal of International Law 363, 364; Mads Andenas and Duncan Fairgrieve, 'Courts and

 | DOI: 10.1163/9789004313750_005

First, why analyse an immensely rich and challenging (and, for that matter, hardly surveyable) subject matter, that of judicial dialogue and cross-fertilisation, by means of a similarly diverse (and, for that matter, somewhat elusive) discipline of law, that of comparative criminal law and justice? My answer is simple enough. In my understanding, a true judicial dialogue between ICTs and HRCs is characterised by a state of affairs whereby courts continuously make reference to each other in their judgments and verdicts.[2] A judicial dialogue thus rests on individual acts of cross-referencing, where one court cites and takes into account extra-jurisdictional reasoning by another court.[3] And this is where comparative criminal law and justice comes into play, as cross-referencing is nothing but comparative criminal law and justice in action.

Second, comparative criminal law and justice enjoys (but also suffers from) extremely vivid and diverse theoretical as well as methodological debates.[4] This calls for an admission and a disclaimer. As to the admission: I seek to lead comparative criminal law and justice from the seclusion it has so readily sought and accepted in recent decades. Indeed, many of the theoretical and methodological debates surrounding comparative criminal law and justice

---

Comparative Law: In Search of Common Language for Open Legal Systems' in Mads Andenas and Duncan Fairgrieve (eds), *Courts and Comparative Law* (OUP 2015) 4.

2 This would be the 'open' and 'official' dialogue between courts that we as lawyers and academics can easily research. I thus disregard all forms of 'disclosed' and 'unofficial' patterns of cross-fertilisation, like joint seminars etc. that are immensely important for mutual learning and joining ranks. On this, see Antje Wiener and Philip Liste, 'Lost Without Translation? Cross-Referencing and a New Global Community of Courts' (2014) 21 Indiana Journal of Global Legal Studies 263. Similarly, I do not look into how comparative insights are used in the internal discussions of a court before a judgment is reached and formulated; at this preliminary stage, it is safe to assume that comparative criminal law and justice play an even more important role. On this, see David S. Law and Wen-Chen Chang, 'The Limits of Global Judicial Dialogue' (2011) 86 Washington Law Review 523.

3 On comparative law, the methods of interpretation and judicial dialogue see Antonios Tzanakopoulos, 'Judicial Dialogue as a Means of Interpretation' in Helmut P. Aust and Georg Nolte (eds), *The Interpretation of International Law by Domestic Courts: Uniformity, Diversity, Convergence* (OUP 2016); Oxford Legal Studies Research Paper no. 71/2014. Available at SSRN: http://ssrn.com/abstract=2497519 accessed 28 July 2016, 73.

4 See eg Albin Eser, 'Strafrechtsvergleichung: Entwicklung-Ziele-Methoden' in Albin Eser and Walter Perron (eds), *Strukturvergleich strafrechtlicher Verantwortlichkeit und Sanktionierung in Europa. Zugleich ein Beitrag zur Theorie der Strafrechtsvergleichung* (Duncker&Humblot 2015) 929, 954 et seq. (who distinguishes no fewer than 34 different concepts of comparative criminal law used in German academia). Also see Mathias Reiman and Reinhard Zimmerman (eds), *The Oxford Handbook of Comparative Law* (OUP 2008); Geoffrey Samuel, *An Introduction to Comparative Law Theory and Method* (Hart 2014).

have a deterring effect on non-comparatists. But, in my eyes, a good many of these debates are but mock battles. They obfuscate that there are several roads that lead to Rome, namely that different approaches and schools of thoughts all have their merits and provide useful insights. This essay thus does not strive for identifying 'the' (one and only) concept of comparative criminal law and justice and how it enlightens the judicial dialogue between ICTs and HRCs. Rather, it advances the idea of theoretical and methodological pluralism as a means to explore the relationship between ICTs and HRCs from several angles and perspectives. This brings me to my disclaimer: I will not survey all that comparative criminal law and justice research has to offer. I cannot even promise to bring a small portion of this research to bear on the interaction between ICTs and HRCs. I simply wish to outline that the theories and methods of comparative criminal law and justice provide a fruitful analytical addition to the research on judicial dialogue.

Third, comparative criminal law and justice is not simply concerned with the legal orders under comparison. Rather, much thought is and has been spent on the comparison as such, especially on the comparing actors[5] and their motives, rationales and preunderstandings as well the comparative methods that are (to be) employed. In this respect, and very summarily speaking, one can identify two approaches: one favouring a realistic or social science agenda—that is describing, explaining and understanding why and how specific actors do (or do not) in fact engage in comparative criminal law and justice; and the other emphasising a normative agenda—that is appraising and evaluating why and how one should (or should not) consider legal reasoning or experience from other ('foreign' or even 'alien') criminal justice systems. Although both approaches often intersect, I will look into them separately to gain further insight into the (one-sided or mutual) interaction between ICTs and HRCs. In keeping with the overarching objective of this book, I will focus on ICTs and why and how they do or should take into account what HRCs have to offer in terms of legal reasoning.

Fourth, I treat said interactions as voluntary, but not *per se* inopportune. Neither are comparative efforts by ICTs or HRCs mandatory in terms of one regime binding the other (which, for example, would require an ICT to adhere to the jurisprudence of the ECtHR), nor is there a foundational divide between ICTs and HRCs (which, for example, would devalue an exchange of positions and legal rationales from the outset). This statement is full of meaning, which I will only sketch briefly. There is strong consensus that ICTs are bound by inter-

5 Academics, the judiciary, policy makers, etc.

national human rights. Yet individual HRCs, like the ECtHR, do not adjudicate on international human rights law *per se*, but rather on separate human rights regimes, like the European Convention on Human Rights. Therefore, as long as ICTs are not members of these regimes (and no ICT is, for example, party to the ECHR), these human rights regimes do not create direct obligations[6] on ICTs. By extension, ICTs are under no immediate duty to observe the jurisprudence of a specific HRC. This positivist account of the state of affairs of international (criminal as well as human rights) law helps us to maintain perspective. On the one hand, it keeps apart what is sometimes hastily merged, that is: international criminal justice and multilateral human rights adjudication as alleged complementary parts in a joint and global battle against human rights violations. From where I stand, ICTs and HRCs have a different approach to human rights violations. For ICTs, human rights are primarily the sword, ie means to justify infringements on personal liberties (namely on the personal liberties of possible human rights violators). For HRCs, in contrast, human rights are primarily the shield, ie means to prevent or hedge infringements on personal liberties (especially infringements upon suspects and defendants in criminal matters).[7] This distinction, on the other hand, does not insinuate that there is an unbridgeable or for that matter: a foundational divide between ICTs and HRCs. Although ICTs deal with extraordinary and indeed unfathomable crimes, they are essentially criminal courts that—by their own self-depiction—must not denigrate due process and the rule of law simply because of the special contexts in and on which they operate. In summary, keeping ICTs and HRCs apart in terms of legal positivism cautions against both rash joinders and rash divisions.

In keeping these four points in mind, I will now turn to drawing on very few, but illustrative theories and methods of comparative criminal law and justice to explore the notion of judicial dialogue, first by taking the realistic approach and by asking what ICTs do and do not do when interacting with

6 See the excellent analysis, accompanied by extensive references, by Julia Geneuss 'Obstacles to Cross-fertilisation: The International Criminal Tribunals' "Unique Context" and the Flexibility of the European Court of Human Rights' Case Law' (2015) 84 Nordic Journal of International Law 404, 405. See more generally Thomas Kadner Graziano, 'Is it Legitimate and Beneficial for Judges to Compare?' in Mads Andenas and Duncan Fairgrieve (eds), *Courts and Comparative Law* (OUP 2015) 25, 38.

7 For this image see eg Harmen van der Wilt, '*Nullum Crimen* and International Criminal Law: The Relevance of the Foreseeability Test' (2015) 84 Nordic Journal of International Law 515; Kai Ambos, *Treatise on International Criminal Law: Volume I: Foundations and General Part* (OUP 2013) 87.

HRCs (Section II), and second by taking the normative approach and asking why ICTs should or should not enter into such a dialogue (Section III).

II Taking the 'Realistic' Approach: What ICTs Do and Do Not Do—and Nothing More Pretentious

1 *Initial Answers*

Let us first examine the 'realistic' questions through the theoretical and methodological lens of comparative criminal law and justice: why and how do ICTs engage in cross-referencing HRCs, thus possibly starting a future or partaking in an ongoing judicial dialogue? And why do they not do so, thus stalling or cancelling such a dialogue?

Evidently, these are sets of empirical questions where the 'Why' and the 'How' elements are intrinsically linked. Viable empirical data, however, is difficult to come by.[8] Coming close to such data, Krit Zeegers arrives at the following conclusion as regards the 'How'—namely by:

> disregard, selectivity, and adaptation. The ICTs sometimes disregard IHRL, for example by asserting the primacy of their own legal frameworks over IHRL or by failing to address human rights issues in their decisions. In addition, the ICTs have employed a selective method, for example by professing adherence to IHRL by relying on specific aspects of IHRL to justify their own approach, while ignoring other aspects of the same human rights norms with which their approach is not in line. Finally, the ICTs have adapted the legal test that would apply to the right in question in IHRL, either by adapting the normative content of a specific human rights norm before the ICTs, resulting in the change of the scope of the respective obligation, or by applying a different legal test to determine whether or not the right in question has been violated.[9]

Apart from that, there is much speculation (being either grounded in anecdotes or 'common sense') on 'how' ICTs make use or do not make use of HRCs, most notably that cross-references to human rights jurisprudence is but

8 See generally, as regards the critique that courts drawing on comparative insights will 'only' engage in 'cherry-picking', Graziano (n 6) 25, 29 et seq. See also, for a quantitative analysis of the cross-references to the case law of the ECtHR that appear in the ICTY judgments and decisions, chapter by Frauke Sauerwein, below.

9 Krit Zeegers, *International Criminal Tribunals and Human Rights Laws* (Springer 2016) 403.

instrumental and an *ex post facto* rationalisation of what has been decided earlier.[10] The conjecture is that, where this jurisprudence fits, it will be quoted, and where it does not, it will be disregarded (selectivity or 'cherry-picking').

The latter, of course, also relates to the 'Why'. ICTs, or so it is assumed, draw on HRCs to draw on their 'expert legitimacy' in fields in which ICTs are not experts (just let me mention criminal procedure in the widest possible sense including witness protection, specific fair trial rights, etc.).[11] And for those who (for good reason) question the 'legitimacy pull' of a selective and adaptive use of comparative insights in the jurisprudence of ICTs, Boris Burghardt offers a last resort:

> Comparative law is not meant to include other legal orders in the context of interpreting international criminal law and procedure. Rather, it communicates outwardly what has been decided inwardly. It is not the potential of comparative arguments in rationalising a decision that is decisive, but their communicative capacity. Comparative law enhances the comprehensibility and hence the acceptability and the connectability of the jurisprudence of ICTs.[12]

---

10 Therefore criticising 'judicial dialogue' as mere 'rhetoric' Sergey Vasiliev, 'International Criminal Tribunals in the Shadow of Strasbourg and Politics of Cross-fertilisation' (2015) 84 Nordic Journal of International Law 371, 378 et seq. On the 'classic' cherry-picking critique see eg Graziano (n 6) 29 et seq. with extensive references; note that Graziano (n 6) 30 et seq. then goes on to disqualify this critique. See also Andrew Friedman 'Beyond Cherry-Picking: Selection Criteria for the Use of Foreign Law in Domestic Constitutional Jurisprudence' (2011) 44 Suffolk University Law Review 873; David S. Law, 'Judicial Comparativism and Judicial Diplomacy' (2015) 163 University of Pennsylvania Law Review 927; Elaine Mak *Judicial Decision-Making in a Globalised World: A Comparative Analysis of the Changing Practices of Western Highest Courts* (Bloomsbury Publishing 2013).

11 Geneuss (n 6) 425.

12 My translation of: 'Die Rechtsvergleichung dient nicht mehr der Einbeziehung fremden Rechts bei der Ermittlung des eigenen Rechts, sondern der Kommunikation des systemimmanent, mittels Auslegung, gefundenen Ergebnisses. Nicht die Begründungsleistung rechtsvergleichender Überlegungen für die völkerstrafrechtliche Rechtsfindung ist entscheidend, sondern ihre Vermittlungsleistung nach außen. Rechtsvergleichung erhöht die Verständlichkeit und damit die Akzeptanz- und Anschlussfähigkeit der völkerstrafrechtlichen Praxis'. See Boris Burghardt, 'Die Rechtsvergleichung in der völkerstrafrechtlichen Rechtsprechung. Von der Rechtsvergleichung als Mittel der Rechtsfindung zur diskursiv-vermittelnden Rechtsvergleichung' in Susanne Beck, Christoph Burchard and Bijan Fateh-Moghadam (eds) *Strafrechtsvergleichung als Problem und Lösung* (Nomos 2011) 235, 251.

All of what has been said so far points to somewhat mundane explanations as to what ICTs do and do not do. Lofty goals like overcoming the fragmentation of international law or the formation of a community of international courts[13] seem out of the picture. And maybe for good reason, if one approaches the supposed judicial dialogue of ICTs and HRCs from the point of view of the legal realist (and not the visionary academic) and asks what courts and judges in fact *do*—and nothing more pretentious.

2 *Instrumental Comparative Criminal Law and Justice*

The foregoing analysis links to what has been labelled the *instrumentalist strand of comparative criminal law and justice research*. It analyses and criticises (as can be expected) the instrumentalisation of comparative criminal law and justice. So far, this strand of research has only been applied to the use (or abuse) of comparative insights in legislative politics.[14] This begs the question whether it can and should be extended to court politics, ie to ICTs using (or abusing) cross-references to HRCs. My answer is no, which will disappoint all who seek to disqualify the instrumentalisation of comparative insights by ICTs simply for this reason.

The pejorative configuration of the instrumentalisation of comparative criminal and justice in legislative politics has a distinct dynamic and background. It points to the phenomenon that interested policy entrepreneurs (like the European Commission, for example) commission like-minded academics, who may well be dependent on the good will of said policy entrepreneurs to receive future funding, to come up with certain comparative results, which were in fact politically pre-determined, but which are later presented as novel and inspired by comparative research. This calls into question the objectivity and fairness of said results, as the prime resource of academic legitimacy is seriously undermined, that is, the neutrality and independence from outside forces when conducting gold standard research. This, then, sheds light on what really matters and what is really at stake when focusing on ICTs cross-referencing HRCs for instrumental reasons: does the instrumentality of comparative arguments in judicial reasoning go against both the neutrality and independence of the judiciary on the one hand and against accepted standards of compara-

---

13 See Mariniello and Lobba (n 1) 364, wherein the authors take issue with the dominant narrative that tends to uncritically ascribe a wealth of positive effects, including the prevention of fragmentation in human rights law, to the process of cross-referencing between HRCs and ICTs.

14 Joachim Vogel 'Diskussionsbemerkungen: Instrumentelle Strafrechtsvergleichung' in Beck, Burchard and Fateh-Moghadam (eds) (n 12) 205, 207 et seq.

tive judicial argumentation on the other? Critics of the instrumentalisation of comparative human rights arguments by ICTs insinuate an affirmative answer, thus (for whatever reasons) raising the bar for judicial comparative argumentation to grand (if not impossible to overcome) heights. 'Only' if the comparison is neutral, universal and 'thick' in all relevant matters does, according to this view, a comparative result or argument hold water. But then the argument has to be as follows: the *ex post facto* rationalisation of a pre-determined solution to a legal problem by means of cross-referencing a HRC in a written judgment of an ICT is illegitimate, because this written judgment is an open and hence neutral quest for 'legalistic truth'. And the selectivity of comparative reasoning is only problematic because comparative arguments must not be teleologically focused and require an all-encompassing reach. Many, I presume, would subscribe to this notion—a notion that has contributed greatly to the seclusion of comparative criminal law and justice, because neutrality, universality and thickness are difficult goals to reach.

I, however, would like to call for a *normalisation of comparative judicial reasoning in written judgments*. It is safe to assume that in a given written judgment or verdict, all arguments weighed are teleologically framed. In this respect, textual, doctrinal or policy arguments are no different from comparative arguments. They may and will often be cherry picked. Or to put it bluntly: It is safe to speculate that cherry picking is not uncommon in judicial reasoning. This may and indeed does reduce the legitimacy pull and the communicative potential of cross-referencing HRCs in ICTs' verdicts. But it certainly does not devalue them altogether. The same holds true for selective or adaptive comparative reasoning. The more selective or adaptive it becomes, the lower is its legitimacy pull and communicative potential.

But again, why does judicial comparative legal argumentation need to be all-encompassing and universal? Turning away for once from the interaction between ICTs and HRCs, take for example a court C that wishes to justify result R by means of a comparative argument. Indeed, it is safe to assume that C will find comparative precedents for R somewhere. However, it is also safe to assume that it will make a difference whether the precedents originate from a legal order known for its human rights violations or, contrarily, for its good human rights record. In other words, it is not the very instrumentality, selectivity or adaptation of comparative arguments that devalues them. What matters is (inter alia) the quality of the argument and the standing of the legal order(s) on which it draws.

3 *Systems Theoretical Comparative Criminal Law and Justice*

A second strand of comparative research that I would like to mention briefly is inspired by *systems theory*. Its functional sub-strand posits[15] that the more developed a legal order is, the more it can draw from within (from its own jurisprudence and the 'prudence' contained therein), ie the less it will look to other legal orders for inspiration or legitimacy. A legal order as a self-contained and independent system recreates itself by its own means so that jurisprudential developments will be more self-referential (eg, citing their own precedents) the more there is to refer to from within, whilst it will seek more external input the less it has available internally. Or, to put it differently: External comparisons are less important the more 'developed' a legal order (or regime) is. In all cases, a 'receiving' legal order has its own 'internal code' so that 'external information' from a 'giving' legal order (comparative insights and experience etc.) has to be and will be recoded internally.

While the previous section focused on the impact of individual or group agency (especially the motives of judges or chambers), systems theory concentrates on the impact of the operations of a legal order as a whole. This also has weight in international criminal law, and neatly explains why ICTs (which still are, when considering case numbers, courts of infant criminal justice systems) draw far more on the ECtHR (which has processed thousands of cases by itself and hence has a vast jurisprudential background) than vice versa. What is more, systems theory also offers an explanation (and a defence) for ICTs adapting the legal doctrines of HRCs to their own needs; this is 'simply' their way of recoding external information internally.

At first sight, a systems theoretical approach to the interaction of ICTs and HRCs cannot explain the (in-)famous *Tadić* ruling that:

> neither Article 14 of the ICCPR nor Article 6 of the European Convention of Human Rights ('ECHR'), which concerns the right to a fair trial, list the protection of victims and witnesses as one of its primary considerations. As such, the interpretation given by other judicial bodies to Article 14 of the ICCPR and Article 6 of the ECHR is only of limited relevance in applying the provisions of the Statute and Rules of the International Tribunal, as these bodies interpret their provisions in the context of their legal framework, which do not contain the same considerations. In interpreting the provisions which are applicable to the

15 See generally Bijan Fateh-Moghadam, 'Operativer Funktionalismus in der Strafrechtsvergleichung' in ibid 43, 46.

> International Tribunal and determining where the balance lies between the accused's right to a fair and public trial and the protection of victims and witnesses, the Judges of the International Tribunal must do so within the context of its own unique legal framework [...]. International Tribunal must interpret its provisions within its own legal context and not rely in its application on interpretations made by other judicial bodies is evident in the different circumstances in which the provisions apply.[16]

After all, the ruling comes from the early times of international criminal justice where one would have expected the ICTY to open itself up widely to HRCs. On this, however, the functional-genetic or dynamic sub-strand of systems theory has much to offer. It posits[17] that in times of systemic existential crisis, ICTs will emphasise their independence and autonomy.[18] And arguably the ICTY faced such a (legitimacy) crisis in *Tadić*; failure to ultimately deliver results would have been fatal not only to the ICTY as such, but probably also to the then still fledgling project of international criminal justice as a whole. The 'self-confidence' of *Tadić*, which flows from its self-reliance and which is even more prominently captured in the way the ICTY distanced itself from the ICJ (keyword: overall vs. effective control test), may have thus very well been borne from the international criminal justice system striving for self-preservation.

Now, whether systems theory holds water is of course open for debate. But a systems theoretical take of comparative criminal law and justice certainly enriches the exploration of the possibilities and limits of a judicial dialogue between ICTs and HRCs. And that is all that I wanted to demonstrate.

16 *Prosecutor v Tadić*, IT-94-1-T, Decision on the Prosecutor's Motion Requesting Protective Measures for Victims and Witnesses, 10 August 1995, para. 27 et seq.

17 See generally Christoph Burchard, 'The International Criminal Legal Process: Towards a Realistic Model of International Criminal Law in Action' in Carsten Stahn and Larissa van der Herik (eds) *Future Perspectives on International Criminal Justice* (Asser Press 2010) 81, 108.

18 See also Vasiliev (n 10) 397 and 401, who considers the autonomous interpretation of ICL an 'efficient buffer' against any legitimacy based critique regarding the 'Europeanisation' of ICL.

III Taking the Normative Approach: What ICTs Should or Should Not Do—and Nothing Less Ambitious

1 *On the Legitimacy of Judicial Comparative Arguments in a Pluralist Setting*

The theory of comparative criminal law and justice not only offers insights into what courts in fact do when or when not cross-referencing extra-jurisdictional material. It also queries why courts (like ICTs) should or indeed should not engage in comparative efforts (like voluntarily referring to the jurisprudence of HRCs). The principal question is whether this is actually a legitimate enterprise at all.[19] This question is heatedly debated on a national level, following Justice Scalia's (in-)famous sortie against the comparative use of foreign law in the interpretation of (U.S.) constitutional law. In his words:

> If there was any thought absolutely foreign to the founders of our country, surely it was the notion that we Americans should be governed the way Europeans are [...]. What reason is there to believe that other dispositions of a foreign country are so obviously suitable to the morals and manners of our people that they can be judicially imposed through constitutional adjudication? Is it really an appropriate function of judges to say which are and which aren't?[20]

This passage, if not in tone, but in substance, essentially mirrors the sentiment in *Tadić*: what have alien legal orders to tell judges in interpreting their own legal orders? In the U.S., this question is linked to the fundaments of constitutional law and theory, namely the separation of powers and the role of judges vis-à-vis the legislator.[21] Yet it would appear to me that there is an even more foundational current in Scalia's opposition to comparative interpretations by the judiciary, that is, how pluralistically arranged legal orders are or are not engaged with each other. Summarily speaking, there are those in comparative criminal law and justice who advocate closure, and those that advocate openness. There are those who seek to highlight unbridgeable (cultural etc.) differences, which are there for good reasons (like for expressing

---

19 Note that in Section I, above, I only summarily dealt with this enterprise being not *per se* inopportune.

20 Antonin Scalia, 'Outsourcing American Law. Foreign Law in Constitutional Interpretation', AEI Working Paper #152, 6; available online www.aei.org/paper/100034 accessed 30 July 2016.

21 As to a brief summary of concerns see Graziano (n 6) 25, 27 et seq.

cultural or historical identities or for guaranteeing the accountability of internal actors, who must not shift responsibility to external actors); and there are those that emphasise union or at least comparable common grounds. So Scalia is directly relevant for our endeavour. His attacks must not be hastily dismissed because they supposedly only speak to national constitutional courts and not to ICTs.

This becomes apparent in Vasiliev's critical evaluation of the 'ICTs/HRCs cross-fertilisation rhetoric'. For him, if I understand him correctly, this rhetoric is a threat.

> The accountability of international criminal tribunals under IHRL can best be ensured if their unqualified autonomy in human rights matters is embraced and put in check, rather than defied and subordinated to the ECtHR's mythical supremacy. The tribunals should step (and be lured) out of the 'Strasbourg shadow' where they have been driven to by the normative discourse that purports to control their consumption of human rights case law. It is time to abandon that discourse. The tribunals' engagement of such jurisprudence is essentially a methodological issue which boils down to questions of when and how the tribunals invoke the ECtHR's jurisprudence and which usages are proper or otherwise. Defining what amounts to 'use' and 'abuse' of foreign jurisprudence in the context of transjudicial communication between international criminal tribunals and human rights courts is future day's work.[22]

Closure and non-comparativism, then, for Vasiliev is better suited to hold ICTs accountable and to ensure their human rights record. Personally, I beg to differ. For me, comparative criminal law and justice may just work, when correctly implemented now and not in some imaginary future, alongside the necessary checks and balances within and without; indeed such checks and balances are missing on the international level. While not striving for unity or community, pluralism in international criminal justice is not about closure, but about openness, the latter being encapsulated in one-sided or mutual comparative efforts. This is my normative take on why ICTs should engage with HRCs by means of judicial comparative interactions, and why I see the judicial dialogue rhetoric as a chance to tame power. Let me briefly explain this.

---

22 Vasiliev (n 10) 403.

2 *Judicial Comparative Criminal Law and Justice as Checks and Balances Within and Without*

At least in theory, judicial comparative interactions can possibly become the necessary checks and balances at the international level, within and without.

The 'within' aspect is what comparative criminal law and justice is traditionally about. When ICTs refer to HRCs, this helps them in critically reviewing their own jurisprudence. Jurisprudence, of course, is often self-referential and thus path-dependent, which can easily lead to blind-spots; this holds especially true in the context that I explore in this essay, ie ICTs weighing infringements upon the personal liberty of a possible criminal offender against the infringements upon human rights for which this very offender is supposedly responsible. Taking seriously what HRCs have to say in general on such weighing processes, and doing so without the strictures of own precedents and doctrines etc., thus becomes an act of self-control for ICTs. This becomes even more important as there are no other legal (leaving aside for now political and academic) mechanisms in place that put ICTs under external checks and balances. Appreciating external comparative insights may thus well serve as the next best governance tool: the internalisation of the external; or in other words: the simulation of external review by way of an internal review through an internalised external (comparative) lens. What is more, checks and balances are not only there to tame power, but also to organise its use more effectively and fairly. Drawing on comparative 'natural experiments' already run in other jurisdictions thus illustrates what paths are worthwhile to follow—and which are not, thus learning from foreign successes or failures.

This brings me to the 'without' aspect, where judicial comparative efforts in the 'comparing' jurisdiction A are actually meant to work as checks and balances for the compared legal orders (B and so forth). This seems like a far-fetched hypothesis to make and, in truth, with regard to the interaction of ICTs and HRCs I do not know of a case study. But since we are talking normatively here, this is what I have in mind: The comparative interaction between the (ordinary) courts of the Member States of the EU in the context of judicial cooperation in criminal matters (for example: Germany having to extradite a French national to Bulgaria etc., which results in a thin comparative review of the state of affairs in Bulgaria) is a real world example of what Eser[23] has termed evaluative/competitive comparative criminal law and justice. As the terminol-

23 See Albin Eser, 'Strafrechtsvergleichung: Entwicklung-Ziele-Methoden' in Eser and Perron (eds) (n 4) 929, 1020 et seq.

ogy suggests, courts no longer refrain from an evaluative and competitive spirit when engaging with compared legal orders for reasons of international comity. Rather they openly check whether what has been comparatively taken into account is legitimate by one's standards, or whether it is not. A cross-referenced legal order or foreign court decision is, henceforth, not necessarily a 'benchmark' (the shadow of Strasbourg as the harbinger of human rights, to mimic Vasiliev[24]). Whether it is a 'benchmark' is openly put to discussion. If it is, then a foreign legal order or a foreign doctrine will and should be persuasive for one's own legal order or doctrines. But if it is not, as openly elaborated, then this will serve as a (admittedly rather weak; but what are we to call for on the international level?) check or balance that is not directly inwardly, but outwardly.

Alleviating judicial comparative efforts to a system of checks and balances, within and without, is admittedly an ambitious agenda. When submitting it to a reality check, two questions arise. First, when having in mind what has been said in Section II. above.: does the 'checks and balances rhetoric' not give courts carte blanche to use or abuse comparative criminal law to their own ends? And second: am I not charging judges with too much (disregarding, if necessary, comity by putting either deficiencies of one's own or even of a foreign jurisdiction in the pillory)?

From my point of view, both questions can summarily be answered by an 'it depends'. It depends very much how critical (in the best intellectual meaning of this word) international courts can and will be with each other. Leaving diplomacy off the table, true (or thick) comparativism is a critical evaluation of foreign meaning (as it is encapsulated in legal doctrines etc.), indeed an evaluation that openly addresses and justifies both the evaluative criteria and evaluation results. This transparency does not cancel out possible uses or abuses of comparative insights for mundane (court political) reasons. But it changes the focus of comparative criminal law and justice in action, and lessens the possibility of 'abuse'. And this is where my normative approach to this discipline and the idea of judicial dialogue finally intersect. The very process of forming enhanced and critical exchanges between international courts, be they orientated towards unity or towards pluralistic legal orders mutually checking and balancing themselves, is something to aspire to.

24 Vasiliev (n 10) 403.

IV Outlook

When looking back on my short essay, I have to admit that I did not do justice to what comparative criminal law and justice has to offer: What has been mentioned has only been mentioned superficially. And I have only mentioned very few aspects, thus leaving aside a great amount. But this may hint that, once out of the 'ghetto',[25] comparatists should have a word on why and how ICTs actually do (not) refer to HRCs and on why and how they should (not) do so.

---

25 See Basil Markesinis, *Comparative Law in the Courtroom and the Classroom* (Hart 2003) 25.

PART 2

The Use of the ECtHR Jurisprudence by ICTs: A Bird's-Eye View

CHAPTER 4

Article 21 (3) of the ICC Statute: Identifying and Applying 'Internationally Recognized Human Rights'

*Volker Nerlich**

Article 21(3) of the Rome Statute of the International Criminal Court[1] places human rights at the apex of the International Criminal Court's applicable law:[2] the application and interpretation of the Court's legal instruments 'must be consistent with internationally recognized human rights'. As the ICC's Appeals Chamber has found, '[h]uman rights underpin the Statute; every aspect of it including the exercise of the jurisdiction of the Court. Its provisions must be interpreted and more importantly applied in accordance with internationally recognized human rights'.[3] Despite its importance, Article 21(3) raises several questions as to its precise ambit and meaning. Some of these questions shall be examined below.

The first section of the present chapter discusses the meaning of the term 'application and interpretation', while the second section scrutinises the term 'internationally recognized human rights' and, in particular, analyses to what extent this term encompasses the jurisprudence of international or regional human rights bodies, domestic legislation and jurisprudence, and 'soft law', such as United Nations General Assembly resolutions relevant to human rights. The concluding section proposes a multi-faceted approach to the application

* Dr. iuris, Humboldt-University of Berlin; LL.M. International and Human Rights Law, University of the Western Cape; Legal Adviser, International Criminal Court; Honorary Professor, Humboldt-University of Berlin. The views expressed are those of the author and cannot be attributed to the International Criminal Court.

1 Rome Statute of the International Criminal Court, UN Doc A/CONF.183/9 of 17 July 1998, entered into force 1 July 2002.

2 See Alain Pellet, 'Applicable Law' in Antonio Cassese, Paola Gaeta and John R.W.D. Jones (eds), *The Rome Statute of the International Criminal Court: A Commentary* (OUP 2002) vol 2 1051, 1079, who speaks of the super-legality of human rights norms in the ICC Statute.

3 *Prosecutor v Lubanga*, ICC-01/04-01/06-772 (OA 4), Judgment on the Appeal of Mr. Thomas Lubanga Dyilo against the Decision on the Defence Challenge to the Jurisdiction [...], Appeals Chamber, 14 December 2006 ('*Lubanga* OA 4 Judgment'), para. 37.

 | DOI: 10.1163/9789004313750_006

of Article 21(3) of the ICC Statute, which takes into account the differences in weight of the sources of human rights norms.

1 'Application and Interpretation'

At first sight, the text of Article 21(3) is somewhat peculiar: logically, the act of *interpretation* of a legal norm precedes its *application*—a provision first needs to be understood before it can be put into action. Why, then, does the text of Article 21(3) inverse this order and refers to the 'application and interpretation' of the ICC Statute? One possible explanation for this is that this was simply an oversight during the drafting process. The provision was included into the draft Statute at a relatively late stage of the negotiations: it appeared for the first time in the reports on the final session of the Preparatory Committee in March/April 1998, which immediately preceded the Rome Conference.[4] It is unclear who proposed the inclusion of the provision and whether it was subject of debate and refined during the session of the Preparatory Committee.[5] Nevertheless, the fact that the text was not put in square brackets in the version of the draft ICC Statute that the Preparatory Committee submitted to the Rome Conference as a basis for further negotiations indicates that there was no controversy surrounding it. Indeed, at the Rome Conference, the debate in relation to what should become Article 21(3) centred on the definition of the term 'gender' as one of the prohibited grounds of discrimination;[6] there does not appear to have been any significant debate as to the remainder of the provision. Given the speed at which the ICC Statute was negotiated, it would therefore not be surprising that this somewhat unconventional formulation was overlooked. No damage would result from this oversight—the Appeals Chamber in the passage cited above simply put the text in the (purportedly) good order.

4 See Preparatory Committee on the Establishment of an International Criminal Court, *Draft Statute for the International Criminal Court/Part 2. Jurisdiction, Admissibility and Applicable Law*, 31 March 1998, A/AC. 249/1998/CRP.20, 3; Preparatory Committee on the Establishment of an International Criminal Court, *Draft Statute for the International Criminal Court/Part 2. Jurisdiction, Admissibility and Applicable Law*, 2 April 1998, A/AC.249/1998/CRP.8, 38–39; Preparatory Committee on the Establishment of an International Criminal Court, *Report of the Preparatory Committee in the Establishment of an International Criminal Court/ Addendum*, 14 April 1998, A/Conf.183/2/Add.1, 47.

5 Research in the preparatory works of the Rome Statute did not yield any results in this regard.

6 See William A. Schabas, *The International Criminal Court: A Commentary on the Rome Statute* (OUP 2010) 398.

However, as Bitti has noted,[7] in the jurisprudence of some Chambers of the ICC, it appears that the 'application and interpretation'/'interpretation and application' of the ICC Statute is not understood as a continuing process in the administration of legal provisions, but as two separate aspects of ensuring human rights compliance of the ICC Statute. According to such a reading, 'interpretation' would refer to the understanding of the Court's legal provisions themselves: Article 21(3) instructs the judges of the Court to choose an interpretation that avoids any conflict with 'internationally recognized human rights'. In other words, in case of doubt, precedence should always be given to a 'human rights friendly' interpretation.

In contrast, 'application' in accordance with human rights could be understood as referring to the process of either 'importing' rules that are not expressly foreseen in the Statute, Rules of Procedure and Evidence or Regulations of the Court, so as to make the ICC's legal framework fully human rights compliant, or declining to apply certain provisions within the ICC's legal framework in order to avoid a violation of human rights. In other words, human rights could supplement or even supersede the express rules of the ICC Statute and its subsidiary instruments. This goes far beyond the process of interpretation.

An example of supplementing the Court's provisions based on human rights requirements is the Appeals Chamber's jurisprudence allowing for a stay of proceedings if a human rights compliant trial can no longer be secured. Such stay of proceedings is not provided for in any of the Court's legal texts and the Appeals Chamber expressly declined to find existence of such a remedy based on the notion of 'abuse of process' known in common law jurisdictions: given that the notion of 'abuse of process' was unknown in the Romano-Germanic tradition, the Appeals Chamber concluded that it did not amount to a 'general principle of law' that may be applied by virtue of Article 21(1)(c) of the ICC Statute.[8] Rather, the legal basis for staying proceedings was found directly in human rights; the Appeals Chamber concluded: 'Where fair trial becomes impossible because of breaches of the fundamental rights of the suspect or the accused by his/her accusers, it would be a contradiction in terms to put the person on trial. Justice could not be done. A fair trial is the only means to do justice. If no fair trial can be held, the object of the judicial process is frustrated and the process must be stopped'.[9]

7 Gilbert Bitti, 'Article 21 and the Hierarchy of Sources of Law before the ICC' in Carsten Stahn, *The Law and Practice of the International Criminal Court* (OUP 2015) 411, 437.

8 *Lubanga* OA 4 Judgement, paras 26–35.

9 *Lubanga* OA 4 Judgment, para. 37; see also ibid para. 39: 'Unfairness in the treatment of the suspect or the accused may rupture the process to an extent making it impossible to piece

An example of human rights superseding provisions of the Court's legal framework was Trial Chamber II's decision[10] to delay the return of witnesses who had been detained in the Democratic Republic of the Congo ('DRC') and had been transferred to The Hague to testify on the condition that they remain in detention throughout and be returned to the DRC once their testimony was concluded, as provided for by Article 93(7) of the Statute.[11] However, while in detention at the seat of the ICC, the witnesses applied for asylum in The Netherlands, alleging breaches of their human rights in the DRC. Having been seized of a request on behalf of the detained witnesses not to return them to the DRC pending the decision on their asylum requests, the Trial Chamber noted the various human rights at stake (in particular, the right to asylum, the principle of *non-refoulement* and the right to an effective remedy) and concluded:

> As the matter stands, the Chamber is unable to apply article 93(7) of the Statute in conditions which are consistent with internationally recognised human rights, as required by the article 21(3) of the Statute. If the witnesses were to be returned to the DRC immediately, it would become impossible for them to exercise their right to apply for asylum and they would be deprived of the fundamental right to effective remedy.[12]

The Trial Chamber also noted that, if the Court were to request The Netherlands to assist in the immediate return of the witnesses, 'it would be constraining the Netherlands to violate the witnesses' right to invoke the *non-refoulement* principle'.[13] On this basis, the Trial Chamber ordered in essence that the two

---

together the constituent elements of a fair trial. In those circumstances, the interest of the world community to put persons accused of the most heinous crimes against humanity on trial, great as it is, is outweighed by the need to sustain the efficacy of the judicial process as the potent agent of justice'.

10 *Prosecutor v Katanga*, ICC-01/04-01/07-3003-tENG, Decision on an Amicus Curiae application and on the 'Requête tendant à obtenir présentations des témoins [...] aux autorités néerlandaises aux fins d'asile' (articles 68 and 93(7) of the Statute), Trial Chamber II, 9 June 2011 ('First Trial Chamber Witness Decision').

11 On the question of the detained witnesses, see in detail Tom de Boer and Marjoleine Zieck, 'ICC Witnesses and Acquitted Suspects Seeking Asylum in the Netherlands: An Overview of the Jurisdictional Battles between the ICC and Its Host State' (2015) 27 International Journal of Refugee Law 573; Joris van Wijk and Marjolein Cupido, 'Testifying behind Bars—Detained ICC Witnesses and Human Rights Protection' in Carsten Stahn (ed), *The Law and Practice of the International Criminal Court* (OUP 2015) 1084.

12 First Trial Chamber Witness Decision (n 10) paras 67–73.

13 ibid para. 73.

witnesses must not be returned to the DRC unless and until The Netherlands had issued a decision on their asylum requests,[14] resulting in the (at least temporary) non-application of Article 93(7)(b) of the Statute, which provides for the return without delay of the witness once his or her testimony is concluded.

While seeking to protect the witnesses' human rights, the Trial Chamber's decision gave rise to another human rights issue—their continued detention at the ICC detention centre pending the Dutch asylum proceedings. While the Trial Chamber initially found that there was a sufficient legal basis for the witnesses to remain in custody,[15] the situation became more and more untenable with the lapse of time. In October 2013, more than two years after the initial decision, the Trial Chamber issued yet another decision regarding the situation of the detained witnesses, rejecting, by majority, the witnesses' request for release from custody.[16] The Chamber found that it was faced with competing obligations, namely to protect the witnesses' human rights (which merited the suspension of the duty in terms of Article 93(7) of the Statute to return them to the DRC) and to keep the detained witnesses in detention, while being unable to review the legality of their detention, which was governed by Congolese law.[17] The Trial Chamber juxtaposed the principle of *non-refoulement*, which it characterised as being of peremptory character, and the right to liberty. It found that the latter 'cannot be considered an intransgressible or peremptory norm of international law' as there 'numerous exceptions' to that right.[18] The Trial Chamber concluded that it lacked competence to rule on the requests for release.[19] Judge Van den Wyngaert attached a dissenting opinion to the decision, strongly criticising the majority and taking the view that the right not to be submitted to arbitrary detention of the witnesses outweighs the Court's obligation vis-à-vis the DRC, and that the witnesses therefore should be immediately released.[20] The legal situation, which has been described as 'Kafkaesque',[21] was

14 ibid 40.
15 ibid para. 81.
16 *Prosecutor v Ngudjolo*, ICC-01/04-01/07-3405-tENG, Decision on the Application for the Interim Release of Detained Witnesses [...], Trial Chamber II, 1 October 2013 ('Second Trial Chamber Witness Decision').
17 Second Trial Chamber Witness Decision (n 16) paras 17 et seq.
18 ibid paras 30, 33.
19 ibid para. 36.
20 Second Trial Chamber Witness Decision (n 16) Dissenting Opinion of Judge Van den Wyngaert, ICC-01/04-01/07-3405-Anx, dated 1 October 2013 and registered on 2 October 2013, paras 19 et seq.
21 See van Wijk and Cupido (n 11) 1090.

further complicated by the ruling of the ECtHR that The Netherlands did not bear responsibility for the legality of the witnesses' detention while in ICC custody.[22]

The Trial Chamber's decision was eventually superseded by a decision of the Appeals Chamber, which had been seized of the case in relation to which the witnesses had testified. The Appeals Chamber took a somewhat different approach to Article 21(3) of the Statute and found that this provision 'does not require the Court to *violate* its obligations pursuant to article 93 (7) (b) of the Statute' to return the witnesses to the DRC.[23] It noted that the human rights obligations vis-à-vis the detained witnesses were owed *by The Netherlands* and not by the Court,[24] and that it is, therefore, 'for The Netherlands to determine whether the Detained Witnesses' asylum claims make it necessary for it to intervene in order to take control of the Detained Witnesses until their respective claims have been finally adjudicated', noting that Dutch authorities would gain physical control and custody over the witnesses when facilitating, at the ICC's request, their return to the DRC.[25] Accordingly, the Appeals Chamber ordered the ICC Registrar to take the necessary steps to return the witnesses immediately to the DRC.[26]

Both cases are indicative of the potentially important impact that human rights have on the ICC's legal framework: they may lead to the application of new rules that supplement the ICC Statute and its subsidiary instruments or even to the non-application of express provisions of the Statute.[27] The overall approach of the ICC jurisprudence demonstrates substantial deference

22 See *Bède Djokaba Lambi Longa v Netherlands* App no 33917/12 (ECtHR, 9 October 2012), paras 68 et seq. Note that this case concerned a witness in the case of *Prosecutor v Lubanga*, in which the same issue arose.

23 *Prosecutor v Ngudjolo*, ICC-01/04-02/12-158, Order on the Implementation of the Cooperation Agreement between the Court and the Democratic Republic of the Congo Concluded pursuant Article 93 (7) of the Statute, Appeals Chamber, 20 January 2014 ('Appeals Chamber Witness Decision'), para. 26 (emphasis in original). See also *Prosecutor v Ngudjolo*, ICC-01/04-02/12-179, Decision on the 'Registry's Urgent Request for Guidance' and further Order […], Appeals Chamber, 21 May 2014, where the Appeals Chamber reiterated that the detained witnesses should be returned to the DRC immediately.

24 Appeals Chamber Witness Decision (n 23) para. 24.

25 ibid para. 29.

26 ibid 3.

27 In fact, even the Appeals Chamber's approach regarding the stay of proceedings may be seen as a non-application of the Statute: the result of a stay of proceedings is that the provisions that give the Court responsibility for the prosecution of crimes under its jurisdiction are not implemented.

to human rights principles: for instance, the Appeals Chamber confirmed the Trial Chamber's imposition of a stay of proceedings on human rights grounds in the *Lubanga* case, even though the conduct of the Prosecutor, which led to the impossibility of disclosure of potentially exculpatory material that the Prosecutor had obtained from third parties on the condition of confidentiality, was as such provided for in the ICC Statute. The Prosecutor also maintained that he had assessed the material in question and had come to the conclusion that it was not of such significance that the trial could not continue without it being disclosed.[28] Nevertheless, the Appeals Chamber considered that, in such a situation, where the material in question could not even be disclosed to the Trial or Appeals Chamber for an independent assessment, the proceedings must be halted—an outcome that on its face seems to be directly in tension with the Court's overall purpose of 'fighting impunity'.[29]

The Trial Chamber's decision in relation to the detained witnesses was equally far-reaching: because of human rights concerns, an unambiguous provision of the ICC Statute was left unapplied, arguably leading to a breach of the Court's obligations vis-à-vis one of its States Parties. Interestingly, as highlighted by the Appeals Chamber's decision, it was not even the Court that owed these human rights to the witnesses concerned: the witnesses did not apply for asylum at the ICC (nor could they have done so), they applied for asylum in The Netherlands.

Such use of Article 21(3) has far-reaching consequences and could, to some extent, lead to a re-writing of the ICC Statute. It is conceivable that other provisions of the ICC Statute could in the future also be found to be at odds with human rights principles and therefore inapplicable at least in specific situations.

There is another, albeit somewhat unrelated, aspect that deserves mentioning in this context: whether the requirement to apply and interpret in compliance with internationally recognised human rights applies exclusively to the ICC's procedural law, or whether it extends to the substantive law of the Court. For instance, is the ICC required (or at least expected) to adopt an interpretation of 'torture' as a crime against humanity or a war crime[30] that aligns with the interpretation of the term by human rights bodies? In the practice of other

---

28 See *Prosecutor v Lubanga*, ICC-01/04-01/06-1486, Judgment on the Appeal of the Prosecutor against the Decision of Trial Chamber I Entitled 'Decision on the Consequences of Non-Disclosure of Exculpatory Materials [...]', Appeals Chamber, 20 October 2008, para. 62.

29 ibid paras 73 et seq.

30 See Articles 7(1)(f) and 8(2)(a)(ii) and (c)(i) of the ICC Statute.

international criminal tribunals, human rights jurisprudence has indeed influenced the interpretation of the substantive law of torture.[31] At the same time, there are also limitations to the relevance of human rights instruments and jurisprudence: the Convention Against Torture and Other Cruel, Inhumane or Degrading Treatment or Punishment[32] limits the definition of torture to acts committed with the involvement of public officials for a particular reason.[33] Both requirements were dropped in the jurisprudence of the ICTY, based on the 'different purpose' of international criminal law and international human rights law.[34] Interestingly, the definition of torture as a crime against humanity under the ICC Statute likewise drops the 'public official requirement'.[35] It could be argued that a human rights compliant interpretation of this provision would actually require the ICC to adopt the 'public official requirement', which would lead, in turn, to lesser protection against acts that, according to the jurisprudence of the ICTY, amount to torture (though such acts would often qualify as other crimes against humanity, such as the crime against humanity of inhumane treatment).

2 'Internationally Recognized Human Rights'

Given the potential impact of Article 21(3) of the ICC Statute, the question of what actually are 'internationally recognized human rights' deserves closer analysis. Binding international human rights instruments obviously qualify as such—notably the International Covenant on Civil and Political Rights.[36] Its Article 14 contains provisions regarding the right to a fair trial, which are of

31 See below, chapters by Elena Maculan and Elizabeth Santalla; Olivier de Frouville, 'The Influence of the European Court of Human Rights' Case Law on International Criminal Law of Torture and Inhuman or Degrading Treatment' (2011) 9 Journal of International Criminal Justice 633.

32 10 December 1984, entered into force 26 June 1987, U.N.T.S. 1465, 85 (CAT).

33 See Article 1 of the CAT.

34 See *Prosecutor v Kunarac*, IT-96-23-T & IT-96-23/1-T, Judgement, Trial Chamber, 22 February 2001, paras 465 et seq. On this issue see further de Frouville (n 31) 637 et seq.; Gerhard Werle and Florian Jessberger, *Principles of International Criminal Law* (3rd edn, OUP 2014) 362 et seq.

35 See Article 7(2)(e) of the ICC Statute: '"Torture" means the intentional infliction of severe pain or suffering, whether physical or mental, upon a person in the custody or under the control of accused; except that torture shall not include pain or suffering arising only from, inherent in or incidental to, lawful sanctions'.

36 16 December 1966, 999 U.N.T.S. 171.

direct relevance to the ICC's core activities. These provisions are, however, in any event part of the Court's applicable law: Article 67(1) of the ICC Statute contains what is almost a carbon copy of Article 14 of the ICCPR—with the ICC Statute in some respects seemingly even going beyond the requirements of Article 14.[37] Similarly, the provisions of Articles 9 and 10 (regarding arrest and detention) and Article 15 (regarding the principle of *nulla poena sine lege*) of the ICCPR all find more or less direct equivalents in the ICC Statute.[38] Thus, the added value of having regard to the text of the ICCPR in these regards is likely to be limited—if the judges of the Court seek guidance from it when interpreting the Statute or its subsidiary legal instruments, they will encounter provisions that are identical or at least very similar to those contained in the ICC Statute.

2.1 *Human Rights Treaty Bodies*

Much more instructive for the Court's endeavour to identify 'internationally recognized human rights' could be the jurisprudence of the international bodies entrusted with interpreting and applying the ICCPR and other human rights instruments. Of particular relevance in this regard is, of course, the United Nations Human Rights Committee ('Human Rights Committee'), which is responsible for interpreting the ICCPR.[39] It does so primarily by way of 'Gen-

37 Notably, Article 67(1)(a) of the ICC Statute, which provide for the right to be informed of the charges in a language that the accused *fully* speaks, and Article 67(1)(f) to have the right to an interpreter or translations of documents if the proceedings or documents are not in a language that the accused *fully* speaks. The corresponding provisions of Article 14(3)(a) and (f) of the ICCPR do not use the term 'fully'. According to the ICC Appeals Chamber, the inclusion of this term in the ICC Statute suggests that the standard at the ICC is higher than that mandated by the ICCPR or the ECHR (see *Prosecutor v Katanga*, ICC-01/04-01/07-522, Judgment on the Appeal of Mr. Germain Katanga against the Decision of Pre-Trial Chamber I Entitled 'Decision on the Defence Request Concerning Languages', Appeals Chamber, 27 May 2008, paras 36 et seq.). The Appeals Chamber recently confirmed that Article 67(1)(a) of the ICC Statute provides for a higher standard than that provided for in the ICCPR or the ECHR (see *Prosecutor v Ntaganda*, ICC-01/04-02/06-1330, Judgment on the Appeal of Mr Bosco Ntaganda against the 'Decision on Defence Requests Seeking Disclosure Orders [...]', Appeals Chamber, 20 May 2016, para. 29, fn. 49).

38 See Article 55 of the ICC Statute, which stipulates the rights of the person under investigation, including in its para. (1)(d) the prohibition of arbitrary arrest and detention. Articles 22 and 23 of the ICC Statute contain the principles of *nullum crimen, nulla poena sine lege*.

39 On the role of the Human Rights Committee, see Sarah Joseph and Melissa Castan, *The International Covenant on Civil and Political Rights: Cases, Materials, and Commentary* (3rd edn, OUP 2013), paras 1.31 et seq.

eral Comments' on specific Articles of the ICCPR and by expressing 'Views' on individual applications in relation to States that are parties to the Optional Protocol to the ICCPR. Although these General Comments and Views are, strictly speaking, not legally binding on the States Parties to the ICCPR, they have nevertheless been described as 'authoritative' interpretations of the ICCPR,[40] which States should accept, in accordance with the principle of good faith. Against this background, and given that the fair trial guarantees in the ICC Statute are directly drawn from the ICCPR, interpretations of the provisions of the ICCPR by the Human Rights Committee are of great significance for the ICC and (subject to what is being said below) may be considered expressions of 'internationally recognized human rights' in terms of Article 21(3) of the ICC Statute. The same is true for the pronouncements of treaty bodies of more specialised human rights treaties, notably the Committee against Torture, the Committee on the Elimination of Discrimination against Women, the Committee on the Elimination of Racial Discrimination, the Committee on the Rights of Persons with Disabilities, the Committee on Enforced Disappearances, the Committee on Economic, Social and Cultural Rights, and the Committee on the Rights of the Child. Their pronouncements may be highly relevant for ensuring a human rights compliant interpretation of the ICC Statute.

2.2 *Regional Treaties and Treaty Bodies*

Although the practice of Human Rights Committee and other universal treaty bodies is particularly apt to be considered when identifying internationally recognised human rights, in the practice of the ICC, references to the Human Rights Committee are relatively sparse. Far more references are made to the jurisprudence of *regional* human rights bodies, notably that of the European Court of Human Rights.[41] This is both easily explainable and surprising.

40 See UN Human Rights Committee, General Comment No 33: The Obligations of States Parties under the Optional Protocol to the [ICCPR], CCPR/C/GC/33, 5 November 2008, paras 13 et seq. in relation to States that are parties to the individual complaints under the Optional Protocol to the ICCPR.

41 A search in the Legal Tools Database for records produced by 'judicial bodies' within the ICC yields 61 results for the search term 'Human Rights Committee', while it yields 277 results for 'European Court of Human Rights'. While these results do not say anything about the value attached to the jurisprudence and while some results may not actually relate to decisions or judgments issued by Chambers (for instance, transcripts are also contained in the search results), this nevertheless is a clear indication of the relative importance of the ECtHR in the jurisprudence of the ICC if compared to the Human Rights Committee.

Easily explainable because the case law of, in particular, the ECtHR is much more voluminous than that of the Human Rights Committee. The ECtHR is deciding each year thousands of cases, while the number of cases dealt with by the Human Rights Committee is small: in 2015 the ECtHR disposed judicially of 45,576 applications, while the Human Rights Committee issued 70 decisions.[42] For that reason alone it is more likely that the ICC would find relevant case law from the ECtHR than from the Human Rights Committee (or indeed from the other regional human rights mechanisms: in 2015, the Inter-American Court of Human Rights issued 18 decisions and judgments, while the African Court on Human and Peoples' Rights has since its inception finalised 28 cases[43]).

The references to ECtHR jurisprudence are nevertheless surprising because they beg the question whether the jurisprudence of a regional human rights body may truly be considered a reflection of 'internationally recognized human rights'. It appears that this question has not received attention in the ICC's jurisprudence. While there are many references to ECtHR jurisprudence, there is no discussion of *why* this jurisprudence is actually of relevance to the Court. Nevertheless, the Court's practice appears to be defensible: first, the European Convention of Human Rights—while being a regional instrument—has a broad membership: 47 States are parties to it, amounting to about one quarter of the States of the World.[44] More importantly, even if regionally enforced, human rights are generally thought of as being universal. There is no indication that that there is anything specifically 'European' about the ECtHR's jurisprudence that would be at odds with 'universal' human rights law and therefore lead to the conclusion that the human rights, as interpreted in the ECtHR jurisprudence, are not 'internationally recognized'. Nevertheless, the specific composition of the ECHR's membership should be borne in mind when relying on its jurisprudence: the ECHR's States Parties' legal systems follow in their vast majority the Romano-Germanic tradition, with only the United Kingdom, Ireland, Cyprus and Malta being based on the Common Law tradition. Thus, there

42 See ECtHR, *Analysis of statistics 2015* (2016), http://echr.coe.int/Documents/Stats_analysis_2015_ENG.pdf 4. The data for the Human Rights Committee are the results of a search in the jurisprudence database of the Office of the High Commissioner for Human Rights (http://juris.ohchr.org/), searching for decisions (both 'Views' and inadmissibility decisions) issued in the year 2015.

43 See http://www.corteidh.or.cr/cf/Jurisprudencia2/index.cfm?lang=en and http://en.african-court.org/#finalised-cases respectively (accessed 3 August 2016).

44 See https://www.coe.int/en/web/conventions/full-list/-/conventions/treaty/005/signatures?p_auth=9CiKDnuF (accessed 7 July 2016).

is arguably a 'Romano-Germanic bias' in the ECtHR's jurisprudence, which could colour, in particular, the interpretation of the right to a fair trial in relation to criminal proceedings, given that the systemic differences are most pronounced in this field.[45]

2.3 *The Case-Specificity of Human Rights Case Law*

An additional challenge when relying on the case law of the Human Rights Committee, the ECtHR or other treaty bodies when identifying 'internationally recognized human rights' is that this case law is often highly case-specific and takes into account the peculiarities of the domestic jurisdiction from which the case originates. Indeed, the jurisprudence of, for instance, the ECtHR is replete with general principles, which, however, need to be applied and assessed taking into account the specific circumstances of the case. Thus, while the case law of treaty bodies may certainly foster a better understanding of human rights requirements, it will rarely contain the direct answer—the broad principle contained in the human rights instrument (eg the 'right to a fair trial') may be concretised to a somewhat narrower principle, such as the right to 'equality of arms' or the principle of adversarial proceedings.[46] Nevertheless, the latter will still require further concretization in order to be operational in a specific case. Thus, human rights case law may provide guidance in identifying internationally recognised human rights, but it is unlikely to provide the actual answer.

This also discloses a potential danger in the reliance on case law of treaty bodies: the decision of, say, the ECtHR that a particular procedural practice is in compliance with fair trial requirements will have been taken in light of the overall context of the jurisdiction in question, including safeguards or counterbalancing measures that are available in that jurisdiction and without which the practice might not have passed muster.[47] Accordingly, when relying on the case law of treaty bodies, it is important not simply to take 'sound bites' of the jurisprudence, but to consider the procedural context. At least as far as the jurisprudence of the ECtHR is concerned, this is facilitated by the fact that

---

45 It has also been noted that the systemic differences between the Romano-Germanic and Common Law traditions for example in the field of the law of evidence explain the ECtHR's deferential review in that regard. See Stefan Trechsel, *Human Rights in Criminal Proceedings* (OUP 2005) 323.

46 See Trechsel (n 45) 84: 'The terms "fair trial" and "fair hearing" are characterized by considerable vagueness'.

47 For an example concerning the use of uncorroborated hearsay evidence, see below, chapter by Yael Vias Gvirsman.

the ECtHR's judgments usually summarise not only the facts of the case, but also the relevant domestic legal framework.[48]

2.4 *Jurisprudence and Legislation of Other Jurisdictions*

Another potential 'source' of 'internationally recognized human rights' are the jurisprudence and legislation of other jurisdictions, both international and domestic. On the international plane, the case law in particular of the ad hoc international criminal tribunals, the ICTY and ICTR, as well as that of the various hybrid jurisdictions could shed light on the scope of fair trial rights. This case law is potentially of great relevance, given that these courts and tribunals deal with similar crimes and often have a similar procedural framework. Many of the issues that the ICC is facing in respect of ensuring the right to a fair trial in complex international proceedings have already been litigated before ICTs. But is the resulting jurisprudence reflective of 'internationally recognized human rights'? There are at least two arguments against such a claim. First, the ad hoc international criminal tribunals and hybrid jurisdictions are not specifically tasked with enforcing human rights provisions in the way that the Human Right Committee and its regional counterparts are. Rather, they make findings regarding human rights incidentally as part of the exercise of their criminal jurisdiction. As such, the jurisprudence lacks the 'specific control' character of human rights bodies—unlike the Human Rights Committee, the ECtHR or other regional human rights bodies, it is not the primary task of ICTs to determine whether or not fair trial rights (or other human rights) were violated.

Second, there are methodological questions as to the appropriateness of relying on the case law of the international and internationalised criminal jurisdictions to identify 'internationally recognized human rights' under Article 21(3) of the Statute. As has been argued elsewhere, the jurisprudence of the ICTY and ICTR is not a source of law for the ICC, though it may be considered as part of the ICC Statute's (widely construed) context in terms of Article 31 of the Vienna Convention on the Law of Treaties[49] ('VCLT') and therefore may be rel-

48 It is worth noting that the Chambers of the ECtHR are assisted by lawyers who are familiar with the legal system from which the case emanates, which provides an additional safeguard for a proper understanding of this context. See ECtHR, *The Role of the Registry*, http://www.echr.coe.int/Documents/Registry_ENG.pdf (accessed 10 July 2016). See also Nina-Louisa Arold Lorenz, Xavier Groussot and Gunnar Thor Petursson, *The European Human Rights Culture—A Paradox of Human Rights Protection in Europe?* (Martinus Nijhoff 2013) 41 et seq.

49 Adopted 23 May 1969, entered into force 27 January 1980, U.N.T.S. 1155, I-18232.

evant for its interpretation.[50] This—rather limited—relevance of the ad hoc tribunals' case law would potentially be turned upside down if the ICTY and ICTR jurisprudence were made applicable by virtue of Article 21(3) of the ICC Statute—which would even give this jurisprudence precedence over the text of the Statute.[51]

Similarly, it is doubtful that domestic case law and legislation form part of 'internationally recognized human rights'. Clearly, there is a wealth of, in particular, jurisprudence from domestic courts that relates to human rights, often analysing how to implement international legal obligations.[52] Accordingly, it may be tempting to identify 'internationally recognized human rights' in this jurisprudence. This, however, would at least be problematic, as the domestic decisions may be influenced by the peculiarities of the jurisdiction in question. Unlike decisions of treaty bodies, which also have to apply human rights in domestic contexts, the domestic decisions are not 'filtered' through international litigation. Thus, particularly if relied upon by lawyers not trained in the jurisdiction in question, domestic case law may be misinterpreted, as the necessary context might easily be ignored or misunderstood. In addition, at least in the absence of a broad comparative assessment of domestic practices and jurisprudence, it is difficult to argue that domestic human rights jurisprudence reflects *internationally* recognised human rights. A loose approach in this regard would run the risk of circumventing the provisions of Article 21(1)(c) of the Statute, which allows for the reliance on general principles of law derived from domestic law only in limited circumstances.

2.5 *The Role of 'Soft Law'*

Another question that arises is that of so-called 'soft' human rights law, the most prominent example of which is arguably the Universal Declaration of Human Rights. Given that the rights contained in the Universal Declaration have since been incorporated into legally binding treaties, notably the ICCPR, more relevant examples of 'soft' human rights law are declarations and resolutions of organs of international institutions. Two such resolutions have been cited in the ICC's jurisprudence quite regularly: the Declaration of Basic

50 See Volker Nerlich, 'The Status of ICTY and ICTR Precedent in Proceedings Before the ICC' in Carsten Stahn and Göran Sluiter (eds), *The Emerging Practice of the International Criminal Court* (Martinus Nijhoff Publishers 2009) 305.

51 See also Bitti (n 7) 436.

52 For instance, in Germany, the ECHR has the force of law; in the United Kingdom, the Human Rights Act (1998) transposes the provisions of the ECHR into domestic law.

Principles of Justice for Victims of Crime and Abuse of Power of 29 November 1985[53] ('1985 Principles') and the Basic Principles and Guidelines on the Right to a Remedy and Reparation for Victims of Gross Violations of International Human Rights Law and Serious Violations of International Humanitarian Law of 6 December 2005,[54] both of which were adopted by the United Nations General Assembly. There are numerous other such resolutions that are potentially relevant to the Court's work.[55]

Do these resolutions, which are non-binding on States, represent 'internationally recognized human rights'? In terms of the literal meaning of Article 21(3) of the Statute, this would indeed appear to be a possible understanding of Article 21(3) of the Statute—'recognized' does not necessarily mean 'binding'. It must also be noted that the 1985 Principles were actually the basis for the inclusion of participatory rights for victims in the ICC Statute—Article 68(3) of the ICC Statute closely mirrors Article 6(b) of the 1985 Principles.[56] Thus, if the negotiators of the ICC Statute were of the view that they could resort to this type of 'soft law', why should the Court not do the same?

---

53 Resolution A/40/34.

54 Resolution A/60/147. This resolution was cited, for example, in *Prosecutor v Lubanga*, Decision Establishing the Principles and Procedures to be Applied to Reparations, ICC-01/04-01/06-2904, Trial Chamber I, 7 August 2012, para. 185 and fns 378–380, 404.

55 See the list of instruments at http://www.ohchr.org/EN/ProfessionalInterest/Pages/UniversalHumanRightsInstruments.aspx (accessed 2 July 2016).

56 See Article 6(b) of the 1985 Principles, which provides that: 'The responsiveness of the judicial and administrative processes to the needs of victims should be facilitated by: [...] (b) Allowing the views and concerns of victims to be presented and considered at appropriate stages of the proceedings where their personal interests are affected, without prejudice to the accused and consistent with the relevant national criminal justice system'. The fact that Article 68(3) of the ICC Statute was 'borrowed' from the 1985 Principles might explain why that provision has resulted in such extensive litigation in the first years of the Court's existence: rather than being a detailed procedural rule, it is a general principle that was originally tailored to be compatible with a vast variety of domestic jurisdictions, some of which are rather opposed to the idea of victim participation in criminal proceedings. The resulting (and necessary) broadness of the provision made it rather difficult to apply in practice.

3 Conclusion: Multiple Facets of 'Internationally Recognized Human Rights'

As seen above, human rights at the ICC have a potent role: not only may they guide the interpretation of the ICC Statute and its subsidiary instruments, they may also mandate the non-application of certain provisions of the Statute (as was done in the case of the detained witnesses) or to the adaption, through case law, of procedures not specifically provided for in the Court's legal instruments (such as in case of the stay of proceedings). Arguably, this strong position of human rights in the Court's legal framework is consonant with the perception of human rights as international *ius cogens*.[57] It is consistent with the letter and spirit of Article 53 of the VCLT that human rights provisions that have acquired the status of *ius cogens* should prevail over the text of the ICC Statute and its subsidiary instruments. As such, Article 21(3) of the ICC Statute is in some ways no more than a variation and concretisation of Article 53 of the VCLT for the purposes of the ICC Statute.[58] Put differently, even without Article 21(3) of the ICC Statute, the ICC, by virtue of Article 53 of the VCLT, would be barred from applying a provision of the Statute that is found to be in breach of a human rights norm that has *ius cogens* status.

At the same time, as has been demonstrated above, internationally recognised human rights may be derived from a variety of sources, including sources that are not binding on States themselves ('soft law') or that are highly case-specific (notably, the jurisprudence of human rights treaty bodies). It would be somewhat perplexing if, in case of conflict, the ICC had to give these sources precedence over its own provisions.

For that reason, a differentiated approach to Article 21(3) of the ICC Statute may be justified. To the extent that human rights reflect *ius cogens*, they override, in case of conflict, the provisions of the ICC Statute—a result that is in keeping with Article 53 of the VCLT.[59] To the extent, however, that the *ius cogens*

---

57 On human rights as *ius cogens* see eg Andrea Bianchi, 'Human Rights and the Magic of *Jus Cogens*' (2008) 19 European Journal of International Law 491.

58 Similarly Pellet (n 2) 1081: 'Without doubt, Article 21(3) of the Statute does not give the ICC express jurisdiction to declare null the totality of a treaty, or even one of its provisions, which is contrary to "internationally recognized human rights", although this would be the effect of a breach of *jus cogens* under article 53 of the Vienna Convention. Nevertheless, it creates a sort of international "super-legality" by clearly authorizing the Court to hold such a norm to be "*ultra vires*" and thus inapplicable'.

59 Note that the Second Trial Chamber Witness Decision (n 16) paras 30, 33, adopted a similar approach when distinguishing between the *peremptory* principle of *non-refoulement* and

character of a human rights norm is not established, the Court should seek guidance from it, but is not required to disregard its own legal framework in case of conflict or tension. This applies notably in respect of human rights 'soft law', which, as has been seen above, is relevant in particular in the field of victim participation and reparations. The Court should, without any doubt, seek guidance from such sources, but it may do so more flexibly than when it comes to *ius cogens* norms. Such an approach may appear incoherent at first. Yet it is merely a reflection of the fact that soft law is as such not binding and allows for more flexibility. Thus, even if, in the application and interpretation of the ICC Statute, the Court does not follow the soft law to the letter, but adapts it to the necessities of the proceedings before the Court, the result may still be consistent with internationally recognised human rights.

---

the right to liberty. Whether the Trial Chamber's conclusion that the right to liberty does not enjoy *ius cogens* status because it knows exceptions is persuasive is open to debate—the right to liberty protects against *arbitrary* detention and it could well be argued that, as soon as detention is arbitrary, it cannot be continued. It is also of note that, as seen above, the Appeals Chamber, in the Appeals Chamber Witness Decision (n 23) para. 26, expressed concern about the non-application of provisions of the Statute on the ground of purported human rights incompatibility.

CHAPTER 5

Article 21(3) of the ICC Statute and 'Internationally Recognized Human Rights' as a Source of Mandatory Judicial Dialogue

*Christophe Deprez**

I Introduction

It is a common view that a strict distinction should be maintained between, on the one hand, human rights jurisprudence and, on the other hand, human rights law proper, ie human rights norms as they emerge from relevant regional and international instruments.[1] According to this view, their respective significance and nature are different—human rights norms being vested with general applicability, with human rights case law only consisting of the casuistic application of these norms to a specific case.[2] Consequently, proponents of this view would argue that human rights treaties are binding upon all subjects falling under their authority, while associated jurisprudence is only of concern to those subjects involved in the specific case at hand.[3]

* The draft version of this article was prepared during a post-doctoral stay at Columbia Law School, New York. I would like to thank those persons and institutions who made this visit possible. I wish to especially thank the *Fonds David-Constant*, whose financial support has been crucial to the project.

1 This view is not restricted to the human rights sphere. On the (widely accepted) dividing line between international law and international judicial practice in general, see John C. Gardner, 'Judicial Precedent in the Making of International Public Law' (1935) 17 Journal of Comparative Legislation and International Law 251, 252; Robert Jennings and Arthur Watts, *Oppenheim's International Law* (9th edn, Longman 1992) 41.

2 See eg Cecilia Medina, 'The Role of International Tribunals: Law-Making or Creative Interpretation?' in Dinah Shelton (ed), *The Oxford Handbook on International Human Rights Law* (OUP 2013) 668. Human rights organs seem to endorse this binary perspective themselves: see eg *Guzzardi v Italy*, App no 7367/76 (ECtHR, 6 November 1980), para. 88 (considering that 'in proceedings originating in an individual application, [the Court] has to confine its attention, as far as possible, to the issues raised by the concrete case before it').

3 See Rosanne van Alebeek and André Nollkaemper, 'The Legal Status of Decisions by Human Rights Treaty Bodies in National Law' in Helen Keller and Geir Ulfstein (eds), *UN Human Rights Treaty Bodies: Law and Legitimacy* (CUP 2012) 407.

 | DOI: 10.1163/9789004313750_007

This chapter seeks to nuance this view. It does so, in particular, with reference to the (undisputable and significant) cross-fertilisation process that emerges between the ICC and human rights bodies.[4] After all, the narrow sense that is usually attached to the term 'cross-fertilisation' describes the phenomenon whereby judges decide to freely dialogue with one another, that is, to resort to external practice where they have no formal obligation to do so.[5] Yet this chapter argues that there is another, mandatory level to the cross-fertilisation mechanism. This is because—in our view—human rights case law is not necessarily intended to remain case-specific, but should, in certain contexts, be considered as bearing general authority.

For the purpose of this chapter, in particular, Article 21(3) of the ICC Statute represents one such context.[6] When human rights case law is to be considered 'internationally recognized' in the meaning of the latter provision, it seems to us that the ICC should carefully apply it, not because it merely chooses to do so, but because its very founding instrument makes such dialogue mandatory.

At a later stage in this chapter, we will show that this is exactly what the ICC has done so far. In its early practice, the Court has repeatedly relied on human rights jurisprudence on account of its 'internationally recognized'—and therefore binding—nature (section IV). But before coming to that, we will first shed some further light on the idea of *mandatory judicial dialogue* (section II), and try to clarify the nature and substance of 'internationally recognized human rights' under Article 21(3) of the Rome Statute (section III).

4 For early literature on cross-fertilisation in general, see, most decisively, Anne-Marie Slaughter, 'A Typology of Transjudicial Communication' (1994) 29 University of Richmond Law Review 99. On the reception of this phenomenon in the context of international criminal justice, see, among recent works, Triestino Mariniello and Paolo Lobba, 'Editorial—The Cross-fertilisation Rhetoric in Question: Use and Abuse of the European Court's Jurisprudence by International Criminal Tribunals' (2015) 84 Nordic Journal of International Law 363 (as well as the other pieces published in that special issue of the Journal).

5 See Slaughter, 'A Typology' (n 4) 103; Anne-Marie Slaughter, 'A Global Community of Courts' (2003) 44 Harvard International Law Journal 191, 193; Julia Geneuss, 'Obstacles to Cross-fertilisation: The International Criminal Tribunals' "Unique Context" and the Flexibility of the European Court of Human Rights' Case Law' (2015) 84 Nordic Journal of International Law 404, 405; Sergey Vasiliev, 'International Criminal Tribunals in the Shadow of Strasbourg and Politics of Cross-fertilisation' (2015) 84 Nordic Journal of International Law 371, 388.

6 Rome Statute of the International Criminal Court, UN Doc A/CONF.183/9 of 17 July 1998, entered into force 1 July 2002 ('ICC Statute' or 'Rome Statute').

II Mandatory Judicial Dialogue on Human Rights before the ICC

As was already pointed out by way of introduction, it seems virtually undisputed throughout literature that human rights norms and human rights jurisprudence are two very different things in nature: the former being general; the latter, case-specific. As De Salvia puts it in reference to the ECtHR, there is 'no *erga omnes* obligation on the other States to conform to a principle set out by the Court in a judgment that concerns only the respondent State'.[7]

This common perception finds its way into the literature on international criminal justice. When the question is raised whether human rights are applicable to the activities of international criminal tribunals—and, in particular, of the ICC—the answer often seems to be different for treaty norms and for their interpretation by competent human rights bodies.

On the one hand, it is widely acknowledged that human rights norms—or, to put it more correctly, some human rights norms—are genuinely binding on the ICC.[8] Since the Court is not a party to the relevant international instruments,[9] the most convincing arguments in this respect usually build on general sources of international law (as an international organisation with legal personality,[10] the ICC should comply with individual rights *qua* customary international law and general principles of law),[11] as well as on Article 21(3) of the Rome Statute

---

7 Michele De Salvia, 'Execution of the Judgments of the European Court of Human Rights: Legal Nature of the Obligations of the States and European Supervision of National Legislative Choices' in The European Commission for Democracy through Law (ed), *The Status of International Treaties on Human Rights* (Council of Europe Publishing 2006) 92. In the very same vein, see John G. Merrills, *The Development of International Law by the European Court of Human Rights* (Manchester University Press 1988) 12.

8 See eg Salvatore Zappalà, *Human Rights in International Criminal Proceedings* (OUP 2003) 5–7; Christoph Safferling, *Towards an International Criminal Procedure* (OUP 2001) 40; Göran Sluiter, 'International Criminal Proceedings and the Protection of Human Rights' (2003) 37 New England Law Review 935, 935; Sergey Vasiliev, 'Applicability of International Fair Trial Standards in International Criminal Proceedings: Between Universalism and Contextuality' (2008) Paper presented at Toogdag Seminar (Utrecht University), 3 http://ssrn.com/abstract=1718960 accessed 15 February 2016.

9 Nor are other international organisations, with the exception of the European Union being a party to the 2006 UN Convention on the Rights of Persons with Disabilities (see https://treaties.un.org/Pages/ViewDetails.aspx?src=IND&mtdsg_no=IV-15&chapter=4&lang=en accessed 15 February 2016).

10 See Rome Statute, Article 4.

11 For the general conclusion that international organisations may be vested with rights and

(which requires the Court to apply and interpret relevant law in a manner that is consistent with 'internationally recognized human rights').[12]

On the other hand, commentators seem reluctant to embrace the idea that international criminal tribunals may be legally bound to follow the jurisprudential views of their human rights colleagues, or, to put it differently, to the idea that cross-fertilisation might be more than a purely rhetorical and discretionary process. In the words of Lorenzo Gradoni, '[i]nternational criminal tribunals have of course no formal duty to accept as valid the interpretations that other jurisdictions or bodies give of the relevant human rights norms'.[13] In the same vein, as Sergey Vasiliev puts it in one of the seminal pieces on the issue:

> A sometimes neglected distinction must at all times be sustained between, on the one hand, the internationally recognised human rights standards and, on the other hand, their interpretations and application-related modalities crafted by [human rights bodies]. While the former constitute the *law* proper and may be mandatory for the tribunals as customary law or general principles, the interpretations of those standards by the said international judicial and monitoring bodies merely constitute the application thereof to the circumstances of a particular case.[14]

---

obligations under international law, see *Interpretation of the Agreement of 25 March 1951 between the WHO and Egypt*, Advisory Opinion (ICJ, 21 May 1980), para. 37. In specific connection with the ICC, see also the obiter dictum in *Djokaba Lambi Longa v The Netherlands*, App no 33917/12 (ECtHR, Decision on admissibility, 9 October 2012), para. 64.

12 For further developments on Article 21(3), see below, Section III.

13 Lorenzo Gradoni, 'The Human Rights Dimension of International Criminal Procedure' in Göran Sluiter and others (eds), *International Criminal Procedure: Principles and Rules* (OUP 2013) 74, 90. This conclusion comes after the author has described the difference between human rights law and case law in the following terms: 'two categories of normative propositions must be distinguished, namely: i) those contained in human rights instruments, such as the [International Covenant on Civil and Political Rights] and its regional counterparts, which articulate general rules and principles [...]; and ii) those extracted from human rights jurisprudence, which are all-things-considered normative statements whereby single cases are adjudicated' (ibid 88).

14 Vasiliev, 'Applicability of International Fair Trial Standards' (n 8) 10. But see, more recently, Sergey Vasiliev, 'Fairness and its Metric in International Criminal Procedure' in Sergey Vasiliev, *International Criminal Trials: A Normative Theory* (OUP forthcoming) 27 http://ssrn.com/abstract=2253177 accessed 15 February 2016 (noting that '[p]recedents form an integral part of the body of [international human rights law] because they give effect to treaty provisions and may be the evidence of custom').

From a strictly conventional perspective, it is certainly true that human rights norms and human rights jurisprudence operate on different levels.[15] However, when it comes to applying human rights to the activities of the ICC, the significance of the traditional *law versus case law* divide should, in our view, be nuanced. Two arguments are particularly worth mentioning in this respect.

Firstly, from an admittedly theoretical standpoint, it can be questioned whether a norm is genuinely distinct from its understanding by competent organs.[16] If it is true that all legal rules need to be interpreted,[17] then indeed one should distinguish between several possible readings of a norm, rather than between such norm—supposedly free from any judicial understanding—and the case law that attaches to it (following this approach, for example, there is no such thing as a self-standing, purely conventional, right to life, but only a range of possible interpretations of this right, whether very literal or more evolutive, such as the requirement that public authorities refrain from any intentional killings that are not absolutely necessary,[18] the positive obligation for the same authorities to ensure an effective investigation after suspicious deaths,[19] etc.). If we accept this line of reasoning as persuasive, then it becomes inconsistent to treat conventional law and judge-made law differently for the purpose of delineating the human rights obligations of the ICC.

15 To only mention the European sphere, it is sufficient to compare Article 46(1) of the ECHR (under which judgments only bind respondent States) and Article 1 of the same instrument (making it clear that 'the rights and freedoms' set forth in the Convention are binding upon all States parties).

16 This fundamental issue has been raised by many, and extends far beyond the sphere of human rights protection. See, among many examples in the literature on general international law, Ingo Venzke, *How Interpretation Makes International Law: On Semantic Change and Normative Twists* (OUP 2012) 1; Duncan B. Hollis, 'The Existential Function of Interpretation in International Law' in Andrea Bianchi and others (eds), *Interpretation in International Law* (OUP 2015) 79; Robert Kolb, *Interprétation et création du droit international* (Bruylant 2006) 3–4 and 103–115.

17 Hans Kelsen, *Pure Theory of Law* (first published 1967, The Lawbook Exchange 2002) 348; Hersch Lauterpacht, *The Development of International Law by the International Court* (Stevens & Sons 1958) 395.

18 See eg *McCann and others v United Kingdom*, App no 18984/91 (ECtHR, 27 September 1995), para. 148; *Juan Humberto Sánchez v Honduras*, App no 11.073 (IACtHR, 7 June 2003), para. 109; *Suarez de Guerrero v Colombia*, Comm no 11/45 (UN Human Rights Committee, 31 March 1982), para. 13(2)–(3).

19 See eg *Osman v United Kingdom*, App no 23452/94 (ECtHR, 28 October 1998), para. 115; *Velasquez Rodriguez v Honduras*, App no 7920 (IACtHR, 29 July 1988), para. 177; *Marcellana and Gumanoy v Philippines*, Comm no 1560/2007 (UN Human Rights Committee, 30 October 2008), para. 7(2).

Secondly, and more concretely, there seems to be no valid reason why the legal foundations for the applicability of human rights to the activities of the ICC could not be equally relevant as regards human rights jurisprudence in particular. If we agree that the ICC should abide by human rights norms to the extent that they are 'internationally recognized', customary, or reflected in general principles of law, then the same should hold true with respect to human rights case law.[20] In that sense the *binding norms versus non-binding jurisprudence* dogma reaches its limit: both law and case law are likely to govern international criminal proceedings *qua* customary international law, general principles of law, or 'internationally recognized human rights'.

In sum, in the dialectics between the ICC and human rights, it is argued here that judicial cross-fertilisation may be a mandatory process, just as much as adherence to human rights norms (in the plain meaning that supposedly stems from their conventional expression) may be a legal requirement.

This, of course, begs the question what substantive rights (or interpretation thereof) are covered by the three normative categories identified above. In the next section and in the remainder of this chapter, we will focus our efforts on the one category that is specific to the ICC: 'internationally recognized human rights'. This is because, as will be observed shortly,[21] while the ICC has repeatedly acknowledged a duty to comply with human rights case law, it has almost exclusively done so with reference to Article 21(3) of the Rome Statute, thereby making 'internationally recognized human rights' the primary source of mandatory judicial dialogue.[22]

20 Göran Sluiter seems to share this opinion when he argues, in connection with the UN sphere of human rights protection, that '[f]ull application of the [International Covenant on Civil and Political Rights] should include the views of the Human Rights Committee' (Sluiter (n 8) 940).

21 See below, Section IV.

22 Throughout this chapter, the well-accepted notion of 'judicial dialogue' is used in a generic way, ie despite the fact that communication between the ICC and human rights bodies is mostly one-sided (but see, on the cursory use of international criminal law and practice by the Strasbourg Court, William A. Schabas, 'Synergy or Fragmentation? International Criminal Law and the European Convention on Human Rights' (2011) 9 Journal of International Criminal Justice 609, 612).

III The Nature and Substance of 'Internationally Recognized Human Rights' under Article 21(3) of the Rome Statute

Article 21(3) of the Rome Statute states that '[t]he application and interpretation of [the sources of law that are of relevance to the activities of the ICC] must be consistent with internationally recognized human rights'. Such generic reference to human rights law—which seems unprecedented in the context of international criminal justice—has been mostly well received in expert literature.[23] As to the ICC itself, it quickly acknowledged the considerable reach of Article 21(3) by recognising, with explicit reference to the latter, that '[h]uman rights underpin the Statute; every aspect of it'.[24]

The exact purpose of 'internationally recognized human rights' may, of course, be discussed. Although the notion is included under Article 21 of the Statute, which is meant to deal with applicable law, from a theoretical perspective the true nature of paragraph 3 may lie somewhere else. Rather than a distinct source of law, 'internationally recognized human rights' seem to be imposed upon the Court as a general constraint *in the interpretation and application of* the law.[25]

And yet, in its early practice, the ICC has progressively vested Article 21(3) with ever-increasing responsibilities. First, when facing several possible understandings of the Rome Statute, the Court has drawn from the provision a general requirement to favour the reading that is in accordance with human rights.[26] Arguably, this is little more than a literal application of Article 21(3).

---

23 See Rebecca Young, 'Internationally Recognized Human Rights before the International Criminal Court' (2011) 60 International and Comparative Law Quarterly 189, 191.

24 *Prosecutor v Lubanga*, ICC-01/04-01/06-772, Judgment on the Appeal of Mr. Thomas Lubanga Dyilo Against the Decision on the Defence Challenge to the Jurisdiction of the Court pursuant to Article 19 (2) (a) of the Statute of 3 October 2006, Appeals Chamber, 14 December 2006 ('Lubanga Judgment on Jurisdiction Appeal'), para. 37.

25 On this view, see William A. Schabas, *The International Criminal Court: A Commentary on the Rome Statute* (2nd edn, OUP 2016) 530; Young (n 23) 193. But see Gilbert Bitti, 'Article 21 and the Hierarchy of Sources of Law before the ICC' in Carsten Stahn (ed), *The Law and Practice of the International Criminal Court* (OUP 2015) 437; Daniel Sheppard, 'The International Criminal Court and "Internationally Recognized Human Rights": Understanding Article 21(3) of the Rome Statute' (2010) 10 International Criminal Law Review 43, 60.

26 See eg *Prosecutor v Katanga*, ICC-01/04-01/07-474, Decision on the Set of Procedural Rights Attached to Procedural Status of Victim at the Pre-Trial Stage of the Case, Pre-Trial Chamber I, 13 May 2008 ('Katanga and Ngudjolo Decision on Victim Status'), para. 78.

Yet, in a more creative manner, the Court further suggested that paragraph 3 also commands to disregard any part of the Statute that would conflict with 'internationally recognized human rights'.[27] Thirdly and lastly, when adequate protection of 'internationally recognized human rights' seemed to require so, ICC judges did not hesitate to assume powers which were not explicitly granted to them by their basic instruments.[28]

In the end, the question whether or not an objective analysis of the Rome Statute leads to the conclusion that Article 21(3) goes as far as to establish human rights as an actual source of applicable law has limited importance. What matters most is that, in practice, the ICC has actually vested paragraph 3 with functions that clearly exceed those of an ordinary tool for interpretation; it has accepted a thorough obligation to uphold relevant human rights (whether through mere interpretation, by ignoring its founding instrument, or by assuming extra-statutory powers).[29]

Given the tremendous potential of Article 21(3) on the development of the practice of the ICC in general, it seems particularly important to try and clarify the exact substance of 'internationally recognized human rights'. However, the extent to which this can be done is questionable.[30]

At the outset, it should be noted that although the concept appears twice in the Statute—under Article 21(3), but also under Article 69(7) in relation to the exclusion of improperly obtained evidence—neither these provisions, nor the RPE, further clarify its scope.

---

27 See eg *Prosecutor v Katanga*, ICC-01/04-01/07-3003, Decision on an *Amicus Curiae* Application [...], Trial Chamber II, 9 June 2011 ('Katanga and Ngudjolo Decision on Witnesses Asylum Requests'), para. 73 (refusing to apply Article 93(7) of the Rome Statute and to return detained witnesses to the Democratic Republic of the Congo, as to do so would have deprived them of their internationally recognised human right to seek asylum).

28 See, most clearly, *Prosecutor v Lubanga*, ICC-01/04-01/06-1486, Judgment on the Appeal of the Prosecutor against the Decision of Trial Chamber I Entitled 'Decision on the Consequences of Non-Disclosure of Exculpatory Materials', Appeals Chamber, 21 October 2008 ('Lubanga Judgment on the Consequences of Non-Disclosure'), para. 77 (admitting that neither the Statute nor the RPE empowered judges to stay proceedings in response to the Prosecutor's failure to disclose exculpatory evidence, but still approving the Trial Chamber's decision to do so, for the sake of 'internationally recognized human rights').

29 This conclusion is shared by Bitti (n 25) 441.

30 Also observing the inherent difficulty of such task, see Young (n 23) 193–194 in particular; Gudrun Hochmayr, 'Applicable Law in Practice and Theory: Interpreting Article 21 of the ICC Statute' (2014) 12 Journal of International Criminal Justice 655, 674.

Furthermore, while the Chambers of the ICC routinely apply the notion in the cases submitted to them,[31] they usually avoid addressing its meaning in a general manner. To the extent of our knowledge, only Judge Pikis has attempted to shed some light on the theoretical boundaries of Article 21(3), in one of the separate opinions he delivered in the *Lubanga* case: '[i]nternationally recognized may be regarded those human rights acknowledged by customary international law and international treaties and conventions'.[32] This definition, however, does not appear to be entirely conclusive (for one thing, it may be asked what significance remains for Article 21(3) if 'internationally recognized human rights' only cover customary law and treaties, ie two sources of law that are already included under Article 21(1)).[33] As to other international criminal tribunals, they do not appear to further clarify the reach of the concept. The ICTY has occasionally relied on the parent notion of 'internationally recognized human rights instruments'[34] but, similarly, without proposing any specific list of such instruments.

Surely the concept of 'internationally recognized human rights' is not specific to the context of international criminal justice. It can also be observed in several international instruments, such as Convention no 169 of the International Labour Organisation,[35] or the 2011 UN Guiding Principles on Business and Human Rights.[36] Even more compelling in this respect are the Dayton Agreements signed in 1995 by several former Yugoslavian entities. Article 1 of the sixth annex to these Agreements lists an impressive (yet non-exhaustive)

---

31 Among many other examples, see those listed below, Section IV.

32 *Prosecutor v Lubanga*, ICC-01/04-01/06-424, Decision on the Prosecutor's 'Application for Leave to Reply to "Conclusions de la défense en réponse au mémoire d'appel du Procureur"', Appeals Chamber, 12 September 2006 ('Lubanga Decision on Leave to Reply'), Separate Opinion of Judge Pikis, para. 3.

33 Daniel Sheppard (n 25) 48–49 raises the same question. On the uncontested opinion that 'the principles and rules of international law' (in the words of Article 21(1) of the Rome Statute) cover customary international law, see Claire Callejon, 'Article 21' in Julian Fernandez and Xavier Pacreau (eds), *Statut de Rome de la Cour pénale internationale. Commentaire article par article*, vol 1 (Pedone 2012) 770; Hochmayr (n 30) 668; Schabas (n 25) 391; Alain Pellet, 'Applicable Law' in Antonio Cassese, Paola Gaeta and John R.W.D. Jones (eds), *The Rome Statute of the International Criminal Court: A Commentary* (OUP 2002) vol 2 1071; Frédéric Mégret, 'The Sources of International Criminal Procedure' in Göran Sluiter and others (eds), *International Criminal Procedure: Principles and Rules* (OUP 2013) 71.

34 See eg *Prosecutor v Tadić*, IT-94-1-T, Decision on the Defense Motion for Interlocutory Appeal on Jurisdiction, Appeals Chamber, 2 October 1995, para. 45.

35 Articles 8(2) and 9(1).

36 Principle 12.

set of 'internationally recognized human rights', such as the right to life, the prohibition of torture, or the right to liberty. It then goes on to spell out an extensive list of relevant international and regional human rights treaties—the ECHR and the UN Covenant on Civil and Political Rights, to name only two. Yet, while these several international instruments—especially the Dayton Agreements—constitute useful guidance in clarifying the substantive scope of Article 21(3) of the Rome Statute, their ultimate significance must be approached carefully. Ultimately, it may still be argued that, in a fragmented international legal order,[37] generic legal concepts must be considered context-specific. In other words, the argument can be made (and seems hard to dispute) that the precise standards, which should be considered internationally recognised for the purpose of—for instance—the Dayton Agreements, are not necessarily identical to those under the Rome Statute.

Finally, in the absence of any conventional definition, it is little surprise that expert literature is not unanimous on the content of 'internationally recognized human rights' under Article 21(3). Several useful views on the issue (which are not always concordant) may be mentioned. Daniel Sheppard believes that 'internationally recognized human rights' are, at a minimum, those provided for in UN general human rights instruments.[38] Lorenzo Gradoni argues that key regional conventions should also be included.[39] According to Joe Verhoeven, human rights can be considered 'internationally recognized' if they find their source in universal or regional treaties and are backed by customary law.[40] Alain Pellet contends that Article 21(3) at least goes beyond the limited content of *jus cogens*.[41]

In sum, it remains a very uncertain task to try and objectively identify a clear list of human rights standards applicable to the ICC under Article 21(3) of the Rome Statute. At the end of the day, this task is to be undertaken by the Court itself. Surely there is a bit of a paradox here: in theory, the ICC is

---

37 On the fragmentation debate in international law, see, among recent pieces, Margaret A. Young, *Regime Interaction in International Law: Facing Fragmentation* (CUP 2012); Mario Prost, *The Concept of Unity in Public International Law* (Hart 2012); Anne-Charlotte Martineau, *Le débat sur la fragmentation du droit international: une analyse critique* (Bruylant 2015).

38 Sheppard (n 25) 63. See also Hochmayr (n 30) 674.

39 Gradoni (n 13) 86. For a more cautious approach, see Stephen Bailey, 'Article 21(3) of the Rome Statute: A Plea for Clarity' (2014) 14 International Criminal Law Review 513, 531–532.

40 Joe Verhoeven, 'Article 21 of the Rome Statute and the Ambiguities of Applicable Law' (2002) 33 Netherlands Yearbook of International Law 2, 14.

41 Pellet (n 33) 1081.

bound by 'internationally recognized human rights' but, in practice, it is also left with much of the power to define the scope of such an obligation.[42] This is nonetheless the essence of any judicial system: just as much as national judges are called upon to interpret domestic legislation (even when such legislation precisely aims to dictate the limits of their own activity), the ICC is the primary actor to ascertain the meaning of the Rome Statute and, thus, of its own powers and limits thereof.

This observation brings us back to cross-fertilisation. For, interestingly enough, the next section will show that, when interpreting Article 21(3) of its Statute, the ICC has not only taken due account of human rights norms, but also of human rights *case law*. This stands in sharp contrast with what we have seen thus far. In this section, several propositions have been put forward regarding the substance of 'internationally recognized human rights'. Yet none of these propositions ever suggested that human rights jurisprudence was likely to be included under that category.[43] As will now be demonstrated, the ICC has been less hesitant. In its first decade of activity, it has endorsed the idea of mandatory judicial dialogue, that is, the perception that human rights case law may be truly binding in the context of international criminal proceedings.

IV Human Rights Jurisprudence as Binding 'Internationally Recognized Human Rights' in the Practice of the ICC

It is well known that the ICC often refers to the human rights practice developed by organs as diverse as the ECtHR,[44] the IACtHR,[45] the African Commission on Human and Peoples' Rights,[46] the UN Human Rights Commit-

42 Already alluding to this paradox, see Mahnoush H. Arsanjani, 'The Rome Statute of the International Criminal Court' (1999) 93 American Journal of International Law 22, 29. Similarly and more recently, see Margaret M. deGuzman, 'Article 21: Applicable Law' in Otto Triffterer and Kai Ambos (eds), *The Rome Statute of the International Criminal Court: A Commentary* (Beck 2016) 948.

43 But see the cursory suggestion made by Young (n 23) 199.

44 Among countless examples, see *Prosecutor v Katanga*, ICC-01/04-01/07-3319, Decision on the Implementation of Regulation 55 of the Regulations of the Court and Severing the Charges Against the Accused Persons, Trial Chamber II, 21 November 2012 ('Katanga and Ngudjolo Decision on Regulation 55'), paras 16, 22, 37 (to mention only a few references).

45 See eg *Prosecutor v Lubanga*, ICC-01/04-01/06-2904, Decision Establishing the Principles and Procedures to be Applied to Reparations, Trial Chamber I, 7 August 2012 ('Lubanga Decision on Reparation Principles'), para. 229.

46 See eg *Prosecutor v Gbagbo*, ICC-02/11-01/11-278-Red, Judgment on the Appeal of Mr Lau-

tee,[47] the UN Committee against Torture,[48] or the UN Committee for the Elimination of Discrimination against Women[49]—to name only a few. However, much less widely acknowledged—though, in our opinion, more critical—is the fact that the ICC regularly considers itself *bound* to do so. In other words, although the Court often relies on external human rights case law as a mere source of (non-binding) inspiration or without clarifying at all the legal significance of such a cross-referencing process,[50] on other occasions, the ICC seems to acknowledge a genuine *obligation* to abide by judge-made human rights standards.

These mandatory references have occasionally been based on custom or general principles of law.[51] This, however, has not been very common, most probably as a result of the organisation of sources of applicable law under Article 21 of the Rome Statute (custom and—even more so—general principles are therein described as subsidiary sources of law).[52] As will now be shown through an account of the Court's relevant jurisprudence, Article 21(3) has so far clearly constituted the primary source of mandatory judicial dialogue before the ICC.

---

rent Koudou Gbagbo Against the Decision of Pre-Trial Chamber I of 13 July 2012 […], Appeals Chamber, 26 October 2012, para. 9; *Prosecutor v Gaddafi*, ICC-01/11-01/11-175, Decision on the Request for Disqualification of the Prosecutor, Appeals Chamber, 12 June 2012, para. 26.

47 See eg Lubanga Decision on Leave to Reply (n 32), para. 6.

48 See eg *Prosecutor v Katanga*, ICC-RoR217-02/08-8, Decision on 'Mr Mathieu Ngudjolo's Complaint under Regulation 221(1) of the Regulations of the Registry […]', Presidency, 10 March 2009 ('Decision on Ngudjolo's Complaint'), para. 27.

49 See eg *Prosecutor v Lubanga*, ICC-01/04-01/06-2901, Decision on Sentence pursuant to Article 76 of the Statute, Trial Chamber I, 10 July 2012, Dissenting Opinion of Judge Benito, para. 21.

50 See Christophe Deprez, 'The Authority of Strasbourg Jurisprudence from the Perspective of the International Criminal Court' (2015) 3 European Journal of Human Rights 278, 281–283 and 293–295.

51 See Katanga and Ngudjolo Decision on Victim Status (n 26), para. 32; Katanga and Ngudjolo Decision on Witnesses Asylum Requests (n 27), paras 64, 68; *Prosecutor v Kony*, ICC-02/04-01/05-252, Decision on Victims' Applications for Participation […], Pre-Trial Chamber II, 10 August 2007, para. 13; *Prosecutor v Ruto*, ICC-01/09-01/11-373, Decision on the Confirmation of Charges pursuant to Article 61(7)(a) and (b) of the Rome Statute, Pre-Trial Chamber II, 23 January 2012 ('Ruto Confirmation of Charges Decision'), para. 41 (although in all these instances, the ICC endorsed human rights case law—either as custom or as general principles—without explicitly mentioning the relevant, specific human rights cases that it was actually applying).

52 See Rome Statute, Article 21(1)(b) and (c).

Admittedly, when the ICC relies on external human rights jurisprudence with explicit reference to Article 21(3), it may sometimes be disputed whether the judges actually mean to attach an 'internationally recognized' character to such jurisprudence *per se*, or, rather, to the human rights norm that the former spells out.[53] Yet it is argued here that, in a number of decisions, the wording makes it quite clear that Pre-Trial, Trial and Appeals Chambers have indeed intended to view human rights *case law* as falling within the realm of binding 'internationally recognized human rights'.

To date and to the extent of our knowledge, this case law relates, in turn, to the right to respect for private and family life, the right to liberty, the right to life, the right to an effective remedy, and the right to a fair trial (including the many ramifications thereof).

As regards *private life*, in the *Lubanga* case, Pre-Trial Chamber I considered internationally recognised the founding ECtHR principle under which possible breaches of the right to respect for private life must be assessed in light of a proportionality test. In the exact words of the Chamber, 'the infringement of the principle of proportionality [as sanctioned by the ECtHR] can be characterised as a violation of internationally recognized human rights'.[54] The language used makes it plain that the Pre-Trial Chamber viewed Strasbourg case law on proportionality, not merely as a convincing (though non-binding) interpretation of the possible implications of Article 21(3), but as binding 'internationally recognized human rights' *per se*. In other words, the wording of the decision indicates that, to the Chamber, Strasbourg practice on proportionality not only represents the ECtHR's own understanding of the right to private life (right to private life which could then, possibly, be considered an 'internationally recognized' norm), but, also, has truly become internationally recognised (case) law in its own right. In sum, in the view of the ICC, the application of Strasbourg practice on proportionality was a duty.

53 Among several uncertain instances, see *Prosecutor v Ntaganda*, ICC-01/04-02/06-785-Red, Decision on Prosecution Requests to Impose Restrictions on Mr Ntaganda's Contacts, Trial Chamber VI, 18 August 2015, para. 42; *Prosecutor v Ntaganda*, ICC-01/04-02/06-786-Red4, Decision on Restrictions in relation to Certain Detainees, Trial Chamber VI, 18 August 2015, para. 33; *Prosecutor v Ntaganda*, ICC-01/04-02/06-335, Third Decision on Bosco Ntaganda's Interim Release, Pre-Trial Chamber II, 17 July 2014, para. 20; *Prosecutor v Gbagbo*, ICC-02/11-01/11-286-Red, Decision on the Fitness of Laurent Gbagbo to Take Part in the Proceedings before this Court, Pre-Trial Chamber I, 2 November 2012, paras 45–48.

54 *Prosecutor v Lubanga*, ICC-01/04-01/06-803-tENG, Decision on the Confirmation of Charges, Pre-Trial Chamber I, 29 January 2007, para. 82.

It is also noteworthy that, more recently, in the *Bemba et al* case, Trial Chamber VII attached the same authority to the ECtHR and IACtHR's reading of another key requirement for any interference with private life to be justified, ie that such interference be in accordance with the law.[55]

Turning to *family life*, the ICC admitted (although in ambiguous terms) the internationally recognised character of the ECtHR's recognition of detainees' entitlement to family visits:

> Noting the terms of article 21(3) of the Rome Statute, providing that the texts of the Court must be applied and interpreted consistently with internationally recognised human rights standards, the recognition of such a right is in accordance with international human rights law which clearly acknowledges that a detained person has the right to receive family visits. [...] The right of detained persons to family visits is also recognised by the jurisprudence of the [ECtHR].[56]

Surely the language used could be more straightforward. In the excerpt, the ICC Presidency fails to directly equate ECtHR case law with binding 'internationally recognized human rights'. Rather, it seems to suggest that the right to family visits is a basic right (ie a human rights norm), which happens to be endorsed by the ECtHR. Yet such a construction is artificial—at least in the European sphere where the entitlement to family visits has no explicit, independent textual expression, but is a *judge-made* ramification of the right to respect for private and family life under Article 8 of the ECHR.[57] When the ICC Presidency holds that the detainees' right to family visits consists of 'internationally recognized human rights', what it does, in fact, is to attach such a nature to external, European human rights practice. To this extent, the Presidency relies on Strasbourg case law, not because it is simply inclined to find the latter convincing, but because Article 21(3) requires that the application and interpretation of ICC law be strictly in line with it.

The same may be observed with respect to the right to *individual liberty*. In the *Ngudjolo* case, the ICC considered internationally recognised the UN Human Rights Committee and ECtHR's view that no financial compensation

55 *Prosecutor v Bemba*, ICC-01/05-01/13-1257, Decision on Kilolo Defence Motion for Inadmissibility of Material, Trial Chamber VII, 16 September 2015, para. 16.

56 Decision on Ngudjolo's Complaint (n 48), paras 27–28 (internal footnotes omitted).

57 See eg *Khoroshenko v Russia*, App no 41418/04 (ECtHR, 30 June 2015), para. 106; *Messida v Italy (no. 2)*, App no 25498/94 (ECtHR, 28 September 2000), para. 61; *Lavents v Latvia*, App no 58442/00 (ECtHR, 28 November 2002), para. 139.

is necessarily due merely because pre-trial detention was (legally) imposed without eventually leading to a conviction.[58] This finding is peculiar in the sense that, in contrast with previous excerpts, here the ICC's reasoning leads to the recognition of the 'internationally recognized' nature of the *absence* of a certain right (the ICC suggests that, in the circumstances described above, it is simply barred from providing any sort of compensation; yet this ignores the true nature of international human rights as a set of *minimum* standards). Be this as it may, in its decision, the Trial Chamber clearly and directly attaches an 'internationally recognized' character to the relevant *practice* of the UN Human Rights Committee and ECtHR (rather than the treaty norms on which this practice is based). Once again, this demonstrates the perception of the Court that it is bound by (some fragments of) human rights *case law* as a result of Article 21(3).

In a much broader fashion as regards substance, but in the very same perspective as a matter of principle, the Court has repeatedly linked Article 21(3) with the whole set of jurisprudential principles developed in the European and Inter-American spheres in connection with provisional detention and release.[59]

Similarly, the ICC has viewed a specific, judge-made aspect of the *right to life* as falling within the ambit of Article 21(3). In the view of Judge Kaul, the finding by Strasbourg judges that competent authorities have a positive obligation to conduct a prompt and effective investigation following the death of a person, must be considered binding *qua* internationally recognised human rights.[60] In the key paragraph of his opinion,[61] Judge Kaul does not even take the trouble to mention the general right to life under Article 2 of the European Convention. Therefore, it cannot be argued that, in his view, it is not the relevant Strasbourg practice itself, but the more general human rights provision at its basis, which is binding as 'internationally recognized human rights'. In the reasoning of Judge Kaul, the connection between Article 21(3) of the Statute

58 *Prosecutor v Ngudjolo*, ICC-01/04-02/12-301, Decision sur la 'Requête en indemnisation en application des dispositions de l'article 85 (1) et (3) du Statut de Rome', Trial Chamber II, 16 December 2015, para. 18.

59 *Prosecutor v Bemba*, ICC-01/05-01/08-14-tENG, Decision on the Prosecutor's Application for a Warrant of Arrest Against Jean-Pierre Bemba Gombo, Pre-Trial Chamber III, 10 June 2008, para. 24. See also *Prosecutor v Harun*, ICC-02/05-01/07-1, Decision on the Prosecution Application under Article 58(7) of the Statute, Pre-Trial Chamber I, 27 April 2007, para. 28.

60 Ruto Confirmation of Charges Decision (n 51), Dissenting Opinion of Judge Kaul, para. 48.

61 ibid.

and the external human rights practice concerned is direct; the latter is, in its own right, binding on the ICC.

In the same vein, according to Trial Chamber I, a link should be made between Article 21(3) and the Inter-American understanding that the *right to an effective remedy* calls for compensation of 'all forms of damage, loss and injury, including material, physical and psychological harm'.[62]

Again in connection with the domain of remedies, in Judge Song's view, also internationally recognised is the European and Inter-American acceptance that victims have a right (or at least a specific interest) that justice be done.[63]

Finally, Article 21(3) has been repeatedly used in connection with *fair trial rights*.

In the *Katanga and Ngudjolo* case, with respect to the protection against self-incrimination, Judge Van den Wyngaert suggested the 'internationally recognized' nature of the ECtHR's conclusion that the mere existence of a relevant legal provision does not constitute sufficient notice that criminal charges may be subject to late re-characterisation.[64]

Furthermore, according to the Appeals Chamber, the same legal value attaches to the ECtHR's conclusion that fair trial includes the right to disclosure of all relevant exculpatory material:

> The Appeals Chamber recalls in this context that article 21 (3) of the Statute stipulates that the Statute must be interpreted and applied consistently with internationally recognized human rights. The Appeals Chamber notes in particular that the Grand Chamber of the ECHR held at paragraph 60 of its judgment of 16 February 2000 in the case of *Rowe and Davis v United Kingdom* [...] that the right to a fair trial requires that 'the prosecution authorities disclose to the defence all material evidence in their possession for or against the accused'.[65]

At first sight, the wording of the paragraph—'The Appeals Chamber *notes*'—would seem to suggest that the ICC only feels bound by the (internationally

62 Lubanga Decision on Reparation Principles (n 45), para. 229.

63 *Prosecutor v Lubanga*, ICC-01/04-01/06-925, Decision of the Appeals Chamber on the Joint Application of Victims [...] Concerning the 'Directions and Decision of the Appeals Chamber' of 2 February 2007, Appeals Chamber, 13 June 2007, Separate Opinion of Judge Song, paras 14–16.

64 Katanga and Ngudjolo Decision on Regulation 55 (n 44), Dissenting Opinion of Judge Van den Wyngaert, para. 47.

65 Lubanga Judgment on the Consequences of Non-Disclosure (n 28), para. 46.

recognised) right to a fair trial in general, but not by the correspondent practice of the ECtHR (which would serve as a mere non-binding clarification of the substance of the former). However, it is argued here that the intermediary of the general right to a fair trial—insofar as it is even perceptible in the reasoning of the Court—is largely fabricated. For the reasons set forth above,[66] it would be artificial to use the right to a fair trial as an empty shell, and to strictly distinguish between a norm (which would be binding on the ICC) and the interpretation of this norm (which would not). In the end, the only consistent reading of the decision by the Appeals Chamber is that the Strasbourg jurisprudence in *Rowe and Davis* itself—and not the supposedly self-standing right to a fair trial at its basis—is binding by virtue of Article 21(3).

With respect to fair trial rights, Pre-Trial Chamber II has further read Article 21(3) as encompassing Strasbourg jurisprudence on the limits of the right to be provided with a translation of relevant documents.[67]

Furthermore, in a broader manner, Pre-Trial Chamber I suggested the 'internationally recognized' character of the European and Inter-American conception that fair trial requirements must be understood as having particularly broad effects.[68]

Lastly, while building on Article 21(3) in the context of Kenyan cases, Judge Trendafilova referred to Strasbourg practice in relation to the temporal scope of the right to a fair trial:

> The Single Judge [...] recalls article 21(3) of the Statute which instructs that the interpretation and application of the law must be consistent with internationally recognized human rights. In light of this, the Single Judge has regard to the existing jurisprudence of, in particular, the European Court of Human Rights to article 6 of the Convention [...], and thus she concludes that the rights guaranteed under article 67 of the Statute, including access to court, apply as soon as the Chamber has issued the summonses to appear in accordance with article 58(7) of the Statute.[69]

66 See above, Section II, in particular text accompanying footnotes 16 and 17.

67 *Prosecutor v Ongwen*, ICC-02/04-01/15-203, Decision Setting the Regime for Evidence Disclosure and Other Related Matters, Pre-Trial Chamber II, 27 February 2015, para. 30.

68 *Prosecutor v Lubanga*, ICC-01/04-01/06-108-Corr, Decision Establishing General Principles Governing Applications to Restrict Disclosure [...], Pre-Trial Chamber I, 19 May 2006, para. 37.

69 *Prosecutor v Muthaura*, ICC-01/09-02/11-38, Decision on Variation of Summons Conditions, Pre-Trial Chamber II, 4 April 2011, para. 11.

What has been written above with respect to the decision of the Appeals Chamber in the *Lubanga* case holds true as far as Judge Trendafilova's finding is concerned. Although the flexible language used ('the Single Judge *has regard* to') may give the impression that Strasbourg practice is considered non-authoritative (which would then leave only the general right to a fair trial under Article 6 of the ECHR with an internationally recognised, and therefore binding, nature), this is only a factitious detour. In the end, what the Single Judge felt bound to apply on account of Article 21(3) of the Rome Statute was not an abstract provision in the European Convention, but the ECtHR's concrete conclusion that fair trial rights ought to be guaranteed at an early stage of the proceedings.

V Conclusion

On the plane of international criminal justice, Article 21(3) of the Rome Statute undoubtedly constitutes an unprecedented call for human rights cross-fertilisation. By requiring the ICC to apply and interpret relevant law in accordance with 'internationally recognized human rights', the provision has quickly led the new permanent international criminal organ to acknowledge that '[h]uman rights underpin the Statute; every aspect of it'.[70] In its first decade of practice, the ICC has vested Article 21(3) with far-reaching—and indeed, unforeseen—effects.[71]

Yet, for the purpose of this chapter, even more critical is the general format of those human rights standards upheld by the Court as a result of Article 21(3). Interestingly, besides human rights norms proper, the various Chambers of the ICC do not seem to rule out the possibility that human rights jurisprudence may also qualify as binding 'internationally recognized human rights'; quite the contrary. An account of their practice in relation to Article 21(3) indicates that they have felt obligated to endorse the views of their human rights colleagues (mostly, but not exclusively, the ECtHR)[72] on issues as diverse as the right to

70 Lubanga Judgment on Jurisdiction Appeal (n 24), para. 37.

71 See above, Section III.

72 See Mariniello and Lobba (n 4) 363; Bitti (n 25) 435; Robert Roth and Françoise Tulkens, 'Introduction [Symposium: The Influence of the European Court of Human Rights' Case Law on (International) Criminal Law]' (2011) 9 Journal of International Criminal Justice 571, 574; Young (n 23) 203; Nicolas Croquet, 'The International Criminal Court and the Treatment of Defence Rights: A Mirror of the European Court of Human Rights' Jurisprudence?' (2011) 11 Human Rights Law Review 91, 122.

life, the right to a fair trial, the requirement for an effective remedy, the right to liberty, and the protection of private and family life.[73]

In this respect, the practice of the ICC departs from the generally accepted conception that law applies to all while judicial findings are only of concern to those involved in the case at hand. Such departure is, in our opinion, to be welcomed. In the specific arena of international criminal justice, the traditional divide between human rights law and case law must be nuanced. Because the ICC is not a party to the relevant international instruments (for instance, the ECHR), it can only be bound by human rights standards through other means: custom, general principles, or Article 21(3) of the Rome Statute. In this context, there seems to be no valid reason why judge-made law should be, a priori, excluded from these categories.[74] More particularly as far as this chapter is concerned, nothing should prevent human rights practice from falling within the scope of Article 21(3) if such practice is indeed 'internationally recognized' (whatever that means).

On a closer look, it seems that the ICC has been aware of this need for nuance. Its Chambers have repeatedly relied on human rights case law as binding 'internationally recognized human rights' within the meaning of Article 21(3) of the Rome Statute.[75] By doing so, the Court echoes the idea that cross-fertilisation does not necessarily take the form of a purely discretionary process. Sometimes, judicial dialogue on human rights is truly mandatory.

73 See above, Section IV.

74 A completely different question is of course to ascertain, on a case-by-case basis, whether a given judicial reading of a human rights norm does indeed fulfil the relevant criteria (eg, in the case of custom, whether the judicial reading at hand is actually backed by state practice and *opinio juris*).

75 This is not to suggest that the ICC has always been consistent as a matter of substance. It may well be the case that the Court sometimes views the practice of human rights organs as non-binding when, in fact, such practice is objectively 'internationally recognized' (or vice versa).

CHAPTER 6

Beyond Anecdotal Reference: A Quantitative Assessment of ICTY References to the Jurisprudence of the ECtHR

*Frauke Sauerwein**

1 Introduction

The relationship between the International Criminal Tribunal for the former Yugoslavia and the European Court of Human Rights[1] can only, from the ICTY's perspective, be described as very fruitful: after all, it includes one of the most numerous recourses to citations of any relationships between international courts and tribunals. Despite this, the two courts are, however, part of different legal regimes. International human rights law (IHRL) protects the individual from certain acts of the State whereas international criminal law (ICL) seeks to pursue and punish individuals who have committed certain abhorrent crimes.[2] Nevertheless, the border between these two areas of law, or even the fact that there is such a border at all, is often not spelled out.[3]

In order to understand the complicated relationship between these two areas of law in general and the mechanisms of cross-fertilisation between the two courts in particular, it is important to analyse the whole picture of the influence of the ECtHR's jurisprudence on that of the ICTY. It is thus necessary to assess the references of the ICTY to the ECtHR in order to understand how and to what extent the transplant of external concepts from one court to the other takes place.[4]

---

* The chapter presents research which is part of a broader study carried out by the author as PhD project. I would like to thank the anonymous reviewer as well as Theodor Shulman and Ximena Soley for comments on drafts of this chapter.

1 When discussing the jurisprudence of the ECtHR, the reports of the European Commission of Human Rights are always included.

2 For further details see Darryl Robinson, 'The Identity Crisis of International Criminal Law' (2008) 21 Leiden Journal of International Law 925.

3 For a good summary of this problematic blur between the two fields of law, see Robinson (n 2).

4 For this concept of transplantation see Triestino Mariniello and Paolo Lobba, 'The Cross-fertilisation Rhetoric in Question: Use and Abuse of the European Court's Jurisprudence by International Criminal Tribunals' (2015) 84 Nordic Journal of International Law 363.

 | DOI: 10.1163/9789004313750_008

As early as in one of its first decisions ever rendered, in *Prosecutor v Tadić*, the ICTY relied on the jurisprudence of the ECtHR in discussing the benefits of a public hearing and the possibility of witness anonymity.[5] Since then, citing the ECtHR's case-law has been a common feature in the case-law of the ICTY until today. It should thus come as no surprise that the relationship between the two courts has been of scientific interest for some time.[6] A striking feature of these initial incursions into the topic is, however, the anecdotal manner in which the ICTY handles its references to the ECtHR. In other words, individual cases are mentioned, but until now nobody has undertaken a comprehensive quantitative assessment of all non-confidential judgments and decisions of the Tribunal. Although Nathan Miller and Michael Nunner separately attempted such an overall analysis of references between courts and tribunals in 2002 and 2009—also with regard to the ICTY and the ECtHR—, the assessment was incomplete and is now outdated.[7]

This paper will contribute to fill in this gap. It solely examines the references by the ICTY to the ECtHR case-law. The first ICTY judges were mostly experts on IHRL or international humanitarian law who cited what they knew best and therefore remained in close contact with IHRL jurisprudence.[8] Moreover, the ICTY had to develop a modern form of ICL and serve as a yard-

5 *Prosecutor v Tadić*, IT-94-1-T, Decision on the Prosecution's Motion Requesting Protective Measures for Victims and Witnesses, Trial Chamber, 10 August 1995, paras 28, 32, 38, 53, 68–70.

6 See only Antonio Cassese, 'The Impact of the European Convention on Human Rights on the International Criminal Tribunal for the Former Yugoslavia' in Paul Mahoney and others (eds), *Protecting Human Rights: The European Perspective: Studies in Memory of Rolv Ryssdal* (Carl Heymanns Verlag 2000) 213; Antonio Cassese, 'The Influence of the European Court of Human Rights on International Criminal Tribunals—Some Methodological Remarks' in Morten Bergsmo (ed), *Human Rights and Criminal Justice for the Downtrodden: Essays in Honour of Asbjørn Eide* (Martinus Nijhoff Publishers 2003) 19; 'Symposium. The Influence of the European Court of Human Rights' Case Law on (International) Criminal Law' (2011) 9 Journal of International Criminal Justice 571.

7 Miller, for example, states that he examined all majority decisions of the ICTY. However, he only mentions twelve decisions and ten judgments until 2001. For this period alone, there were 31 decisions and fourteen judgments counting only majority decisions. Nunner mainly uses the data compiled by Miller, to which he only marginally adds own research. Nathan Miller, 'An International Jurisprudence? The Operation of "Precedent" Across International Tribunals' (2002) 15 Leiden Journal of International Law 483; Michael Nunner, *Kooperation internationaler Gerichte: Lösung zwischengerichtlicher Konflikte durch herrschaftsfreien Diskurs* (Mohr Siebeck 2009). See also Erik Voeten who finds 161 references of the ICTY to the ECtHR but does not discuss these references in detail. Erik Voeten, 'Borrowing and Nonborrowing among International Courts' (2010) 39 Journal of Legal Studies 547, 571.

8 Robinson (n 2) 961.

stick for all later ICTs. To understand the role of the ECtHR in the case-law of these ICTs, it is therefore important to primarily assess its influence on the ICTY.

I will first discuss the relationship between IHRL and ICL and thereby sketch the framework in which cross-fertilisation between the ICTY and the ECtHR takes place (II). I will then give a detailed assessment of the number of ICTY cases referring to the ECtHR and the European Commission of Human Rights (III) before presenting the variety of the citations (IV). Finally, I will highlight problematic aspects of these citations through an exemplary discussion of cases concerning provisional release (V).

II The References' Framework: The Relationship between IHRL and ICL

To understand the references made by the ICTY to the ECtHR, it is necessary to sketch the overall framework in which these references take place. This framework is set by the relationship between IHRL and ICL. IHRL constitutes one of the three roots of ICL besides international humanitarian law and national criminal law.[9] Moreover, IHRL has a two-sided character:[10] not only does it protect individuals from acts of States, but it also imposes the duty on States to prosecute individuals who have committed certain crimes.[11] Therefore, one might see ICL as a prolongation of this second and offensive trait of IHRL.[12] Moreover, there are some areas in which these different fields overlap.[13] This is especially true in areas that use the same concepts, be they questions of

9 ibid 925.

10 Françoise Tulkens, 'The Paradoxical Relationship between Criminal Law and Human Rights' (2011) 9 Journal of International Criminal Justice 576; William A. Schabas, 'Droit pénal international et droit international des droits de l'homme: faux frères?' in Marc Henzelin and Robert Roth (eds), *Le droit pénal à l'épreuve de l'internationalisation* (LGDJ 2002) 165, 165–167.

11 ibid.

12 See also M. Cherif Bassiouni, 'The Proscribing Function of International Criminal Law in the Process of International Protection of Human Rights' (1982) 9 Yale Journal of World Public Order 193, 195.

13 Paul Tavernier, 'Les Tribunaux Pénaux Internationaux et le droit international des droits de l'Homme' in Mireille Delmas-Marty, Emanuela Fronza and Elisabeth Lambert-Abdelgawad (eds), *Les source du droit international pénal: L'expérience des Tribunaux Penaux Internationaux et le Statut de la Cour Pénale Internationale* (Société de législation comparée 2004) 396.

substantive or procedural law. For example, both the ICTY and ECtHR prohibit torture and guarantee fair-trial rights.

Nevertheless, these commonalities bear the risk of concealing crucial differences between the two areas of law and even between seemingly similar concepts like torture.[14] These differences emanate from the role of the individual and the State, respectively, in IHRL and ICL.[15] IHRL imposes certain duties on the State. Even in cases which concern its offensive dimension, human rights courts condemn the State for its inactivity. Unlike ICTs, human rights courts do not establish the individual criminal responsibility of certain individuals for certain crimes. In ICL, ICTs have to balance the rights of the victims with the rights of the accused and fundamental criminal principles. These comprise, inter alia, the principles of legality, legal certainty, strict construction of criminal law, and personal culpability.[16] This is reflected in the United Nations General Secretary's Report on the ICTY which stated that the ICTY should only apply rules of law which are 'beyond any doubt part of customary law' in order to secure the principle of legality.[17] In using the progressive jurisprudence of human rights courts, which is centered on a teleological and victim-focused rationale, ICTs might violate these rights.[18] Of course, there are areas in which cross-fertilisation is less or more problematic. For example, the role of the individual with respect to procedural questions is quite similar in both legal regimes: the individual is protected against actions of the power-wielding entity that may endanger his or her right to a fair trial—be it a State or an international organisation like the United Nations. However, questions

---

14 Elena Maculan, 'Judicial Definition of Torture as a Paradigm of Cross-fertilisation: Combining Harmonisation and Expansion' (2015) 84 Nordic Journal of International Law 456; Michelle Farrell, 'Just How Ill-treated Were You? An Investigation of Cross-fertilisation in the Interpretative Approaches to Torture at the European Court of Human Rights and in International Criminal Law' (2015) 84 Nordic Journal of International Law 482.

15 See only Schabas (n 10). This different role is accepted by the ICTY in *Prosecutor v Kunarac*, IT-96-23-T&IT-96-23/1-T, Judgment, Trial Chamber, 22 February 2001, para. 470; *Prosecutor v Kupreškić*, IT-95-16-T, Trial Chamber, Judgment, 14 January 2000, para. 589; *Prosecutor v Krnojelac*, IT-97-25-T, Judgment, Trial Chamber II, 15 March 2002, fn. 1438. On this see Robert Cryer, 'The Interplay of Human Rights and Humanitarian Law: The Approach of the ICTY' (2010) 14 Journal of Conflict and Security Law 511.

16 See only Robinson (n 2); Patricia Pinto Soares, 'Tangling Human Rights and International Criminal Law: The Practice of International Tribunals and the Call for Rationalized Legal Pluralism' (2012) 23 Criminal Law Forum 161.

17 Report of the Secretary-General Pursuant to Paragraph 2 of Security Council Resolution 808 (1993), 3 May 1993, UN Doc S/25704, paras 33, 36.

18 Robinson (n 2).

concerning substantive law, such as the definition of torture, may have to be evaluated differently in each legal regime because of these differences.[19]

It is therefore important that the ICTY takes the differences between IHRL and ICL into account when referring to human rights jurisprudence. Moreover, it should refer to the jurisprudence of the ECtHR in a coherent manner,[20] because inconsistencies in citations may affect the analysis of the different contexts and conceal incorrect translations from human rights jurisprudence to that of the ICTY. In this chapter I will therefore evaluate to what extent the ICTY follows this ideal way of referring to the ECtHR jurisprudence.

III References to the Jurisprudence of the ECtHR

I will first tackle the question to what degree the ICTY's jurisprudence is 'fertilised' by its human rights counterpart in a quantitative way by presenting the number of cases that refer to the jurisprudence of the ECtHR. Relying on references in separate opinions, I will, moreover, show that the influence of this jurisprudence even goes beyond these direct references.

1 *Number of ICTY Cases Referring to Jurisprudence of the ECtHR*

In researching the database of the ICTY,[21] it is possible to evaluate the influence of the ECtHR on the ICTY quantitatively: until the end of the year 2014, the ICTY refers explicitly to the ECtHR in 43 judgments, 139 decisions, and 30 separate opinions.[22] These impressive numbers do not even include sole references to

19 Maculan (n 14); Farrell (n 14).

20 See also Antonio Cassese's 'wise approach': Cassese, 'The Influence' (n 6) 20–21.

21 http://icr.icty.org/ accessed 15 January 2016. All public judgments and decisions in both English and French were searched using the search terms 'European Court of Human Rights, ECtHR, ECHR, Eur Ct HR, Eur Court, European Commission of Human Rights, cour européenne des droits de l'homme, CEDH, Cour EDH, EDH, Cour Eur'.

22 I count decisions and judgments of the first and the second instance separately and also include contempt cases and decisions of the disciplinary board. Furthermore, cases in which a chamber merely mentions that a previous case was decided on the basis of case-law of the ECtHR are included because the chamber includes the European jurisprudence in its own findings with this comment. Similarly, discussions of the role of the ECtHR are included. To better assess the importance of the ECtHR's jurisprudence, references to the European Commission on Human Rights were counted without further specification as references to the ECtHR. In contrast, cases in which the jurisprudence of the ECtHR is only listed in the glossary or discussed in the annex are not included. For further details see annex to this paper and the author's PhD project.

the European Convention on Human Rights but only explicit recurrences to ECtHR case-law. If one counts the references to ECtHR jurisprudence, which are thus defined rigidly as several citations—even if they appear in different parts of the same judgment but concern the same question of law[23]—, one can count 144 references in 139 decisions and 66 references in 43 judgments.[24] This number offers a remarkable first impression of the quantitative impact of the ECtHR jurisprudence.[25] Moreover, in 32 decisions and three judgments, the Tribunal simply presents arguments of the parties referring to the jurisprudence of the ECtHR. Such a simple presentation without the Tribunal's own discussion cannot, however, be counted as a true direct reference and will therefore not be discussed further in this chapter.

In assessing the importance of those direct citations proportionally, it bears mentioning that in 42[26] out of 141 judgments,[27] ie in 29.8 % of all judgments, there is at least one reference to the ECtHR. If one excludes judgments in contempt cases, this number rises to 33.6 %.[28] In contrast, the ICTY cites the ECtHR in only approximately 1.9 % of the total amount of all non-confidential decisions.[29] However, the total number of decisions covers many very short, one-page decisions in which there are no citations at all. The statistics concerning judgments are thus the most significant when assessing the degree of cross-fertilisation between both courts.

In order to analyse the question to what extent legal concepts of IHRL are transplanted into a criminal framework, it is necessary to also evaluate the

23 See for a related but different counting system Miller (n 7) 488, who only counts separately where 'definite distinctions' can be drawn.

24 This number includes neither the simple presentation of arguments of the parties nor references in separate opinions.

25 In contrast, the ECtHR only refers to the ICTY in eight decisions and eighteen judgments. For further details see the author's PhD project.

26 The judgment *Prosecutor v Blaškić*, IT-95-14-AR108 *bis*, Judgment on the Request of the Republic of Croatia for Review of the Decision of Trial Chamber II of 18 July 1997, Appeals Chamber, 29 October 1997, is not mentioned in the official 'Judgment List'; therefore, I only count 42 judgments instead of 43 judgments in order to calculate the percentages.

27 This number comprises all judgments on the 'Judgment List' until the end of the year 2014 (http://www.icty.org/en/cases/judgement-list accessed 11 January 2016) and the contempt cases, (http://www.icty.org/action/contemptcases/27#casetabs accessed 11 January 2016).

28 37 out of 110 judgments.

29 As of 29 August 2014 (relying on information obtained from ICTY Outreach that there was a total amount of 7193 non-confidential decisions at this date).

different areas of law in which cross-fertilisation occurs: 173 references concern the rights of the accused in procedure and detention and other procedural questions, 30 references concern questions of substantive law, and eight references other matters like the role of the ECtHR jurisprudence. The first predominantly covers the right to a fair trial and its special guarantees, which are determined in Articles 20–21 ICTY Statute and Article 6 ECHR,[30] and questions regarding provisional release.[31] Concerning matters of substantive law, the ICTY strongly relies on the jurisprudence of the ECtHR in questions relative to torture and rape.[32] All in all, a quantitative analysis of the ICTY's jurisprudence evinces that the ICTY heavily relies on the ECtHR jurisprudence in different and varied matters of law. This analysis, however, is still insufficient to show the whole picture.

2 *Separate Opinions*

The ICTY is not only influenced by the European jurisprudence in the cases in which it explicitly cites the ECtHR. A full-scale assessment of the relationship between the two courts must therefore ask in which cases there is no citation although the ECtHR's case-law would have been relevant to the topic in question. Unfortunately, it is difficult to ascertain the practical impact of this question. How can these cases be found? I try to touch upon this problem by taking into consideration cases in which the majority decision does not refer to the ECtHR but a separate opinion does. In these cases, it cannot have been completely out of the question to cite the ECtHR. Moreover, separate opinions can, to a certain extent, provide insight into the deliberation of judges. They often supplement the reasoning of the majority and reveal differences between the judges concerning this reasoning.[33] Therefore, separate opinions can indicate cases in which the ECtHR played a role for the Tribunal's reasoning even though it does not mention the Court in the majority opinion. The ICTY refers

30 34 references in judgments and 87 references in decisions. This comprises a wide range of questions like the admittance and weighing of evidence (17 references), the right to self-representation (five references), the principle of equality of arms (ten references), the impartiality of judges (ten references), the presumption of innocence (three references), the principle of legality (six references), etc.

31 38 decisions.

32 Out of 30 references concerning aspects of substantive law, sixteen deal with torture or rape.

33 Dean Spielmann, 'Opinions séparées et secret des délibérations à la Cour eurpéenne des droits de l'homme' (2007) 126 Journal des tribunaux 310.

to the jurisprudence of the ECtHR in 30 separate opinions.[34] In 16[35] of those, the majority decision does not mention the ECtHR.

I would like to draw attention to just one very extreme case that, almost like a caricature, illustrates the importance of separate opinions as a possible indicator for cases in which the ECtHR played a role in the Tribunal's reasoning and illustrates huge inconsistencies in how it implements the ECtHR's case-law. In the *Decision on Prosecution Motion for Production of Defence Witness Statements* in the case against *Tadić*,[36] the issue arose whether the prosecution could have access to earlier statements by a defence witness before cross-examining this witness. The judges decided, with a majority of 2:1, that such access may not be provided. As regards cross-fertilisation by ECtHR case-law, the reasoning of the decision is significant: there simply is none. The decision merely includes the following cryptic words: 'For the reasons set out in the separate opinions attached to this Decision'.[37] Attached to the decision are three separate opinions of all three judges; two concurring and entitled 'separate', one dissenting. Hence, this decision vaguely points to two of the three opinions without clarifying its reasoning.

Judge Stephan does not mention the jurisprudence of the ECtHR in his opinion at all.[38] Instead, he analyses Articles 20 and 21 of the ICTY Statute and the ICTY's Rules of Procedure and Evidence before mostly discussing national jurisprudence. Judge Vorah[39] expressly approves of the reasoning of his colleague but goes further and also discusses international case-law. Starting from the description of the right to a fair trial in international conventions, he underlines the importance of the principle of equality of arms while discussing in detail reports of the European Commission of Human Rights as well as jurisprudence of the ECtHR and the European Court of Justice. In other words, while the decision of the majority only refers to its separate opinions, one of these focuses only on national jurisprudence whereas the other one adopts the reasoning of the first opinion and also analyses international law. Although the decision refers to both separate opinions, in fact there seems to be a dissent between the two judges concerning the role of references to international jurisprudence and especially that of the ECtHR.

34 See also annexed table. I count each opinion of the same majority decision separately.

35 All 16 concern separate opinions to decisions.

36 *Prosecutor v Tadić*, IT-94-1-T, Decision on Prosecution Motion for Production of Defence Witness Statements, Trial Chamber, 27 November 1996.

37 ibid para. 2.

38 ibid, Separate Opinion of Judge Stephens.

39 ibid, Separate Opinion of Judge Vorah.

Otherwise, the decision to outsource the reasoning of the ruling to two separate opinions does not make any sense. This is underlined by the dissenting opinion of Judge McDonald. She criticises both the analysis of national and international jurisprudence by her colleagues and strongly rejects the application of the case *Jespers v. Belgium* of the European Commission of Human Rights in the context of the ICTY.[40]

Although the ICTY overturned this decision in substance—while referring to the ECtHR—in the following years[41] and, fortunately,[42] no other case could be found in which the entire reasoning was transferred to the separate opinions, this decision highlights the significance of ECtHR jurisprudence in cases in which this jurisprudence is not explicitly mentioned in the reasoning of the ICTY decision. It is a rare and extreme example in which both the reasoning of the majority and the reference to the ECtHR is so imperfect that one can only guess the latter's influence on the ICTY's jurisprudence. There are a number of other decisions or judgments where the legal reasoning of ICTs is present and allows for critical examination. However, this underlines two important aspects. Firstly, the influence of the ECtHR case-law on the ICTY surpasses direct references in majority opinions. Secondly, it sheds light on a problem which is also existent—in a less pronounced manner—in other references: in many cases it remains unknown why the ICTY decides to cite the European court explicitly in some cases and not in others.

IV Categorising the References to the ECtHR

We saw that there is no coherence regarding the question of whether the ICTY cites the ECtHR. As a second step, I will therefore evaluate if the ICTY cites its human rights counterpart in a consistent manner once it decides to cite it. I will examine the legal basis of the citations (1) and four different ways of citing: generally pointing to the ECtHR's jurisprudence (2), references in footnotes (3), citing ICTY jurisprudence while highlighting its human rights origin (4), and detailed discussions (5). Of course, these ways are not peculiar to the

40 ibid, Separate and Dissenting Opinion of Judge McDonald.

41 Christiane Kamardi, *Die Ausformung einer Prozessordnung sui generis durch das ICTY unter Berücksichtigung des Fair-Trial-Prinzips* (Springer 2009) 315–317.

42 Actually, outsourcing the reasoning violates the right to a reasoned decision. On this right see Vladimir Tochilovsky, *Jurisprudence of the International Criminal Courts and the European Court of Human Rights: Procedure and Evidence* (Martinus Nijhoff Publishers 2008) 523–525.

references analysed in this chapter, but reflect how any citation may occur. This analysis can, however, highlight the different degrees of cross-fertilisation and the specific problems they imply (6).

1 *Legal Basis for Referring*

The Statute of the ICTY is silent on the question of referring to IHRL jurisprudence. In analysing the different cases, it is possible to deduce different options: the ECtHR's jurisprudence may be referred to due to similarities between Article 21 ICTY Statute and Article 6 ECHR, both of which guarantee the right to a fair trial;[43] it may help to prove the existence of practice in order to define customary law;[44] the ICTY may assess it as an argument of the Parties;[45] moreover, a reference may be appropriate in light of Article 31(3)(c) of the Vienna Convention on the Law of Treaties.[46] However, the ICTY never really details on which legal basis it grounds its references. It is therefore necessary to look more closely into the variety of citations and the way they deal or do not deal with the differences between IHRL and ICL.

2 *General References to ECtHR Case-Law*

Firstly, in some rare cases, the ICTY points to the ECtHR's jurisprudence in general: 'Rules 65 (B) and (D) [...] must therefore be read in the light of the ICCPR and ECHR and the relevant jurisprudence.'[47] This way of referring seems to be relevant in the shorter decisions, especially during the Tribunal's first years, and concerns the interpretation of Article 21 ICTY Statute or the RPE.[48] The Tribunal thereby puts itself in the tradition of IHRL, underlines that it protects the rights of the accused, and thereby adds further legitimacy to its decision

43 See only *Prosecutor v Prlić*, IT-04-74-AR73.6, Decision on Appeals against Admitting Transcript of Jadranko Prlić's Questioning into Evidence, Appeals Chamber, 23 November 2007, para. 51.

44 See only *Prosecutor v Kupreškić* (n 15), para. 540; Noora Arajärvi, *The Changing Nature of Customary International Law: Methods of Interpreting the Concept of Custom in International Criminal Tribunals* (Routledge 2014).

45 See only *Prosecutor v Biljana Plavsić*, IT-00-39&40/1-S, Trial Chamber, 27 February 2003.

46 Aldo Zammit Borda, 'A Formal Approach to Article 38(1)(d) of the ICJ Statute from the Perspective of the International Criminal Courts and Tribunals' (2013) 24 European Journal of International Law 649.

47 *Prosecutor v Limaj*, IT-03-66-AR65.2, Decision on Haradin Bala's Request on Provisional Release, Bench of the Appeals Chamber, 31 October 2003, para. 12.

48 See only *Prosecutor v Ljubičić*, IT-00-41-PT, Decision on Second Application for Provisional Release, Trial Chamber, 26 July 2005, para. 16.

without, however, discussing the ECtHR's case-law. This reference is very superficial and conveys that its interpretation of procedural law corresponds to that of the ECtHR. In many cases this may well be; however, it also bears the risk of concealing divergent views on certain questions of law.

3 *References in Footnotes*

Secondly, one finds references to the ECtHR in footnotes. Sometimes, only the name of the European case is given; often, the ICTY briefly explains the case. This concerns questions of both procedural and substantive law. For example, in a decision in the case against *Šešelj* regarding the question of how much time suffices for the defence to prepare, the Tribunal mentions several cases of the ECtHR and describes which period of time was deemed sufficient in which situation;[49] and, in its judgment in *Prosecutor v Krnojelac*, the Trial Chamber referred, inter alia, to case-law of the European Commission of Human Rights in order to define the term expulsion.[50]

Such references in footnotes highlight again that the ICTY cites the ECtHR to give further weight to its argumentation,[51] without, however, discussing the case-law of the latter in a refined manner. In some cases—especially concerning questions of procedural law—a short reference to a similar decision of the ECtHR may be sufficient to support an argument. Moreover, the citation in *Krnojelac* sets a positive example of how to deal with IHRL: it is one of few cases in which the ICTY expressly acknowledges the differences between IHRL and ICL,[52] 'in particular the distinct role and function attributed to States and individuals in each regime.'[53] Unfortunately, this is a very rare example of the Tribunal acknowledging the difference between the legal regimes. Moreover, even in this case, the ICTY merely states shortly and without further elaboration that the concept of expulsion is consistent in both regimes.[54] In brief, this way of citing does not constitute a sufficiently elaborate framework through which to discuss and compare the context of the different cases.

49 *Prosecutor v Šešelj*, IT-03-67-PT, Decision on Provision of Previous Testimony in Audio Format, Trial Chamber I, 22 November 2006, fn. 20.

50 *Prosecutor v Krnojelac* (n 15), para. 476 and fn. 1438.

51 ibid fn. 857: 'is supported'.

52 See also *Prosecutor v Kunarac* (n 15); *Prosecutor v Kupreškić* (n 15).

53 *Prosecutor v Krnojelac* (n 15), fn. 1438.

54 ibid.

4 *Emphasising That ICTY Jurisprudence Originates from ECtHR Case-Law*

Sometimes the ICTY only bases its conclusions on its own jurisprudence in a footnote while emphasising that these conclusions were originally drawn from the ECtHR's case-law.[55] In most cases, this manner of citing is used to further endorse the ICTY's jurisprudence in cases concerning the rights of the accused.[56] However, the ICTY also uses it in questions of substantive law; for example, it highlights its assessment that once rape has been proved, severe pain or suffering as required by the definition of torture has also been established.[57]

Perhaps this way of citing best reveals the use of ECtHR case-law by the ICTY: the Tribunal shows the roots of its jurisprudence, demonstrates that it descends from human rights jurisprudence, and thereby adds more legitimacy to its own jurisprudence. However, this may bear the risk of creating misunderstandings and generalising specific questions because the Tribunal does not analyse the ECtHR's jurisprudence at all, but only sees it through the lens of its case-law.

5 *Detailed Discussions*

Finally, there are lengthy and detailed discussions of cases in the text of ICTY judgments. In some cases, the ICTY uses this way of referring when one of the parties or an amicus curiae emphasises the importance of ECtHR case-law in their motions. Then, it often distinguishes the situations of the different cases in order to show why the ECtHR's jurisprudence is not applicable in the case at hand.[58] But the Tribunal also discusses the Court's jurisprudence in detail without the parties relying on it. For example, in its judgment in *Prosecutor v Delalić*,[59] the Trial Chamber develops a detailed definition of rape and discusses to what extent it can be characterised as torture. For this, it first presents several cases of the European Commission of Human Rights and the

---

55 For a typical example see *Prosecutor v Popović*, IT-05-88-T, Judgment, Trial Chamber II, 10 June 2010, vol 1, para. 60 and fn. 92 ('See *Prosecutor v. Stanislav Galić*, Case No. IT-98-29-AR73.2, Decision on Interlocutory Appeal Concerning Rule 92 bis(C), 7 June 2002, fn. 34, referring to judgements of the European Court for (*sic*) Human Rights'). This way of citing can be found in 13 decisions and six judgments of the ICTY.

56 ibid.

57 *Prosecutor v Brđanin*, IT-99-36-T, Judgment, Trial Chamber II, 1 September 2004, para. 485 and fn. 1264.

58 See only, *Prosecutor v Plavsić*, IT-00-39&40/1-S, Sentencing Judgment, Trial Chamber, 27 February 2003.

59 *Prosecutor v Delalić*, IT-96-21-T, Trial Chamber, 16 November 1998.

ECtHR, describes the facts of these cases, asks which treatment reached the threshold of torture, and even quotes passages of these judgments.[60] In its further reasoning, it analyses, inter alia, the case *Aydin v Turkey*[61] for several pages in order to determine whether rape can constitute torture.[62] In the end, the Tribunal follows the ECtHR and concludes that rape constitutes torture if certain elements are met.[63]

At first sight, this reference seems to be the clear opposite of the examples given above. The ICTY relies heavily on the jurisprudence of the ECtHR and discusses it in detail. However, in this case, which deals, moreover, with questions relevant for the definition of the crime, the ICTY does not problematise its use of IHRL.[64] Furthermore, it develops this definition without establishing international customary law in a traditional way[65] but bases its conclusion mainly on the case-law of the ECtHR and the Inter-American Commission on Human Rights. In doing so, it incorporates IHRL without reflecting the principle of legality as advised by the UN Secretary-General in his initial report on the ICTY.[66] Hence, even when the ICTY discusses the ECtHR's case-law in detail, it often does not spell out the relationship between IHRL and ICL, but just uses it when it is helpful for the case at hand.

6 *Inconsistent and Insufficiently Contextualised Citations*

The references of the ICTY to the ECtHR can be both extensive and superficial. A passing reference in a footnote certainly carries a different weight than a discussion of an ECtHR case that continues for several pages. This is underlined by the different functions these citations serve in the context of the judgment: sometimes the ICTY simply cites while discussing arguments of the parties; in other instances, it uses the reference to determine customary law or common

60 ibid paras 462–466.

61 *Aydin v Turkey*, App no 23178/94 (ECtHR, 25 September 1997).

62 In this context, it also refers to the similar jurisprudence of the Inter-American Commission on Human Rights, the ICTR, and that of the Special Rapporteur on Torture: *Prosecutor v Delalić* (n 59), paras 467, 481–493.

63 ibid para. 496.

64 In the context of torture, such a problematisation first occurs several years later in *Prosecutor v Kunarac* (n 15). However, in this case the ICTY merely rejects a definition of the Convention against Torture and Other Cruel, Inhuman or Degrading Treatment or Punishment citing ECtHR case-law in support of this rejection, paras 478–479.

65 Regarding the establishment of international customary law by the ICTs see Noora Arajärvi (n 44).

66 See above (n 17).

principles of law either as a guideline for interpretation or to legitimise its own jurisprudence.[67] Nevertheless, the ICTY mostly regards its usage of the ECtHR's case-law as rather unproblematic and there is no real difference between how it cites its own case-law and how it refers to that of the ECtHR. Thus, some judges even felt compelled to stress that the cases of the ECtHR 'are often cited as though they are binding on the Tribunal, when, in fact, they are only of persuasive authority.'[68] Moreover, the ICTY only seldom addresses the differences between IHRL and ICL and the question to what extent external notions can be transplanted from one context into the other. Instead, its citations are often unsystematic and erratic. Certainly, the citation of the ECtHR may be more problematic in cases of substantive law with relevance for the principle of legality than in those of procedural law; and the ECtHR's jurisprudence should be considered more carefully in the former case. However, this cannot conceal the need for more consistency in approaching the ECtHR's case-law.

V Exemplifying the Problematic Usage of the ECtHR's Jurisprudence by the ICTY: Decisions Concerning Provisional Release

The aforementioned quantity and manner of referring to the jurisprudence of the ECtHR illustrates a close connection between the ICTY and the ECtHR. However, the unsystematic approach of the ICTY to the ECtHR's case-law might disguise differences between IHRL and ICL. Due to the principle of legality, this is most pronounced in questions of substantive law, which can entail criminal sanctions against individuals. In contrast, questions regarding procedural aspects concern similar situations affecting the rights of the accused before both courts. Hence, citing the ECtHR in these matters seems to be rather unproblematic prima facie. Nevertheless, the inconsistent manner of citation described above can also create problems in this area of law; this culminates in cases in which key aspects of ECtHR jurisprudence even seem to be reversed. Therefore, I deliberately chose the matter of provisional release as an example for a seemingly unproblematic aspect of procedural law in order to underline

67 For a detailed discussion of these functions see the author's PhD project.

68 Patrick Robinson, 'Presentation' in *Dialogue between Judges: Fifty Years of the European Court of Human Rights Viewed by Its Fellow International Courts* (European Court of Human Rights 2009) (http://echr.coe.int/Documents/Dialogue_2009_ENG.pdf accessed 15 January 2016) 17, 19–20. See also *Prosecutor v Šainović*, IT-99-37-AR65, Decision on Provisional Release, Appeals Chamber, Dissenting Opinion of Judge David Hunt, 30 October 2002, para. 75.

this problematic usage of the ECtHR's case-law by the ICTY (1) as well as the need for a more refined way of dealing with this case-law (2).

1 *Referring to the ECtHR in Cases on Provisional Release*

The question whether an accused is released on remand impacts his individual rights. On the one hand, he has to be assumed innocent until his conviction. Detention restricts his personal liberty and puts his rights at a higher risk.[69] On the other hand, he has to be kept from escaping and destroying evidence.[70] The ECtHR and ICTY follow different approaches in this regard. Whereas Article 5(3) ECHR clearly states that detention may not exceed a reasonable time,[71] the Statute of the ICTY is silent on this matter.[72] Consequently, the original version of Rule 65(B) RPE stated that provisional release should only be granted in exceptional circumstances.[73] Although this requirement was removed in 1999,[74] the ICTY practice remained hazy and indecisive as regards the length of the detention as well as the question which elements must be present to grant provisional release. In 2008, the Appeals Chamber ruled that provisional release will only be granted in the case of compelling humanitarian grounds.[75] This practice was strongly criticised by several judges and seen as the reintroduction of the old 'exceptional circumstances' rule.[76] In autumn 2011, Rule 65(B) RPE was changed again, now stating that 'compelling humanitarian grounds may be considered in granting such release.'

A good example for the different approaches in granting provisional release adopted by the ECtHR and ICTY is the *Decision on the Accused Prlić's Motion for*

---

69 Salvatore Zappalà, *Human Rights in International Criminal Proceedings* (OUP 2003) 66–67.

70 ibid.

71 See also Article 9(3) of the International Covenant on Civil and Political Rights: 'It shall not be the general rule that persons awaiting trial shall be detained in custody'.

72 Concerning an analysis of the provisional release at the ICTY and its evolution see Krit Zeegers, 'Provisional Release before the *Ad Hoc* Tribunals' in Charles Riziki Majinge (ed), *Rule of Law through Human Rights and International Criminal Justice: Essays in Honour of Adama Dieng* (Cambridge Scholars Publishing 2015) 228.

73 Rule 65(B) RPE original version. All versions of the RPE are accessible under www.icty.org/sid/136 accessed 15 January 2016.

74 Rule 65(B) RPE version of 17 November 1999.

75 See only *Prosecutor v Prlić*, IT-04-74-AR65, Decision on Prosecution's Consolidated Appeal against Decisions to Provisionally Release the Accused Prlić, Stojić, Praljak, Petković and Ćorić, Appeals Chamber, 11 March 2008, para. 21.

76 See only *Prosecutor v Stanišić*, IT-03-69-AR.65.7, Decision on Franco Simatović's Appeal against the Decision Denying His Urgent Request for Provisional Release, Appeals Chamber, Dissenting Opinion of Judge Güney, 23 May 2011; Zeegers (n 72) 252–257.

Provisional Release,[77] which centres on the humanitarian grounds requirement. Here, the Trial Chamber admits that the motion could be decided differently in the light of the ECtHR case-law due to the different construction of Article 5(3) ECHR, under which 'detention of an accused during his trial constitutes an exception and not the rule.'[78] However, the ECtHR would always proceed 'with an in concreto analysis of the decisions of national jurisdiction.'[79] The Chamber, in contrast, is bound by the requirement of compelling humanitarian reasons as laid down by the Appeals Chamber to justify the provisional release.[80] In this case, the Chamber abundantly cites ECtHR jurisprudence before denying its entire relevance with one short remark regarding the requirement of humanitarian grounds. In his dissenting opinion to the *Decision on Simatović's Appeal against the Decision Denying His Urgent Request for Provisional Release*, Judge Güney sharply criticises this practice, stating that 'establishing such a stringent criterion prior to the trial judgment is not supported by any international human rights instruments or by any other international criminal law jurisdictions.'[81]

However, these differences have not deterred the ICTY from citing the ECtHR in its case-law on provisional release. In the *Decision on Momičilo Krajišnik's Notice of Motion for Provisional Release*, the Trial Chamber even explicitly states that the first change of Rule 65(B) in 1999 'does not alter the position that provisional release continues to be the exception and not the rule.'[82] It underlines that even if the accused has satisfied all requirements of this Rule, it will be still at the discretion of the ICTY to grant provisional release.[83] In this case, the accused had been in prison for 18 months and it was assumed that the trial would commence around five months later.[84] The Chamber acknowledges that according to international treaties, the accused should be released if he 'cannot be brought to trial within a reasonable period of time.' However, the ECtHR

77 *Prosecutor v Prlić*, IT-04-74-AR65, Decision on the Accused Prlić's Motion for Provisional Release, Trial Chamber III, 9 April 2009.

78 ibid para. 42.

79 ibid.

80 ibid.

81 Dissenting Opinion of Judge Güney to the Decision on Franco Simatović's Appeal against the Decision Denying His Urgent Request for Provisional Release (n 76), para. 3.

82 *Prosecutor v Krajišnik*, IT-00-39-&40-PT, Decision on Momičilo Krajišnik's Notice of Motion for Provisional Release, Trial Chamber, 8 October 2001, para. 12. It justifies this position 'by the absence of any power [...] to execute its own arrest warrants'.

83 ibid para. 14.

84 Dissenting Opinion of Judge Robinson to the Decision on Momičilo Krajišnik's Notice of Motion for Provisional Release (n 82), para. 43.

'has found that extensive periods of pre-trial detention may be reasonable'; in doing so, it quotes *W. v Switzerland* and *Ferrari-Bravo v Italy*, where four years and eleven months were deemed reasonable.[85] Thus, it uses exceptional ECtHR cases to legitimise its general approach of denying provisional release. What is the exception in the ECtHR jurisprudence is thereby turned into the norm in the ICTY's jurisprudence.

However, the ICTY also uses the ECtHR's case-law to justify its decision when granting provisional release. In those cases, the ICTY often cites *Ilijkov v Bulgaria*,[86] pointing out that the ECtHR has 'repeatedly held that the gravity of the charges cannot by itself serve to justify long periods of detention on remand.'[87] This hints at a positive influence of the ECtHR's jurisprudence on the exercise of the rights of the accused at the ICTY. However, in stressing that the gravity of the charges cannot by itself justify long periods of detention, the Tribunal still underlines that this criterion is an important element to be taken into account while assessing a motion on provisional release. In combination with the humanitarian grounds requirement, this still places the burden of proof on the accused[88] and legitimises a restrictive policy of denying provisional release.

In conclusion, one has to emphasise that the ICTY follows a different approach than the ECtHR in cases concerning provisional release. In contrast to the principles of the ECHR, release remains the exception. Nevertheless, the ICTY has no problem citing exceptional cases of the ECtHR to justify long pre-trial detentions without clarifying this in a coherent discussion of the ECtHR's case-law.

2 *Call for a More Refined Way of Dealing with ECtHR Jurisprudence*

These examples from the jurisprudence concerning provisional release show an ambiguous way of dealing with ECtHR jurisprudence. On the one hand, the ICTY often cites it in this context. On the other hand, the Tribunal follows a

85 Decision on Krajišnik's Notice of Motion for Provisional Release (n 82), paras 15, 22. This was criticised by Judge Robinson in his dissenting opinion to the decision arguing that detention should never be the rule.

86 *Ilijkov v Bulgaria*, App no 33977/96 (ECtHR, 26 July 2001).

87 This statement is an element used in many decisions concerning provisional release; see only *Prosecutor v Stanišić*, IT-03-69-PT, Decision on Provisional Release, Trial Chamber, 28 July 2004, para. 22.

88 Göran Sluiter, 'Procedural Lawmaking at the International Criminal Tribunals' in Shane Darcy and Joseph Powderly (eds), *Judicial Creativity at the International Criminal Tribunals* (OUP 2010) 315, 327–330.

different approach than the ECtHR, where the rights of the accused seem to be better protected. Moreover, the rules of when to grant provisional release were often changed during the past years, which has led to the unequal treatment of different defendants.[89] In view of the high importance of the rights of the accused in the context of ICL, the approach of the ICTY has to be viewed critically. It should either cite the ECtHR jurisprudence in a consistent way, and ensure that both systems provide similar guarantees, or refrain from citing the ECtHR in this context. Otherwise, the citation of ECtHR cases only disguises the different approaches and leads to legal uncertainty.

All in all, the example of cases concerning provisional release shows that even in questions which do not touch upon matters of substantive law, there is a tension between the original case-law of the ECtHR and the way it is used and interpreted by the ICTY. This tension is partly caused by the inconsistent approach of the ICTY to this case-law. Therefore, one has to call for a refined and systematic approach that can replace the former.

Conclusion

References to the ECtHR are very common in the jurisprudence of the ICTY. The ECtHR's jurisprudence plays a decisive role in all possible ways and at all stages of the criminal proceedings. Its importance concerning quantity as well as quality is evident. Nevertheless, the scope of the ECtHR's influence does not exhaust itself in direct citations, as a mere glance at cases in which only a separate opinion includes an explicit citation evinces. The quality of citation ranges from general, superficial invocations of the ECtHR to in-depth analyses of certain ECtHR cases. Categorising the citation of ECtHR jurisprudence, however, reveals that the Tribunal does not critically assess its references.

Contrary to the Statute of the ICTY, which is silent on this matter, the Rome Statute explicitly states in Article 21(3) that the application and interpretation of law must be consistent with internationally recognised human rights. Such a statement, however, cannot sufficiently regulate the problematic use of jurisprudence regarding human rights: it merely legitimises, for the first time, the references to this jurisprudence. Perhaps Article 21(3) could be used against a similar development in the area of provisional release at the International Criminal Court, but this is yet to be seen. It does not help with regard to the unchallenged and erratic usage of human rights jurisprudence.

89 ibid 330.

The ICTY—or, in view of its imminent closure, the other ICTs—should, therefore, develop clear rules as to when it is helpful to refer to another court in general and to a human rights court in particular. In citing external jurisprudence, the ICTs should, on the one hand, assess all of the relevant jurisprudence of the court to which they refer, refraining from only citing exceptional cases. Moreover, they should keep in mind that they are acting in a criminal system which should primarily adhere to fundamental criminal principles. Therefore, it is very important that the current erratic approach be replaced with a systematic one.

Annex: Number of ICTY Cases Referring to Jurisprudence of the ECtHR[90]

Year	Number of cases: decisions	Number of references[91] in decisions	Number of cases: judgments	Number of references in judgments	Separate opinions	Cases in which the ICTY only presents arguments of the parties referring to the ECtHR
1995	2	2	0	0	1	0
1996	3	3	0	0	2	0
1997	6	8	1	2	0	1
1998	7	7	2	5	0	0
1999	2	2	2	3	0	1
2000	4	5	4	8	1	4
2001	6	6	5	8	1	0
2002	13	13	3	7	3	0
2003	16	16	3	3	3	1
2004	13	13	2	2	0	2
2005	14	14	4	5	2	6
2006	10	12	3	3	2	4
2007	11	11	2	2	1	3
2008	5	5	3	3	1	4

90 All cases until the end of the year 2014 have been examined.

91 One 'reference' shall be defined as several citations, even if those are in different parts of the same judgment, as long as the citations concern the same question of law.

(cont.)

2009	8	8	2	3	0	5
2010	6	6	2	3	2	1
2011	5	5	2	3	4	2
2012	2	2	0	0	3	0
2013	3	3	1	1	3	1
2014	3	3	2	5	1	0
Total	139	144	43	66	30[92]	35[93]

92 To 22 decisions and five judgments.

93 32 decisions and three judgments.

PART 3

Cross-fertilization and Substantive Issues: Crimes and Punishment

CHAPTER 7

The *Nulla Poena sine Lege* Principle: A Symptomatic Sign of Interactions between Strasbourg and The Hague

Damien Scalia

1 Introduction

While the obligation for international criminal tribunals to consider human rights is not explicitly mentioned in their mandates, on many occasions these tribunals refer to the case law of regional courts in the area of human rights or, at the very least, use this branch of international law in the decisions they make.[1] According to Professor Cassese, the approach taken by the ICTs when referring to sources of law is 'wild':

> in general the 'wild' approach tends to place law that is 'external' to the international criminal court [...] on the same level as the law governing that court. In other words, the International Criminal Tribunal makes reference to, or applies, national and European Court case law without distinguishing it from the decisions of the Tribunal itself or of other international criminal courts.[2]

In parallel, the International Criminal Court's Statute explicitly mentions human rights principles and international human rights law as sources of law.[3] Indeed, Article 21 of the Rome Statute refers to 'internationally recognized human rights' as those that can serve in the interpretation and application

1 *Prosecutor v Tadić*, IT-94-1, Judgment, Appeals Chamber, 2 October 1995, para. 45; *Prosecutor v Furundžija*, Judgment, Trial Chamber, 10 December 1998, para. 183; Gloria Gaggioli, *L'influence mutuelle entre les droits de l'homme et le droit international humanitaire à la lumière du droit à la vie* (Pédone 2013).

2 Antonio Cassese, 'The Influence of European Court of Human Rights on International Criminal Tribunals—some Methodological Remarks' in Morten Bergsmo (ed), *Human Rights and Criminal Justice for the Downtrodden. Essays in Honour of Asbjørn Eide* (Marinus Nijhoff Publishers 2003) 19, 24.

3 Article 21 of the Rome Statute.

 | DOI: 10.1163/9789004313750_009

of other sources of law that are mentioned in the same Article. In this context, they are not referred to as an applicable source of law *per se*, but as a framework for interpreting and applying the law.[4] In fact, whatever source of law the Court may refer to, it has to do so in a manner that respects human rights. The principles of human rights law deemed internationally recognised should therefore be respected in the context of international criminal law, as is outlined in Article 21(3) of the Rome Statute.[5] At the same time, as Pellet remarks, the introduction of this category of rules, backed-up by a special judicial authority, is not an innovation; the International Criminal Tribunal for the former Yugoslavia makes reference to the same human rights law as a source of its jurisprudence.[6] Nevertheless, while this obligation is recognised, it does not mean that human rights are fully respected, as I will demonstrate in this chapter, taking into account a fundamental principle of criminal law: the principle of legality of penalties.

Indeed, in this 'judicial dialogue' between international criminal law and international human rights, the *nulla poena sine lege* principle (as fundamental principle of a democratic penal system) is an example of the use of human rights case law by the international criminal tribunals and court. Human rights case law is mostly used to legitimate decisions and interpretations or creation of law; in other words, references to human rights allow international criminal law to correspond to the *universal values legitimacy*.[7] According to Cassese, 'we can say that an institution enjoys such legitimacy when it is grounded on, or at least is not contrary to, peremptory norms of international law (*jus cogens*) or, more generally, is based on those 'principles of justice as fairness' to which Rawls drew attention'.[8]

---

4 Ida Caracciolo, 'Applicable Law' in Flavia Lattanzi and William A. Schabas (eds), *Essays on the Rome Statute of the International Criminal Court* (Il Sirente 1999) 211, 228.

5 According to Pre-Trial Chamber II, these humans rights are also included in Article 21(2) of the Rome Statute. See *Prosecutor v Bemba*, ICC-01/05-01/08, Decision Pursuant to Article 61(7)(a) and (b) of the Rome Statute on the Charges of the Prosecutor Against Jean-Pierre Bemba Gombo, Pre-Trial Chamber, 15 June 2009, para. 39.

6 Alain Pellet, 'Applicable Law' in Antonio Cassese, Paola Gaeta and John R.W.D. Jones (eds), *The Rome Statute of the ICC: A Commentary* (OUP 2002) vol 2 1051, 1080. For explanation of the references of Human Rights Law by the ICTs, see Damien Scalia, 'Human Rights in the Context of International Criminal Law: Respecting Them and Ensuring Respect for Them' in Gloria Gaggioli and Robert Kolb (eds), *Research Handbook on Human Rights and Humanitarian Law* (Edward Elgar Publishing 2013) 575.

7 Antonio Cassese, 'The Legitimacy of International Criminal Tribunals and the Current Prospects of International Criminal Justice' (2012) 25 Leiden Journal of International Law 491, 492.

8 Cassese (n 7) 492.

In order to demonstrate this analysis, I will make the case that while the ICTs and ICC recognise the applicability of the *nulla poena sine lege* principle (in referring to the human rights law or as contained in the Rome Statute), this principle is not strictly respected in the pronounced penalties (Sections III and IV). Moreover, the same analysis can be made concerning the application of this principle to the executed penalties (Section V). That being said, before developing this argument, it is crucial to examine the *nulla poena sine lege* principle as defined by the ECtHR. Indeed, the European Court has developed the definition of this principle which could be taken into consideration as a point of reference in order to analyse the case law of the ICTs and ICC (Section II). I take into consideration the ECtHR definition because it is the most comprehensive definition of the principle: it embraces criteria developed by other human rights organs at the international level.[9] Moreover, as I will present below, international criminal tribunals make reference to ECtHR case law in order to define the principle.

II Definition of the *Nulla Poena sine Lege* Principle in the European Jurisprudence

Before analysing the cross-fertilisation between international criminal law and human rights, it is necessary to define the principle of legality of penalties. According to Article 7 of the European Convention on Human Rights, the *nulla poena sine lege* principle states that '[A penalty shall not be imposed that is heavier] than the one that was applicable at the time the criminal offence was committed'. It can also be found in Article 11(2) of the Universal Declaration of Human Rights and Article 15 of the International Covenant on Civil and Political Rights.

Historically, in civil law systems, the legality principle (*nullum crimen, nulla poena sine lege*) was defined by two formal criteria: 1) a written law adopted by 2) a legislator.[10] This definition has changed at the international level and, especially due to the case law of the ECtHR, at the national level too. Today the principle is defined by three material criteria: the quality (clarity and precision), the accessibility and the foreseeability of the law.[11]

9 Damien Scalia, *Du principe de légalité en droit international pénal* (Bruylant 2011).

10 Djoheur Zerouki, *La légalité criminelle, Enrichissement de la conception formelle par une conception matérielle* (Université Jean Moulin 2001).

11 *Sunday Times v the United Kingdom*, App no 6538/74 (ECtHR, 26 April 1979), para. 49.

The quality of the law implies clear and precise formulation.[12] These criteria are not absolute and have to be interpreted by 'appropriate legal advice',[13] allowing individuals 'to assess, to a degree that is reasonable in the circumstances, the consequences which a given action may entail'.[14] Moreover, the ECtHR has recognised that 'the wording of many statutes is not absolutely precise. The need to avoid excessive rigidity and to keep pace with changing circumstances means that many laws are inevitably couched in terms which, to a greater or lesser extent, are vague'.[15] It has also noted 'the impossibility of attaining absolute precision in the framing of laws', especially in fields where values change according to the evolution of society's conceptions.[16] Thus, the Court accepts that a legal system can resort to 'one of the standard techniques of regulation by rules', that is 'to use general categorisations as opposed to exhaustive lists'.[17] Precision and clarity must be appreciated within the global context of the text concerned. A vague provision can thus become more precise when read jointly with other provisions of the same law.[18]

Additionally, the law must also be accessible. The concept of accessibility has been explained as follows:

> the law must be adequately accessible: the citizen must be able to have an indication that is adequate in the circumstances of the legal rules applicable to a given case [...] a norm cannot be regarded as a 'law' unless it is formulated with sufficient precision to enable the citizen to regulate his conduct: he must be able—if need be with appropriate advice—to foresee, to a degree that is reasonable in the circumstances, the consequences which a given action may entail.[19]

Thus, the interpretation of accessibility is ambivalent.

Finally, the law has to be foreseeable. This criterion can be satisfied only when the first two criteria have been met. Additionally, one must be able 'to foresee, to a degree that is reasonable in the circumstances, the consequences

---

12 *Kokkinakis v Greece*, App no 14307/88 (ECtHR, 25 May 1993), para. 52.

13 *Sunday Time* (n 11), para. 40.

14 *Cantoni v France*, App no 17862/91 (ECtHR, 15 November 1996), para. 35.

15 *Kokkinakis* (n 12), para. 40.

16 *Barthold v Germany*, App no 8734/79 (ECtHR, 25 March 1985), para. 60.

17 *Cantoni v France* (n 14), para. 31.

18 *G. v Liechtenstein*, App no 10980/84 (EurCommHR, 30 October 1984) cited in Zerouki (n 10), para. 308.

19 *Sunday Times* (n 10), para. 49.

which a given action may entail'.[20] In fact, this criterion has to be analysed by converse implication: unreasonable, unexpected and surprising elements cannot satisfy the foreseeability criterion.[21] Thus, a 'sudden' change in the case law, to the disadvantage of the accused, and which the latter could not have expected, violates the principle of legality. Moreover, external facts must enable the applicant to foresee that a turnaround in the case law might happen, or that an act which did not constitute a criminal offence and whose criminalisation would have been very difficult to foresee might nonetheless be treated as criminal in given circumstances. Two factors seem to be relevant in this matter. Firstly, the evolution of customs and society may make a right foreseeable, even if the right seems contradicted by a current criminal norm. In this regard, the marital rape case of *S.W. v United Kingdom* is revealing.[22] Secondly, the gravity of the offence must be seen as entailing the foreseeability of the law.[23]

As regards sentences, the ECtHR has confirmed that: 'the notion of the legality of a sentence implies not only that the sentence has a legal basis but that the law itself fulfils the conditions of accessibility and foreseeability'.[24] Moreover, in relation to sentencing, the ECtHR also recognises that the *lex mitior* principle should be applied. This principle states that a punishment cannot be more severe than the punishment prescribed by the law at the time a crime was committed.[25]

At the end, it is important to highlight that the 'law', the cornerstone of the *nulla poena sine lege* principle, encompasses both the *lex scripta* and the law in a more general sense, which includes case law. However, in a recent case, the ECtHR declared that 'general principles of law' cannot be sources of either incrimination or penalty;[26] the principle of legality is thus violated by a criminal offence based solely on general principles of law. One could take the same approach to examining penalties and the *nulla poena sine lege* principle.

---

20 *Cantoni v France* (n 14), para. 35; *Sunday Times* (n 11), para. 49.

21 Zerouki (n 10) 311.

22 *S.W. v United Kingdom*, App no 20166/92 (ECtHR, 22 November 1995), para. 44.

23 *Pessino v France*, App no 40403/02 (ECtHR, 10 October 2010), para. 36.

24 *Gragnic v France*, App no 15312 (EurCommHR Report, 29 June 1994), para. 32.

25 *Scoppola v Italia (no 2)*, App no 10249/03 (ECtHR, 17 September 2009).

26 *Maktouf and Damjanović v Bosnia and Herzegovina*, App no 2312/08 and 34179/08 (ECtHR, 18 July 2013); Damien Scalia, 'L'application du principe de légalité des peines aux crimes (les plus) graves: l'orthodoxie retrouvée' (2014) 99 Revue trimestrielle des droits de l'homme 689.

III Principle of Legality of Penalties before ICTs

As I will present here, the *nulla poena sine lege* principle is recognised by international criminal law. Nevertheless, the respect for this principle is questionable.

The recognition of the applicability of the principle of legality is made both by the ICC and ICTs. Concerning the ICC, the *nulla poena sine lege* principle is recognised in the Rome Statute (Article 23) as well as in the case law.[27] Concerning the ICTs, even if their statutes do not state the principle, they have recognised the applicability of the principle of legality.[28] Moreover, it has to be respected by the 'law' of the ICTs, including their founding instruments and their case law. Indeed, it is a fundamental principle of any democratic penal system and it has been stated in the report which establishes the ICTY.[29]

In order to recognise this applicability, an important reference is made to human rights law in a number of cases.[30] In this context, international judges have used both international conventions and case law from the ECtHR and the American Court of Human Rights (ACtHR) to define this principle: 'while the Statute of the International Tribunal lists offences over which the International Tribunal has jurisdiction, the Tribunal may enter convictions only where it is satisfied that the offence is proscribed under customary international law at the time of its commission'.[31] Despite this recognition, in practice the *nulla poena sine lege* principle is routinely violated. Nevertheless, the analysis is different for ICTs and the ICC.

Nevertheless, with regard to the foreseeability criterion, it is difficult to forecast sentences.[32] First, the Statutes of the ICTY and ICTR mention only one

27 *Prosecutor v Katanga*, ICC-01/04-01/07, Decision on Sentence Pursuant to Article 76 of the Statute, Trial Chamber, 23 May 2014, para. 39.

28 *Prosecutor v Mpembara*, ICTR-01-65-T, Trial Chamber, 11 September 2006, para. 26; *Prosecutor v Blagojević*, IT-02-60-T, Judgment, Trial Chamber, 17 January 2005, para. 625; *Prosecutor v Tadić*, IT-94-1-T and IT-94-1Abis, Judgment in Sentencing Appeals, Appeals Chamber, 26 January 2000, Separate Opinion of Judge Cassese, para. 4; *Prosecutor v Erdemović*, IT-96-22, Sentencing Judgment, Trial Chamber, 29 November 1996, para. 38.

29 *Report of the Secretary-General pursuant to paragraph 2 of Security Council Resolution 808(1993)*, S/25704, 3 May 1993, paras 34, 111 and 113.

30 *Prosecutor v Blaskić*, IT-95-14, Judgment, Appeals Chamber, 29 July 2004, para. 141.

31 ibid.

32 On this subject, see eg Ines M.W. de Roca and Christopher M. Rassi, 'Sentencing and

penalty for all crimes: life imprisonment. According to the criteria defining the legality principle (ie 'to assess, to a degree that is reasonable in the circumstances, the consequences which a given action may entail'),[33] a single penalty for all crimes does not allow one to assess the consequences (in terms of penalty) which a given crime may entail. Second, the Statutes of the ICTY and ICTR, in attempting to address the principle of legality with respect to sentencing, require the sentencing chamber to have recourse to the general practice regarding prison sentences in the courts of the former Yugoslavia and Rwanda, respectively.[34] However, judges have stated that this criterion is only indicative.[35] Such a decision clearly violates the criterion of foreseeability of the *nulla poena sine lege* principle imposed by the ECtHR. Indeed, in order to be foreseen, accused persons should be able to evaluate the penalties enumerated in the law applicable at the time of the crime. If this law is only indicative, it is impossible to foresee the penalties tied to the crime.

One could argue that the ECtHR is not strictly bound by the ICTs. However, a recent decision concerning crimes committed during the war in the former Yugoslavia issued by the ECtHR allows such scepticism to be rejected. This decision was issued in the *Maktouf and Damjanovic* case.[36] In this judgment, the European Court had to address the question of the violation of the *nulla poena sine lege* principle in a specific case where the applicants had been convicted for war crimes under a new law (provisions of the 2003 Criminal Code of Bosnia Herzegovina) for crimes that were committed under an older one (1976 Criminal Code, which was, according to the interpretations made by European judges at national tribunals, more lenient[37]). The ECtHR decided that 'since there exists a real possibility that the retroactive application of the 2003 Code operated to the applicants' disadvantage as concerns the sentencing, it cannot be said that they were afforded effective safeguards against the imposition of a

---

Incarceration in the Ad Hoc Tribunals' (2008) 44 Stanford Journal of International Law 1; Robert Cryer and others, *An Introduction to International Criminal Law and Practice* (2nd edn, CUP 2010) 499.

33 *Cantoni v France* (n 14), para. 35.

34 Article 24(1) of the ICTY Statute and Article 23(1) of the ICTR Statute.

35 *Prosecutor v Popović*, IT-05-88-T, Judgment, Trial Chamber, 10 June 2010, para. 2142; *Prosecutor v Milutinović*, IT-05-87-T, Judgment, Trial Chamber, 26 February 2009, para. 1160; *Prosecutor v Stakić*, IT-97-24-A, Judgment, Appeals Chamber, 22 March 2006, para. 398.

36 *Maktouf and Damjanović* (n 26).

37 The case was difficult because the sentences imposed on the applicants were in the latitude of both the 1976 Criminal Code and the 2003 Criminal Code.

heavier penalty, in breach of Article 7 of the Convention'.[38] According to this conclusion, one could argue that the jurisprudence and provision of the Statute of the ICTY is a retroactive application of a new law, which is more punitive than the Criminal Code of the former Yugoslavia (the 1976 Criminal Code): the law in the former Yugoslavia condemned war crimes or crimes against humanity by imprisonment for 20 years, and,[39] while the death penalty was indeed provided for war crimes, before the time of the war, only the maximum of 20 years had ever been applied—this has been recognised by the ICTY case law.[40] This means that all sentences of more than 20 years of imprisonment pronounced by the ICTY are in conflict with this jurisprudence.

The lack of respect of the *nulla poena sine lege* principle is also present in the area of aggravating and mitigating circumstances. The mitigating and aggravating circumstances that may be taken into account are not exhaustively listed in the Statutes or RPE of the ICTY and ICTR. This is an arguable breach of the criterion of quality (ie the precision) and has led some authors to call for sentencing guidelines, containing, for example, 'an indicative list of aggravating and mitigating circumstances; [...] an approximate weight to attribute to aggravating and mitigating circumstances'.[41]

As it stands now, such circumstances are considered somewhat erratically, as trial chambers have considerable discretion in determining what they wish to consider.[42] As an example, the good morals of the accused prior to the conflict have been taken into account sometimes as mitigating circumstances, sometimes as aggravating circumstances, and have sometimes been deemed to be irrelevant.[43] The age of the accused at the time of the offences has also been treated inconsistently: in *Furundžija*, the fact that the accused was 23 years old was held to be a mitigating circumstance,[44] but in other cases, the same

38 *Maktouf and Damjanović* (n 26), para. 70. For a detailed analysis of the *Maktouf and Damjanovic Case*, see Scalia (n 26).

39 *Erdemović* (n 28), paras 34–40.

40 ibid.

41 Silvia D'Ascoli, *Sentencing in International Criminal Law: The UN ad hoc Tribunals and Future Perspectives for ICC* (Hart Publishing 2011).

42 *Prosecutor v Naletilić*, IT-98-34-T, Judgment, Trial Chamber, 31 March 2003, para. 742. For an extensive quantitative analysis of sentencing data in the case law of the ICTY and ICTR, see D'Ascoli (n 41).

43 *Prosecutor v Barayagwiza*, ICTR-99-52-A, Judgment, Appeals Chamber, 28 November 2007, para. 1069; *Prosecutor v Plavsić*, IT-00-39&40/1-S, Judgment, Trial Chamber, 27 February 2003; *Prosecutor v Tadić*, IT-94-1-T, Sentencing Judgment, Trial Chamber, 14 July 1997, para. 59.

44 *Furundžija* (n 1), para. 284.

mitigating circumstance was applied where the accused were observed to be between 32 and 37 years old.[45] The jurisprudence remains vague on various issues; it does not set down a hierarchy of crimes and no sentencing guidelines have been issued by the ICTY or the ICTR. It has been argued that this is one factor underlying the failure of the tribunals to develop a fair and consistent sentencing regime.[46] Moreover, the mitigating and aggravating circumstances that may be taken into account are not exhaustively listed in the Statutes or RPE of the ICTY and ICTR. The legality principle is not strictly respected, ie the consequences of a given action are not foreseeable.

Thus, the criteria identified by the ECtHR to define the principle of legality of penalties are not fulfilled by the ICTY and ICTR Statutes and case law, especially due to the fact that there is only one sentence for all crimes. The foreseeability, as well as the quality and the accessibility of law are not strictly respected. International criminal tribunals seem not to comply with the principle of the legality of sentences.

IV Principle of Legality of Penalties before ICC

Concerning the ICC, the founding instruments are more detailed and seem to respect the legality of penalties principle. Nevertheless, while these texts and the case law bring more explanation and meet more criteria underpinning the principle, the vagueness of the founding instruments and the arbitrariness of the Judges (when they take into consideration factors to establish the quantum of the sentence) leave the foreseeability and accessibility criteria aside.

Firstly, it is necessary to present the provisions governing the sentences in the founding instruments of the ICC. Article 77 of the Rome Statute contains a provision favouring a fixed term of imprisonment to a maximum of 30 years, and adds the possibility of 'a term of life imprisonment when justified by the extreme gravity of the crime and the individual circumstances of the convicted person'. For its part, Article 78(1) completes this provision by stating that it is necessary to 'take into account such factors as the gravity of the crime and the individual circumstances of the convicted person'. Clarifying these Articles, Rule 145 adds that:

---

45 *Prosecutor v Serushago*, ICTR-98-39-S, Judgment and Sentence, Trial Chamber, 5 February 1999, para. 39; see also *Prosecutor Blaskić*, IT-95-14-T, Judgment, Trial Chamber, 3 March 2000, para. 778.

46 Ola Olusanya, *Sentencing War Crimes and Crimes against Humanity under the International Criminal Tribunal for the Former Yugoslavia* (Europa Law Publishing 2005).

> 1. In its determination of the sentence pursuant to article 78, paragraph 1, the Court shall:
>
> [...]
>
> (b) Balance all the relevant factors, including any mitigating and aggravating factors and consider the circumstances both of the convicted person and of the crime;
>
> (c) In addition to the factors mentioned in article 78, paragraph 1, give consideration, inter alia, to the extent of the damage caused, in particular the harm caused to the victims and their families, the nature of the unlawful behaviour and the means employed to execute the crime; the degree of participation of the convicted person; the degree of intent; the circumstances of manner, time and location; and the age, education, social and economic condition of the convicted person.
>
> 2. In addition to the factors mentioned above, the Court shall take into account, as appropriate:
>
> (a) Mitigating circumstances such as:
>
> (i) The circumstances falling short of constituting grounds for exclusion of criminal responsibility, such as substantially diminished mental capacity or duress;
>
> (ii) The convicted person's conduct after the act, including any efforts by the person to compensate the victims and any cooperation with the Court;
>
> (b) As aggravating circumstances:
>
> (i) Any relevant prior criminal convictions for crimes under the jurisdiction of the Court or of a similar nature;
>
> (ii) Abuse of power or official capacity;
>
> (iii) Commission of the crime where the victim is particularly defenceless;
>
> (iv) Commission of the crime with particular cruelty or where there were multiple victims;
>
> (v) Commission of the crime for any motive involving discrimination on any of the grounds referred to in article 21, paragraph 3;
>
> (vi) Other circumstances which, although not enumerated above, by virtue of their nature are similar to those mentioned.

Therefore, the founding instruments are more detailed in explaining the circumstances or factors which should be taken into account in determining the sentence against a condemned individual. Nevertheless, some problems are still present in these provisions, leading to the conclusion that the principle of legality is not strictly respected. First, the Statute states only one fixed term imprisonment for all crimes. In so doing, the ICC Statute is similar to the ICTY and ICTR Statutes in that there is no specified sentence for any specific crime. Second, there is no *a priori* hierarchy between crimes under the jurisdiction of the Court in the Statute. Thus, the degree of precision required by the ECtHR's criteria seems not to be respected.

That being said, Articles 77 and 78 of the Rome Statute, together with Rule 145 of the Rules of Procedure and Evidence, supply an important list of the aggravating and mitigating circumstances that should be taken into consideration when pronouncing penalties. Nevertheless, the list of criteria that judges have to take into account is non-exhaustive, and, therefore, not foreseeable: this is especially problematic for the aggravating circumstances for which the last provision of Rule 145 states that 'other circumstances which, although not enumerated above, by virtue of their nature are similar to those mentioned could be taken into consideration'. Regarding the criteria under the definition of the *nulla poena sine lege* principle and the criterion of foreseeability, this list is problematic especially because of the fact that aggravating circumstances are taken into account to the disadvantage of the convicted person. Moreover, there is no hierarchy established between all criteria listed as mitigating or aggravating circumstances.

This lack of clarity and precision in the founding instruments could have been filled by the sentences pronounced by the ICC. However, this has not exactly been the case, principally due to the arbitrariness of the Judges in taking into account the factors related to the crimes, the condemned or the victims. In order to demonstrate this, I will briefly present the three decisions on sentence issued by the ICC; ie in the *Lubanga* case,[47] the *Katanga* case[48] and the *Bemba* case.[49] The purpose of this Section is not to explain every aspect of each decision on sentence issued by the ICC, but only to present the elements of comparison of the decisions which lead us to think that the *nulla poena sine lege* principle is not strictly respected. In this vein, two main elements demonstrate the arbitrariness of the respective Trial Chambers and the lack of respect of the criteria defining the legality principle: the weakness of the analysis of the gravity of the crimes and the absence of certain factors without explanation.

47 *Prosecutor v Lubanga*, ICC-01/04-01/06, Decision on Sentence pursuant to Article 76 of the Statute, Trial Chamber, 10 July 2012.

48 *Prosecutor v Katanga*, ICC-01/04-01/07, Decision on Sentence pursuant to Article 76 of the Statute, Trial Chamber, 23 May 2014.

49 *Prosecutor v Bemba*, ICC-01/05-01/08, Decision on Sentence pursuant to Article 76 of the Statute, Trial Chamber, 21 June 2016.

Gravity of Crimes

According to the Article 78 of the Statute of the ICC and the Rule 145 of the RPE of the ICC, the Court must take into account the gravity of the crime as the first criterion allowing it to determine the quantum of the sentence. While this is recognised by the Decisions issued by the ICC,[50] the Trial Chambers of the ICC, at least in two decisions, do not give a comprehensive analysis of this criterion. In the *Lubanga* Decision, according to D'Ascoli, 'there is no substantial analysis devoted to the gravity of the *specific* crimes Lubanga is convicted of, their relative seriousness and the damage caused. Furthermore, the ascertained gravity of Lubanga's crimes remains an empty statement where the Chamber does not seem to make concrete conclusions about this 'seriousness', especially in its determination of the penalty. In fact, [...] there is no specific discussion of how the gravity of Lubanga's crimes, and the damage caused by such crimes, is reflected in and has impacted the length of the sentence imposed'.[51] The same would apply regarding the *Bemba* Decision. Indeed, the Trial Chamber, in explaining the gravity criterion, takes into account the conduct of the convicted person,[52] which is contrary to the interpretation thereof accepted by the *Katanga* Decision.[53] Moreover, the Chamber does not seem to draw concrete conclusions about the gravity of the crimes;[54] rather, it merely states that the decision was taken 'in its discretion and in light of the particular circumstances of the case',[55] which leaves an important power to the Judges. Furthermore, the Chamber seems to take into consideration the gravity of the crimes also as aggravating circumstances,[56] contrary to the *Katanga* Decision.[57] Indeed, in the *Lubanga* Decision, the Judges seem to take into consideration other crimes than those for which Lubanga was convicted: in the Decision on Sentence, the Judges noted other crimes (mainly sexual violence) for which Lubanga was not tried.[58]

It is important to highlight that I do not reject the necessary degree of discretion on the part of the Chamber to consider relevant factors in assessing

---

50 *Lubanga* (n 47), para. 36; *Bemba* (n 49), para. 15.

51 Silvia D'Ascoli, 'The First Decision on Sentence of the International Criminal Court in the Lubanga Case. Great (Unmet) Expectations' in Triestino Mariniello (ed), *The International Criminal Court in Search of its Purpose and Identity* (Routledge 2015) 193, 201.

52 *Bemba* (n 49), paras 15–17.

53 *Katanga* (n 48), para. 35.

54 See eg *Bemba* (n 49), para. 33.

55 *Bemba* (n 49), para. 33.

56 See eg *Bemba* (n 49), paras 34–47.

57 *Katanga* (n 48), para. 35.

58 *Lubanga* (n 47), paras 60–76.

gravity, as recognised by the Judges themselves.[59] But in order to respect the criteria defining the *nulla poena sine lege* principle (especially those of clarity and foreseeability), it is important for the Chamber, on the one hand, to correctly explain the approach used to establish the gravity criterion and, on the other hand, to decide in accordance with the previous case law of the same court. This is not the case in the three decisions issued by the ICC, principally because of the lack of analysis contained in these decisions and the arbitrariness of the Judges. Indeed, these decisions do not provide a satisfactory answer to the questions related to the gravity of crimes and the hierarchy between them.

Absence of Certain Factors

In the *Lubanga* Decision, as well as in the *Bemba* Decision, the Chambers seem to wander between all circumstances without giving any further explanation as to why some of them are taken into account or not and they establish no hierarchy between the circumstances. 'For example, [in the *Lubanga* Decision] the Chamber failed to consider the "forced abductions and pressured recruitment", the "impact of the crimes on the victims", the "abuse of power or official capacity" and the "broader social impact of the crimes"'.[60] The Chamber does not explain why it did not take these circumstances into account. The same applies to the *Bemba* Decision: the Chamber failed to consider the same circumstances for all crimes,[61] and, once again, it seems to consider some criteria concerning the gravity of crimes, or even the criteria defining crimes, as aggravating circumstances as well. For example, in the evaluation of the 'particularly defenceless victims' as aggravating circumstances related to the crime of rape, the Chamber takes into consideration the fact that the victims were unarmed.[62] However, this criterion is in itself an element of the definition of the crime against humanity or war crime. Thus, it seems that some of the same criteria are used twice, both in the definition of crimes and as aggravating circumstances.

Concerning the mitigating circumstances, in the *Lubanga* Decision the Trial Chamber seems to wander in the same way. According to D'Ascoli, the analysis of mitigating circumstances 'appears rather brief, especially when considering all the factors discussed by the Lubanga Defence in its submission concerning sentencing [...] there is no specific motivation or reasoning given to explain the Chamber's findings on the mitigating circumstances submitted by

59 *Bemba* (n 49), para. 15.

60 D'Ascoli (n 51) 207.

61 *Bemba* (n 49), paras 21–58.

62 ibid, para. 43.

the Defence'.[63] Furthermore, the Chamber ignores Lubanga's family situation and his clean criminal record. The *Katanga* and *Bemba* Decisions are more detailed as regards the mitigating circumstances and take all of them into consideration.

These two main elements demonstrate the fact that there is certain arbitrariness in the decisions related to the sentences issued by the Court. In the same vein, it is important to highlight that the weight of each criterion used to determine the sentence is very difficult to understand. D'Ascoli, when examining the *Lubanga* Decision, is left asking 'why a sentence of 14 years' imprisonment [was pronounced against Lubanga]? The reader would expect to find an answer to this question in the relevant part of the Decision addressing the determination of the sentence'.[64] However, 'no specific reasoning is developed for the determination of the sentence'.[65] Indeed, if the Chamber does explain why a sentence of life imprisonment is inappropriate, it does not explain or motivate the sentence (14 years). It 'seems as though the trial chamber has simply pulled the number out of the air'.[66] If this impression of a sentence 'pulled from thin air' could be understood as a sign of the inexperience of the ICC because it was the first sentence it pronounced, the same impression in the *Katanga* and the *Bemba* cases is utterly unacceptable. Unfortunately, the reader has the same impression when he/she reads both of these decisions, too.[67] The most surprising element is the fact that in both decisions, the respective Trial Chambers do not refer (in the part named 'Determination of Sentence') to previous decisions, ie the *Lubanga* Decision for the *Katanga* Decision, and the *Lubanga* and the *Katanga* Decisions for the *Bemba* Decision. Indeed, the quanta of sentence pronounced by the Judges are not compared with the previous pronounced quantum/a. However, the criterion of foreseeability obliges a consistency between all pronounced sentences. In other words, it is necessary to have an ordinal proportionality, as defined by von Hirsch, in order to respect the *nulla poena sine lege* principle. Here, there can be no doubt that the fact that the founding instruments are silent on the quantum for each crime (and give only a fixed term for any crime) implies that the *nulla poena sine lege* principles is not fulfilled.

63 D'Ascoli (n 51) 208–209.

64 ibid 210.

65 ibid.

66 Gideon Boas et al (eds), *International Criminal Law Practitioner Library—Volume III. International Criminal Procedure* (Cambridge University Press 2011) 375, 420–421.

67 *Bemba* (n 49), paras 90–96; *Katanga* (n 48), paras 141–147.

V Executed Sentences and Recourse to Human Rights

The relation between international criminal law and human rights law is also present in the executed sentences. In this area, a recent decision by the President of the Mechanism of the International Criminal Tribunals (MICT) is symptomatic of the use of human rights by international criminal judges and of the lack of respect for the *nulla poena sine lege* principle. This decision was given in the *Galić* case in June 2015.[68]

In the area of early release, settled case law granted release after the execution of two thirds of the sentence of imprisonment, taking into consideration potential rehabilitation, the gravity of the crimes and cooperation with the Prosecutor.[69] Nonetheless, after Galić was condemned to life imprisonment, no one could determine how to calculate two thirds of life imprisonment. Indeed, in the constituent texts of the ICTY (in contrast to the ICC Statute, which states that after 25 years of imprisonment, early release can be requested), there are no plans for such a situation and no case law exists. The disappointing decision of 23 June 2015 was the first of its kind. The President of the MICT had to determine when a person sentenced to life imprisonment could apply for early release. To review the case briefly, Galić was arrested in 1999, sentenced in 2003 to 20 years' imprisonment and, in 2009, by the Appeals Chamber of the ICTY, to life imprisonment. He is currently serving his sentence in Germany. The decision of 23 June was not justified, so it was accompanied by a decision explaining the reasons for the refusal of early release.[70]

In his explanation, the President of the MICT began by dismissing in a single sentence the question of the application of German law, which allows early release of a person sentenced to life after 15 years of imprisonment. Even if the jurisprudence of this MICT decision is justified, I remain confident that, according to the constituent texts of ICTs and principles of criminal law (especially equal treatment and legal certainty), this ruling is dubious. Furthermore, the President went on to accept the principle that persons sentenced to life imprisonment were entitled to early release. He justified this conclusion based

68 *Prosecutor v Galić*, MICT-14-83.ES, Reasons for the President's Decision to Deny the early Release of Stanislav Galić and Decision on Prosecution Motion, Presidency, 23 June 2015.

69 See eg *Prosecutor v Nikolić*, MICT-14-65-ES, Public redacted version of the 14 March 2014 Decision on early release, Request for early release Momir Nikolić, President, 12 October 2015; *Prosecutor v Zelenović*, MICT-15-89-ES, Public Redacted Version of the 28 August 2015, Decision of the President on the early Release of Dragan Zelenović, President, 15 September 2015.

70 *Galić* (n 68).

on the principle of individualisation of punishment as well as international standards.[71]

In accordance with this decision, the President set the deadline for a request for early release. The Prosecutor offered to translate the sentence of life imprisonment into time corresponding to the maximum sentence imposed by an international or internationalised criminal court—the proposed term was the sentence Charles Taylor's sentence by the Special Court for Sierra Leone: 52 years.[72] The President rejected this interpretation. After making an inventory of international (human rights) law, it was concluded that there was no international consensus about a potential early release or review of the prison sentence after a delay despite the ICC Statute and a relatively stable jurisprudence of the ECtHR. Indeed, Article 110 of the Rome Statute provides that 'when the person has served two thirds of the sentence, or 25 years in the case of life imprisonment, the Court shall review the sentence to determine whether it should be reduced'. Moreover, the ECtHR has accepted, for a long time, the fact that after 25 years of imprisonment, there is an obligation to review the sentence.[73]

Nevertheless, in order to reject this apparent consensus of international law in the area of early release, the President of the MICT based his reasoning solely on a recent reversal appearing before the ECtHR (which must be confirmed): the *Bodein v France* case. In the latter, the Strasbourg Court had accepted a period longer than 25 years to review a sentence of life imprisonment. However, in citing this case law, the President of the MICT seems to have forgotten that the ECtHR decision was based on a French national law that applied in the *Bodein* case, while in the same decision he rejected the German national law. Thus, to refuse the early release of Mr Galić, the President of the MICT did indeed use human rights law—but his decision relied on only a single decision (one yet to be confirmed) and ran contrary to general human rights law.

After that, the President of the MICT returned to the Prosecutor's proposal but based only on the most significant sentence imposed, at that time, by the ICTY, namely 45 years.[74] He concluded that a person sentenced to life imprisonment was eligible for early release after two thirds of 45 years, ie 30 years of imprisonment. This demonstration is regrettable for several reasons: firstly, the reasoning seems to meet neither the criteria underpinning the legality principle nor the test of legitimacy. Indeed, the principle of legality (as defined by the

---

71 ibid paras 20–25.

72 ibid para 26; *Cantoni v France* (n 14), para. 35.

73 *Vinter and others v United Kingdom*, App no 66069/09, 130/10, 3896/10 (ECtHR, 9 July 2013).

74 ibid para. 35.

ECtHR as seen previously) is not respected by this conclusion. International human rights law (as well as international criminal law as stated by the ICC Statute) has clearly indicated that after 25 years a condemned individual has the right to review his sentence. Moreover, the case law of the ICTY and the MICT has clearly accepted early release after execution of two thirds of the sentence. Secondly, legal certainty in this case seems difficult to achieve. Indeed, what would happen if the ICTY and the ICTR had to sentence a person to 60 years in prison? Would the deadline for early release then be after 40 years? This example could be viewed as unrealistic, but in December 2015, the Appeals Chamber of ICTR passed a sentence of 47 years of imprisonment.[75] In this case, what will happen with this period of 30 years? If the reasoning of the President of the MICT is to be followed, the two-thirds period has to be identified as more than 31 years.

The purpose here seems to be to legitimise the decision the President would like to achieve rather than to respect human rights law.

VI Conclusion

Reference to international human rights law is a frequent occurrence in international criminal jurisdictions. In many cases, the reference and influence are made in order to ensure the respect of the rights of accused.[76] At the same time, influence and references to international human rights law do not necessarily imply respect for this law, as has been analysed here with a focus on the *nulla poena sine lege* principle and concerning the penalties pronounced or executed by international criminal tribunals and courts. Van der Wilt has stated that 'the dramatic challenges of the *nullum crimen* principle will soon extinguish in view of the codification of international criminal law, developments in customary international law and erratic implementation of international standards in domestic legislation will compel courts to face the foreseeability question'.[77] Concerning the question of the *nulla poena* principle, however, the foreseeability test has not yet been fulfilled—due to many elements that I have developed

75 *Prosecutor v Nyiramasuhuko*, ICTR-98-42-A, Judgment, Appeals Chamber, 14 December 2015, Disposition.

76 Triestino Mariniello and Paolo Lobba, 'The Cross-fertilisation Rhetoric in Question: Use and Abuse of the European Court's Jurisprudence by ICTs' (2015) 84 Nordic Journal of International Law 363.

77 Harmen van der Wilt, 'Nullum Crimen and International Criminal Law: The Relevance of the Foreseeability Test' (2015) 84 Nordic Journal of International Law 519.

in this paper: a single penalty for all crimes, an erratic evaluation of (mitigating or aggravating) circumstances and the fact that the case law concerning early release was overturned. It seems that the codification of international law will not yet extinguish dramatic challenges to the principle.

CHAPTER 8

Critical Remarks on the *Accessibility/Foreseeability* Standard as Applied in International Criminal Justice

Giulio Vanacore

1 Introduction

How far does the principle of legality in supranational criminal law go? Initially, this principle fulfilled the function of protecting an individual from punishment for a crime that was not provided for by criminal law.[1] Due to the overwhelming case law of the European Court of Human Rights, the principle has, however, undergone somewhat of a metamorphosis.[2] Today, legality also means that persons can be criminally sanctioned when they understand the scope of a criminal provision, they consciously breach it and they *foresee* the consequences of such breach. In this case, even an unwritten provision must be clear and sufficiently accessible. It must also be in force before the act is committed and the consequence of its breach must be *foreseeable*.

The partial metamorphosis of the principle of legality was not, however, entirely automatic.

As will be discussed below, the International Criminal Court has also adopted this broader interpretation. It was eloquently explained by Judge van den Wyngaert in her concurring opinion in the *Ngudjolo* judgment.[3] She was

1 See for example Article 22 (*Nullum crimen sine lege*), Article 23 (*Nulla poena sine lege*) and Article 24 (Non-retroactivity *ratione personae*) of the Rome Statute.

2 See eg *Achour v France*, App no 67335/01 (ECtHR, 29 March 2006), para. 41; *Kononov v Latvia*, App no 36376/04 (ECtHR, 17 May 2010), para. 185; *Korbely v Hungary*, App no 9174/02 (ECtHR, 19 September 2008), para. 71. The starting point of the ECtHR case law is Article 7 of the ECHR, which reads as follows: '1 No one shall be held guilty of any criminal offence on account of any act or omission which did not constitute a criminal offence under national or international law at the time when it was committed. Nor shall a heavier penalty be imposed than the one that was applicable at the time the criminal offence was committed. 2 This Article shall not prejudice the trial and punishment of any person for any act or omission which, at the time when it was committed, was criminal according to the general principles of law recognised by civilised nations'.

3 *Prosecutor v Ngudjolo*, ICC-01/04-02/12, Judgment pursuant to Article 74 of the Statute, Con-

 | DOI: 10.1163/9789004313750_010

commenting on the potential reception of Klaus Roxin's theory on *control over the crime* (*Tatherrshaft*) into Article 25(3)(a) of the ICC Statute. In particular, Judge van den Wyngaert discussed the extent to which national *Dogmatik*[4] could be used to disentangle the interpretative problems of co-perpetration and indirect perpetration. Despite providing practical ways to fill interpretational gaps within the Rome Statute, the problem with using concepts from legal systems, which are foreign to those of the defendant, is that it raises questions as to the defendant's *awareness of the criminal illicitness of his actions*. A solution, put forward in the conclusion to this paper, may be to encourage theoretical studies that develop a truly international criminal *Dogmatik*, and which would provide interpretative tools to ICC judges intent on remedying existing voids within the Statute.

II A *Dogmatik* Alternative for Accessibility and Foreseeability: Culpability

According to the ECtHR case law, the principle of legality is breached if a criminal provision is neither sufficiently accessible to the defendant, nor the consequence of its breach foreseeable. Such reasoning, however, is not always immediately acceptable. Many legal systems, including the Italian one, consider unawareness of criminal law to fall within the scope of culpability.[5] More

curring Opinion of Judge Christine Van den Wyngaert ('Concurring opinion'), Trial Chamber II, 18 December 2012, para. 20.

4 This paper reflects a marked preference for keeping the word *'Dogmatik'*, without trying to translate it. Fletcher made the same choice in George Fletcher, 'The Theory of Criminal Liability and International Criminal Law' (2012) 10 Journal of International Criminal Justice 1030.

5 Obviously one could counter that there is a conceptual difference between the ECtHR's *foreseeability* and the traditional Continental Law concept of *knowledge* or *knowability* of a criminal provisions, as one of the parameters to assess the *Dogmatik* category of *culpability* in the structure of crime (see *infra* in the text). The former concept could be said to include the latter. Part of what can be foreseen could be outside of the scope of real knowledge or potential knowability. Instead, what is known or can be known is certainly inside the scope of foreseeability. In other terms, what can be known can also be predicted, while the opposite is not always true. The concept of foreseeability can thus be imagined as a circle which encompasses a smaller circle, namely that of knowability. This way of reasoning leads to a fundamental conclusion: the ECtHR has strengthened the guarantees of those who violate criminal law. Indeed, if *foreseeability*, which falls within the *new* concept of *legality*, is something bigger than the traditional *knowability*, which falls within the traditional

precisely, ignorance of the law, which is justified only if it is inevitable, is a ground for excluding culpability.[6] One of the latest legal conundrums for the Italian legal system was whether foreigners, and in particular people from Arab or gypsy communities, should be excused for committing crimes which were not punishable in their original culture and legal systems. Such crimes were sometimes very serious—for instance, beating relatives, sending children out to beg or subjecting women to sexual mutilation. In Italy, lawyers refer to *cultural excuses*. They have tried, unsuccessfully, to place these situations in different theoretical (or *Dogmatik*) categories known as: typical justification (like the exercise of right[7]), non-typical justification or atypical excuse. Case law has so far excluded all these theoretical proposals: culpability has to step in, even in these cases, since it cannot be said that foreigners' ignorance of Italian law is unavoidable. At best, judges have adjusted sentences downward either by recognising mitigating circumstances or by referring to the criteria for the right range of punishment.[8]

Continental law *Dogmatik* category of *culpability*, then the principle of legality is more often breached than the negation of culpability recognised. Nevertheless, even if these thoughts are acceptable, the discourse articulated in the text does not seem to lose its rationale.

6 See in this regard the historical judgment of the Italian *Corte Costituzionale* (no 364/1988) which reinterpreted Article 5 of the Italian Criminal Code. The principle *ignorantia legis non excusat*, envisaged in that Article, was interpreted and perceived as *relative*. The Italian judges held that ignorance of the law excludes culpability when it appears *unavoidable*, and as such *excusable*. Two decisions of the *Corte Costituzionale* followed in the same vein: no 1085/1988 and no 322/2007. The linchpin of this innovative approach was a novel interpretation of Article 27 of the Italian Constitution, which provides for the principle of culpability and qualifies criminal responsibility as 'personal'. Since 1988, culpability has meant responsibility for a *culpable* act, ie only for an act undertaken at least with negligence (*culpa*), with the exclusion of both excusable conduct (like the ones engaged in with an unavoidable ignorance of the law) and strict liability results. On the classical debate on the distinction between *objective unlawfulness* and *subjective culpability*, see Edmund Mezger, 'Die subjektiven Unrechtselemente' (1924) 89 Der Gerichtssaal 207; more recently Hans Achenbach, *Historische und dogmatische Grundlagen des strafrechtssystematischen Schuldlehre* (J. Schweitzer 1974) 24.

7 Article 51 of the Italian Criminal Code 'Exercise of a Right and Fulfilment of a Duty'.

8 See in this regard the decision of the Italian *Corte di Cassazione*: 16 December 2008 no 46300 (concerning the case of an immigrant abusing his relatives, pursuant to his original *cultural norm* which would justify the use of force by husbands and fathers against wives and sons); 17 December 2009, no 48272; 5 July 2011, no 26153 (holding that the *pater familias* figure is anachronistic and violates the principle of equality between spouses); 24 November 2011, no 43646 (pursuant to which non-therapeutic circumcision must be justified by reference to a legal provision, lest it be considered an offence: if practiced by a non-professional physician it

What is crucial for the purposes of this analysis is that these *foreigner cases* would probably not be treated by the ECtHR in terms of culpability (or justification) but would, in all likelihood, be analysed in terms of legality. This is something conceptually new and, above all, quite distinct.[9] Legality is indeed a concept, which relates to the provision in question, the system and its correctness in terms of values. Culpability, on the other hand, considers the relationship between the person and the facts, and is linked to social blameworthiness and stigmatisation.[10] It also assumes that the legality of the relevant provision has been confirmed from the outset.

Not every criminal system is ready to recognise a breach of legality when a law is not sufficiently accessible and the consequences of breaking it are not foreseeable. Many systems have other *Dogmatik* solutions to these issues, starting with culpability.[11]

---

constitutes the crime of 'Improper and Unauthorised Practice' under Article 348 of the Italian Criminal Code).

9 The reference here is to the *Dogmatik* category of culpability, entrenched in the concept of blameworthiness. Following the Continental *theory of crime*, a crime can fall into two main categories: unlawfulness (*Unrecht* in German, *illiceità* in Italian, *ilicitud* in Spanish) or culpability (*Schuld* in German, *colpevolezza* in Italian, *culpabilidad* in Spanish).

10 Hereafter we will refer to a *normative* idea of culpability (or culpability *in a general sense*). A concept of the culpability category which is linked not only to *mens rea*, ie which has a *normative* connotation, not just a *psychological* one (the last being also called culpability *in a special sense*), was firstly developed in Germany by Reinhard Frank, *Das Strafgesetzbuch für das Deutsche Reich* (1st edn, Hirschfeld 1897) 73. According to Frank, the category of culpability in itself would no longer be a mere box in which to include *mens rea*, ie intention and negligence (giving rise to a merely psychological vision of culpability, or culpability in a special sense). Following Frank's theory, the function of culpability is not simply that of expressing an intentional or negligent link between the perpetrator and the act; rather, it is a complex category, comprehensive of all those elements which admit social blame for the act. These elements for the German author are: 1) soundness of mind or mental capacity (ie *capacitas culpae*: *Zurechnungsfähigkeit* in German, *imputabilità* in Italian, *imputabilidad* in Spanish), 2) knowability of the fact's illicitness, 3) intention or negligence and 4) all those exceptional circumstances or abnormal motivations accompanying the agent's behaviour which preclude his blameworthiness by the legal system in question. *See* Reinhard Frank, 'Über den Aufbau des Schuldbegriffs' in Reinhard Frank (ed), *Festschrift für die juristische Fakultät in Gießen* (A. Töpelmann 1907) 530.

11 In traditional Common Law theory there is no space for a distinction between the *Dogmatik* categories of unlawfulness and culpability. As a result, no difference is drawn between the grounds for excluding unlawfulness (justifications) and those excluding culpability (excuses). Any circumstances which prompt a not-guilty verdict fall within the general category of *defences*. Defences have a manifest procedural origin. Mistakes of law

III From *Dogmatik* to Principles: No Culpability within the Convention

Moving from *Dogmatik*-based reasoning to principles-based thinking, the principle of culpability is undoubtedly connected to that of legality. The principle of culpability presupposes a personal mental link between agent and action.[12] This principle would, however, be an empty shell without the concept of strict legality: people can only be considered criminally liable when there are provisions criminalising their behaviour, and such provisions are made sufficiently available. This acknowledged link between legality and culpability does not imply that the latter is always an obvious and implicit corollary of the former, as is illustrated by absolute liability offences in legality-obeying systems.

The ECtHR, for its part, does not seem to have fully appraised the culpability principle in its case law, while it has overburdened legality by including all cases of foreseeability within its realm.[13] The Strasbourg Court rarely recognises the principle of culpability, even in cases where a thorough discussion on culpability as a fair and fully liberal guarantee in attributing criminal liability would be necessary. This is partly because there is no provision within the Convention on the necessary personal and mental link in criminal law. It could also be a consequence of the probable rejection of *Dogmatik*-based reasoning by Strasbourg judges. Sometimes the principle of culpability has been mentioned as a procedural tool to distribute the burden of proof, to preserve presumption of innocence in criminal trials and thus to interpret Article 6(2) of the ECHR. However, denial of the principle's full relevance and legitimacy is proven by those judgments in which the Court is inclined to recognise *strict liability* as a valid form of imputation in criminal law.[14] Strict

---

are mere defences, having a general exculpatory effect. See, for a historical reconstruction of justifications and excuses in the Common Law tradition, John C. Smith, *Justification and Excuse in the Criminal Law* (Stevens & Sons 1989) 7. See also, for a comparative perspective, Francesco Viganò, *Stato di necessità e conflitti di doveri* (Giuffrè 2000) 161. In any event, what is relevant for the purpose of this chapter is that Common Law, as well as Continental Law, does not consider ignorance of the law to be a matter to be dealt with under the legality umbrella.

12 Thomas Weigend, 'Subjective Elements of Criminal Liability' in Markus D. Dubber and Tatjana Hörnle (eds), *The Oxford Handbook of Criminal Law* (OUP 2014) [490], 490–492.

13 Giuseppina Panebianco, 'The *Nulla Poena sine Culpa* Principle in European Courts Case Law' in Stefano Ruggeri (ed), Human Rights in European Criminal Law (Springer 2015) 53.

14 See *Salabiaku v France*, App no 10519/83 (ECtHR, 7 October 1988), para. 27; in a similar vein, *Västberga Taxi Aktiebolag and Vulic* v *Sweden*, App no 36985/97 (ECtHR, 23 July 2002), para. 112; *Janosevic v Sweden*, App no 34619/97 (ECtHR, 23 July 2002), para. 100.

liability falls outside the scope of the principle of culpability, at least as far as a broad, modern and liberal interpretation is concerned. Strict liability entails only objective imputation: a causal link between an action and its outcome is sufficient. No subjective link between a person's mind and actions is needed. By holding that the UK's 2003 Sexual Offences Act was compatible with the Convention, the ECtHR confirmed its rejection of the culpability principle, and recognised strict liability as legitimate. It deemed that, in cases of sexual violence, a defendant's ignorance of the victim's age was entirely irrelevant. The case before the ECtHR concerned the criminal conviction of a 15-year-old boy who had claimed before the British courts that he was excusably unaware of the victim's real age when he had a consensual sexual relationship with her. The victim, a 12-year-old girl, repeatedly told the accused that she was 15. The ECtHR upheld this peculiar case of strict liability and maintained that, between the State's right to safeguard the normal sexual growth of minors under 13 and the right to the accused's full defence, the first had to prevail.[15]

IV Accessibility and Foreseeability outside the Convention and inside International Criminal Justice

The notions of accessibility and foreseeability as pillars of the legality principle have also been used outside the ECtHR, before international criminal jurisdictions, such as *ad hoc* tribunals and the ICC. This is a classic example of *legal fertilisation* between international jurisdictions.[16]

15 See *G v United Kingdom*, App no 37334/08 (ECtHR, 30 August 2011). For a completely opposite view on the same issue (ie the mistaken age of the victim in consensual but still criminal sexual practice), cf Italian Constitutional Court, judgment no 322/2007 (n 6), www.giurcost.org/decisioni/2007/0322s-07.html accessed 28 February 2016. The Italian Constitutional Court refused to impute the agent's objective non-awareness of the victim's age. The principle of culpability dictates that no criminal liability can be imposed in the case of an excusable (ie inevitable) mistake of either fact or law. For strict liability offences within English, U.S. and French criminal legal systems, see Weigend (n 12) 491–492.

16 For a critical analysis of the relationship between international criminal law as applied by international criminal jurisdictions and ECtHR, see William A. Schabas, 'Synergy or Fragmentation?' (2011) 9 Journal of International Criminal Justice 613, who argue that the result of this *cross-fertilisation* dialogue may well be described as synergy, rather than as fragmentation (ibid 632).

In its Decision on Joint Challenge to Jurisdiction in *Hadžihasanović*, the Trial Chamber II of the ICTY had to decide whether the doctrine of superior responsibility in internal armed conflict violated the *nullum crimen sine lege* principle.[17] In order to do so, the Chamber strongly relied on some passages of the ECtHR spousal rape case[18] to maintain that the term *law* in Article 7 of the European Convention 'implies qualitative requirements, notably those of accessibility and foreseeability' according to which 'Article 7 cannot be read as outlawing the gradual clarification of the rules of criminal liability through judicial interpretation'.[19] In justifying the legality of the superior responsibility mode of liability in internal armed conflict, the Chamber also added that 'in interpreting the principle of *nullum crimen sine lege*, it is critical to determine whether the underlying conduct at the time of its commission was punishable' and 'in order to meet the principle of *nullum crimen sine lege*, it must only be foreseeable and accessible to a possible perpetrator that his concrete conduct was punishable at the time of commission'.[20]

However, not all international criminal decisions accept that an assessment of legality includes an examination as to whether the accused was aware of the illicitness of his acts.[21] Many decisions, particularly those handed down from the ICC, include a reformulation of the defence's claims in order to maintain that awareness of a conduct's illicitness is not a matter that relates to legality, but rather to *mistake of law*.[22] This policy resembles the Romano-Germanic approach to culpability rather than the ECtHR's extended vision of legality.

17 *Prosecutor v Hadžihasanović*, IT-01-47-PT, Decision on Joint Challenge to Jurisdiction, Trial Chamber II, 12 November 2002.

18 *SW v United Kingdom*, App no 20166/92 (ECtHR, 22 November 1995), para. 44, referring to 'a reasonably foreseeable development of the law' (ibid para. 43).

19 ibid paras 35–36.

20 *Hadžihasanović* (n 17), para. 62. The Trial Chamber there also stated that 'the emphasis on conduct, rather than on the specific description of the offence in substantive criminal law, is of primary importance'.

21 For example, *Prosecutor v Lubanga*, ICC-01/04-01/06, Decision on Confirmation of Charges, Pre-Trial Chamber I, 29 January 2007, paras 302–316. A thorough commentary on the decision is made by Thomas Weigend, 'Intent, Mistake of Law and Co-perpetration in the *Lubanga* Decision on Confirmation of Charges' (2008) 6 Journal of International Criminal Justice 471.

22 Weigend (n 21) 475. On statutory regulation of mistake of law, Albin Eser, 'Mental Element—Mistake of Fact and Mistake of Law' in Antonio Cassese, Paola Gaeta and John

In *Lubanga*, the defence argued that the defendant could not have known of the prohibition on enlisting children in 2002 because both the Democratic Republic of Congo and Uganda had failed to transpose the relevant articles of the ICC Statute into national law, and thus had not made them accessible to the population.[23] The Pre-Trial Chamber rejected this argument by holding that:

> [t]he terms enlisting, conscripting and using children under the age of fifteen years to participate actively in hostilities are defined with sufficient particularity in [...] the Rome Statute and the Elements of Crime, which entered into force on 1 July 2002, as entailing criminal responsibility and punishable as criminal offences.[24]

Therefore

> [t]here is no infringement of the principle of legality if the Chamber exercises its power to decide whether Thomas Lubanga Dyilo ought to be committed for trial on the basis of written (*lex scripta*) pre-existing criminal norms approved by the States Parties to the Rome Statute (*lex praevia*), defining prohibited conduct and setting out the related sentence (*lex certa*), which cannot be interpreted by analogy in malam partem (*lex stricta*).[25]

Rather surprisingly, the Pre-Trial Chamber did not cite the ECtHR's case law at all, contrary to the decisions of previous international criminal jurisdictions. The judges in *Lubanga* maintained that 'the Defence is not relying on the principle of legality, but on the possibility of excluding criminal responsibility on account of a *mistake of the law in force*'.[26] Since, however, the first sentence of Article 32(2) of the ICC Statute provides that '[a] mistake of law as to whether a particular type of conduct is a crime within the jurisdiction of the Court shall not be a ground for excluding criminal responsibility', *ignorantia legis* cannot be excused in the realm of the ICC and thus the arguments of the defence were dismissed.[27]

R.W.D. Jones (eds), *The Rome Statute of the International Criminal Court: A Commentary* (OUP 2002) vol 1 889, 941.

23 Weigend (n 21) 474.

24 *Lubanga* (n 21), para. 302.

25 ibid para. 303.

26 ibid para. 301.

27 ibid paras 306, 312–314. Moreover the specific mistake by *Lubanga* cannot be characterised

V Foreseeability and Mistake of Law within the ICC Statute. A Likely Solution from *Cross-fertilisation*

As a result, framing cases of non-foreseeability as mistakes of law implies denying their relevance from the outset in the realm of the ICC Statute, in keeping with the stark wording of the first sentence of Article 32(2). Within the ICC Statute, there is indeed *no* scope to consider avoidable mistakes of law. While, as seen above, a full theorisation of the culpability principle before the ECtHR can help to deny conventional legitimacy to criminal offences imputed without *mens rea*,[28] the situation is slightly different under the ICC Statute. A viable and immediate solution to preventing strict liability in cases of excusable ignorance before the ICC could be to consider *accessibility/foreseeability* as a standard which envisages a stable link between an individual's conduct and the provision criminalising it and as a tool to ascertain infringements of the legality principle.

What is really important is that liberal values and main guarantees are fully respected before the ICC, as in every criminal legal system. These bedrock values include one of fundamental importance: the need for a stable personal and mental link between a perpetrator's actions and the behaviour that is criminalised by law. In the ICC Statute, the drafters of Article 30 on *mens rea* were careful not to leave any margin for liability without intent and knowledge. However, strict liability, which seemed to have been evicted through the front door of Article 30, could return through the back door by means of the first sentence of Article 32(2).

Objective forms of liability are indeed not only those imputations of material results covered by neither intention nor negligence, but also those which do not take into account a perpetrator's subjective ability to foresee a fact's wrongfulness. The wording of Article 32 in this regard leaves no room for doubt: *ignorantia legis* can never be excused as far as direct mistakes of law are concerned. There is no excusability founded on unavoidability before the ICC.

Article 32 resembles Article 5 of the Italian Criminal Code, which was interpreted in an uncompromising manner, such as the ICC provision, before the

as a mistake on a *normative element* as such falling under the second sentence of Article 32(2) and relevant only when it excludes the *mens rea*. See *Lubanga*, ibid para. 316; as well as Weigend's insightful remarks thereon (n 21) 475–476.

28 See above, Section III on the absence of the culpability principle within the Convention and ECtHR case law cited therein.

Italian Constitutional Court in 1988.[29] The problem for the ICC is that no constitutional court is available to declare the deviation from the culpable standard of Article 32 on mistake of law. From the perspective of a Continental criminal law scholar, accustomed to *Dogmatik*, it can be said that the Statute explicitly acknowledges a *restricted*, merely psychological, version of the culpability category (or culpability in a special sense) but not a *general* and normative vision of it.[30] This vision is extremely important to avoid all cases of strict liability since it has the merit of expanding culpability beyond *mens rea* to include, among other elements, *knowability of a fact's illicitness*.

There are two viable solutions in order to fill this gap in the ICC Statute. The first is to amend Article 32 in order to include the possibility of excusable mistakes and the concept of unavoidability. The second more pragmatic option is to use the ECtHR foreseeability standard as the key to firmly establishing a necessary personal link between the individual and the criminal provision. This solution would be a typical case of positive cross-fertilisation between the ECtHR and the ICC.

This second interpretative course was not, however, taken into consideration by the Pre-Trial Chamber in the *Lubanga* decision. Resorting to foreseeability as a parameter to evaluate legality would cover the shortages of the ICC Statute as regards the culpability principle and the *Dogmatik* category of normative culpability. The *foreseeability meter*, as used by the ECtHR, represents *rebus sic stantibus* a forced solution given the strict wording of Article 32. The probable key to allowing for this cross-fertilisation may be Article 21(1)(b), on applicable sources of law, which provides: '[t]he Court shall apply … (b) [i]n the second place, where appropriate, applicable treaties and the principles and rules of international law', read together with Article 21(3), which states that '[t]he application and interpretation of law pursuant to this article must be consistent with internationally recognized human rights'. Foreseeability, as a ground to evaluate the legitimacy of attributing criminal liability, may be seen as a *principle of international law* and, at the same time, as a fundamental *internationally recognised human right*. In this regard, fundamental achievements in criminal law matters by the ECtHR case law could be taken as *appropriate* and *applicable* interpretations of a relevant international treaty (the Convention). If one excludes this possibility, there is no other normative tool in the Statute which would prevent strict liability with regard to ignorance of the law.

---

29 Italian *Corte Costituzionale*, judgment no 364/1988 (n 6).

30 See above (n 10) for an explanation on the *normative* concept of culpability (or culpability *in a general sense*).

Not accepting the use of foreseeability to overcome the severity of Article 32, it may well be argued that the substantive rights of those accused before the ICC are less safeguarded, in terms of legality of statutory criminal provisions, than those guaranteed to applicants before the ECtHR and concerning legitimacy of national criminal provisions. This is a serious risk if one believes that the accused's rights—in this case regarding pillar principles of criminal law such as legality and culpability—should be standardised to the fullest possible degree, and above all for international trials.

VI Accessibility and Foreseeability even for the Criminal Provisions under the *General Part* (and Their Interpretation)?

Another issue worthy of analysis is whether the concepts of accessibility and foreseeability only apply to provisions describing criminal conduct or whether the ECtHR's concept of legality can go even further and apply to the so-called *general part* of a criminal statute. A *general part* is composed of the complex provisions relating to the rules, principles and single elements that are common to every crime or offence. This includes, for instance, provisions on *mens rea*, the grounds for excluding responsibility, complicity, rules of causality and omission, and the articulated forms of co-authorship. Looking at the ICC Statute, the *general part* includes Articles from 22 to 33.

Is it correct to affirm that even those general provisions should be covered by accessibility and foreseeability? Is it necessary, for example, for the provision on *mens rea* to be accessible to the accused, and the consequences of its breach *foreseeable*? Moreover, does the *interpretation* of such general provisions have to fulfil ECtHR legal requirements to be considered applicable in a case?

When the criminal trial is set in motion—not at a national level but at an international level, as is the case for ICC proceedings—the issue is far more complex. At a national level, it is rare for a provision to be deemed inaccessible given that it is generally part of the national legal system of the accused. Hence there is a presumption that the accused knew—or at least should have known—of the existence of the provision. However, in international proceedings, the same presumption is not as easy to embrace, since the accused could be catapulted before an international criminal jurisdiction without previously knowing all its legal peculiarities.

Crimes heard before the ICC are the most heinous and brutal acts that any person from any part of the world can commit (see for example, Articles 6–8 of the ICC Statute). But can the same be said about the provisions falling under the *general part* of the Statute? For instance, can one say with absolute certainty that the Court's interpretation of Article 25(3)(a),[31] which has been applied in several decisions and which is based on the German criterion of 'control over the crime' (*Tatherrschaft*) and 'control over the organisation' (*Organisationsherrshaft*),[32] is a general provision that is sufficiently accessible to people from, say, African countries?

The problem was recently raised by Judge van den Wyngaert in her concurring opinion attached to the *Ngudjolo Chui* judgment before the ICC.[33] The question she posed was not whether Article 25(3)(a) *alone* was sufficiently accessible and foreseeable for the accused, but, rather, whether the Court's prevailing *interpretation* of that Article was sufficiently accessible for the accused to predict the criminal consequences of its breach. The Judge's short but illuminating contribution to the issue was the following:

> Individuals must have been in a position to know at the time of engaging in certain conduct that the law criminalized it. The Grand Chamber of the European Court of Human Rights has given considerable weight to the elements of 'accessibility' and 'foreseeability' in its assessment of the legality principle. I doubt whether anyone (inside or outside the DRC) could have known, prior to the Pre-Trial Chamber's first interpretations of

31 Article 25(3)(a) of the ICC Statute reads as follows: 'In accordance with this Statute, a person shall be criminally responsible and liable for punishment for a crime within the jurisdiction of the Court if that person: (a) Commits such a crime, whether as an individual, *jointly with another* or *through another person*, regardless of whether that other person is criminally responsible' (emphasis added). These modes of liability have been interpreted with the aid of Roxin's theory of 'control over the crime' and 'control over the organisation'.

32 On this, among others, see *Prosecutor v Katanga*, ICC-01/04-01/07-717, Decisions on the Confirmation of Charges, Pre-Trial Chamber I, 30 September 2008, para. 480; *Prosecutor v Lubanga*, ICC-01/04-01/06-803-tEN, Decision on the Confirmation of Charges, Pre-Trial Chamber, 29 January 2007, paras 326–341; *Prosecutor v Ruto*, ICC-01/09-01/11-373, Decision on the Confirmation of Charges Pursuant to Article 61(7)(a) and (b) of the Rome Statute, Pre-Trial Chamber II, 23 January 2012, paras 291–292; *Prosecutor v Muthaura*, ICC-01/09-02/11-382-Red, Decision on the Confirmation of Charges Pursuant to Article 61(7)(a) and (b) of the Rome Statute, Pre-Trial Chamber II, 23 January 2012, para. 296; *Prosecutor v Banda and Jerbo*, ICC-02/05-03/09-121-Conf-Corr, Corrigendum of the Decision on the Confirmation of Charges, Pre-Trial Chamber I, 7 March 2011, para. 126; *Prosecutor v Bemba*, ICC-01/05-01/08-424, Decision Pursuant to Article 61(7)(a) and (b) of the Rome Statute on the Charges of the Prosecutor Against Jean-Pierre Bemba Gombo, Pre-Trial Chamber II, 15 June 2009, para. 348.

33 Concurring Opinion (n 3).

Article 25(3)(a), that this article contained such an elaborate and peculiar form of criminal responsibility as the theory of 'indirect co-perpetration', much less that it rests upon the 'control over the crime' doctrine.[34]

VII A Role for Criminal *Dogmatik* in International Criminal Law?

As a result of the ICC case law there is no longer a relationship between legality, foreseeability and a *criminal provision*—now it is between legality, foreseeability and what German jurists would call criminal *Dogmatik*. Can *Dogmatik* help the international criminal judge interpret international criminal provisions? Can *Dogmatik* fill the gaps in an international criminal statute? If the answer is yes, what kind of *Dogmatik* can be used to establish accountability for international crimes? In particular, is it appropriate to base the interpretation of a fundamental provision such as Article 25 of the ICC Statute upon a theory which comes from just one legal system, namely the German one?

These questions are even more complex in the light of the fact that all the defendants before the ICC have so far been nationals of African States, hence people belonging, in the main, to Common law, French law or the Arab law traditions. Basing accountability of these accused upon Roxin's theory of *control over the crime* (*Tatherrshaft*),[35] and its variant of *control over an organisation* (*Organisationsherrshaft*),[36] is problematic from the point of view of accessibility to this German doctrine and the *foreseeability* of its effects on the outcome of the proceedings before the Court, as well as the possible punishment to be imposed. In other words, can accused people from legal systems which do not belong to the German tradition fully accede to Roxin's theory, as applied by the Chambers in The Hague, in order to understand when they would be considered co-authors (or perpetrators through another person) in a likely trial before the Court? It is true that German criminal theory has been

34 ibid para. 20.

35 Klaus Roxin, *Täterschaft und Tatherrschaft* (Walter de Gruyter 1963).

36 On the application of Roxin's theory before the Court, see Thomas Weigend, 'Perpetration through an Organization: The Unexpected Career of a German Legal Concept' (2011) 9 Journal of International Criminal Justice 91; Stefano Manacorda and Chantal Meloni, 'Indirect Perpetration *versus* Joint Criminal Enterprise: Concurring Approaches in the Practice of International Criminal Law?' (2011) 9 Journal of International Criminal Justice 159; Florian Jeßberger and Julia Geneuss, 'On the Application of a Theory of Indirect Perpetration in *Al Bashir*: German Doctrine at The Hague?' (2008) 6 Journal of International Criminal Justice 853.

largely welcomed in Spanish-speaking legal systems and has been introduced in many criminal statutes in Latin American countries. The *Fujimori* judgment in Peru could indeed be seen as a paradigm of Roxin theory application outside Germany.[37] However, it is also true that it is difficult to find traces of this theory in African countries. African legal systems have English, French, or Arab criminal law roots, mainly as a result of colonialism.

Again, this is not an issue of *knowing* of a relevant criminal provision, for example, on genocide. Nor is it an issue of accessibility to a statutory *general part* provision, as Article 25(3)(a) would be. Here, what is at stake is accessibility to the interpretation of that Article according to a theory that is fully recognised by just one legal system—and its Spanish-speaking affiliates.

Judge van den Wyngaert tried to justify an alternative interpretation of Article 25(3)(a), in a way that was different from the German one. It was much more linked, in her opinion, to the text of the Statute, and maintained the principles of accessibility and foreseeability by the accused, who may have not known anything about German legal theory.

A discussion on the merits of this alternative path of co-authorship falls outside the scope of this paper. However, one may want to reflect on what would have happened if a strict reading of the statutory provisions had not been a convenient way out of the legal storm. In other words, again, can *Dogmatik* coming from the outside step in when the provisions do not offer alternative means of interpretation?

It is disputed whether generally recognised theoretical foundations exist in international criminal law. Looking merely at the story of joint criminal enterprise, the likely answer is no. So far, no common and widely accepted form has been established to base accountability on the case of multi-person liability;[38] there is also no shared view on the way—or indeed the need—to differentiate between commission and participation, a perpetrator from a mere participant in a crime. *Dogmatik* can undoubtedly help in resolving complex issues, particularly when Statutes are silent.

---

37 In this regard, see Kai Ambos, 'The *Fujimori* Judgment: A President's Responsibility for Crimes Against Humanity as Indirect Perpetrator by Virtue of an Organized Power Apparatus' (2011) 9 Journal of International Criminal Justice 137; Francisco Muñoz-Conde and Héctor Olásolo, 'The Application of the Notion of Indirect Perpetration through Organized Structures of Power in Latin America and Spain' (2011) 9 Journal of International Criminal Justice 113.

38 On the notion and structure of joint criminal enterprise, see Stefano Manacorda, *Imputazione collettiva e responsabilità personale. Uno studio sui paradigmi ascrittivi nel diritto penale internazionale* (Giappichelli 2008) 252–273.

Another way ICC judges resolve critical cases is by reference to the *stare decisis* Common law rule. The Court applies it widely with the aim of creating binding legal precedents. Probably the use of *Dogmatik* is conceptually opposed to the *stare decisis* rule. When a case cannot be adjudicated, national theories which apply to international criminal law can step in: in order to avoid the *stare decisis* rule, the use of national theories can be deemed more suitable. The latter solution is much more well-accepted by Continental law lawyers. In truth, the path the Court seems to follow to fill normative gaps is a combination of these two approaches: a theory (like Roxin's) is firstly chosen and adapted to international criminal trials. This theory, in its adapted form, is then reproduced in subsequent trials. In the end, *Dogmatik* becomes mandatory simply as a judicial precedent, hiding nothing less than a *stare decisis* rationale.

This is a path which probably reconciles Common law and Continental law views as far as filling gaps in a criminal statute is concerned. On the other hand, however, this path must deal with the position and role of the accused in a criminal investigation and trial. It risks not taking correctly into account the concepts of accessibility and foreseeability, as defined by the ECtHR. Theories must be widely accepted by a number of legal systems in order to be deemed accessible and, consequently, foreseeable. The aim of the ICC has always been to create a jurisdiction where lawyers from different traditions can happily cohabit. However, the danger is that the rights of the accused—probably the most important aspect of a criminal proceeding—are forgotten, and the jurisdiction is transformed into something truly Kafkaesque.[39]

39 Linking legality to modes of liability may prompt legal scholars to explore the complementarity principle. The ICC Statute affirms that the Court is *complementary to national criminal jurisdictions*. Many have interpreted this as meaning that the ultimate aim of the ICC is to be a Court of *last resort*. Are these considerations reconcilable with an interpretation of statutory provisions, such as Article 25(3)(a), which borrows an exclusively national theory falling outside the boundaries of both the legal systems of the accused and the conditions of accessibility and foreseeability? Further, is the debated effect of the harmonisation of national criminal jurisdictions, likely to result from the complementarity principle seen from a *downward* perspective, put into question? This paper does not aim to answer these complex questions and to approach the challenging relationship between legality, modes of liability and complementarity. See on the complementarity principle, among others: Jann Kleffner, *Complementarity in the Rome Statute and National Criminal Jurisdictions* (OUP 2008); Mohamed El Zeidy, *The Principle of Complementarity in International Criminal Law: Origin, Development and Practice* (Martinus Nijhoff Publishers 2008).

VIII A Future of Shared *Dogmatik* Solutions in International Criminal Law? Conclusions

In the author's opinion, the solution may lie in trying to create a truly international criminal law *Dogmatik*. This would be preferable to taking a single national theory and applying it directly in international trials. However, it inevitably implies years of study, debates among scholars, attempts and failures, and careful dedication to the complexity of domestic principles, rules, and theories.[40]

However, we must not forget one of the reasons why *Dogmatik* was born, and developed, in Germany. The intent, in the second half of the 19th century, was to create a truly national system, secured by the same legal roots, after the unification of all the different *Länders*, with their crucial legal diversities in criminal law too.[41]

The aim of international scholars should be the same: to try to link all criminal systems together so as to create widely accepted theories for the interpretation of statutory provisions and for accountability under the ICC Statute. The latter is a successful example of a global international criminal law text, where diverse perspectives have been shared with a view to including in a single code the basic rules for founding responsibility for international crimes. Obviously the proposed solution would mean that some systems and legal thinking would have to cede something belonging to their own traditions in favour of others. Albeit lengthy and bristling with theoretical problems, this appears to be the only viable way to find an acceptable compromise between, on the one hand, filling statutory gaps (and of coherently interpreting a global *general part* of criminal law) and, on the other, enforcing the ECtHR's ideas of accessibility and foreseeability, in order to safeguard accused persons from any legal abuse.

---

40 In a similar vein, see Fletcher (n 4) 1030–1031. In criticising Gunther Jakobs' words ('there could never be a system of international criminal law because there is no *Dogmatik* in the international system'), Professor Fletcher holds that 'we should actively encourage the writing of theoretical works that lay out the foundational principles of international criminal law [...] My impression of most of the literature published on the ICC, however, runs in a different direction [...] What we need more than ever [...] are debates among scholars about the correct interpretation of special offences as well as the general principles of liability'.

41 In a similar vein, Thomas Vormbaum, *Storia moderna del diritto penale tedesco* (2nd edn, Cedam 2013).

CHAPTER 9

The Judicial Dialogue between the ECtHR and the ad hoc Tribunals on the Right to Rehabilitation of Offenders

Alice Riccardi

Introduction

Paraphrasing the International Criminal Tribunal for the former Yugoslavia Trial Chamber judgment in the *Furundžija* case, human dignity is the 'basic underpinning and indeed the very *raison d'être*' of both international criminal law (ICL) and international human rights law (IHRL).[1] The consequence of such a common normative (and also historical) root is a judicial synergy between international criminal tribunals and human rights jurisdictions, whereby both have made use of each other rulings.[2] This judicial relationship may suggest that ICTs and human rights courts constitute a 'community of courts',[3] where processes of cross-fertilisation—namely the 'effective merging of normative meanings among two or more legal orders'[4]—take place. Recently, academic interest in the idea that ICTs and human rights courts are part of such a judicial comity has flourished; notably, scholars are currently discussing whether the 'community of courts thesis' would resist a realist critique, or are engaged in defining criteria and methods for cross-fertilisation to occur legitimately and fairly.[5]

1 *Prosecutor v Furundžija*, IT-95-17/1-T, Judgment, Trial Chamber, 10 December 1998, para. 183.

2 William A. Schabas, 'Synergy or Fragmentation? International Criminal Law and the European Convention on Human Rights' (2011) 9 Journal of International Criminal Justice 609, 612. See also Solomon T. Ebobrah, 'International Human Rights Courts' in Cesare P.R. Romano, Karen J. Alter and Chrisanthi Avgerou (eds), *The Oxford Handbook of International Adjudication* (OUP 2013) 225.

3 Anne-Marie Slaughter, 'Judicial Globalisation' (2000) 40 Virginia Journal of International Law 1103, 1112. See also Melissa A. Waters, 'Mediating Norms and Identity: The Role of Transnational Judicial Dialogue in Creating and Enforcing International Law' (2005) 93 Georgetown Law Journal 487; Anne-Marie Slaughter, 'A Typology of Transjudicial Communication' (1994) 29 University of Richmond Law Review 99, 112–113.

4 Antje Wiener and Philip Liste, 'Lost Without Translation? Cross-Referencing and a New Global Community of Courts' (2014) 21 Indiana Journal of Global Legal Studies 263, 295.

5 Among others see Sergey Vasiliev, 'International Criminal Tribunals in the Shadow of

 | DOI: 10.1163/9789004313750_011

This contribution enters this debate by testing the cross-fertilisation narrative between ICTs and the ECtHR vis-à-vis a specific case study.[6] The case study chosen concerns the right to rehabilitation of offenders. The recent recognition of life sentence prisoners' right to rehabilitation by both the ECtHR and the two ad hoc Tribunals might indeed *prima facie* appear as a fluctuating, albeit clear, form of transjudicial communication. A summary reading of the ECtHR Grand Chamber judgment in the *Vinter* case of 9 July 2013,[7] together with the decision on the early release of Mr Galić adopted by the President of the Mechanism for International Criminal Tribunals of 23 June 2015,[8] might in fact suggest a sharing of normative perceptions on rehabilitation, indicating a shift towards a judicial comity. However, in order to properly speak of a 'community of courts', it is necessary that the communicating courts follow a transparent process of reciprocal transplantation and avoid altering the original understanding of the norm being imported. Conversely, the case study at hand shows that at a closer look the two mentioned pronouncements merely represent the final part of a longer story of misinterpretations, pragmatic use of external precedents and non-engagement. In this light, the aim of this contribution is to study these judicial intersections in order to assess whether ICTs and human rights courts may *really* be said to be part of a global community founded on shared normative perceptions. In addition, this case study may be paradigmatic for re-orienting the cross-fertilisation narrative between ICTs and human rights jurisdictions, especially because questions regarding rehabilitation go to the core of the ICTs' 'uniqueness dogma'[9]—ie the argument that IHRL shall be re-interpreted by ICTs in order to adapt its standards to the contextual specificities of international criminal proceedings.

This chapter is accordingly divided into two sections. The first section sets the stage by describing the respective contexts in which the discussions on

---

Strasbourg and Politics of Cross-Fertilisation' (2015) 84 Nordic Journal of International Law 371, 374.

6 A casuistic approach to test the 'community thesis' has recently been upheld in Antje Wiener and Philip Liste (n 4) 263.

7 *Vinter and others v United Kingdom*, App no 66069/09, 130/10 and 3896/10 (ECtHR, 9 July 2013), para. 114.

8 *Prosecutor v Galić*, MICT-14-83-ES, Reasons for the President's Decision to Deny the Early Release of Stanislav Galić and Decision on Prosecution Motion, Presidency, 23 June 2015, para. 22.

9 Julia Geneuss, 'Obstacles to Cross-Fertilisation: The International Criminal Tribunals' "Unique Context" and the Flexibility of the European Court of Human Rights' Case Law' (2015) 84 Nordic Journal of International Law 404, 412–414.

rehabilitation took place. The second section illustrates how ad hoc Tribunals and the ECtHR have 'dialogued', by describing the modalities through which each jurisdiction imported principles concerning rehabilitation from the case law of the other. It shall be highlighted that the aim of this contribution is not to exhaustively describe the maturation of the respective jurisprudence on rehabilitation; rather, it seeks to identify the reciprocal judicial intersections, with the purpose of clarifying how these took place. Accordingly, the second section focuses on three selected examples of transjudicial communication, in order to explore whether the said jurisdictions understood the reciprocal contexts in question and employed transparent methods of importation or contestation. Following this analysis, the author concludes that the chosen examples show a normative convergence on rehabilitation; however, this convergence does not expose an 'emerging global jurisprudence',[10] but simply the existence of context-specific trajectories.

1 The Context

This chapter focuses on the transjudicial communication between the ad hoc Tribunals and the ECtHR on the topic of rehabilitation, meant broadly as both a theory of punishment and a rationale underpinning the execution of sentences.[11] As a theory of punishment, rehabilitation posits that in order to prevent crime and to address the societal ills that caused the criminal to offend, rehabilitation shall be offered by society, which, in turn, increases the criminal's ability to succeed in maintaining law-abiding behaviour in the future.[12] As an enforcing rationale, rehabilitation rests on the idea that everyone can,

10 Anne-Marie Slaughter, 'A Global Community of Courts' (2003) 44 Harvard International Law Journal 191, 193.

11 It falls outside the scope of this contribution to analyse the influence of rehabilitation on the determination of sentences *in concreto* and on the practical aspects of enforcing sentences according to a rehabilitative model. For an overview see Jessica M. Kelder, Barbara Hola and Joris van Wijk, 'Rehabilitation and Early Release of Perpetrators of International Crimes: A Case Study of the ICTY and ICTR' (2014) 14 International Criminal Law Review 1177.

12 In general see Francis Allen, *The Decline of the Rehabilitative Ideal* (Yale University Press 1981). See also Francis T. Cullen and Paul Gendreau, 'Assessing Correctional Rehabilitation: Policy, Practice, and Prospects' in Julie Horney (ed), *Criminal Justice 2000. Volume III: Policies, Processes, and Decisions of the Criminal Justice System* (U.S. Department of Justice, National Institute of Justice 2000).

if treated, be reintegrated into society as a crime-free actor. This theoretical background constituted the basis upon which Article 10(3) of the International Covenant on Civil and Political Rights was drafted, providing that the 'penitentiary system shall comprise treatment of prisoners the essential aim of which shall be their reformation and social rehabilitation'. Commenting upon this provision, the Human Rights Committee specified that '[n]o penitentiary system should only be retributory; it should essentially seek reformation and social rehabilitation of the prisoner'.[13] Article 5(6) of the American Convention on Human Rights confirms that punishment shall be aimed at prisoners' reform and social re-adaptation. In the same vein, the Inter-American Commission on Human Rights affirmed that States must bear in mind that 'punishment consisting of deprivation of liberty shall have as an essential aim the reform, social readaptation and personal rehabilitation of those convicted; the reintegration into society and family life'.[14] Similarly, the Council of Europe (CoE) maintained that member States are 'in duty bound to ensure [...] the social rehabilitation of offenders'.[15] International and regional bodies entrusted with providing authoritative interpretation of IHRL conventions have therefore identified in rehabilitation a right afforded to individuals deprived of their liberty—a right the existence of which cannot at present be contested in the realm of IHRL.

Nevertheless, the ECtHR had a hard time in expounding the positive obligations stemming from this right. For their part, the ad hoc Tribunals did not assume that guilty individuals are entitled to rehabilitation. The respective contexts in which the dialogues between ad hoc Tribunals and the ECtHR on rehabilitation took place were in fact very complex ones on both sides.

As to the ad hoc Tribunals, discussions on rehabilitation took place in connection with the broader debate on the aims of prison sentences in ICL. As is widely known, ICTS' Statutes do not embody provisions establishing penological justifications for sentencing (or rationales of sentencing), nor has the international judiciary delineated a definitive set of guidelines in this respect.[16] Sim-

13 Human Rights Committee, CCPR/C/21/Rev.1/Add.7, General Comment No. 21 (1992), para. 10.

14 Inter-American Commission on Human Rights, 'Resolution 1/08. Principles and Best Practices on the Protection of Persons Deprived of Liberty in the Americas' (2008), recital 4.

15 European Convention on the Supervision of Conditionally Sentenced or Conditionally Released Offenders (1964), preamble.

16 See Bruce Broomhall, 'Part 7: Penalties' in Otto Triffterer (ed), *Commentary on the Rome Statute of the International Criminal Court* (2nd edn, Beck-Hart-Nomos 2008) para. 5; Robert Sloane, 'The Expressive Capacity of International Punishment: The Limits of the National Analogy and the Potential of International Criminal Law' (2007) 39 Stanford

ilarly, no aim is positively assigned to the execution of sentences.[17] However, '[t]he determination of a "fair" sentence, that is to say a sentence consonant with the interest of justice, depends on the objectives sought'.[18] In other words, whereas the definition of punishment may be value-neutral, the practice of punishment must instead be justified in terms of different considerations—eg values or social goals—for it to be legitimate. Moreover, the objectives sought influence the magnitude of sentences, since the relationship between the gravity of the crime and the quantum of punishment shall eventually be proportional to something—ie to the aim pursued through punishment itself. A cursory review of the ad hoc Tribunals' case law reveals that a plethora of rationales have been invoked by judges in meting out sentences, in pursuance of their 'unfettered discretion'; and that both forward- and backward-looking theories of punishment have been advanced.[19] Among other rationales, rehabilitation has enjoyed mixed fortune: initially ruled out—as if ICTs, in pursuing their mission of putting an end to impunity for crimes under international law, were re-interpreting IHRL to the detriment of the accused—rehabilitation gained recognition only at the end of the 2000s, although it has not yet been assigned the same force it possesses in the realm of IHRL.

At the ECtHR, discussions on rehabilitation arose in the context of the compatibility between life imprisonment without parole and the prohibition of inhumane and degrading treatment provided in Article 3 of the European Convention on Human Rights. Although penalties have, in general, been overlooked in IHRL, with the gradual disappearance of the death penalty, life imprisonment became the prominent issue under the scrutiny of human rights bodies and courts.[20] Within the CoE, interest in the compatibility between life

Journal of International Law 1, 1; Ralph Henham, 'The Philosophical Foundations of International Sentencing' (2003) 1 Journal of International Criminal Justice 64, 85; Daniel B. Pickard, 'Proposed Sentencing Guidelines for the International Criminal Court' (1997) 20 Loyola of Los Angeles International and Comparative Law Journal 123, 124.

17 See in general Roisin Mulgrew, *Towards the Development of the International Penal System* (CUP 2013).

18 *Prosecutor v Blaškić*, IT-95-14, Judgment, Trial Chamber, 3 March 2000, para. 761.

19 Although conceding that different theories of punishment can overlap in concrete cases, still the portrayal of overabundant and possibly conflicting rationales is counterproductive for the respect of the rights of the accused and the perception of ICTs' legitimacy. See in general Mirjan R. Damaška, 'What is the Point of International Criminal Justice' (2008) 83 Chicago-Kent Law Review 329, 331.

20 See also among other examples European Committee for the Prevention of Torture and Inhumane or Degrading Treatment or Punishment, CPT/Inf (2012), Report on the Visit to Bulgaria from 4 to 10 March 2012, 4 December 2012, para. 32.

imprisonment and the prohibition of inhumane and degrading treatment grew in the early 2000s.[21] In this respect, the Lord Chief Justice of the United Kingdom stated that '[t]here seems to be a tide in Europe that is setting against the imposition of very lengthy terms of imprisonment that are irreducible'.[22] This tide originated from the ECtHR's increasing disquiet with some practices characterising the sentencing and penitentiary systems of members States;[23] and concretised when the Strasbourg Court started receiving applications directly challenging life imprisonment without parole on the basis that it would amount to inhumane or degrading treatment, leaving prisoners in a prolonged state of distress.[24] These applications claimed that Article 3 of the ECHR entailed a positive obligation for States to ensure that individuals are detained under conditions 'compatible with the respect for human dignity and that the manner and method of the execution of the measure do not subject them to distress or hardship exceeding the unavoidable level of suffering inherent in detention'.[25] However, the path towards the recognition of rehabilitation only received closure in 2013 with the *Vinter* case, as further described below.

II Modalities of Transjudicial Communication

It has been noted that '[p]ure cross-fertilisation through transjudicial communication is likely to be very difficult to track', for the 'listening' courts seek ideas from other courts, but rarely give credit to the source of such ideas.[26] This is particularly true when the given idea does not concern a legal technicality, but rather a principle of a normative nature, as in the case study at hand. The interactions between ad hoc Tribunals and the ECtHR regarding rehabilitation fluctuated over the years; to grasp them is not an easy exercise, for their communication has often taken place on an informal level, and inaccurate methods of normative translation have been employed. The study of

21 Somehow coinciding with the publication of Dirk van Zyl Smit, *Taking Life Imprisonment Seriously in National and International Law* (Kluwer Law International 2002).

22 *R v Bieber* [2008] EWCA Crim 1601, [2009] 1 WLR 223.

23 *Stafford v United Kingdom*, App no 46295/99 (ECtHR, 28 May 2002), para. 78.

24 According to William A. Schabas, 'Introduction' in Hans G. Franck and William A. Schabas (eds), *The Barbaric Punishment: The Death Penalty* (2003) 22, life imprisonment without parole is 'of terrifying and dehumanising brutality [and] raises its own human rights questions'.

25 *Kudla v Poland*, App no 30210/96 (ECtHR, 20 October 2000), para. 94.

26 Slaughter, 'A Typology' (n 3) 118.

these intersections is, however, important as it allows some problems inherent to the practice of cross-fertilisation between ICTs and the ECtHR to surface. The following pages thus analyse three different examples of transjudicial communication on rehabilitation that have (consciously or unconsciously) resulted in the coexistence of a matrix of reciprocal judicial behaviours. The three examples cover all possible modalities of communication among courts: the first example is one in which both judicial contexts refer to the other in order to advance a normative claim; the second is one of negative cross-fertilisation, whereby the ICTY refused to embrace an IHRL norm; in the third example, both jurisdictions converge towards the same norm, although without explicitly cross-referencing each other. The investigation of these three modalities discloses first and foremost a complicacy in identifying a structure or methodology of communication between the courts; furthermore, it exposes the misuse of cross-fertilisation and allows for the suggestion of general ideas for its enhancement.

A *Cross-referencing as a Tool to Advance a Normative Claim*

It is contended that in order to properly speak of a judicial comity and of cross-fertilisation, a certain amount of 'hermeneutic understanding' of the context in which the norm was originally developed is necessary.[27] In fact, while cross-fertilisation may happen as a result of mere cross-referencing, this does not necessarily entail that the meaning attached to a given idea in its original context is left untouched in the receiving system.

As anticipated in the introduction, a cursory reading of the ECtHR Grand Chamber *Vinter* judgment, together with the MICT President's decision on the early release of Mr Galić, might suggest a 'judicial comity' between the two jurisdictions, for they cross-reference each other in the apparent sharing of a normative perception, namely the recognition of 'the human dignity of all offenders. No matter what they have done, they should be given the opportunity to rehabilitate themselves'.[28] Yet, a closer look to their interactions discloses (in particular on the part of the ECtHR) little 'hermeneutic understanding' between their respective contexts.

27 Neil Walker, 'Postnational Constitutionalism and the Problem of Translation' in Joseph H.H. Weiler and Marlene Wind (eds), *European Constitutionalism Beyond the State* (CUP 2003) 37.

28 Dirk Van Zyl Smit, Pete Weatherby and Simon Creighton, 'Whole Life Sentences and the Tide of European Human Rights Jurisprudence: What Is to Be Done?' (2014) 14 Human Rights Law Review 59, 65.

As is widely known, in *Vinter*, the Grand Chamber established that the absence of a real prospect of release through an appropriate mechanism established by law for persons sentenced to life imprisonment with whole life orders amounts to inhumane and degrading treatment contrary to Article 3 of the ECHR. In order to cement its position that 'there is now clear support in European and international law for the principle that all prisoners, including those serving life sentences, be offered the possibility of rehabilitation',[29] the ECtHR strategically focused on the recognition of the right to rehabilitation to the most odious of offenders.[30] Indeed, the idea to prove that '[t]hose who commit the most abhorrent and egregious of acts and who inflict untold suffering upon others, nevertheless retain their fundamental humanity and carry within themselves the capacity to change',[31] must have been considered a win-win situation by the judges.

In particular, the Grand Chamber recalled the sentencing provisions of ICTs—namely of the ICC, the ICTY, the ICTR, but also of the SCSL and of the STL[32]—and affirmed that they confirmed an international 'commitment to the rehabilitation of life sentence prisoners',[33] since they all incorporate a mechanism for sentence review even in case of life imprisonment, the most eloquent sign of a rehabilitation-oriented sentencing policy.

As a matter of fact, aside from the ICC Statute, to claim in such a *tranchant* manner that ICTs—generally taken—are committed to rehabilitation is highly problematic. First, none of their statutes explicitly discuss whether an individual sentenced to life imprisonment is eligible for early release. As to the SCSL specifically, in the *AFRC* case it held that rehabilitation is more appropriate as an aim of punishment in the domestic context, rather than in international criminal trials.[34] Furthermore, the sentence of 50 years of

---

29 *Vinter* (n 7), para. 114.

30 By quoting, inter alia, the German Federal Constitutional Court ruling in the *Life Imprisonment* case recognising rehabilitation 'even for extremely serious cases like genocide', see *Lebenslange Freiheitsstrafe*, 45 BVerfGE 187 (1977), Decision; GFCC *War Criminal* case, 72 BVerfGE 105 (1986), Decision; and Italian Constitutional Court, Judgment no 192, 14 July 1976—which support the sentencing rationale of rehabilitation as the 'aim of every sentence and the right of every prisoner'. See *Vinter* (n 7), paras 69–72.

31 *Vinter* (n 7), Concurring Opinion of Judge Power-Forde.

32 *Vinter* (n 7), para. 66.

33 ibid para. 118.

34 *Prosecutor v Brima*, SCSL-04-16-0624, Sentencing Judgment, Trial Chamber, 19 July 2007, para. 14. See generally Shahram Dana, 'The Sentencing Legacy of the Special Court for Sierra Leone' (2014) 42 Georgia Journal of International and Comparative Law 615, 660–663.

imprisonment imposed upon Charles Taylor at the age of 65 shows little interest in his potential for reintegration,[35] and might even result in a *de facto* impossibility for him to ever be eligible for early release.[36] As to the ad hoc Tribunals, at the time of the pronouncement of the *Vinter* judgment, no application for early release had ever been filed by an individual sentenced to life imprisonment. Consequently, to affirm that ICTs as a whole endorsed a 'commitment to the rehabilitation of life sentence prisoners' in 2013, was a step too far.

In fact, and ironically, the first ever application for early release of an individual sentenced to life imprisonment filed before an ad hoc Tribunal was *subsequent* to the *Vinter* judgment. Further, and even more ironically, following this application, the MICT President, in discussing whether a life sentence prisoner might ever be considered eligible for early release, turned to the ECtHR case law and explicitly referred to the *Vinter* judgment in that it supports 'the rehabilitative principle and respect for human dignity [which], inter alia, require that all prisoners, including those serving life sentences, be afforded both a possibility of review of their sentence and a prospect of release'.[37]

Therefore, the ECtHR's reference to the jurisprudence of the whole panorama of ICTs as an unequivocal demonstration of a rehabilitation-oriented penal policy barely fits into the abovementioned 'hermeneutic understanding' test; furthermore, it shows that, however opportune the ECtHR's conclusion might be, cross-referencing may be driven by mere pragmatic considerations (eg resolving a contingent legal dilemma), rather than sincere normative sharing.

On the other hand, non-engagement may also be problematic when a transparent methodology of negative cross-referencing is not employed. Indeed, as shown in the following paragraph, in its early case law the ICTY adopted a troublesome way to justify its decision to move away from the interpretation given by human rights bodies to the offenders' right to rehabilitation.[38]

B *Negative Cross-fertilisation*

It can be argued that the debate on cross-fertilisation gained momentum in the wake of the 1995 *Tadić* Protective Measures Decision. Therein, the ICTY affirmed its freedom to (i) assign limited relevance to the interpretation given

---

35 *Prosecutor v Taylor*, SCSL-03-01-1389, Judgment, Appeals Chamber, 26 September 2013.

36 On the disproportionality of Mr Taylor sentence see in general Kevin J. Heller, 'The *Taylor* Sentencing Judgment: A Critical Analysis' (2013) 11 Journal of International Criminal Justice 835.

37 *Galić* (n 8), para. 22.

38 See above (n 13).

to fair trial rights by other judicial bodies and to (ii) interpret human rights provisions in light of the 'context of its unique legal framework', ie the adjudication of horrific crimes.[39] Although few international lawyers would readily object to the argument that 'one ought not to transpose legal constructs [...] whenever these constructs do not harmonise with the specific features' of the international criminal justice system,[40] still the conclusion drawn by the ICTY that it was more similar to a 'military tribunal, which often has limited rights of due process and more lenient rules of evidence'[41] was particularly worrisome. In the context of sentencing, this assumption resulted in the ICTY's initial refusal to embrace rehabilitation. Indeed, until 2003, only four of 16 ICTY trial judgments referred to rehabilitation as a sentencing rationale,[42] following the refusal of the Appeals Chamber in the *Čelebiči* case to engage with rehabilitation, in the following terms:

> The cases which come before the Tribunal differ in many respect from those which ordinarily come before national jurisdictions, primarily because of the serious nature of the crimes being prosecuted [...] Although both national jurisdictions and international and regional human rights instruments provide that rehabilitation should be one of the primary concerns for a court in sentencing, this cannot play a predominant role in the decision-making of a Trial Chamber of the Tribunal.[43]

As evident in this ruling, the ICTY Appeals Chamber adopted the approach implicitly recognised in *Tadić*, namely assigning limited relevance to the interpretation given to a human right by external judicial organs (and treaty bod-

---

39 *Prosecutor v Tadić*, IT-94-1-T, Decision on the Prosecutor's Motion Requesting Protective Measures for Victims and Witnesses, Trial Chamber, 10 August 1995, paras 17–30. See also *Prosecutor v Barayagwiza*, ICTR-97-19-AR72, Judgment, Appeals Chamber, 3 November 1999, para. 40.

40 Antonio Cassese and others (eds), *Cassese's International Criminal Law* (3rd edn, OUP 2013) 16.

41 *Tadić* (n 39), para. 28.

42 Cases in which accused pleaded guilty are excluded from this calculation. The four trial judgments referred to are those rendered in the *Kupreškić*, *Kunarac*, *Krnojelac* and *Galić* cases.

43 *Prosecutor v Mucić*, IT-96-21-A, Judgment, Appeals Chamber, 20 February 2001 ('*Čelebići* case'), para. 806. Notably, this is also the judgment in which the ICTY Appeals Chamber concluded that 'it is inappropriate for it to attempt to list exhaustively the factors that it finds should be taken into account by a Trial Chamber in determining a sentence' (ibid para. 718).

ies).[44] In other words, while recognising the existence of the right and its corollaries, it simply decided not to engage with it in light of, seemingly, the serious nature of crimes under international law. This approach led one author to affirm, in 2003, that 'it is not possible to conclude, at this stage of development of the international criminal law system, that the convicted person has a right to rehabilitation'.[45]

The *Čelebiči* ruling represents one of the rare instances of negative cross-fertilisation,[46] which Teitel and Howse consider a 'reaction to the suggestion that a tribunal must be *bound* by the rulings of another tribunal—obligated to follow those rulings as *authority* rather than to the extent persuasive'.[47] However, when a court refuses—because of its purported uniqueness—to engage with a human right, it should do so cautiously.

The intrinsic problem of the *Čelebiči* approach does not really reside in its outcome (which the present author does not share, but which gathered some sympathy among scholars),[48] but rather in the paucity of legal explanations accompanying it. Although it holds true that a 'thick' translation[49] of human rights standards in international criminal proceedings may be difficult to achieve because of the specificities of ICTs, a method to secure correct (non)engagements ought to be put in place. It has been recently argued in this regard that ICTs should focus less on the 'outcome of the translation than on the method of incorporation'.[50] In light of a defence appeal brief elaborating, for roughly 20 pages on the issue of rehabilitation and the wealth of sources

---

44 For the same approach see also *Prosecutor v Kamuhanda*, ICTR-99-54A-A, Judgment, Appeals Chamber, 19 September 2005, para. 357.

45 Salvatore Zappalà, *Human Rights in International Criminal Proceedings* (OUP 2003) 206.

46 Another famous example is the debate between the ICTY and the International Court of Justice concerning the legal test for attribution to a State of the conduct of a non-State actor in the territory of another State. See *Prosecutor v Tadić*, IT-94-1-A, Judgment, Appeals Chamber, 15 July 1999, paras 115–145.

47 Ruti Teitel and Robert Howse, 'Cross-Judging: Tribunalization in a Fragmented but Interconnected Global Order' (2009) 41 International Law and Politics 959, 965 (emphasis in original).

48 See among others Mirko Bagaric and John Morss, 'International Sentencing Law: In Search of a Justification and Coherent Framework' (2006) 6 International Criminal Law Review 191, 248; Jens D. Ohlin, 'Towards a Unique Theory of International Criminal Sentencing' in Göran Sluiter and Sergey Vasiliev (eds), *International Criminal Procedure: Towards a Coherent Body of the Law* (Cameron May 2009) 383.

49 A term used in Neil Walker (n 27) 36.

50 Geneuss (n 9) 424.

and case law cited therein,[51] the ICTY Appeals Chamber's approach in *Čelebiči* was too elusive. One may speculate that the judges were, in selecting rationales of sentencing, mainly influenced by the first limb of Article 24(2) of the ICTY Statute, which provides that sentences shall reflect the gravity of the crimes, rather than by its second limb, according to which sentences shall be determined taking into account the personal circumstances of the convicted person.[52] Such justification cannot, however, suffice to positively evaluate the ICTY attitude towards human rights in its early case law. When deciding to depart from an interpretative practice of a human right, ICTs must assume the role of explaining the reasons for such a departure—explanations that are virtually absent in the example at hand—especially when refusing to embrace such an interpretation entails a restriction upon the rights of the accused.[53] In fact, 'the defensive function of human rights law—the constraints of the use of coercive powers against individuals—is by no means less important [in international criminal proceedings] than on the domestic level'.[54]

In this regard, Julia Geneuss recently suggested that practices of cross-fertilisation between ICTs and human rights courts should proceed in two steps. First, the importing court must focus on the 'directory' authority of the external judicial source; when it is an ICT importing from a human rights court, although the latter has no mandatory force upon the former, its rulings (or the statements of human rights bodies) 'should' nonetheless be followed—because of their inherent level of expertise.[55] Second, the importing court must focus on the persuasiveness of the ruling. In the example at hand, therefore, ICTs must appreciate such persuasiveness and 'decide whether and how they want to translate' an IHRL standard into the unique context of international criminal proceedings. At this stage, if they decide to adhere to a human rights court's ruling, ICTs' judges can 'add additional factors that reflect the unique context in

51 *Prosecutor v Mucić*, IT-96-21-A A 2129-A, Response of the Appellant Zdravko Mucić to the Prosecution's Fourth Ground of Appeal Brief, 17 September 1999, paras 23–41.

52 Both Ralph Henham, 'Contextualized Rationales of Sentencing in International Criminal Law' (2007) 5 Journal of International Criminal Justice 762 and William A. Schabas, *The UN International Criminal Tribunals: The Former Yugoslavia, Rwanda and Sierra Leone* (CUP 2006) 563 share this opinion.

53 Masha Fedorova and Göran Sluiter, 'Human Rights as Minimum Standards in International Criminal Proceedings' (2009) 3 Human Rights and International Legal Discourse 18, 33.

54 Geneuss (n 9) 413.

55 ibid 426, citing Grant Lamond, 'Persuasive Authority in the Law' (2010) 17 The Harvard Review of Philosophy 16, 24.

which they operate and might omit those factors that are not relevant because they only matter in the domestic context'.[56]

In *Čelebiči*, the Appeals Chamber did not follow this method; on the contrary, it merely looked at the 'classical', nationally-interpreted notion of rehabilitation,[57] and ruled out its relevance vis-à-vis the specificities of international criminal proceedings. This said, subsequent cases have employed a method similar to the one delineated by Geneuss and reached the conclusion that rehabilitation also matters in ICL (albeit with the limits imposed by its uniqueness), as further analysed in the following paragraph.

C Context-Specific Convergence towards the Same Norm

International courts rarely cite other courts; however, tacit processes of acculturation—ie 'the adoption of behavioural patterns of the surrounding culture'[58]—exist among the international judiciary, and can be detected when courts' respective reasoning is virtually identical,[59] where their methodologies of analysis resemble each other, or simply when they are aware of disseminating their ideas. Anne-Marie Slaughter defined this latter type of cross-fertilisation as one aimed to 'provide inspiration for the solution of a particular legal problem'.[60] Admittedly, in the 2000s numerous judicial bodies worldwide discussed whether individuals convicted for a crime are entitled to rehabilitation.[61] In the same period, evidence of a process of acculturation also began to appear at the ad hoc Tribunals. Indeed, in and around 2004, a jurisprudential *revirement* concerning the notion of rehabilitation occurred specifically at

---

56 Geneuss (n 9) 426.

57 Namely as 'the loss of freedom which [...] provides the impulse and context for the convicted person's reflection on the wrongfulness of his or her acts and on the harm and suffering they have caused'. See also *Prosecutor v Jokić*, IT-01-42/1-S, Sentencing Judgment, Trial Chamber, 18 March 2004, para. 35; *Prosecutor v Kordić*, IT-95-14/2, Judgment, Appeals Chamber, 17 December 2004, para. 1233.

58 Ryan Goodman and Derek Jinks, 'International Law and State Socialisation: Conceptual, Empirical and Normative Challenges' (2005) 54 Duke Law Journal 983, 992.

59 John G. Merrills, *The Development of International Law by the European Court of Human Rights* (2nd edn, Manchester University Press 1993) 18.

60 Anne-Marie Slaughter, 'A Typology' (n 3) 117.

61 See among others: *Vélez Loor v Panamá* (IACtHR, 23 November 2010), para. 204; *Graham v Florida* (2010) 130 S Ct 2011 (United States of America); *de Boucherville v the State of Mauritius* (2008) UKPC 70 (Mauritius); *Montero Aranguren y otros (Retén de Catia) v Venezuela* (IACtHR, 28 March 2006), para. 146; *R v Latimer* (2001) 1 SCR 3 (Canada); *Lau Cheong v Hong Kong Special Administrative Region* (2002) HKFCA 18 (Hong Kong); *Dodo v the State* (2001) CCT 1/01 ZACC 16 (South Africa).

the ICTY. There, Trial Chambers held for quite a long time that rehabilitation 'depends on the states in which the convicted persons will serve their sentences, and not on the International Tribunal', and that rehabilitation would therefore have no relevance before international criminal jurisdictions.[62] Subsequently, this stance was reversed for it contrasts with (i) the role that rehabilitation plays in sentencing and (ii) the functions of ad hoc Tribunals in the enforcement phase of sentences.

As to sentencing, in 2003 in the *Nikolić M* case, ICTY judges effectively held that 'the concept of rehabilitation can be thought of broadly and can encompass all stages of the criminal proceedings, and not simply the post-conviction phase'.[63] Rehabilitation, as further recognised in 2005 by the ICTY Appeals Chamber in the *Nikolić D* case, must already be considered when imposing the sentence, rather than its mere possibility postponed to the execution phase of the proceedings.[64] This novel interpretation led a growing number of ICTY Trial Chambers to embrace rehabilitation among other rationales of sentencing. Indeed, in 2005, the ICTY affirmed that '[f]rom a human rights perspective each accused [...] ought to have a chance to be reintegrated into society'.[65] This attitude stemmed from the idea that although rehabilitation has 'not yet achieved the same dominance as retribution and deterrence in the sentencing history of the Tribunal, [it] is important for achieving the goals of the Tribunal'.[66] In other words, ICTY judges started to feel the 'directory' authority of human rights sources,[67] and to acknowledge additional factors reflecting the unique context in which they operate. In fact, they re-interpreted rehabilitation in ICL as 'the process of coming face-to-face with the statements of victims, if not the victims themselves, can inspire—if not reawaken—tolerance and understanding of "the other" [...] Reconciliation and peace would thereby be promoted'.[68] In particular, this convinced the ICTY to take into high consider-

62 *Prosecutor v Kunarac*, IT-96-23 & 23/1, Judgment, Trial Chamber, 22 February 2001, para. 844.

63 *Prosecutor v Nikolić M*, IT-02-60/1, Sentencing Judgment, Trial Chamber, 2 December 2003, para. 93.

64 *Prosecutor v Nikolić D*, IT-94-2-A, Judgment, Appeals Chamber, 4 February 2005, para. 97. See also *Prosecutor v Stakić*, IT-97-24-A, Judgment, Appeals Chamber, 22 March 2006, paras 388–393.

65 *Prosecutor v Nikolić D*, IT-94-2-S, Sentencing Judgment, Trial Chamber, 18 December 2003, para. 282.

66 *Prosecutor v Brđanin*, IT-99-36-T, Judgment, Trial Chamber, 1 September 2004, para. 1092.

67 See above (n 56).

68 *Nikolić M* (n 63), para. 93. See also *Prosecutor v Ćešić*, IT-95-10/1-S, Sentencing Judgment,

ation guilty pleas in determining the sentence, in contrast to the general State practice according to which guilty pleas do not mitigate the sentence in cases of the most grave crimes, since 'the rationale behind the mitigating effect of a guilty plea in this Tribunal is much broader, including the fact that the accused contributes to establish the truth [...] and to reconciliation in the affected communities'.[69] This trend eventually prevailed, to the extent that the majority of the ICTY and the totality of the ICTR guilty verdicts pronounced after 2004 explicitly embraced rehabilitation among other sentencing rationales.[70] However, it ought to be underlined that no judgment by an ad hoc Tribunal ever affirmed that rehabilitation shall prevail over other rationales, such as retribution and deterrence.

As to the execution of sentences, it must not be forgotten that ad hoc Tribunals enjoy primacy over national jurisdictions. In this role, the ICTY followed the trend of taking into consideration the rehabilitative potential of the accused in its practice concerning early release, which was consolidating at the same time. The ICTY commuted its first sentence in 2001[71] and the contours of early release—a legal device not specifically provided for in the Statute, which only refers to pardon and commutation of sentences[72]—started to become apparent in the second half of the 2000s. Rule 125 of the ICTY RPE, which

Trial Chamber, 11 March 2004, para. 28; *Prosecutor v Mrđa*, IT-02-59-T, Judgment, Trial Chamber, 31 March 2004; *Jokić* (n 58), para. 35; *Prosecutor v Babić*, IT-03-72-S, Sentencing Judgment, Trial Chamber, 29 June 2004, para. 46.

69 *Nikolić D* (n 65), para. 233.

70 Namely, the trial judgments in the: *Brđanin* (n 66), para. 1092; *Prosecutor v Strugar*, IT-01-42-T, Judgment, Trial Chamber, 31 January 2005, fn. 1290; *Prosecutor v Hadžihasanović*, IT-01-47-T, Judgment, Trial Chamber, 15 March 2006, para. 2073; *Prosecutor v Orić*, IT-03-68-T, Judgment, Trial Chamber, 30 June 2006, para. 721; *Prosecutor v Krajišnik*, IT-00-39-T, Judgment, Trial Chamber, 27 September 2006, para. 1134; *Prosecutor v Martić*, IT-95-11-T, Judgment, Trial Chamber, 12 June 2007, para. 484; *Prosecutor v Milošević D*, IT-98-29/1-T, Judgment, Trial Chamber, 12 December 2007, para. 987; *Prosecutor v Haradinaj*, IT-04-84-T, Judgment, Trial Chamber, 3 April 2008, para. 488; *Prosecutor v Delić*, IT-04-83-T, Judgment, Trial Chamber, 15 September 2008, para. 559; *Milutinović*, IT-05-87-T, Judgment, vol 3, 26 February 2009, para. 1146; *Prosecutor v Popović*, IT-05-88-T, Judgment, Trial Chamber, 10 June 2010, para. 2130; *Prosecutor v Gotovina*, IT-06-90-T, Judgment, vol 2, 15 April 2011, para. 2598; *Prosecutor v Perišić*, IT-04-81-T, Judgment, Trial Chamber, 6 September 2011, para. 1796; *Prosecutor v Tolimir*, IT-05-88/2-T, Judgment, Trial Chamber, 12 December 2012, para. 1211; and *Prosecutor v Karađžić*, IT-95-5/18-T, Judgment, Trial Chamber, 24 March 2016, para. 6025.

71 *Prosecutor v Aleksovški*, IT-95-14/1, Order of the President for the Early Release of Zlatko Aleksovski, Presidency, 14 November 2001.

72 cf UN Security Council, S/25266, Letter Dated 10 February 1993 from the Permanent Repre-

complements Article 28 of the ICTY Statute, was amended to establish that, in granting convicted individuals' applications, the ICTY President shall consider, inter alia, the prisoner's demonstration of rehabilitation.[73] An ICTY Trial Chamber commenting on this criterion underlined that 'from a human rights perspective each accused, having served the necessary part of his sentence, ought to have a chance to be reintegrated into society'.[74] Such 'necessary part' of the sentence was progressively set by ICTY Presidents at the expiration of two-thirds of the sentence;[75] this standard became a universal yardstick when, in 2008, the ICTY President affirmed that it reflects the domestic law of the majority of enforcing States and that it was an obligation incumbent upon the Tribunal 'to treat all ICTY detainees in a similar manner, despite the State in which they are serving their sentence'.[76]

In the same years, the ECtHR was also actively engaged in expounding the boundaries of the positive obligations arising from the prohibition of inhumane and degrading punishment. In 2001, for the first time it did 'not rule out the possibility that the imposition of an irreducible life sentence may raise an issue under Article 3 of the Convention'.[77] In 2006, it further affirmed that the notion of 'hope' was key to the assessment of the compatibility of a parole system with Article 3 of the ECHR.[78] Then, in 2008, in the *Kafkaris* case, it affirmed that 'it is clear from the relevant case law that the existence of a system providing for consideration of the possibility of release is a factor to be taken into

---

sentative of France to the United Nations Addressed to the Secretary-General, 10 February 1993, paras 157–159. The expression "early release" was officially used for the first time in ICTY, IT/146, Practice Direction on the Procedure for the Determination of Applications for Pardon, Commutation of Sentence and Early Release of Persons Convicted by the International Tribunal, 7 April 1999.

73 See ICTY RPE Revision 7, 18 January 1996, rule 125. See also ICTY, IT/146/Rev.3, Practice Direction on the Procedure for the Determination of Applications for Pardon, Commutation of Sentence, and Early Release of Persons Convicted by the International Tribunal, 16 September 2010.

74 *Nikolić D* (n 65), para. 282.

75 Mulgrew (n 17) 57. In critical terms see Jonathan H. Choi, 'Early Release in International Criminal Law' (2014) 6 The Yale Law Journal 1626.

76 *Prosecutor v Tadić*, IT-94-1-ES, Decision of the President on the Application for Pardon or Commutation of Sentence of Duško Tadić, Presidency, 17 July 2008, para. 17. Recently, the MICT applied the same standard also to those convicted by the ICTR in *Prosecutor v Ruzindana*, MICT-12-10-ES, Decision of the President on the Early Release of Obed Ruzindana, Presidency, 13 March 2014, para. 778.

77 *Einhorn v France*, App no 71555/01 (ECtHR Admissibility, 16 October 2001), para. 27.

78 *Legér v France*, App no 19324/02 (ECtHR, 11 April 2006), para. 90.

account when assessing the compatibility of a certain life sentence with Article 3'[79]—although it concluded that 'at the present time there is not yet a clear and commonly accepted standard amongst the member States of the Council of Europe concerning life sentences'.[80] Interestingly, in a partly dissenting opinion attached to the judgment, five judges expressed their unease with the majority's failure to affirm that rehabilitation is an established value under the ECHR, pointing in particular to (a set of unspecified) 'recent developments in international criminal justice reflect[ing] a similar approach',[81] ie that 'besides the punitive purpose of sentences, they must also encourage the social reintegration of prisoners' since 'it is accepted that the "legitimate requirements of the sentence" entails reintegration'.[82]

As is evident, the analysed case law shows that both the ad hoc Tribunals and the ECtHR were, during the same time period, converging towards the same conclusion, namely that convicted individuals are entitled to rehabilitation. Yet, they only engaged *en passant* in reciprocal cross-referencing; further, their respective conclusions are context-specific as they adapted the notion of rehabilitation to their own frameworks. In conclusion, in this example, no court is deferential to the other, and no one is hegemonic over the other. Indeed, one of the main concerns expressed by scholars in relation to the cross-fertilisation between ICTs and the ECtHR is that the former (provided that no binding rule to consult respective precedents exists), cannot be expected to invariably follow the latter, which is not the universal authentic interpreter of IHRL, but only the guardian jurisdiction of the European human rights convention.[83] However, in this example of convergence, independent judicial bodies equally and autonomously reach their respective legal conclusions in application of the law binding upon them and in light of the object and purpose of their respective legal bases. What emerges, therefore, rather than a global jurisprudence, is the existence of context-specific trajectories. Moreover, and most importantly, all courts participate in the *production* of human rights norms—eventually bringing about harmonisation in the interpretation of IHRL. Whereas a deferential approach to the interpretation of human rights may hide a discretional choice in the selection of precedents on which to rely, a non-deferential approach (coupled with context-specific explanations of why and how a given norm

79 *Kafkaris v Cyprus*, App no 21906/04 (ECtHR, 12 February 2008), para. 99.

80 ibid para. 104.

81 ibid Jointly Partly Dissenting Opinion of Judges Tulkens, Cabral Barreto, Fura-Sandstrom, Spielmann and Jebens, para. 4.

82 ibid para. 5.

83 A concern expressed by Vasiliev (n 5) 392.

applies) may instead be key to the dissemination of uniform human rights standards. Cross-fertilisation may not in fact necessarily lead to harmonisation, for hermeneutic translation of a norm from its original to the incorporating context is rare; instead, a non-deferential approach guarantees that the norm is realised through the lens of the diverse positive framework in which it is applied.

Conclusions

The practice analysed in this contribution reveals that it may be difficult to speak concretely of a judicial normativity between ICTs and the ECtHR. In particular, each of the three modalities of interaction on rehabilitation described above show that it is problematic to rely on the notion of cross-fertilisation for three reasons.

First, cross-fertilisation *stricto sensu*—as opposed to mere cross-referencing—requires familiarity with the 'lending' system; the absence of such awareness affects the very possibility of transplanting a given rule into another context and also the idea that the communicating courts are part of a global community sharing normative perceptions. In the *Vinter* case,[84] the ECtHR Grand Chamber unwarrantedly grouped together the pluralist experiences of ICTs—as if they were themselves a community of courts—to pinpoint a norm and use it to prove its case that such a norm is universally valid. Although this operation contributed to a clarification of States' human rights obligations in sentencing, it originated from an inaccurate understanding of the lending context. Furthermore, the norm affirmed by the ECtHR afterwards (re)entered the context from which it was improperly extrapolated,[85] in a contorted circulation of legal ideas.

Second, although ICTs and human rights courts have certain overlapping elements, they have starkly different normative contexts, to the extent that cross-referencing is oftentimes also construed in terms of contestation. This type of interaction notably emerged in the *Čelebići* case,[86] where the ICTY Appeals Chamber refused to engage with the human right to rehabilitation due to the ostensible uniqueness of the Tribunal. Therefore, even if ICTs feel the authority of the human rights court's normative context, they may nevertheless

84 See above (n 32).
85 See above (n 37).
86 See above (n 43).

exclude the possibility that a norm developed therein is also persuasive. This gives rises to another set of problems related to the method of incorporation and/or contestation. Whereas the ICTY was correct in not considering human rights courts and bodies' utterances as inherently persuasive—for ICTs ought to feel free to develop 'through interpretation and taking into account of their specific situations and exigencies, their own human rights judicial policy'[87]—the case study nonetheless shows that ICTs should put forward a test for excluding such persuasiveness, especially when this refusal may be detrimental to the rights of the accused. Further research is therefore necessary in order to delineate a test or methodology for ICTs in appraising the persuasiveness of a human rights court's ruling vis-à-vis the specificities of international criminal proceedings.

Third, the respective development of ICL and ECtHR jurisprudence on rehabilitation in recent years shows that, although a convergence on rehabilitation is undeniable, this convergence has occurred for distinct reasons. Indeed, each court independently travelled towards a common normative concept while tracing its own trajectory; furthermore, each court adapted such concept to its own specificities and accordingly modelled the legal consequences stemming therefrom. Non-deferential approaches have the merit of understanding that the meaning and effectiveness of a given utterance in one context may change if transplanted into another. This, rather than hinting at a comity of courts, may at most suggest an 'ordered pluralism'.[88] In other words, although transjudicial communication will continue to exist and can help in advancing the universalism of human rights, it shall still not result in a uniform system; rather, through transjudicial communication we shall continue to 'expect to find […] distinct context-specific understanding though generated through cross-referencing'.[89]

87 Lorenzo Gradoni, 'International Criminal Courts and Tribunals: Bound by Human Rights Norms … or Tied Down?' (2006) 19 Leiden Journal of International Law 847, 855.

88 Mireille Delmas-Marty, *Les forces imaginantes du droit (II), Le pluralisme ordonné* (Le Seuil 2006).

89 Wiener and Liste (n 4) 275.

CHAPTER 10

Judicial Dialogue and the Definition of Torture: The Importation of ICTs from European Jurisprudence

Elena Maculan

I Introduction

Judicial dialogue is a growing phenomenon in the domain of International Criminal Law (ICL) and International Human Rights Law (IHRL). These two areas of law partially share the same object and content, as well as the common goal of protecting human rights (HR).[1] Therefore, interaction between the relevant bodies in both fields is normal and should be welcomed in that it helps in determining a common 'syntax' to be applied in matters of common concern.

However, the so-called 'jurisprudential cross-fertilisation',[2] the outcome of this dialogue, may hide certain negative aspects. The use of external references may raise concerns as to both the methodological aspects and the impact of such a dialogue within the evolution of concepts and principles.

The current paper analyses the use made by the ad hoc International Criminal Tribunals (ICTs) of the European Court of Human Rights (ECtHR) and other HR bodies' case law with regard to the definition of torture. It is a perfect case study through which to shed some light on these possible 'shadowy sides' of judicial cross-fertilisation.

After a description of this jurisprudence (Section II), the paper addresses the methodological issues inherent in the practice of borrowing precedents from external jurisprudence, in the contexts of the selection of sources (Section III(1)) and the interpretation thereof (Section III(2)). Secondly, it will

1 Robert Roth and Françoise Tulkens, 'Introduction Symposium: The Influence of the European Court of Human Rights' Case Law on (International) Criminal Law' (2011) 9 Journal of International Criminal Justice 571, 572–573.

2 Anne-Marie Slaughter, 'A Typology of Transjudicial Communication' (1994) 29 University of Richmond Law Review 99, 117; William W. Burke-White, 'A Community of Courts: Toward a System of International Criminal Law Enforcement' (2002) 24 Michigan Journal of International Law 63.

 | DOI: 10.1163/9789004313750_012

examine whether European and HR case law actually provide reliable sources from which ICTs may borrow concepts and interpretive solutions (Section III(3)), in light of the differences between their respective frameworks.

II The Phenomenon: Judicial Dialogue in Defining Torture

Making reference to IHRL norms and case law is a *method* extensively used by the ICTs when defining substantive concepts and procedural safeguards.[3] This is because, on the one hand, compliance with HR standards is a condition of legitimacy for ICTs' decisions in terms of both procedural standards and subject matter.[4] On the other hand, IHRL provides normative content to the younger and less well-developed domain of ICL. Therefore, HR bodies' case law becomes a primary point of reference for ICL bodies when confronted with a three-fold objective.

Firstly, the jurisprudence of other judicial bodies performs a *gap-filling*[5] or *supplementary*[6] function, by providing applicable concepts wherever these are not defined in the relevant Statute. Secondly, HR case law may perform an *interpretive* function,[7] by helping in the interpretation of certain constitutive elements not clearly set out in the norms or in resolving specific applicative issues. Thirdly, since HR bodies enjoy an undisputed persuasive authority, quoting their jurisprudence furthers the *legitimacy* of the findings made by the tribunal itself.[8]

The definition of torture provides a perfect case study of this phenomenon. Faced with the lack of a normative definition of the crime in the relevant Statutes—a lack that has been remedied by the ICC Statute—,[9] ICTs have sys-

---

3 Elisabeth Lambert-Abdelgawad, 'Les Tribunaux Pénaux pour l'ex-Yugoslavie et le Rwanda et l'appel aux sources du droit international des droits de l'homme' in Mireille Delmas-Marty, Emanuela Fronza and Elisabeth Lambert-Abdelgawad (eds), *Les sources du droit international pénal* (Société de Législation comparée 2004) 115.

4 Lorenzo Gradoni, 'The Human Rights Dimension of International Criminal Procedure' in Göran Sluiter and others (eds), *International Criminal Procedure: Principles and Rules* (OUP 2013) 74.

5 Fabián Raimondo, 'General Principles of Law, Judicial Creativity and the Devolpment of International Criminal Law' in Shane Darcy and Joseph Powderly (eds), *Judicial Creativity at the International Criminal Tribunals* (OUP 2010) 46.

6 Lambert-Abdelgawad (n 3) 98.

7 Both Raimondo (n 5) 46; Lambert-Abdelgawad (n 3) 98.

8 Raimondo (n 5) 46; Lambert-Abdelgawad (n 3) 98; Slaughter (n 2) 119.

9 Rome Statute of the International Criminal Court, UN Doc A/CONF.183/9, 17 July 1998, entered

tematically needed to resort to HR case law in order to determine the constitutive elements of the offence and to resolve issues of application.

Torture is in fact not only an international crime, insofar as it may amount to a war crime or to a crime against humanity;[10] also, and even before, it is a gross HR violation, one that is expressly prohibited by many HR instruments of a general scope[11] and by a number of specific international and regional instruments.[12] Hence, it represents a real intersection point among IHRL, International Humanitarian Law (IHL), and ICL,[13] despite the existence of significant differences among the definitions of the offence envisaged in the relevant instruments.[14]

---

into force 1 July 2002 ('Rome Statute' or 'ICC Statute'), Article 7.2(e); and Elements of Crimes, ICC-ASP/1/3(part II-B) of 9 September 2002, Articles 8.2(a)(ii) and 8.2(c)(i) provide definitions of torture as a crime against humanity and as a war crime, respectively.

10 Control Council Law No. 10, Article II(1)(C); Statute of the International Criminal Tribunal For The Former Yugoslavia, UN Doc. S/RES/827 of 25 May 1993 ('ICTY Statute'), Article 5(f); Statute of the International Criminal Tribunal for Rwanda, UN Doc. S/RES/955 of 8 November 1994 ('ICTR Statute'), Article 3(f); and ICC Statute, Article 7(1)(e) enshrine torture among the underlying conducts for crimes against humanity. Torture is also a war crime under ICTY Statute, Article 2(b); ICTR Statute, Article 4(a); and ICC Statute, Articles 8(2)(a)(ii) and 8(2)(c)(i). Besides, torture has been punished under the offence of persecution and under the residual offence of 'other inhuman treatment of a similar kind', both as crimes against humanity.

11 Universal Declaration of Human Rights, Article 5; International Covenant on Civil and Political Rights, Article 7; American Convention of Human Rights, Article 5; European Convention on Human Rights, Article 3; African Charter on Human and Peoples' Rights, Article 5. Furthermore, it is prohibited under International Humanitarian Law: *see* Geneva Convention I (Articles 12 and 50), II (Articles 12 and 51), III (Articles 17, 87, 130), IV (Articles 32 and 147) and Article 3(1)(a) common to the four Conventions; Additional Protocol I (Article 2) and II (Article 2).

12 Declaration on the Protection of All Persons from Being Subjected to Torture and Other Cruel, Inhuman or Degrading Treatment or Punishment, A/RES/30/3452 of 9 December 1975 (DAT); Convention against Torture and Other Cruel, Inhuman or Degrading Treatment or Punishment, A/Res/39/46 of 10 December 1984 (CAT). At a regional level, European Convention for the Prevention of Torture and Inhuman or Degrading Treatment or Punishment, CPT/Inf/C(2002)1[EN] of 26 November 1987; Inter-American Convention To Prevent And Punish Torture (IACAT) of 9 December 1985.

13 Olivier de Frouville, 'The Influence of the European Court of Human Rights' Case Law on International Criminal Law of Torture and Inhuman or Degrading Treatment' (2011) 9 Journal of International Criminal Justice 633, 635. A similar remark is made by *Prosecutor v Furundžija*, IT-95-17/1-T, Judgment, Trial Chamber, 10 December 1998, para. 183; *Prosecutor v Aleksovski*, IT-95-14/1-T, Judgment, Trial Chamber, 25 June 1999, para. 54.

14 The main differences lie in three elements: the need for a severity threshold of the pain

It should be no surprise, then, that judicial or quasi-judicial bodies operating in these three areas of law look to one another in order to resolve interpretive issues about its scope and application.

In this regard, when addressing the key elements of the definition of the offence, both the ICTY and, to a lesser extent, the ICTR, have widely borrowed concepts from HR instruments and case law. As we will see, despite quoting several different instruments, the jurisprudence of the ECtHR has played a prominent role.

This influence has caused three main effects:

1. The gradual abandoning of the public official requirement.
2. The determination of a severity threshold for an act to amount to torture, by virtue of a relative assessment of the specific circumstances of each case. Jurisprudence has also identified a core of acts that amount to torture *per se*, among which rape has been included.
3. The development of distinctive criteria between torture and inhuman treatment, based on a severity scale of the suffering inflicted, on the existence of specific purposes or on the combination of both.

1 *The Public Official Requirement*

The first point where European case law has clearly exerted great influence is the progressive abandonment of the public official requirement. This requirement implies that the acts of torture are perpetrated by a State official or a person acting in an official capacity or at least with his/her acquiescence or consent, and it is envisaged by all relevant HR instruments that define torture.[15]

---

or suffering caused by the torturous act (which is not required by the IACAT), the requirement of a public official being involved (which is not envisaged in the ICC Statute for torture as a crime against humanity), and the provision for a catalogue of specific purposes pursued by the perpetrator when undertaking the torturous act (which varies in number and grounds, as well as in its exhaustive or merely representative nature, and which is absent for torture as a crime against humanity in the Rome Statute). All of such unevenness casts doubts on the existence of any coherent notion of torture under general International Law: Nigel S. Rodley, 'The Definition(s) of Torture in International Law' (2002) 55 Current Legal Problems 467, 469; Christoph Burchard, 'Torture in the Jurisprudence of the Ad Hoc Tribunals: A Critical Assessment' (2008) 6 Journal of International Criminal Justice 159, 161.

15 On the contrary, the requirement is not envisaged for torture as a crime against humanity under the Rome Statute, which requires instead that the perpetrator has the victim in his/her custody or under his/her control.

Yet the European Court has sometimes condemned the respondent State for breach of Article 3 ECHR when this State failed to undertake the necessary measures to prevent, investigate or punish acts of torture that were committed by *private individuals*.[16] Furthermore, the ECtHR has condemned certain States for violation of Article 3 of the ECHR because of having expelled, returned or extradited a person to a State where there were substantial grounds for believing that the person would be in danger of being subjected to torture.[17]

This evolution is consistent with the idea that the prohibition against torture imposes upon States the duty not only to prohibit and punish this offence, but also to forestall its occurrence.[18]

A similar evolution can be seen in the jurisprudence of the ad hoc Tribunals: whilst the first judgments argued that the involvement of a public official was one of the constitutive elements of torture,[19] the *Kunarac* trial judgment marks a decisive overruling on the issue.[20] The reasoning reminds that IHRL imposes upon States a set of duties in order to protect human rights and it may declare State responsibility for any breaches thereof; whereas in IHL—and ICL—'individual criminal responsibility for violation of international humanitarian law does not depend on the participation of the State'.[21] Accordingly, torture as a HR violation requires the involvement of an individual acting in an official capacity, that is, representing the State, whereas the same offence in the fields of IHL and ICL does not presume such a requirement.

The Trial Chamber finds support for this interpretation in the European case law, by arguing that it expressly held that the breach does *not* need to involve any public official.[22]

---

16 *HLR v France*, App no 24573/94 (ECtHR, 29 April 1997), para. 40; *Costello Roberts v United Kingdom*, App no 13134/87 (ECtHR, 25 March 1993), paras 27–28; *A. v United Kingdom*, App no 35373/97 (ECtHR, 17 December 2002), para. 22; *Z. and others v United Kingdom*, App no 29392/95 (ECtHR, 10 May 2001), para. 73; *Aksoy v Turkey*, App no 21987/93 (ECtHR, 18 December 1996), para. 98; *Kurt v Turkey*, App no 15/1997/799/1002 (ECtHR, 25 May 1998), para. 140.

17 See eg *HLR v France* (n 16); *Soering v United Kingdom*, App no 14038/88 (ECtHR, 7 July 1989), para. 91; *Cruz Varas and others v Sweden*, App no 15576/89 (ECtHR, 20 March 1991), paras 69–79; *Chahal v United Kingdom*, App no 22414/93 (ECtHR, 15 November 1996), paras 79–80.

18 *Furundžija* (n 13), paras 147–157.

19 *Prosecutor v Akayesu*, ICTR-96-4-T, Judgment, Trial Chamber, 2 September 1998, para. 594; *Furundžija* (n 13), para. 162, and *Furundžija*, IT-95-17/1-A, Judgment, Appeals Chamber, 21 July 2000, para. 111.

20 *Kunarac*, IT-96-23 & 23/1-T, Judgment, Trial Chamber, 22 February 2001, paras 465ff.

21 ibid para. 470.

22 ibid para. 479 and fns 1190–1191. Nevertheless, the language used by the ECtHR on this

This overruling was upheld by the Appeals Chamber in the same case[23] and was followed by later decisions,[24] as well as by the definition of torture as a crime against humanity in the ICC Statute. As a result, we may conclude that the involvement of a public official is no longer a requirement for an act to be labelled as torture under ICL.[25]

2 *The Severity of the Torturous Acts*

A second element in which ICTs have borrowed interpretive solutions from European case law is the determination of a severity threshold for the pain or suffering inflicted by the torturous act. This threshold is necessary in order to identify the punishable acts,[26] but also, according to the ECtHR, to distinguish torture from inhuman and degrading treatment.[27]

It must be said that European case law itself has exhibited inconsistencies as to this determination. The most outstanding example is the *Northern Ireland* case,[28] in which the combined use of wall-standing, hooding, subjection to noise, and sleep, food and drink deprivation was deemed to amount to torture by the European Commission; however, it was considered not of a sufficient intensity to be qualified as such by the European Court. As a result, it was labelled as inhuman and degrading treatment, which in any case is a violation of Article 3 ECHR.[29]

---

point seems rather cautious ('the Court *does not rule out the possibility*': HLR *v France* (n 16), para. 40, emphasis added).

23 *Prosecutor v Kunarac*, IT-96-23 & 23/1-A, Judgment, Appeals Chamber, 12 June 2002, paras 145–148.

24 *Prosecutor v Kvočka*, IT-98-30/1-T, Judgment, Trial Chamber, 2 November 2001, para. 139 (upheld on appeal on 28 February 2005, paras 280–284); *Prosecutor v Krnojelac*, IT-97-25-T, Judgment, Trial Chamber, 15 March 2002, para. 187 (which simply quotes the *Kunarac* precedent without delving into the issue); *Prosecutor v Brđanin*, IT-99-36-T, Judgment, Trial Chamber, 1 September 2004, paras 488–489; *Prosecutor v Limaj*, IT-03-66-T, Judgment, Trial Chamber, 30 November 2005, para. 240. See also *Prosecutor v Semanza*, ICTR-97-20-T, Judgment, Trial Chamber, 15 May 2003, paras 342 ff., making reference to the precedent set by the ICTY in the *Kunarac* Appeals Chamber's Judgment.

25 This conclusion has been confirmed in *Prosecutor v Semanza*, ICTR-97-20-A, Judgment, Appeals Chamber, 20 May 2005, paras 247 ff.

26 DAT, CAT and the ICC Statute both under Article 7 and Article 8 call for the pain or suffering inflicted being *severe*. In contrast, the IACAT does not set out this requirement.

27 See below, following Section.

28 *Ireland v United Kingdom*, App no 5310/71 (ECtHR, 18 January 1978) ('*Northern Ireland* case').

29 This decision has been much criticised and has not been followed in subsequent cases:

Although these inconsistencies exist, European jurisprudence has offered an extremely useful criterion through which to assess this interpretive issue, namely, the principle of *relative assessment*. This principle, which appeared for the first time in the *Northern Ireland* case, establishes that the severity threshold needs to be addressed on a case-by-case basis. More specifically, it depends on general circumstances, such as the duration of the treatment and its physical effects, as well as on circumstances relating to the victim, such as gender, age, and state of health.

The principle has subsequently been imported by the ICTs. The *Aleksovski* trial judgment, seeking a definition of the war crime of 'outrages upon personal dignity', makes reference to the definition of inhuman treatment propounded by the ECtHR and to the test developed in the *Northern Ireland* case.[30] The same principle also appears in the *Kvočka* trial judgment, which relies on the *Čelebići* precedent as well as on the *Northern Ireland* case, in stating that, facing the impossibility of delineating a precise threshold, the assessment has to take into account both the objective severity of the harm inflicted and certain subjective criteria and specific features of the victim.[31]

Accordingly, solitary confinement has been deemed in itself not as a form of torture; yet, in view of its strictness or duration, and provided it pursues one of the prohibited purposes of torture, it may be labelled as such.[32] Once again, this consideration is grounded on European precedents.[33]

The ICTY has, in addition, taken from the European jurisprudence the idea that some acts are *per se* so severe as to amount to torture, meaning that one does not even need to assess the specific circumstances of the case, because those acts surely reach the severity threshold. The conducts falling in this category have the clear advantage of lessening the prosecutorial burden of proof, since no medical certificate of the suffering inflicted is required.[34]

William A. Schabas, 'The Crime of Torture and the International Criminal Tribunals' (2006) 37 Case Western Reserve Journal of International Law 349, 357.

30 *Aleksovski* (n 13), para. 53.

31 *Kvočka* (n 24), paras 142–143. In the same terms, *Brđanin* (n 24), paras 483–484; *Limaj* (n 24), para. 237; *Prosecutor v Martić*, IT-95-11-T, Judgment, Trial Chamber, 12 June 2007, para. 75. By applying this relative assessment, the ICTR, in *Prosecutor v Ntagerura*, ICTR-99-46-T, Judgment, Trial Chamber, 25 February 2004, concluded that the acts of kicking and beating the detainees were not of sufficient gravity to amount to torture, since they did not prevent two of them from escaping from detention.

32 *Krnojelac* (n 24), para. 183.

33 ibid fn. 544. See also *Kvočka* (n 24), para. 144, fn. 303.

34 Burchard (n 14), 164.

While recognising that 'an exhaustive list of torturous practices is impossible to devise',[35] the ICTY, relying on external references, has tried to set out a list of these conducts, such as beating, sexual violence, threats to torture relatives, mutilation of body parts, and mock execution.[36]

Rape, too, has been deemed as an act that amounts *per se* to torture,[37] in view of the fact that 'sexual violence necessarily gives rise to severe pain or suffering, whether physical or mental'.[38] Therefore, rape can be charged as torture provided it meets the necessary requirements,[39] that is, when it was inflicted for one of the purposive elements encompassed by the definition of torture.[40] In stating, furthermore, that 'such conduct could met the purposive requirements of torture as, during armed conflicts, the purposive elements of intimidation, coercion, punishment or discrimination can often be integral components of behaviour',[41] the ICTY apparently affirms that in a context of armed conflict rape always meets this requirement.

To support these findings, the ICTY quotes the *Mejía v Perú* case before the Inter-American Commission of Human Rights (IAComHR), in which a rape inflicted on a schoolteacher by some soldiers was deemed to constitute torture.[42] The Trial Chamber also makes reference to the *Aydin v Turkey* case before the ECtHR, which labelled as torture the rape repeatedly inflicted on the applicant while she was detained in a police station, probably with the aim of obtaining information on members of the PKK with which the victim allegedly cooperated.[43] The European precedent suggests that it is hardly imaginable that a rape inflicted by a person acting in official capacity on a victim who is under detention does not involve at least one of the prohibited purposes of torture.

35 *Kvočka* (n 24), para. 147.

36 ibid paras 144–149. See also *Martić* (n 31), para. 76, which adds some further conducts.

37 While in earlier judgments the ICTY stated that it *may* constitute severe pain or suffering: *Prosecutor v Mucić*, IT-96-21-T, Judgment, Trial Chamber, 16 November 1998 ('*Čelebići* case'), para. 496.

38 *Kunarac* (n 23), para. 150; *Brđanin* (n 24), para. 485.

39 Similarly, *Čelebići* case (n 37), para. 496; *Kvočka* (n 24), para. 145; *Semanza* (n 24), paras 480 ff.

40 *Čelebići* case (n 37), para. 471; *Akayesu* (n 19), para. 687. The latter judgment also considers the perpetration of the act by a public official as a constitutive element, although we have seen that later decisions abandoned this requirement.

41 *Čelebići* case (n 37), para. 471.

42 ibid para. 483.

43 ibid paras 487–489. See *Aydin v Turkey*, App no 57/1996/676/866 (ECtHR, 25 September 1997).

3 *Distinguishing between Torture and Inhuman and Degrading Treatment*

As has been mentioned, the severity threshold has been used by the ECtHR as a criterion through which to distinguish torture from inhuman and degrading treatment. The latter conduct, which is also prohibited by the ECHR, as well as by the other HR instruments dealing with torture, has traditionally been conceived on a lower scale in a progression of severity towards torture. The distinction between the two categories is relevant not only on symbolic grounds, due to the special stigma attached to the (sole) offence of torture, but also because, according to the relevant international instruments, only torture gives rise to the possible exercise of extra-territorial jurisdiction.[44]

Despite this conceptual separation, the relevant international instruments do not clarify what distinguishes the two categories.[45] Hence, the ECtHR has been developing two interpretive criteria to make this determination.

The first criterion considers torture as an *aggravated* form of inhuman treatment, where 'aggravated' is interpreted as 'more severe', thus implying a greater intensity of the harm or suffering inflicted. In the *Greek* case, for the first time, the European Commission argued for this progression of seriousness,[46] although it did not clearly establish where exactly to place the threshold between the two categories. For instance, later judgments found that keeping the victim under inappropriate conditions of detention amounts to inhuman or degrading treatment, but not to torture.[47]

In the *Northern Ireland* case, the ECtHR stated that torture involves 'suffering of a particular intensity or cruelty', and that it has a 'special stigma' attached.[48] In addition, in *Selmouni v France*, the Court expressly recognised that the

44 Robert Roth, 'Just Short of Torture: Abusive Treatment and the Limits of International Criminal Justice' (2008) 6 Journal of International Criminal Justice 215.

45 Only the DAT expressly affirms that torture is an aggravated form of ill-treatment (Article 1.2).

46 *Denmark and others v Greece*, App no 3321/67, 3322/67, 3323/67, 3344/67 (Commission Decision, 31 May 1978) ('*Greek* case'), para. 186. Although the decision did not exactly equate the 'aggravated' suffering with a 'more severe' one, this is how subsequent decisions by the ECtHR have interpreted that reasoning: see Michelle Farrell, 'Just How Ill-treated Were You? An Investigation of Cross-fertilisation in the Interpretative Approaches to Torture at the European Court of Human Rights and in International Criminal Law' (2015) 84 Nordic Journal of International Law 482, 495–496.

47 *Greek* case (n 46); *Kudla v Poland*, App no 30210/96 (ECtHR, 26 October 2000), paras 82–100. See also the decisions quoted in *Kvočka* (n 24), para. 169, fn. 329.

48 *Northern Ireland* case (n 28), para. 167. Similarly, *Ilhan v Turkey*, App no 22277/93 (ECtHR, 27 June 2000), para. 85; *Salman v Turkey*, App no 21986/93 (ECtHR, 27 June 2000), paras

classification of a conduct may change over time; it concluded, accordingly, by labelling as torture a conduct that under its former understanding would have fallen within the definition of 'other forms of ill-treatment'.[49]

The ICTY has often followed this ECtHR approach: in the *Furundžija* judgment it emphasised that European case law has found that 'torture is deliberate inhuman treatment causing very serious and cruel suffering', and that the intensity of pain and suffering inflicted is the distinctive feature of the former as opposed to the latter.[50] The Tribunal has also stated that, if the acts fail to meet the requirements for them to be regarded as torture, they might be charged under the counts of inhuman or cruel treatment.[51]

The second interpretive solution proposed by the ECtHR focuses on the requirement for a specific purpose as a distinctive feature of torture.[52] Actually, many relevant international instruments define torture as the infliction of a pain or suffering for one of the purposes they list, such as obtaining information or a confession, punishing or intimidating the victim,[53] but they do not require the same element for the cruel or inhuman treatment. Whenever such purposive element cannot be proven, the conduct cannot amount to torture, while it may be punished as inhuman treatment.[54]

114–116; *Tomasi v France*, App no 12850/87 (ECtHR, 27 August 1992), paras 108 and 115; *Ribitsch v Austria*, App no 18896/91 (ECtHR, 4 December 1995), paras 35–38.

49 The Court concluded that a certified trauma caused by beatings over a period of various days may be considered as a proof of torture: *Selmouni v France*, App no 25803/94 (ECtHR, 28 July 1999), para. 101.

50 *Furundžija* (n 13), para. 160 and fn. 179, quoting the *Northern Ireland* case (n 28) and the *Greek* case (n 46). The *Kvočka* trial judgment followed the same lead, although it did not make any reference to European case law, but only to the *Čelebići* precedent (*Kvočka* (n 24), para. 161).

51 *Čelebići* case (n 37), para. 468; *Krnojelac* (n 24), para. 181; *Limaj* (n 24), para. 236.

52 *Greek* case (n 46), para. 186; *Northern Ireland* case (n 28), paras 66–67; *Tyrer v United Kingdom*, App no 5856/72 (ECtHR, 25 April 1978), para. 13; *İhlan v Turkey*, App no 22277/93 (ECtHR, 27 June 2000), para. 87; *Dikme v Turkey*, App no 20869/92 (ECtHR, 11 July 2000), para. 95; *Denezi and others v Cyprus*, App no 25316–25321/94, 27207/95 (ECtHR, 23 May 2001), para. 384. The IACtHR also agrees on the point: *Cantoral Benavides v Perú* (IACtHR, 18 August 2000), para. 97.

53 The number and ground of these purposes vary among the relevant instruments. Moreover, the CAT affirms that the list is representative, and so does the ICTY in *Čelebići* case (n 37), para. 470. An opposite view, considering the catalogue as exhaustive, was held in *Kunarac* (n 20), para. 485. In contrast, the ICC Statute does not require any specific purpose for an act to be labelled as a crime against humanity of torture, whereas it does for torture as a war crime.

54 *Egmez v Cyprus*, App no 30873/96 (ECtHR, 21 December 2000), para. 78; *Denizci v Cyprus*,

This criterion is also applied in some decisions by the ICTY, such as in the *Blagojević* and the *Čelebići* trial judgments, the latter dealing with the war crime of 'wilfully causing serious great suffering or serious injuries'.[55]

Thirdly, European jurisprudence has applied a combination of both criteria, namely, both the severity of the suffering and the specific purpose for which it was inflicted. The ICTY, too, has mainly followed this path.[56] In the *Čelebići* judgment, the Trial Chamber finds that the key distinctive features are both 'a sliding scale of severity' of the pain or suffering and the purpose for which the ill-treatment was inflicted.[57] The Chamber grounds this conclusion within references to European case law.[58]

Furthermore, the Trial Chamber argues that the category of cruel and inhuman treatments perform a residual function for those conducts that fall short of meeting the requirements for torture.[59]

III A Critical Assessment

The jurisprudence described above shows that ICTs constantly borrow interpretations and concepts from the ECtHR and other HR bodies' case law when defining torture as an international crime. Nevertheless, such a pattern raises concerns as both to methodological aspects—the selection of external sources and the interpretation thereof—and to a core question, namely, whether IHRL is a proper frame of reference for bodies that operate in the field of ICL.

1 *The Selection of Sources and the Preference for Strasbourg Case Law*

As a first consideration, one might question the grounds on which the ICTs select the normative instruments and the case law to which they make ref-

---

App no 25316–25321/94 and 27207/95 (ECtHR, 23 May 2001), paras 384–386. See also Judge Herndl's dissenting opinion as to the finding on torture in *Selmouni* (n 49) precisely on the ground that the purposive element had not been proved.

55 *Čelebići* case (n 37), para. 508; *Prosecutor v Blagojević*, IT-02-60, Judgment, Trial Chamber, 17 January 2005, para. 586. The ICC has followed this path too, by refusing to confirm charges of torture as a war crime when the Prosecutor failed to adequately prove that acts had been committed for a specific purpose: *Prosecutor v Bemba*, ICC-01/05-01/08-424, Decision Pursuant to Article 61(7)(a) and (b) of the Rome Statute on the Charges of the Prosecutor, Pre-Trial Chamber II, 15 June 2009, paras 290, 298–300.

56 *Krnojelac* (n 24), para. 181; *Brđanin* (n 24), para. 483; *Martić* (n 31), para. 75.

57 *Čelebići* case (n 37), paras 534–535.

58 ibid para. 535.

59 ibid para. 542.

erence. ICTs' jurisprudence dealing with the crime of torture relies on European precedents, on decisions of the HRC and, to a lesser extent, on the IACtHR, as well as it considers international treaties and soft law instruments. For instance, the *Čelebići* judgment, in determining the severity threshold for an act to be labelled as torture, quotes case law of the HRC and of the ECtHR, and a Report by the Special Rapporteur on Torture, apparently drawing no distinction among them.[60] The judgment also makes extensive reference to other sources of law when dealing with the possible labelling of rape as torture: it quotes precedents by the IAComHR, by the ECtHR and by the ICTR, as well as Reports by UN Special Rapporteurs and Commission of Experts.[61]

Hence, in ICTs' jurisprudence there appears to be no such thing as a clear and consistent criterion for the selection of the sources on which they rely. Rather, the jurisprudence of ICTs combines different instruments, irrespective of their natures, as a mandatory norm, as a soft law instrument or as a finding made by another judicial body. The selection is based on the substantive relevance for the case at issue and on the *persuasive authority* of the bodies from which the source derives.[62]

Among this plurality of sources, the ECtHR jurisprudence has clearly played a prominent role.[63] This may be explained, firstly, on the ground of the relatively high number of cases in which the Court has dealt with torture and inhumane treatment.

Secondly, in some instances the ECtHR is the sole system to have addressed a specific interpretive issue. For example, the criteria to distinguish between torture and inhuman treatment were developed by the ECtHR, whereas both the HRC and the IACtHR have adopted a comprehensive approach by overlooking such distinction.[64]

Thirdly, it may be argued that European jurisprudence is found to be more appropriate by and for the ICTs, since its interpretation of torture is broader than the definition envisaged in the CAT, thus allowing Tribunals to apply it to a wider range of cases. The progressive abandonment of the public official

---

60 ibid paras 461–469.

61 ibid paras 480–493.

62 Lambert-Abdelgawad (n 3) 113; Roth and Tulkens (n 1) 571–575.

63 Although, initially, ICTs almost sweepingly adopted the definition of torture contained in the CAT, deeming it a representation of customary international law: Burchard (n 14) 162.

64 *Čelebići* case (n 37), para. 461. Both the HRC and the Inter-American bodies have simply stated whether there has been a violation generally of Article 7 ICCPR and Article 5 ACHR, respectively: see eg *Mejía v Perú*, Case no 10.970, Report no 5/96 (IAComHR, 1 March 1996).

requirement by both the ECtHR and the ICTs, for example, expands their definition of torture to wider than that envisaged in the CAT.

Therefore, European case law is a primary source of reference when dealing with torture; not necessarily because it is *more* authoritative than, for example, the IACtHR or the HRC precedents,[65] but for the simple reason that it has dealt more often and more thoroughly with a range of interpretive issues related to the definition of torture.[66]

As a second consideration, we might point out that having resort to HR instruments and case law, and mainly to European jurisprudence, is a constant for ICTs. The references to these sources have nonetheless been decreasing in more recent years. Insofar as the tribunals gather their own settled case law about torture, they quote their own precedents on the matter, thereby relying on external sources only indirectly.[67]

Yet, as soon as one of these statements is challenged, the ICTY recovers its referencing practice. This is perfectly evident in the *Brđanin* appeal judgment, in which the appellant challenged the level of seriousness required for an act to be regarded as torture.[68] In rejecting the appellant's claim, the Appeals

65 De Frouville (n 13) 640. Still, it has been pointed out that the relationship between the ECtHR and the ICTs 'seems to be marked by a curious asymmetry in cross-referencing and mutual influence, which is reinforced by a quasi-ideological normativity demanding the tribunals' deference to the Strasbourg Court': Sergey Vasiliev, 'International Criminal Tribunals in the Shadow of Strasbourg and Politics of Cross-fertilisation' (2015) 84 Nordic Journal of International Law 371, 373.

66 The same conclusion applies to a range of substantive and procedural matters, for which the European case law is systematically quoted as a source of reference by the ad hoc tribunals: see Antonio Cassese, 'L'influence de la CEDH sur l'activité des Tribunaux pénaux internationaux' in Antonio Cassese and Mireille Delmas-Marty (eds), *Crimes internationaux et juridictions internationales* (Presses Universitaires de France 2002) 143. Extending the scope of the analysis also to European influence on the ICC and on some hybrid tribunals, see also William A. Schabas, 'Synergy or Fragmentation? International Criminal Law and the European Convention on Human Rights' (2011) 9 Journal of International Criminal Justice 609; Emanuela Fronza, 'Human Rights and Criminal Law: Reference to the Case Law of Human Rights Bodies by International Criminal Tribunals' in Robert Kolb and Damien Scalia (eds), *Droit international pénal* (2nd edn, Helbing Lichtenhahn 2012) 392.

67 See eg *Naletilić*, IT-98-34-T, Judgment, Trial Chamber, 3 May 2006, para. 299. In turn, ECtHR has begun to make reference to ICTs case law: de Frouville (n 13) 646–648.

68 *Prosecutor v Brđanin*, IT-99-36-A, Judgment, Appeals Chamber, 3 April 2007, paras 244–252. The applicant claimed that this requirement should be interpreted in accordance with the 'Bybee memorandum' from the United States' Office of Legal Counsel. The latter adopts a higher severity threshold, thereby narrowing the scope of the offence.

Chamber holds that the applicable standard is the requirement of 'severe' pain or suffering set out by the CAT and reflecting a customary international norm.[69] Further support for this conclusion is found in the *travaux preparatoires* of the CAT, as well as in the ECtHR case law.[70]

2 *Judicial Transplant or Readjustment?*

Besides the issue of which sources of reference are quoted by the ICTs, another remarkable question is *how* these sources are used, that is, whether the ICTs adopt those interpretations wholesale or somehow adjust them to their own needs and goals.

In some instances ICTs go further than the precedents on which they rely, either because they infer from those precedents more than is actually stated, or because they autonomously add a reasoning that does not appear therein.

An example of the latter pattern can be found in the *Čelebići* judgment. When determining the distinguishing features of torture as opposed to inhuman treatment, the ICTY names both the severity of the pain or suffering and a specific purpose for which the ill-treatment was inflicted. It finds support for this combination of elements in ECtHR and HRC precedents.[71] It also adds another criterion, that is, the commission of the act under official sanction, although this element was not elicited from the case law analysed. It may be argued that the Chamber considered such a point to be implicit, since all the ECtHR cases upon which it relied involved acts performed by military or police forces upon detainees. However, this criterion amounts to an autonomous finding by the ICTY, one not supported by the external references that are quoted.

In contrast, the borrowing of jurisprudence is sometimes flawed through a misinterpretation of the source, meaning that the importing judicial body derives from it more than is explicitly stated. Whether this operation is due to an unconscious misunderstanding or, on the contrary, it is consciously performed in order to achieve a predetermined outcome, it is difficult to confirm.

We might consider as an example the solution proposed by the ICTY regarding the issue of the possible application of cumulative charges, under the offences of torture and inhuman treatment, for one and the same conduct.

69 The Appeals Chamber finds that the 'Bybee memorandum' does not reflect a change in customary international law. Furthermore, it has subsequently been superseded by the 'Levin memorandum', which does not endorse the same interpretation: *Brđanin* (n 68), para. 248.

70 ibid para. 250 and fns 487–489.

71 *Čelebići* case (n 37), paras 461–472.

The issue was addressed in the *Kupreskić* judgment, which opts for the application of the principle of consumption, on the ground of an alleged—but not existing—statement by the ECtHR.[72] The Trial Chamber derives from the *Aksoy* case before the ECtHR the criteria to regulate these cases, namely, the principle of consumption and the goal and values pursued by the norms. As a result, whenever two offences pursue the same goal and safeguard the same basic values, and, as a second requirement, one is *lex specialis* with respect to the other, a conviction for the more serious offence fully encompasses the blameworthiness of the lesser one. With regard to the offences at stake, a conviction for torture encompasses the conviction for inhuman or degrading treatment, deemed less severe than the former. Nonetheless, what the quoted European decision actually held, after finding that the facts amounted to torture, is that, 'in view of the gravity of this conclusion, it is not necessary for the Court to examine the applicant's complaints of other forms of ill-treatment'.[73] Hence, the ICTY conclusion goes considerably beyond what the European decision quoted actually states.[74]

A similar step forward is provided by the ICTY when it maintains that a rape perpetrated by a public official during an armed conflict *normally* amounts to torture, on the ground of certain ECtHR decisions.[75] After having found that a rape inflicted by a person acting in official capacity on a victim who is under detention usually involves at least one of the prohibited purposes of torture, the Trial Chamber adds that such scenario is 'inherent in situations of armed conflict'.[76] In other words, it states that normally a rape committed by a public official in a context of armed conflict amounts to torture. While the former inference is actually suggested by the European case law on which the Chamber relies, the latter does not appear therein. It is true that the ICTY does not expressly state that this conclusion stems from the European jurisprudence, yet it apparently quotes this case law to support it.

In a similar vein, the *Furundžija* Trial Chamber judgment makes reference to the same cases—*Aydin v Turkey* and *Meijía v Perú*—in order to support the finding that an act of rape may be charged under the label of torture whenever it is inflicted in the course of detention and interrogation and provided it is committed by a person in official capacity and for one of the purposes envis-

72 *Prosecutor v Kupreskić*, IT-95-16-T, Judgment, Trial Chamber, 14 January 2000, paras 688 ff.

73 *Aksoy* (n 16), para. 64.

74 The ICTY finds further support to this conclusion in a quick comparative analysis of domestic systems: *Kupreskić* (n 72), paras 693–695 and fn. 956.

75 *Čelebići* case (n 37), para. 495.

76 ibid para. 495.

aged by the definition of torture.[77] Once again, the ICTY goes even further, since it argues that not only the direct victim of rape, but also relatives being forced to watch the act can be considered victims of torture. The same consideration applies to the conduct of forcing the victim to be present at the torture or execution of a relative.[78] This view is also shared by later judgments,[79] even if they rely not on HR bodies' case law, but instead on ICTY precedents.

In conclusion, it could be said that the ICTs do look in external jurisprudence for concepts, solutions, and/or support, although by no means do they adopt them sweepingly at all times. They, rather, adjust those references to achieve a correlation with the specific cases with which they are dealing—an action that is perfectly normal and correct—or even with some goals or outcomes that they have previously identified by themselves. The latter operation, albeit very common in the jurisprudential circulation, is not methodologically correct, especially when it involves what could be construed as a misuse of the external references.

3 *Is European and HR Case Law a Suitable Frame of Reference for ICTs?*

Beyond the possible misuses and readjustment of the external jurisprudential references, a question that lies at the core of this practice of judicial dialogue is whether it is a correct approach from a methodological and 'principled' perspective.

The matter is linked to the complex relationship between ICL and IHRL, which are 'false brothers'.[80] This means that, despite sharing many principles and concepts, they differ in terms of structure, functions, and restraints. Thus, although both share the ultimate goal of protecting human rights, IHRL deals with State responsibility, whereas ICL addresses the power of imposing individual criminal responsibility. In addition, while HR bodies focus on victims and their suffering and claims, ICL should be concerned with the perpetrator of the

---

77 *Furundžija* (n 13), para. 163.

78 ibid paras 162, 267.

79 *Kvočka* (n 24), para. 145; *Aleksovski* (n 13), para. 56.

80 William A. Schabas, 'Droit pénal international et droit international des droits de l'homme: faux frères?' in Marc Henzelin and Robert Roth (eds), *Le droit pénal a l'épreuve de l'internationalisation* (Librairie générale de droit et jurisprudence 2002) 165. Tavernier uses the image of 'Siamese twins', who cannot but live together despite having different 'personalities': Paul Tavernier, 'Les tribunaux pénaux internationaux et le droit international des droits de l'homme' in Delmas-Marty, Fronza and Lambert-Abdelgawad (n 3) 395.

offence and with his/her safeguards. The latter approach is consistent with the liberal inspiration of ICL and necessity to overcome that 'identity crisis' of ICL sharply denounced by Robinson some years ago.[81]

These essential differences affect the principles, limits, and interpretive methods with which the judicial bodies have to comply, their being stricter in ICL than in IHRL.[82]

Hence, an evolutionary interpretation of the concept of torture is permissible in the field of human rights and under its preventive approach in dealing with State responsibility.[83] It may, though, cause unfair outcomes if it were to be transposed into the domain of ICL, insofar as it may broaden the scope of an offence to the detriment of the accused and would thus infringe the basic principles of criminal law.

For instance, there seems to be no problem with the progressive widening beyond the category of State authorities of the responsibility for torture in the application of the ICCPR and the ECHR, which entail only State responsibility and are not limited by the rule of strict interpretation.[84]

Such an expansive shift in the field of ICL, as the *Krnojelac* Trial Chamber judgment has pointed out, would serve to 'enlarge the scope of the crime of torture beyond what it was at the time relevant to the indictment',[85] thereby infringing the principle of the non-retroactivity of criminal norms.

Similarly, the European Court has, according to its mandate and functions, in defining torture, focused upon the pain and suffering experienced by the victim. The relative assessment test in itself has been applied from an impact of pain and suffering perspective, rather than for objective elements related to the

81 Darryl Robinson, 'The Identity Crisis of International Criminal Law' (2008) 21 Leiden Journal of International Law 925. This crisis is described as the inner contradiction of ICL, which claims adherence to the fundamental principles of liberal criminal systems, but has, in fact, come to embrace a number of illiberal doctrines incompatible with those principles.

82 As suggested in *Kunarac* (n 20), para. 482. In this judgment the ICTY makes an overruling of its previous finding (*Čelebići* case (n 37), para. 459; *Furundžija* (n 13), para. 160) that the definition of torture envisaged in the CAT reflected a customary norm. The *Kunarac* judgment points out instead that the definition of torture under the CAT is meant to apply only at the inter-state level and, moreover, only 'for the purposes of' that Convention. As a result, it can serve only 'as an interpretational aid' within the ICTY system.

83 Schabas, 'Droit pénal international' (n 80) 167.

84 Sandesh Sivakumaran, 'Torture in International Human Rights and International Humanitarian Law: The Actor and the Ad Hoc Tribunals' (2005) 18 Leiden Journal of International Law 541, 553.

85 *Krnojelac* (n 24), para. 186. Similarly, *Brđanin* (n 24), para. 481, fn. 1257.

perpetrator's conduct.[86] The conduct of the perpetrator does not play a pivotal role in the Court's interpretation. This choice is consistent with the victim-focused teleological reasoning adopted by the ECtHR. However, it cannot acritically be transplanted into ICTs jurisprudence, where the focus is precisely on the conduct of the perpetrator and the principles of strict construction and culpability apply.

Lastly, stating that rape committed by State agents against a detainee normally amounts to torture not only goes against the *in dubio pro reo* principle, but it might also cause an unjustified double charge for one and the same conduct, thereby infringing upon the *ne bis in idem* principle.

This is not to say that ICL allows no evolution in the definition and structure of international crimes; the rapid development of this domain throughout the past decades proves quite the opposite. Due attention must be paid to the fundamental safeguards inherited by ICL from its Criminal Law component, such as the principles of legality, strict construction, non-retroactivity, culpability, *in dubio pro reo*, and *ne bis in idem*. All of these principles aim at granting a liberal and fair approach. They are thus intrinsically part of the legitimacy of ICL as a whole.

Judges should carefully consider the effects of the interpretation they purport: if it causes an *expansion* of the scope of the crime beyond what the relevant instruments say—for example, by broadening the definition of torture to acts committed by private individuals instead of by State officials—this outcome should have been at least reasonably foreseeable at the time of the conduct. Also, it should be doubted that an emerging jurisprudential trend by a HR body—such as saying that the involvement of a public official is not required—might prevail over an opposite statement found in the CAT and all relevant HR instruments.

This clarification suggests a further consideration: when IHRL itself does not provide a uniform concept or solution—as happens with torture—the choice of giving precedence to Strasbourg case law, while grounded in its substantial relevance and persuasiveness, might cause an undesirable 'regionalisation' of the concept, one that does not reflect the 'generally acceptable' or 'internationally recognized' HR standards.

4 *Concluding Remarks*

The evolution of the ICTs' definition of torture under the influence of the European jurisprudence offers a litmus test of the dynamics and effects of judicial

86 Farrell (n 46) 511.

cross-fertilisation. Although this phenomenon may be very useful when facing normative lacunae or interpretive issues, and although it enhances the development of a common 'grammar' in the protection of human rights, it hides some shadowy areas that should be carefully scrutinised. On the one hand, the ICTs' practice of borrowing from HR bodies' case law may occasionally result in methodological flaws as to *what* to rely on, and *how* to rely on whichever aspect is adopted. On the other, it should be a careful and *critical* reference to those solutions and reasoning, a reference that relates and adjusts them to the different framework of the importing system, that is, of the ICL. Here, the fundamental principles require different interpretive techniques and stricter restraints than those in IHRL.

As a result, it may be the case that no single definition of torture can be achieved, given that it may vary among the domains of IHRL, IHL, and ICL. The *harmonising effect* caused by the phenomenon of judicial cross-fertilisation may be considered *per se* in positive terms, since it both helps to overcome the fragmented normative definition of torture and fosters the creation of a common understanding of the offence.[87] However, any 'shadowy sides' possibly lying within must not be overlooked; these must be examined in the context of the specific domain of ICL. If what it costs in order to have a harmonised definition of torture results in the infringement of fundamental safeguards in criminal matters, possibly the idea that different concepts of torture will endure should, rather, be accepted. This reality would not necessarily assume an undesirable fragmentation of human rights, but simply its natural 'branching out'.[88]

87 Elena Maculan, 'Judicial Definition of Torture as a Paradigm of Cross-fertilisation. Combining Harmonisation and Expansion' (2015) 84 Nordic Journal of International Law 456, 473–474.

88 Vasiliev (n 65) 397.

CHAPTER 11

Confronting the Divergent Notions of Torture and Other Ill-Treatment under the Rome Statute through the Lens of Cumulative Conviction

*Elizabeth Santalla Vargas**

1 Introduction

The criminalisation of torture as a crime against humanity and as a war crime under the Rome Statute, while capturing significant jurisprudential developments, presents incongruent features which go beyond the divergence posed by the contextual elements.[1] In short, while the involvement of a public official, as required by the Convention against Torture,[2] was abandoned in the criminalisation of torture as a crime against humanity and as a war crime, the purpose requirement was maintained in the latter. The criminalisation of torture as a crime against humanity rather incorporated a custodial element or the victim's control exerted by the accused (Article 7(2)(e) of the Rome Statute).[3] It has been asserted that the underlying reason for including the purpose requirement as a war crime was the intention to differentiate it from the crime of inhuman treatment.[4]

---

* The author wishes to thank the encouragement and input provided by the editors and the peer reviewers during the drafting process. This article was concluded in August 2016.

1 See Elizabeth Santalla Vargas, 'La Múltiple Faceta de la Tortura y los 'otros tratos' en la jurisprudencia de la Corte Interamericana de Derechos Humanos y de los Tribunales Penales Internacionales' in Eduardo Ferrer and Alfonso Herrera (eds), *Diálogo Jurisprudencial en Derechos Humanos entre Tribunales Constitucionales y Cortes Internacionales* (Tirant lo Blanch 2013) 1315, 1340 ff. Originally in Kai Ambos *et al* (eds.), *Sistema Interamericano de Protección de los Derechos Humanos y Derecho Penal Internacional* (Konrad Adenauer 2010).

2 Convention against Torture and other Cruel, Inhuman or Degrading Treatment or Punishment, adopted by GA Res 39/46 of 10 December 1984, entered into force 26 June 1987 ('Convention against Torture'), Article 1(1).

3 Rome Statute of the ICC, UN Doc A/CONF.183/9 of 17 July 1998, entered into force 1 July 2002 ('Rome Statute').

4 See Knut Dörmann, 'War Crimes under the Rome Statute of the ICC, with a Special Focus on the Negotiations on the Elements of Crimes' in Armin von Bogdandy and Rüdiger (eds), 7 *Max Planck Yearbook of United Nations Law* (Nijhoff 2003) 366–370. See also, Manfred Nowak

 | DOI: 10.1163/9789004313750_013

It is acknowledged that the ad hoc Tribunals jurisprudence largely influenced the criminalisation of torture under the Rome Statute framework. Remarkably, the early case law that dealt with the task of elucidating the constituent elements of the offence in the context of the ICTY statutory framework resorted to human rights law (conventional IHL did not provide definitions in this respect).[5] In so doing, the public official requirement of the Convention against Torture was gradually overcome, as an approach that would be confined to such a purview would clearly clash with the non-State actor prevalence, or at least formal recognition, in the realm of IHL and thus the underlying goals and scope of international criminal law. The compatibility of the purposive element with IHL is arguably less problematic. Importantly, the spectrum of the element, by considering that customary international law was not confined to the non-exhaustive list of purposes enunciated by the Convention against Torture,[6] was expanded to include, inter alia, of particular relevance in the realm of IHL, humiliation[7] that, inextricably linked to the safeguarding of human dignity, arguably lies at the heart of the prohibition of torture and other ill-treatment. In line with these jurisprudential developments, the formula adopted in the Elements of Crimes: 'for such purposes as',[8] allows for a broader consideration. The question arises, therefore, as to the underlying rationale for including the purposive element with respect to torture as a war crime but not as a crime against humanity when such an element derives from

---

and Ralph Janik, 'Torture, Cruel, Inhuman, Degrading Treatment or Punishment' in Andrew Chapham and others (eds), *The 1949 Geneva Conventions: A Commentary* (Oxford 2015) 328, para. 31.

5 See Knut Dörmann, 'Contribution by the ad hoc Tribunals for the former Yugoslavia and Rwanda to the Ongoing Work on Elements of Crimes in the Context of the ICC' (2000) 94 Asil Proceedings of the Annual Meeting 286.

6 *Prosecutor v Mucić*, IT-96-21-T, Judgment, Trial Chamber, 16 November 1998 ('*Čelebići* Trial Judgment'), para. 470.

7 *Prosecutor v Furundžija*, IT-95-17/1-T, Judgment, Trial Chamber, 10 December 1998, para. 162. The elements of the war crime of torture were upheld on appeal. See *Prosecutor v Furundžija*, IT-95-17/1-A, Judgment, Appeals Chamber, 21 July 2000, para. 111. See also *Prosecutor v Kvočka*, IT-98-30/1-T, Judgment, Trial Chamber, 2 November 2001, para. 141; *Prosecutor v Kvočka*, IT-98-30/1-A, Judgment, Appeals Chamber, 28 February 2005, para. 289. In *Krnojelac* the Trial Chamber explicitly rejected the customary law status of humiliation as a prohibited purpose. Having the discussion on appeal revolved around the question of superior responsibility, the Appeals Chamber did not pronounce on such a divergent view. See *Prosecutor v Krnojelac*, IT-97-25-T, Judgment, Trial Chamber II, 15 March 2002, para. 186; *Prosecutor v Krnojelac*, IT-97-25-A, Judgment, Appeals Chamber, 17 September 2003, para. 161.

8 Elements of Crimes, Article 8(2)(a)(ii)-1 (element 2).

the human rights law archetype.[9] This is even more intriguing if one takes into account that the distinction between torture and other ill-treatment could not be deemed particularly relevant in the development of conventional IHL.[10] Against this backdrop, one may argue that the custodial element of torture as a crime against humanity resembles the underlying traditional perspective embedded in the Convention against Torture that encapsulated the prohibition of torture within the State actor paradigm.[11]

What the consequences and implications are for such a divergent criminalisation (of torture as a war crime and as a crime against humanity) will be analysed with respect to the discussion prompted by *ne bis in idem* in the context of the cumulative charging/conviction contention and the formulation of the *idem* component of the principle under the Rome Statute. In addition, instances of reliance on the ECtHR's case law approach to the *idem* component by ICTs will be analysed in the light of the previous discussion.

II Normative Divergence and Cumulative Conviction

The underlying rationale, *raison d'être* and coherence of such criminalisation may be scrutinised for the first time in *Ongwen*, a case before the ICC concerning a former senior commander of the Sinia Brigade of the Lord Resistance Army (LRA). The case, part of the situation in Uganda, involves a non-State armed group (the LRA). Both torture as a war crime and as a crime against humanity form part of the charges. In addition, cruel treatment and outrages upon personal dignity as war crimes and other inhuman acts as a crime against humanity are also part of the charges.[12] It may be further noted that, inter alia, torture and cruel treatment form part of the underlying acts underpinning the charge of persecution on political grounds.[13] All of those charges have been confirmed at the confirmation of charges procedural phase.[14]

9 Considering that the rationale behind such an approach remains unclear and that it might have been the result of an oversight during the drafting process, see Nowak and Janik (n 4) 329, para. 35.

10 ibid 319, para. 5 (referring to the structural conception and drafting history of the Geneva Conventions).

11 For a similar view, see Nowak and Janik (n 4) 321, para. 9.

12 *Prosecutor v Ongwen*, ICC-02/04-01/15-375-AnxA-Red, Document Containing the Charges, Annex A, Pre-Trial Chamber II, 22 December 2015, paras 22, 35, 38, 49, 61.

13 ibid paras 25, 39, 52, 65.

14 *Prosecutor v Ongwen*, ICC-02/04-01/15, Decision on the Confirmation of Charges against

In justifying its cumulative charging policy, the Prosecution stressed that although the physical acts are substantially the same, the legal elements differ.[15] The Defence, in turn, requested the Chamber to refrain from confirming cumulative charges in the interest of fairness to the extent that charges 'are based on the same facts'.[16] It may be noted that the Prosecution's position echoes the ICTY's cumulative charging policy that was affirmed and regarded as a constant practice by virtue of its occurrence in a procedural phase where the totality of the evidence has not yet been assessed.[17] In fact, the Prosecution's rebuttal to the Defence's contention[18] posited that any conflict with *ne bis in idem* could only be triggered by cumulative conviction.[19]

The discussion is thus reminiscent of the ICTY's debate concerning *ne bis in idem* and cumulative conviction. It may be recalled that the controlling test in this regard asserted in *Čelebići*—followed in subsequent case law[20]—posited the relevance of identifying the existence of a materially distinct element in the crime at stake requiring proof of a fact which the other offence

---

Dominic Ongwen, Pre-Trial Chamber II, 23 March 2016 ('*Ongwen* Confirmation of Charges Decision').

15 Confirmation of Charges hearing, 21 January 2016. See transcript, ICC-02/04-01/15-T-20-Red-ENG, at lines 24–25, p. 17 and 3–6, p. 18.

16 Confirmation of Charges hearing, 25 January 2016. See transcript, ICC-02/04-01/15-T-22-ENG, at lines 17–19, p. 52.

17 *Prosecutor v Mucić*, IT-96-21-A, Judgment, Appeals Chamber, 20 February 2001 ('*Čelebići* Appeal Judgment'), para. 400.

18 Confirmation of Charges hearing, 26 January 2016. See transcript, ICC-02/04-01/15, at lines 20–24, p. 10 (considering that the *Čelebići* test entails an artificial application, in particular by allowing the *chapeau* requirements be sufficient for enabling cumulative charging).

19 Confirmation of Charges hearing, 26 January 2016. This stance further echoes the STL Appeals Chamber's view: '[t]he *non bis in idem* principle is triggered not at the *charging* stage, but rather when *guilt* is determined'. See STL-11-01/I/AC/R176bis, Interlocutory Decision on the Applicable Law: Terrorism, Conspiracy, Homicide, Perpetration, Cumulative Charging, Appeals Chamber, 16 February 2011 ('STL Decision on the Applicable Law'), para. 288. See also, Carl-Friedrich Stuckenberg, 'Cumulative Charges and Cumulative Convictions' in Carsten Stahn (ed), *The Law and Practice of the ICC* (OUP 2015) 840, 858.

20 See eg *Prosecutor v Jelisić*, IT-95-10-A, Judgment, Appeals Chamber, 5 July 2001, para. 82; *Prosecutor v Kupreškić*, IT-95-16-A, Judgment, Appeals Chamber, 23 October 2001, paras. 387, 388; *Prosecutor v Kunarac*, IT-96-23&IT-96-23/1-A, Judgment, Appeals Chamber, 12 June 2002, para. 168. The test was also found applicable in the context of the ECCC. See, *Prosecutor v Kaing ('Duch')*, 001/18-07-2007-ECCC/SC, Judgment, Appeals Chamber, 3 February 2012, paras. 298, 300 (with further case law of the ICTY, ICTR, SCSL and the ICC applying the test).

does not require.[21] Where the test is not met, a conviction would be entered in connection with the offence requiring the materially distinct element.[22] In fact, the test—having been previously relied upon also by ICC Pre-Trial[23] and Trial Chambers[24]—has been endorsed by the recently adopted ICC Chamber Practice Manuals, explicitly allowing for confirmation of cumulative charges—apart from evidentiary considerations—to the extent that they contain a *materially distinct legal element*. In so doing, deference is given to the Trial Chamber to resolve issues of concurrence of offences.[25] It is worth noting that the Decision on the Confirmation of Charges in *Bemba*, that also adopted the *Čelebići* test,[26] while referring to the approaches adopted in the context of cumulative charging at both the national and international level, arguably made reference to the notion of protected legal value[27]—couched in various terms—in national case law as well as in the aforementioned decisions of the ICTY.[28] Notably, the Decision on the Confirmation of Charges in *Ongwen* has referred to a 'different protected interest' as an alternative factor (to the materially distinct element criterion).[29]

It is further interesting to note that the *Kupreškić* Trial Judgment's discussion on cumulative charging had drawn, inter alia, on the application by both the European Commission and the ECtHR of Article 3 of the ECHR. As pointed out by the Chamber, relying on *Aksoy v Turkey*,[30] both 'bodies have refrained

---

21 *Čelebići* Appeal Judgment (n 17), para. 412.

22 ibid para. 413.

23 For the application of the test in *Bemba*, see Stuckenberg (n 19) 852. See also, STL Decision on the Applicable Law (n 19), paras 286–293.

24 *Prosecutor v Katanga*, ICC-01/04-01/07-3436, Judgment, Trial Chamber II, 7 March 2014, para. 1695. *Prosecutor v Bemba*, ICC-01/05-01/08-3343, Judgment, Trial Chamber III, 21 March 2016, para. 748.

25 ICC Chambers Practice Manual, February 2016, 19 (reproduces verbatim the text of the first version).

26 *Prosecutor v Bemba*, ICC-01/05-01/08-424, Pre-Trial Chamber II, 15 June 2009 ('*Bemba* Confirmation of Charges Decision'), para. 202.

27 The notion that is applied as a test for analysing cumulative charging/conviction has not been defined in the case law analysed here. In the author's view, its application evokes the underlying value(s) that justifies that certain undesirable and/or prohibited conduct is considered criminally reprehensible. In so doing, such value(s) is deemed worthy of protection by criminal law.

28 *Bemba* Confirmation of Charges Decision (n 26), para. 200, fns 275 and 276 (cases referring to 'different protected interests', 'different values', 'differing social interests').

29 *Ongwen* Confirmation of Charges Decision (n 14), para. 32.

30 *Aksoy v Turkey*, App no 21987/93 (ECtHR, 18 December 1996), para. 64.

from a multiple characterisation of the same action falling foul of Article 3'.[31] Such an approach[32] may have been linked to the understanding that under Article 3 of the ECHR no different consequences arise with respect to the three categories of ill-treatment, ie torture, inhuman and degrading treatment or punishment.[33]

In identifying the underlying rationale of the ECtHR's approach in *Aksoy v Turkey*, that the *Kupreškić* Trial Chamber[34] deemed illustrative of the stance adopted by the ECtHR, the Chamber considered that all ill-treatment violations of Article 3 of the ECHR appeared to have been understood as safeguarding the same values. Such an observation, led the Chamber to consider an additional test, namely the ascertainment of 'whether the various provisions at stake protect different values',[35] a test that the Chamber found to be rooted in both common and civil law legal traditions. It further elaborated that 'under this test, if an act or transaction is in breach of two criminal provisions protecting different values, it may be held that the act or transaction infringes *both* criminal provisions'.[36]

The Chamber posited, however, that national case law did not reveal the application of the test in isolation but rather in conjunction with or in support of traditional approaches (the *Blockburger* test[37]—that led to the *Čelebići* test—and its counterpart in civil law legal systems, namely reciprocal specialty[38]) as well as the principles of consumption and specialty.[39] Although admitting that war crimes and crimes against humanity may protect specific values, in addition to the general underlying values of core crimes as 'they are

---

31 *Prosecutor v Kupreškić*, IT-95-16-T, Judgment, 14 January 2000 ('*Kupreškić* Trial Judgment'), para. 692.

32 A more recent case, *El Masri v Turkey*, somehow denotes a change of stance. The ECtHR's finding of inhuman and degrading treatment in addition to torture was predicated upon events that while concerning different episodes of the same situation were closely related. *El-Masri v the former Yugoslav Republic of Macedonia*, App no 39630/09 (ECtHR, 13 December 2012), para. 223.

33 William A. Schabas, *The European Convention on Human Rights: A Commentary* (OUP 2015) 169.

34 For an overview of the discussion, see John Ackerman and Eugene O'Sullivan, *Practice and Procedure of the ICTY. With Selected Materials from the ICTR* (Kluwer Law International 2000) 257–260.

35 *Kupreškić* Trial Judgment (n 31), para. 693.

36 ibid para. 694.

37 For the development and content of the test, see ibid para. 681.

38 ibid paras 684–685.

39 ibid para. 695.

designed to ensure respect for human dignity',[40] the Chamber deemed disputable the application of the 'the different values test' unless supported by reciprocal specialty.[41] It thus applied the test in corroboration of the latter while analysing cumulative charging with respect to persecution and murder as a crime against humanity.[42] A different approach, accordingly, has been adopted by the Pre-Trial Chamber in *Ongwen* where consideration of a 'protected interest' was made in a disjunctive manner.[43]

In contrast, in *Bemba*, in adhering to the *Čelebići* test, the Trial Chamber relied, inter alia, on *Zolotokhin v Russia* which has inclined to the factual assessment as the decisive test for establishing the *idem* component in the context of the ECHR.[44] However, in *Zolotokhin* the ECtHR substituted the various approaches previously undertaken in its case law, including consideration to the 'protected social value', with a purely factual assessment.[45] The soundness of resorting to an interpretation that in the area of State responsibility is not necessarily cognisant of considerations relevant in the context of individual criminal responsibility is thus open to scrutiny.

In the context of the Rome Statute, as aforementioned, the purposive element only applies to torture as a war crime. Transposing the *Čelebići* test, both torture as a war crime and as a crime against humanity would always be maintained. In the war crimes scenario the purposive element of torture entails a materially distinct element with respect to other ill-treatment. As a crime against humanity, apart from the contextual element, the custodial element would in turn do so. Questions arise, therefore, as to whether the various offences constituting ill-treatment, distinct from torture, do not *per se* protect different values that may render permissible its consideration as autonomous offences, even if arising out of the same conduct, and so not necessarily subsumed by torture. Arguably, considerations as to the underlying protected legal value—a notion that may prove dissonant in the purview of international State responsibility—may furnish some insight in this respect and may enable a more balanced analysis that is mindful of the rights of the accused inherent in the safeguards against (impermissible) cumulative conviction.

40 ibid para. 702.
41 ibid para. 704.
42 ibid para. 710.
43 See above (n 29).
44 *Zolotukhin v Russia*, App no 14939/03 (ECtHR, 10 February 2009), para. 82.
45 ibid paras 77, 78, 70.

1 *Does the Divergent Criminalisation of Torture and Other Ill-treatment Foster further Discussion on the Relationship between* Ne Bis in Idem *and Cumulative Conviction?*

The terminological disparity in framing the *ne bis in idem* principle, incorporated in all Statutes of ICTs, may raise doubts as to the utility of analysing the jurisprudence of the ad hoc Tribunals. Such a concern may lie in addition to considerations of its general relevance as a guiding interpretive tool of the principles of international law within the purview of Article 21(1)(b) of the Rome Statute, as far as procedural law is concerned. What is more, to the extent that the principle has been explicitly provided for in the Rome Statute, questions arise as to whether resorting to such a subsidiary source of law[46] is necessary at all. While the Statutes of the ICTY (Article 10(1)), the ICTR (Article 9(1)), and the SCSL (Article 9(1)) refer to *acts* of serious violations of IHL, the Statute of the ICC uses *conduct* (Article 20). As such, some commentators advocate for advancing uniformity in terminology aiming at reinforcing the essence of the principle as a judicial guarantee and a fundamental right of the accused.[47] Thus the question lingers as to whether a substantial disparity in scope and content applies to *ne bis in idem* when couched in terms of *acts* or *conduct*. In addressing this question, in accordance with the general rules of interpretation, the drafting history of the provisions at stake as well as jurisprudential interpretation are relevant. This is arguably even more compelling if one considers that the equally authentic versions of the Statute[48] present a range of diverse terminology arguably entailing differences in content—which also applies to the authentic versions of the ICTY Statute—rendering a literal interpretation nugatory.[49]

---

46 See Gilbert Bitti, 'Article 21 and the Hierarchy of Sources of Law before the ICC' in Carsten Stahn (ed), *The Law and Practice of the ICC* (OUP 2015) 411, 427–430.

47 Stefano Manacorda and Giulio Vanacore, 'The Right Not to Be Tried Twice for International Crimes: an Overview of the *Ne Bid in Idem* Principle within the Statutes of the ICC and the ICTs' in Triestino Mariniello (ed), *The ICC in Search of its Purpose and Identity* (Routledge 2015) 61. In the author's interpretation the term *acts* or *crimes* advances such a goal, ibid 77.

48 Rome Statute, Article 128.

49 Due to linguistic constraints only the English, French and Spanish versions have been consulted. While the English version of the Rome Statute uses *conduct* in both Articles 20(1) and 20(3), the French version uses *actes* in Article 20(1) and *comportement* in Article 20(3). In turn, the Spanish version uses *conductas* in Article 20(1) and *hechos* in Article 20(3). Only the Spanish version of Article 20(3) can be literally assimilated to *facts*. It may be deemed, however, an inaccurate translation as the expression *hechos también prohibidos en virtud de los artículos 6, 7 u 8* may be actually referring to conduct, bearing

Interestingly, the drafting history of Article 20 of the Rome Statute reveals that initial consideration was given to the same terminology applied by the ad hoc Tribunals' Statutes, ie *acts* rather than *conduct*.[50] The underlying reasons for such a change in the adopted text, however, are not self-evident[51] and no further explanation seems to be available nor it seems that much attention was paid to the usage of a different term (*conduct* rather than *acts*) in formulating the *idem* component.[52] Against this background, one may find sound reasons to assert that the terminological disparity does not substantially bear upon the content and scope of the principle. In fact, the application of the principle in the ad hoc Tribunals case law denotes that the aforesaid terms were regarded as embracing a similar understanding. One may note that, for instance, in

---

in mind that mere facts do not entail criminal consequences and cannot be deemed to correspond literally neither to *conduct* nor to *comportement*. While the ICTY Statute uses *acts* in the English version, the French version uses *faits*, which corresponds to *hechos* in Spanish (and so this version refers to *hechos*).

50 Schabas points out that two separate provisions appeared in the PrepCom's report of 1996. One of them was based upon Article 42 of the ILC's draft. Some Delegations submitted revised texts. See William A. Schabas, *The ICC: A Commentary on the Rome Statute*, Article 20 (*Ne bis in idem*) (OUP 2010) 374–375. The US delegation proposal included the term *acts* (8 March 1998).

51 An explanation might lie in the overall aim of avoiding preference towards a particular legal tradition in the Rome Statute drafting. For the *idem* component, see Immi Tallgren and Astrid Reisinger Coracini, 'Article 20—*Ne bis in idem*' in Otto Triffterer and Kai Ambos (eds), *The Rome Statute of the ICC. A Commentary* (3rd edn, C.H. Beck, Hart, Nomos 2016) 901, 903–904 (with further references). See also Gerard Conway, '*Ne Bis in Idem* in International Law' (2003) 3 International Criminal Law Review 217.

52 The PrepCom's Report on the Establishment of an ICC incorporated *conduct* in Article 18 (*ne bis in idem*) with no explanation as to the departure from the term 'acts' that had prevailed in the ILC's draft of the Statute, which constituted the basis for the work of the PrepCom, see UN Diplomatic Conference of Plenipotentiaries on the Establishment of an ICC, 15 June–17 July 1998, A/CONF.183-2, 14 April 1998, 29. Tallgren and Reisinger Coracini point out that such a change was introduced by the Chairman's working paper for the last session of the PrepCom in 1998. Upon controversy raised by some delegations as to the expression 'conduct constituting a crime', the Chairman had proposed maintaining the ILC's draft, ie 'acts constituting a crime'. Some delegations, however, preferred 'conduct'. See Tallgren and Reisinger Coracini (n 51) 916, para. 27, fn. 96; 923, para. 40. Attention was rather paid to the nature of the crimes, see eg Report of the Ad hoc Committee on the Establishment of an ICC, Summary of the Proceedings during the Period 3–13 April 1995, A/AC.244/2, 21 April 1995, 22 (Article 42, paras 105–106). See also, *Prosecutor v Gaddafi*, ICC-01/11-01/11-344-Red, Decision on the admissibility of the case against Saif Al-Islam Gaddafi, Pre-Trial Chamber I, 31 May 2013 ('PTC *Gaddafi* Admissibility Decision'), para. 87, fn. 138.

Ntakirutimana, the Appeals Chamber referred to *conduct* in addressing the alleged violation of the principle:

> double jeopardy principles are offended by two convictions with mental elements established by the *same conduct* but each with an *actus reus* distinguishable from the other in time, location, and identity of the victims.[53]

It further recalled its holding in *Musema*:

> multiple criminal convictions entered under different statutory provisions but based on the same *conduct* are permissible only if each statutory provision involved has a materially distinct element not contained in the other.[54]

It continued by referring to the same *facts* that may enable cumulative convictions with respect to genocide and extermination and prevent it in the case of murder and extermination as crimes against humanity.[55] In *Orić*, while denying Orić's application for leave to appeal the Single Judge's Decision, the aforesaid discussion on *ne bis in idem* in *Ntakirutimana* was confirmed as a consistent interpretation of the Statute[56] by the Appeals Chamber of the MICT.[57] In analysing Orić's alleged criminal conduct,[58] the Single Judge's Decision considered, inter alia, the alleged victims and the nature of the offences subject to the proceedings before the War Crimes Chamber of the State Court of Bosnia-Herzegovina concluding that those factors could not constitute the same acts entailing violations of IHL for which Orić had been prosecuted—and acquitted before the ICTY. As the domestic proceedings are concerned with alleged war crimes against prisoners of war, the victims play a particular role in contributing to identifying the nature of the offence.[59] Such an

53 *Prosecutor v Ntakirutimana*, ICTR-96-10-A and ICTR-96-17-A, Judgment, 13 December 2004, para. 20 (emphasis added).

54 ibid para. 542 (emphasis added).

55 ibid para. 542.

56 Article 7 of the MICT Statute mirrors Article 10 of the ICTY Statute.

57 *Prosecutor v Orić*, MICT-14-79, Decision on an Application for Leave to Appeal the Single Judge's Decision of 10 December 2015, Appeals Chamber, 17 February 2016, para. 11.

58 *Prosecutor v Orić*, MICT-14-79, Decision on Second Motion Regarding a Breach of *Non Bis in Idem*, Single Judge, 10 December 2015, para. 9.

59 ibid para. 8.

analysis denotes that in contrasting the diverse proceedings in question not only the facts are relevant, but importantly the overall appraisal of the conduct criminally reprehensible. The nature of the offence is arguably of crucial consideration (particularly) in the context of the ad hoc Tribunals by virtue of the normative relation between ordinary and international crimes.[60] It may be further noted that an interchangeable usage can also be found in literature.[61]

In the context of the Rome Statute, it is accepted that the term *conduct* embraces a similar meaning in both the complementarity and *ne bis in idem* provisions (Articles 17(1)(c) and 20(3), respectively).[62] The term, while not explicitly defined in the ICC jurisprudence, has been interpreted thus far as encompassing a factual component predicated upon specific incidents that in the context of the 'same case' admissibility assessment requires the analysis of 'the conduct alleged in those incidents being an integral part of the case against the suspect'.[63] In turn, *incident* 'is understood as referring to a historical event, defined in time and place, in the course of which crimes [...] were allegedly committed'.[64] It appears, therefore, that in interpreting the term *conduct*—in both scenarios: under Articles 17 and 20, while an important factor is the factual element, the term is not to be confined to a purely factual assessment but can rather be construed more broadly encompassing the link-

60 ICTY Statute, Article 10(2)(a).

61 See eg Christine Van den Wyngaert and Tom Ongena, '*Ne bis in idem* Principle, Including the Issue of Amnesty' in Antonio Cassese, Paola Gaeta and John R.W.D. Jones (eds), *The Rome Statute of the ICC: A Commentary* (OUP 2002) vol 1, 705, 724. The commentary reads in part: 'a person tried for murder (an ordinary crime) by a national court could be retried for genocide by the ICTY or ICTR on the basis of the same conduct' (ibid 719). William A. Schabas and Mohamed El Zeidy commenting Article 17 of the Rome Statute, in Otto Triffterer and Kai Ambos (eds), *The Rome Statute of the ICC. A Commentary* (3rd edn, C.H. Beck, Hart, Nomos 2016) 781, 787, para. 7.

62 Schabas and El Zeidy (n 61) 810, para. 53.

63 *Prosecutor v Gaddafi*, ICC-01/11-01/11-547-Red, Judgment on the appeal of Libya against the decision of Pre-Trial Chamber I of 31 May 2013 entitled 'Decision on the admissibility of the case against Saif Al-Islam Gaddafi', Appeals Chamber, 21 May 2014 ('*Gaddafi* Admissibility Appeal Judgment'), para. 70. In the Prosecutor's view, the terms *same conduct, acts* or *facts* were to be understood as synonymous of the *idem* requirement, distinct to the *same offence, same crime or same elements* that embody a legal qualification. See *Prosecutor v Gaddafi*, ICC-01/11-01/11-384-Red, Prosecution Response to the 'Document in Support of the Government of Libya's Appeal against the Decision on the admissibility of the case against Saif Al-Islam Gaddafi', Prosecutor, 22 July 2013, para. 57.

64 ibid para. 62.

age of such factual scenario to the legal qualification of the offence. It may be noted that in the *Gaddafi* Admissibility Appeal Judgment, the Appeals Chamber referred to conduct 'described in the incidents under investigation which is imputed to the suspect'.[65] The mere existence of facts can only be imputed to a suspect where its causation (by act or omission) or attribution[66] is, at the outset, criminally reprehensible, namely a conduct committed by a human being or attributed to him/her—as opposed to mere facts with no criminal consequences—bearing criminal implications. Such an approach goes in tandem with the 'substantially the same conduct test', which does not require identity in terms of legal qualification (in the context of complementarity).[67] In fact, the Decision on Admissibility in *Gaddafi* held that the *ne bis in idem* principle under Article 20(3) does not require the same legal characterisation of the crime.[68] The extent to which the nature of the offence becomes irrelevant for the *ne bis in idem* analysis remains, arguably, a question surrounded by ambiguities, particularly as far as the cumulative conviction analysis is concerned. As opposed to the terminological preference for *conduct*, the intended legislative departure from the ad hoc Tribunal Statutes with respect to the underlying distinction between ordinary and international crimes[69] finds an explanation in the drafting history, which reflected the uncontroversial view that the complementarity regime embodies a presumption in favour of domestic jurisdictions.[70]

Strikingly, the Appeals Chamber did not engage in further analysis of the Pre-Trial Chamber's holding as to the irrelevance of the nature of the offence (ordinary vs international crimes) in the *ne bis in idem* analysis for the purpose of admissibility. The contours of the principle are thus open for further exploration. Such an analysis may require further consideration as to the pertinence, and the extent to which, the so-called *in abstracto* application of the principle can actually further the complementarity paradigm that, while not requiring identical legal characterisation nor identity of conduct (ascribing to

65 *Gaddafi* Admissibility Appeal Judgment (n 63), para. 62.

66 In accordance with the applicable modes of criminal liability as recognised in international criminal law (in the Rome Statute, Articles 25 and 28).

67 *Gaddafi* Admissibility Appeal Judgment (n 63), para. 67.

68 PTC *Gaddafi* Admissibility Decision (n 52), paras 86–88.

69 ibid para. 88.

70 For a similar view in relation to Libya's argument, see Michele Tedeschini, 'Complementarity in Practice: The ICC's Inconsistent Approach in the Gaddafi and Al-Senussi Admissibility Decisions' (2015) 7 Amsterdam Law Forum 76, 89 (with further reference). For Libya's argument, see *Gaddafi* Admissibility Appeal Judgment (n 63), para. 64.

the 'substantially the same conduct' test), is arguably meant to foster domestic prosecution of 'the most serious *crimes* of *international concern*'[71] or international crimes.[72] As such, questions arise as to whether the nature of the offence does not bear upon the overall appraisal of a conduct, at least with respect to some crimes in particular. Put differently, if the term is not to be attributed a purely factual connotation, not only the contextual elements but also specific material elements that characterise and distinguish international crimes from one another, are arguably relevant in its appraisal.[73] In fact, the Chamber noted that various offences that had been charged domestically, including torture, required under Libyan legislation the so-called 'public official' element, that in *Gaddafi*'s case raised concerns as to its applicability (as he allegedly exercised *de facto* control).[74] The Chamber, nonetheless, seemed to accept Libya's contention that provided sufficient evidence of such *de facto* control be furnished, the statutory requirement would be met.[75] Leaving aside doubts arising, inter alia, from the principles of legality, the *in dubio pro reo* guiding criminal interpretation in case of *lacunae*, and so forth, the soundness of such a purported application of the law, lends itself to scrutiny. The question lingers as to whether torture as an 'ordinary offence' that has traditionally been criminalised within the limited public-official scenario, can be deemed to entail substantially the same conduct as torture as a crime against humanity and a war crime, bearing in mind that torture under both categories of core crimes is not confined to the said public-official scenario. Although the case did not trigger the analysis concerning the specific question of torture (the charges before the ICC include the crimes against humanity of murder and persecution),[76] the aforesaid discussion leads to delve into the legal consequences that the diver-

71 Rome Statute, Article 1.

72 Rome Statute, preamble: 'Recalling that is the duty of every State to exercise its criminal jurisdiction over those responsible for international crimes'. For the *in concreto* and *in abstracto* domestic approaches, see Conway (n 51) 244.

73 The Office of the Public Counsel for the Victims asserted that charging of ordinary crimes would meet the test 'provided that national criminal legislation encompasses all the material elements of the crimes alleged in the specific case before the [ICC]'. See PTC *Gaddafi* Admissibility Decision (n 52), para. 71. The Chamber did not directly address the argument.

74 He 'did not occupy a formal official position within the Libyan State'. PTC *Gaddafi* Admissibility Decision (n 52), paras 109, 112.

75 ibid para. 109.

76 The Office of the Public Counsel for the Victims considered that the scope of the crimes domestically charged was considerably narrower than the crimes against humanity of murder and persecution. See PTC Gaddafi Admissibility Decision (n 52), paras 148–149.

gent criminalisation of torture under the Rome Statute poses in relation to *ne bis in idem* in both the admissibility and cumulative conviction analysis.

It is further interesting to note that the relevance of analysing the nature of the offence permeated the discussion on admissibility in *Gbagbo*, where the Trial Chamber found that 'economic crimes' and 'crimes against the State' do not cover the same conduct as the relevant conduct alleged in the proceedings before the ICC.[77] In analysing the scope of the conduct the Chamber took into account factual considerations in tandem with its legal characterisation under domestic law. Mindful of the previous jurisprudence, it regarded the latter's relevance as an indicative factor of the 'actual subject-matter of the domestic proceedings under consideration'.[78] In contrast, it considered that the 'crimes against individuals' that had also been instituted domestically, merited further analysis as their nature was the same as of those underpinning the proceedings before the ICC.[79] No specification, however, as to the single offences falling under such a label is provided in the Judgment.[80] In any event, the finding of admissibility was based on grounds of insufficiency of investigative efforts by the national authorities.[81]

Leaving aside the technical intricacies that may be construed at the doctrinal level considering the way the principle has been framed[82] in a particular normative framework, also in this scenario, a common point of analysis may be deemed the concurrence—or not—of the underlying legal value or the commonality amongst protected legal values underlying the criminal provisions at stake. Such an analysis, however, while being purportedly self-evident in some instances—for instance, in contrasting genocide with homicide (as an ordinary offence)[83]—may require a further reflection where the 'physical element' is the same and so capable of triggering the application of various criminal pro-

---

77 *Prosecutor v Gbagbo*, ICC-02/11-01/12-47-Red, Decision on Côte d'Ivoire's Challenge to the Admissibility of the Case against Simone Gbagbo, Trial Chamber I, 11 December 2014 ('*Gbagbo* Judgment on Admissibility'), paras 44, 47, 49. The finding was confirmed on appeal, see *Prosecutor v Gbagbo*, ICC-02/11-01/12-75-Red, Judgment on the Appeal of Côte d'Ivoire [...], Appeals Chamber, 27 May 2015 ('*Gbagbo* Appeal Judgment on Admissibility'), para. 99.

78 *Gbagbo* Judgment on Admissibility (n 77), para. 49, fn. 87. See also, *Gbagbo* Appeal Judgment on Admissibility (n 77), para. 71.

79 *Gbagbo* Judgment on Admissibility (n 77), para. 50.

80 A vast amount of information in the subsequent paragraphs was redacted.

81 *Gbagbo* Judgment on Admissibility (n 77), para. 78.

82 See Tallgren and Reisinger Coracini (n 51) 901.

83 See *Prosecutor v Bagaragaza*, ICTR-05-86-AR 11*bis*, Decision on Rule 11 *bis* Appeal, Appeals Chamber, 30 August 2006, para. 17 (consideration was given not only to the significant

visions whose protected legal value may not be markedly different. Torture and the other ill-treatment may be deemed a case in point.

As aforementioned, consideration of the underlying protected legal value permeated the early ICTY case law that was first confronted with the question of cumulative charging. The *Kupreškić* Trial Judgment, previously commented, followed[84] its Decision on the Defence Challenge to the Form of the Indictment, which reasoned that

> the Prosecutor may be justified in bringing cumulative charges when the articles of the Statute referred to are designed to protect different legal values and when each article requires proof of a legal element not required by the other.[85]

It may be noted that the separate and dissenting opinion to the *Čelebići* Appeal Judgment—which set the landmark as far as cumulative conviction is concerned—, while explicitly rejecting the *Kupreškić* conjunctive test as a general principle of international criminal law or as common to the dominant legal traditions, acknowledged that the protected value 'is both the rationale for and, inherent in, different acts being labelled different crimes, and it be generally given effect by the application of the 'different elements' test'.[86] Conversely, the STL's Interlocutory Decision on the Applicable Law adhered to the *Kupreškić* conjunctive test by holding that cumulative charging is permissible when not only distinct legal elements can be identified but also 'the rules envisaging each offence relate to substantially different values'.[87] This may not seem surprising as Judge Cassese acted as presiding Judge in this Decision as well as in the aforementioned *Kupreškić* and *Krnojelac* Decisions. In fact, the Interlocutory

---

difference in terms of criminalisation but also to the underlying legal values of such crimes). See also, Manacorda and Vanacore (n 47) 61.

84 *Kupreškić* Trial Judgment (n 31), para. 639.

85 *Prosecutor v Kupreškić*, IT-95-16, Decision on Defence Challenges to Form of the Indictment, 15 May 1998, p. 2. By the same token, in *Krnojelac* the underlying distinction between crimes against humanity and war crimes in the context of the cumulative charging analysis was approached from the distinct protected legal values embodied in both categories of core crimes (in addition to the identification of differentiated legal elements), see *Prosecutor v Krnojelac*, IT-97-25, Decision on the Defence Preliminary Motion on the Form of the Indictment, Trial Chamber II, 24 February 1999, para. 8.

86 *Čelebići* Appeal Judgment (n 17) Separate and Dissenting Opinion of Judge David Hunt and Judge Mohamed Bennouna, para. 17.

87 STL Decision on the Applicable Law (n 19) dispositive section, p. 152 (point 15).

Decision pondered the existence of underlying substantially different values as the decisive factor for assessing the permissibility of cumulative charging where the offences can be deemed formally distinct. It further emphasised that such an approach may foster the achievement of truth and justice through the criminal process in a fair and efficient manner.[88]

The implications of such an analysis, however, may bear more significantly on the potential opportunity to shape a coherent interpretation of the criminalisation of torture and other ill-treatment in its relationship with human rights and humanitarian law. In fact, the practice of cumulative convictions became recurrent in international criminal law proceedings due to various factors of which particularly relevant to the criminalisation of torture and other ill-treatment may be the fact that most offence definitions 'grew out of custom and uncoordinated treaties'.[89] Further aspects arising out of the distinct but closely intertwined relationship between torture and the other ill-treatment may prompt further analysis. Indeed, while core crimes may be generally deemed to be aimed at ensuring, inter alia, respect for human dignity,[90] torture and the other ill-treatment offences are arguably particularly driven by such a goal.[91] In turn, while the aforementioned categories of ill-treatment embrace a common underlying legal value, the distinct legal elements of each offence prompt consideration of the specific protected legal values embodied in their criminalisation.

In this vein, it may be noted that humiliation, as previously mentioned, has been explicitly recognised by some ICTY case law as capable of triggering the characterisation of torture.[92] By the same token, in the context of the ECHR, a violation of Article 3 may be triggered by humiliation that may render a punishment or treatment capable of amounting to inhuman or degrading treatment or torture.[93] In *Dedovskiy and others v Russia* the ECtHR found that the use of rubber truncheons against the applicants—who were in detention—was retaliatory in nature and

88 ibid paras 299, 301.

89 Stuckenberg (n 19) 840. For the disparity of conventional definitions, see eg Santalla Vargas (n 1) 1317–1320.

90 With reference to the ICTY Statute, see *Kupreškić* Trial Judgment (n 31), para. 702.

91 For a similar view, see eg UNHCR Manual on Refugee Protection and the ECHR (April 2003, updated August 2006), Part 4.1. Selected Case Law on Article 3: '[t]he right protected under Article 3 of the ECHR relates directly to an individual's personal integrity and human dignity', 1. See also, *El-Masri v Turkey* (n 32), para. 207.

92 See above (n 7).

93 See Schabas (n 33) 171.

> intended to arouse in the applicants feelings of fear and humiliation and to break their physical and moral resistance. The purpose of the treatment was to debase the applicants and drive them into submission. In addition, the truncheons blows must have caused them intense mental and physical suffering, even though they did not apparently resort in any long-term damage to health. In these circumstances, the Court finds that the applicants were subjected to treatment which can be described as torture.[94]

By applying—in general—the materially distinct legal element test the crime of outrages upon personal dignity would be subsumed by the war crime of torture. In accordance with the Elements of Crimes, humiliation—and degradation or other violation upon one's dignity—characterises and differentiates the crime of outrages upon personal dignity from torture.[95] If humiliation is also accepted as a purpose falling under the statutory definition of the war crime of torture under the Rome Statute,[96] which would be in tune with the jurisprudence at both systems of international responsibility as indicated above, the distinctive legal element would be the infliction of severe physical or mental pain or suffering.[97] Provided that severe infliction is proved, cumulative conviction would be impermissible. Such an outcome may result in the prevalence of torture by virtue of an element that is currently questioned by part of literature[98] as the distinguishing feature of torture, as evinced in *Dedovskiy and others v Russia*. While it is accepted that a lower threshold of severity applies for degrading treatment and outrages upon personal dignity vis-à-vis other ill-treatment, including torture,[99] the distinction in practice may be blurred. In accordance with the Elements of Crimes, humiliation, degradation or other

---

94 *Dedovskiy and others v Russia*, App no 7178/03 (ECtHR, 15 May 2008), para. 85.

95 Elements of Crimes, Article 8(2)(c)(ii), elements 1 and 2.

96 ibid Article 8(2)(c)(ii)-4, element 2 ascribing to the non-exhaustive formula: 'for such purposes as'.

97 ibid Article 8(2)(c)(ii)-4, element 1.

98 The UN Special Rapporteur on the Question of Torture, Manfred Nowak, considered that the decisive criteria for distinguishing torture from other ill-treatment 'may best be understood to be the purpose of the conduct and the powerless of the victim, rather than the intensity of the pain or suffering inflicted, as argued by the [ECtHR] and many scholars'. UN/Doc. E/CN.4/2006/6, 23 December 2005, para. 39.

99 See Nowak and Janik (n 4) 327, para. 29 and 321, para. 9, pointing out that the Elements of Crimes require the same threshold of gravity for torture—as a crime against humanity and as a war crime—as well as for inhuman or cruel treatment.

violation upon personal dignity require a certain degree of severity which is likely to involve severe mental pain or suffering.[100] Put differently, such an element of the crime of outrages upon personal dignity would likely be proved by the demonstration of severe mental pain or suffering (probably also of severe physical pain or suffering).[101] Against this backdrop, the application of the materially distinct element *per se* may prove perfunctory. Perhaps additional consideration as to the protected legal value criterion may contribute to drawing a distinction amongst the offences from a *raison d'être* perspective. To the extent that the role of the Elements of Crimes is to assist the ICC in the interpretation and application of core crimes,[102] its non-binding nature[103] arguably allows for adopting such an approach as far as cumulative conviction is concerned. Such a posture may eventually lead to depart from a strict application of the elements in furtherance of normative coherence which, in turn, may better uphold the rights of the accused and the search for justice.

III Conclusions

The underlying rationale of the divergent criminalisation of torture and other ill-treatment as crimes against humanity and war crimes under the Rome Statute has not been thus far comprehensibly scrutinised. Current developments ensuing from judicial proceedings before the ICC have flagged the question in the context of the cumulative charging/conviction discussion, denoting that such divergent criminalisation fosters a further discussion on the interpretation and application of the principle of *ne bis in idem* in relation to torture and other ill-treatment. The discussion, having arisen in the early jurisprudence of

100 As opposed to the ICTY case law that generally used 'severe' while referring to torture and 'serious' with respect to inhuman or cruel treatment, the Elements of Crimes use severe for all ill-treatment, including the crime of outrages upon personal dignity.

101 *Prosecutor v Aleksovski*, IT-95-14/1-T, Judgment, Trial Chamber, 25 June 1999, para. 55: referring to the Commentary of the Geneva Conventions which provided: 'outrages upon personal dignity refer to acts which, without directly causing harm to the integrity and physical and mental well-being of persons, are aimed at humiliating and ridiculing them'. It further added that, '[i]t is enough that the act causes real and lasting suffering to the individual arising from the humiliation or ridicule' (ibid para. 56). On appeal the Appeals Chamber took into account the physical and psychological harm to confirm the level of gravity supporting the conviction of outrages upon personal dignity. See *Prosecutor v Aleksovski*, IT-95-14/1-A, Judgment, Appeals Chamber, 24 March 2000, para. 37.

102 Rome Statute, Article 9(1).

103 See Bitti (n 46) 421 (with references to the *traveaux préparatoires* and ICC case law).

the ICTY, leads one to question not only its relevance and applicability vis-à-vis the Rome Statute framework but also whether the divergences in terms of criminalisation featuring in a normative structural system posed by such a framework, as opposed to the ad hoc Tribunals model, prompt a further scrutiny as to the *raison d'être* of the specific offences triggering ill-treatment.

Against this background, the ECtHR's case law approach to *ne bis in idem*, may not prove suitable for the system of individual criminal responsibility, where notions of particular relevance in such a context, such as the protected legal values underlying criminalisation, may reinforce legitimacy. Indeed, while possibly rendering a similar result, such consideration may contribute to dispelling concerns as to what may appear a perfunctory differentiation amongst offences. The characterisation of the ICC Chamber Practice Manual as a 'living document'[104] may allow for further consideration as to the pertinence of incorporating such a factor into account while assessing cumulative charging (and conviction), an endeavour that may be deemed already initiated in the judicial practice of the ICC.[105]

To the extent that the question of *ne bis in idem* under the Rome Statute is intrinsically linked to admissibility considerations, a further spectrum of analysis is posed by the terminology adopted in the Rome Statute, ie *conduct*. The question of torture and other ill-treatment arguably fosters further reflection as to the incipient consideration of the dichotomous relationship between ordinary and international crimes. This is particularly so, as the former scenario has largely been confined to the traditional understanding of torture thus undermining the relevance of the other ill-treatment. After all, the *jus cogens* prohibition of torture and other ill-treatment arguably implies that all such conduct that particularly encroaches upon human dignity be given the same enforcement consideration under international law.

---

104 ICC Chambers Practice Manual (n 25) 5.

105 *Ongwen* Confirmation of Charges Decision (n 14).

PART 4

Fairness of International Criminal Proceedings: The (Side) Effects of Cross-fertilization

CHAPTER 12

Absent Witnesses and the Right to Confrontation: The Influence of the Jurisprudence of the European Court of Human Rights on International Criminal Law

Yvonne McDermott

1 Introduction

The right of an accused person to challenge the witnesses and evidence against them is a universal fair trial right, which is reflected in the Statutes of the international criminal tribunals. Arguably, it is more challenging for international criminal tribunals to respect this right compared to their domestic counterparts. This is because the tribunals themselves have to ensure the safety and appearance of witnesses who may be unwilling to come forward; unlike domestic courts, they do not have a police force that they can rely upon in this regard.[1] In addition, because the events tried by international criminal tribunals have often happened years (or sometimes decades) before the trial, witnesses may no longer be alive or available to testify. To this end, Trial Chambers may be asked to rely on a previous statement made by a witness in lieu of his or her live testimony in court,[2] or on the hearsay evidence

1 Antonio Cassese, 'Reflections on International Criminal Justice' (1998) 61 Modern Law Review 1, 9–10.

2 As provided for in Rules 92*bis*, *ter*, *quater* and *quinquies* of the Rules of Procedure and Evidence of the International Criminal Tribunal for the former Yugoslavia, UN Doc IT/32/Rev.50 (2015) ('ICTY RPE'); Rule 92*bis* of the Rules of Procedure and Evidence of the International Criminal Tribunal for Rwanda, UN Doc ITR/3/Rev.23 (2015) ('ICTR RPE'); Rules 92*bis*, *ter*, and *quater* of the Rules of Procedure and Evidence of the Special Court for Sierra Leone, adopted on 16 January 2002, as amended 31 May 2012 ('SCSL RPE'); Rules 155–159 of the Rules of Procedure and Evidence of the Special Tribunal for Lebanon, adopted on 20 March 2009, as corrected 3 April 2014 ('STL RPE'), and Rule 68 of the Rules of Procedure and Evidence of the International Criminal Court, UN Doc PCNICC/2000/1/Add.1 (2000), as amended by resolution ICC-ASP/12/Res.7, 27 November 2013. See further, Patricia M. Wald, 'Dealing with Witnesses in War Crime Trials: Lessons from the Yugoslav Tribunal' (2002) 5 Yale Human

 | DOI: 10.1163/9789004313750_014

of another person with whom the unavailable witness spoke about the events at issue.[3]

In admitting such evidence, international criminal tribunals have to consider the fact that witnesses in international criminal trials 'are precious commodities',[4] and as such, they should not be endangered or excessively inconvenienced by their cooperation with the tribunal, as that may well discourage future witnesses from coming forward and without witnesses, there can be no trials. However, the tribunals also have to ensure that their judgments are adequately founded in a solid evidentiary base, as to do otherwise would seriously hamper the legitimacy and reputation of their institutions.[5] Moreover, the admission to the evidentiary record of the testimony of witnesses who are not present poses a threat to the accused's right to confrontation, as that testimony cannot be subjected to the same level of scrutiny as it would face if the witness were present before the court.

These challenges are not unique to the international criminal context, of course. Domestic courts frequently make decisions on whether to admit the testimony of a witness in written form, or to accept the testimony of another person whom that witness spoke to in place of his or her first-hand account. Unsurprisingly, a not insignificant number of such cases have later re-emerged before human rights tribunals when the defendant convicted in such trials alleges that his or her right to confront the witnesses against him or her was not respected. Before the European Court of Human Rights (ECtHR), a quite detailed body of case law has developed on this question. As shall be shown, the ECtHR's standards on the conformity of convictions that were based in no small part on the accounts of unavailable witnesses with the right to a fair trial has evolved significantly over time.

This chapter examines the influence of that case law on the practice of the international criminal tribunals. Part II sets out the ECtHR standards on the right of confrontation where witnesses are unavailable. It will show that

---

Rights & Development Law Journal 217, 227; Peter Murphy, 'No Free Lunch, No Free Proof' (2010) 8 Journal of International Criminal Justice 539.

3 For example, *Prosecutor v Akayesu*, ICTR-96-4-A, Judgment, Appeals Chamber, 1 June 2001, paras 277–309; *Prosecutor v Aleksovski*, IT-95-14/1-AR73, Decision on Prosecutor's Appeal on Admissibility of Evidence, Appeals Chamber, 16 February 1999, para. 15; *Prosecutor v Lubanga*, ICC-01/04-01/06-1399, Decision on the Admissibility of Four Documents, Trial Chamber I, 13 June 2008. See further the chapter of Yael Vias Gvirsman, in this volume.

4 See Wald (n 2) 238.

5 Nancy Combs, *Fact-Finding without Facts* (CUP 2010) 6–7.

(contrary to popular belief, and the interpretation of these authorities by the international criminal tribunals), the notion of 'balancing' the rights of the accused with the rights of witnesses did not arise in the ECtHR's jurisprudence until relatively recently. It highlights a move away from the previous centrality of the ECtHR's 'solely or to a decisive extent' standard, and expresses concerns with the notions of 'counterbalancing' and 'fairness as a whole' that have become central to the ECtHR's case law in this area. Part III distinguishes between different types of witness protection mechanisms applicable in international criminal trials. It will show a clear departure from ECtHR principles in some respects, particularly as regards the 'solely or decisive extent' standard. By contrast, the more likely a piece of evidence is to be instructive in the outcome of the trial—in other words, the higher its probative value—the more likely it is to be admitted. Evidence will only be excluded where its probative value is substantially outweighed by its prejudice to a fair trial of an accused. Part IV examines the use (and possible misuse) of ECtHR case law on decisions surrounding absent witnesses in international criminal trials. It will show that, rarely, the international criminal tribunals have distinguished themselves from human rights bodies to argue that the same human rights standards cannot apply to them. More frequently, the tribunals have implicitly recognised the value of human rights case law and the potential applicability of those same standards before international criminal courts, but have been highly selective in the use of those standards. On one notable occasion, for example, an ECtHR decision was used as justification for reaching the precise opposite conclusion than the ECtHR had reached in that decision. The paper concludes with a discussion of why the international criminal tribunals might choose to apply ECtHR standards (albeit quite selectively) in their procedural decisions, given that these legal regimes stand independently, and the international criminal tribunals are by no means bound by the case law of the ECtHR].

II ECtHR Case Law on Absent Witnesses and the Right to Confrontation

The ECtHR has considered a large number of cases where the right of the accused to confront the witnesses against him or her has been allegedly violated. Many of these cases concern witnesses who refused to testify owing to fears for their safety, while other cases concern situations where witnesses were unwilling to testify, or became unavailable by the time of trial. The general rule is that the ECtHR will not interfere with national courts' role in the admission and assessment of evidence before them; rather, the Court will consider whether proceedings as a whole, including the evaluation of evidence, were fair.[6]

One of the earliest leading cases in this field, *Kostovski v. Netherlands*, concerned an individual who was convicted of robbery on the basis of the account of a witness who testified anonymously owing to fears of reprisals.[7] Kostovski had been given the opportunity to pass questions to the witness via the magistrate, but only two of his 14 questions were ultimately answered, because it was felt that the others would reveal the witness's identity.[8] The ECtHR, in finding a violation, stated that the accused must 'be given an adequate and proper opportunity to challenge and question a witness against him, either at the time the witness was making his statement or at some later stage of the proceedings.'[9]

The Court also noted that the conviction was based solely or to a decisive degree upon the anonymous evidence—this is a standard that was followed in numerous later cases,[10] but as shall be shown, has waned in significance in recent years.

The language in *Kostovski* appears to give precedence to the rights of the accused in criminal proceedings, even where there are fears of retribution on the part of a witness. The ECtHR stated that in principle, statements should be made at a public hearing in the presence of the accused, and if pre-trial statements were to be used, this was only permissible 'provided the rights of the defence [to examine that witness] have been respected'.[11] Thus, the conflict of interests that arose in this case was not one requiring 'balance' as such, but rather one where the fundamental rights of the accused had to be respected above all else.

The ECtHR's gradual turn towards balancing the rights of the accused with the rights of witnesses began to appear in the well-known case of *Doorson v. Netherlands*, decided seven years after *Kostovski*. This case concerned a drug

6 *Barberà v Spain*, App no 10590/83 (ECtHR, 6 December 1988), para. 68.

7 *Kostovski v Netherlands*, App no 11454/85 (ECtHR, 20 November 1989).

8 ibid para. 16.

9 ibid para. 41.

10 For example, *Doorson v Netherlands*, App no 20524/92 (ECtHR, 26 March 1996); *Van Mechelen v The Netherlands*, App no 21363/93 (ECtHR, 23 April 1997); *Verdam v The Netherlands*, App no 35253/97 (ECtHR, 31 August 1999); *Luca v Italy*, App no 33354/96 (ECtHR, 27 February 2001); *Kok v The Netherlands*, App no 43149/98 (ECtHR, 4 July 2000); *Visser v Netherlands*, App no 26668/95 (ECtHR, 14 February 2002). The principle appears to derive from *Unterpertinger v Austria*, App no 9120/80 (ECtHR, 24 November 1986), para. 33.

11 *Kostovski* (n 7), para. 41.

trafficker who was convicted on the basis of anonymous testimony. The ECtHR, in taking a less forceful stance than its earlier position in *Kostovski*, stated that:

> It is true that Article 6 … does not explicitly require the interests of witnesses in general, and those of victims called upon to testify in particular, to be taken into consideration. However, their life, liberty or security of person may be at stake, as may interests coming generally within the ambit of Article 8 of the Convention. Such interests of witnesses and victims are in principle protected by other, substantive provisions of the Convention, which imply that Contracting States should organise their criminal proceedings in such a way that those interests are not unjustifiably imperilled. Against this background, principles of fair trial also require that in appropriate cases the interests of the defence are balanced against those of witnesses or victims called upon to testify.[12]

In other words, the ECtHR recognised that other Convention rights may come into competition with the rights of the accused, and insofar as is possible, those other rights will have to be taken into account. It is worthy of note, however, that the Court did not say that the rights of witnesses and victims had to be balanced against the rights of the accused in all circumstances; rather, it stated that 'in appropriate cases', such a balancing exercise would have to be entered into. Furthermore, the negative formulation of this statement—that the rights of victims and witnesses should not be 'unjustifiably imperilled'—is notable; a more positive formulation would require courts to pay equal regard for the rights of these individuals. Lastly, the Court did not refer to 'rights' as such, but to the 'interests' of victims called to testify and other witnesses.

Doorson, like *Kostovski* before it,[13] also considered a second form of 'balance' in relation to fair trial rights where witnesses are unwilling to come forward. It noted that domestic legal authorities might invoke 'counterbalancing' procedures to remedy 'the handicaps under which the defence labours'.[14] Such measures might include juror instructions to treat the untested evidence with caution, or granting the defence the opportunity to challenge the reliability of the anonymous witness. However, the ECtHR held that, notwithstanding such counterbalancing measures, a conviction should not be based solely or to a decisive extent on anonymous witness testimony.[15] As the national court had

12 *Doorson* (n 10), para. 70.
13 *Kostovski* (n 7), para. 43.
14 *Doorson* (n 10), para. 76.
15 ibid.

not based its finding of guilt solely or decisively on anonymous testimony, the ECtHR found that the applicant's rights under Article 6 of the Convention had not been breached.[16]

In 2009, the ECtHR was faced with a joint case where the applicants' convictions had been decisively based on unexamined witness testimony, where the witnesses were absent from the trial.[17] In *Al-Khawaja and Tahery*, one of the applicants had been convicted of indecent assault, where one of the two victims died before the trial and her statement to police was read to the jury. The other applicant had been convicted of wounding with intent to cause serious bodily harm after the statement of one witness, who was too afraid of possible reprisals to attend the trial, was read to the jury. The ECtHR found that both men's right to a fair trial had been breached.[18]

Before the Grand Chamber,[19] the government of England and Wales challenged the 'solely or to a decisive extent' rule, drawing largely on the UK Supreme Court's judgment in *R v. Horncastle*,[20] where the Supreme Court refused to follow the ECtHR's earlier ruling in the case (a decision later praised as evidencing judicial dialogue between Strasbourg and ECHR member states[21]). In an apparent departure from the earlier ruling in *Doorson*, the Grand Chamber concluded that where a conviction is based solely or decisively on the evidence of absent witnesses, the Court will subject the proceedings to 'the most searching scrutiny', but that such convictions would not automatically result in a breach of Article 6.[22] Worryingly, in concluding that Al-Khawaja's rights were not violated but that Tahery's had been, the Grand Chamber appeared to consider whether there was strong corroborative evidence to support the untested witness statements in the cases as a 'counterbalancing' factor.[23] As Laura Hoyano has convincingly argued, this interpretation appears to misconstrue the very notion of 'balance'.[24] Rather than finding factors that assisted

16 ibid.

17 *Al-Khawaja and Tahery v UK*, App nos 26766/05 and 22228/06 (ECtHR, 20 January 2009).

18 ibid.

19 *Al-Khawaja and Tahery v UK*, App nos 26766/05 and 22228/06 (ECtHR, 15 December 2011), paras 129–146.

20 *R v Horncastle and others* [2009] UKSC 14.

21 Noreen O'Meara, 'Reforming the European Court of Human Rights: The Impacts of Protocols 15 and 16 to the ECHR', in Katja S. Ziegler and others (eds), *The UK and European Human Rights: A Strained Relationship?* (Oxford: Hart, 2015) 71, 90.

22 *Al-Khawaja and Tahery* (n 19), para. 147.

23 ibid paras 156 and 165.

24 Laura Hoyano, 'What Is Balanced on the Scales of Justice? In Search of the Essence of the Right to a Fair Trial' (2014) Criminal Law Review 4.

the defendants and outweighed the prejudice suffered by them by the admission of such statements, the Grand Chamber's interpretation found a 'balance' through 'other evidence further loading the prosecution's pan on the scales of justice',[25] or effectively, a further imbalance. This turn in the case law is concerning, and the dangers inherent in this approach is illustrated by cases that have followed in the years since the Grand Chamber's judgment.

Later ECtHR cases have made it explicit that *Al-Khawaja and Tahery* represented an explicit departure from the Court's previous reliance on the 'sole or decisive' rule,[26] and have further conflated the notion of 'counterbalancing' with the strength of the prosecution case as a whole. It is now firmly established that the Court will conduct a three-pronged test in determining whether the trial as a whole was fair.[27] The first step asks whether there was good reason for the non-attendance of the witness, and whether all reasonable attempts were taken to secure his or her testimony. Recent case law has found that this step is not decisive—in other words that a trial can still be found to be fair where a key witness did not attend trial, and there was no good reason for his or her non-appearance. For example, in *Seton v. UK*, the Court found that this prong of the three-step test was not conclusive, but rather 'a very important factor to be weighed in the balance when assessing the overall fairness, and one which might tip the balance in finding a breach'.[28] In that case, the relevant witness was actually in prison, so the state could easily have secured his attendance at trial. The Court found that there was no breach because the evidence was not decisive to the outcome of the trial. Judges Spielmann, Sajò, Karakaş and Keller, in their joint concurring opinion in the case of *Schatschaschwili v. Germany*, disagreed with this approach; the learned judges would have preferred for the ECtHR to take the position that the unjustified absence of a witness whose testimony is of some importance to the trial is a breach of the rights of the accused, even if that witness's statement was not the sole or decisive basis for a decision.[29]

The second step in the ECtHR's three-pronged approach is the 'sole or decisive' test, outlined above. In the past, the fact that a witness was unavailable and his or her untested testimony was the sole or decisive basis for the conviction would, have been sufficient for the ECtHR to determine that there was a

25 ibid 14.

26 *Schatschaschwili v Germany*, App no 9154/10 (ECtHR, 15 December 2015), para. 112.

27 ibid paras 110–111.

28 *Seton v UK*, App no 55287/10 (ECtHR, 31 March 2016), para. 59.

29 *Schatschaschwili v Germany* (n 26), Joint Concurring Opinion of Judges Spielmann, Sajò, Karakaş and Keller.

breach of the accused's rights. By today, whether the decision was based solely or decisively on the untested testimony is just one of three questions that the Court will go through in determining whether there was a breach, albeit one that will give rise to 'the most searching scrutiny' of the case as a whole if this question is answered in the positive.[30]

The third and final question that the ECtHR will ask is whether sufficient counterbalancing measures were in place to rebalance the burden that the defence laboured under. The judgment in *Schatschaschwili* gave some helpful examples of counterbalancing measures that may be put in place.[31] These included whether the trial court approached the evidence with caution, and indicated that it was given less weight; whether the absent witness's testimony had been recorded; whether the defence had been able to question the witness at an earlier stage in the case, or put questions to him or her in writing, and whether the defendant was given the opportunity to challenge the testimony by giving his or her own version of events.[32] Increasingly, following *Al-Khawaja and Tahery*, further corroborative evidence, such as hearsay evidence from someone the absent witness spoke to, similarities with another witness or witnesses' account, and further factual evidence, have been seen as counterbalancing measures.[33] In *Seton v. UK*, the Court appeared to be influenced by the fact that other evidence against the accused was 'overwhelming'.[34] This turn in the jurisprudence is worrying, insofar as it conflates two distinct elements of the three-stage test: whether the testimony was sole or decisive, and whether there were counterbalancing measures in place to mitigate against that. If a piece of evidence was the sole or decisive basis of a conviction, it seems nonsensical to suggest that the existence of other evidence somehow corroborating that evidence 'counterbalances' that fact.

More recently, the ECtHR has moved beyond the notion of ensuring that the rights of witnesses are not 'unjustifiably imperiled' to a more holistic reading of the fairness of proceedings 'as a whole'. A good example of this is the case of *Hummer v. Germany*, where the ECtHR stated that its:

30 *Hummer v Germany*, App no 26171/07 (ECtHR, 19 July 2012), para. 45; *Al-Khawaja and Tahery* (n 19), para. 147.

31 *Schatschaschwili v Germany* (n 26), para. 126.

32 ibid.

33 ibid.

34 *Seton v UK* (n 28), para. 68.

> primary concern under Article 6(1) is to evaluate the overall fairness of the criminal proceedings. In making this assessment the Court will look at the proceedings as a whole having regard to the rights of the defence but also to the interests of the public and the victims that crime is properly prosecuted and, where necessary, to the rights of witnesses.[35]

This suggests a further, more explicit, move towards 'balancing' the rights and interests of the various parties—and even the general public—in assessing the fairness of proceedings. As the right to a fair trial is solely owed to the accused, and given the danger that permitting fairness to be 'balanced' against external interests, there is a real danger here that the ECtHR risks diluting its previous high standards on the rights of the accused.[36]

III Unavailable Witnesses before the International Criminal Tribunals

Before turning to the use of ECtHR case law on unavailable witnesses by the international criminal tribunals, it is important to distinguish between the different types of protective measures that the tribunals apply in order to protect witnesses, because there is a clear interplay with such measures and witness unavailability. Protective measures are granted when the tribunal deems them necessary to protect the safety, privacy, wellbeing or dignity of witnesses.[37] The party making the request for protective measures must indicate the objective reasons underlying the request—a subjective fear expressed by witnesses or a general unwillingness to testify unless their safety is guaranteed will not suffice.[38] The ICTR, however, accepted the volatility of the security situation in Rwanda as a basis for granting protective measures to witnesses.[39]

---

35 *Hummer* (n 30), para. 37.

36 For a further discussion on the theme of 'balance' in the criminal law, see Yvonne McDermott, *Fairness in International Criminal Trials* (OUP 2016), chapter 4.

37 Rome Statute of the International Criminal Court, Article 87(4).

38 *Prosecutor v Strugar*, IT-01-42-T, Decision on the Prosecution Motion to Admit Evidence via Video-Conference Link, Trial Chamber II, 20 January 2004; *Prosecutor v Muvunyi*, ICTR-2000-55A-T, Decision on Prosecutor's Extremely Urgent Motion Pursuant to Trial Chamber II Directive of 23 May 2005, Trial Chamber II, 20 June 2005, paras 16–17; *Prosecutor v Lubanga*, ICC-01/04-01/06-T-153-Red2, Transcript, 24 March 2009, p. 63, lines 19–25.

39 *Prosecutor v Simba*, ICTR-01-76-I, Decision on Defence Request for Protection of Witnesses, Trial Chamber I, 25 August 2004, para. 6.

Protective measures granted can include delayed disclosure of the witness's identity;[40] the exclusion from the press or public from the gallery;[41] the use of a pseudonym to protect the witness's identity;[42] allowing the witness to give testimony by other means than live in-court testimony to protect them from confrontation with the accused, such as via video-link or other means;[43] or granting additional support where the witness is a child, an elderly person, a victim of sexual violence, or suffering from trauma.[44] There are special rules on permissible questioning when the witness is a victim of sexual violence.[45] In rare cases, witnesses have been relocated with new identities, but as the specialized units within the tribunals responsible for witness protection make these arrangements extra-judicially, little is known about such arrangements. Such measures, however, do not result in the unavailability of witnesses, and so they find a way of ensuring witness protection whilst still protecting the rights of the accused.

By far the most controversial witness protection measure that can be granted by judges is full anonymity. An early decision in the *Tadić* case before the ICTY determined that anonymity could be granted to witnesses, provided that there was a 'real fear for the safety of the witness or his or her family'; that the testimony of the witness was important to the prosecution case; that there was nothing to indicate that the witness was *prima facie* unreliable, and that the witness's safety could not be secured through domestic witness

---

40 Rule 76(4), ICC RPE; *Prosecutor v Katanga*, ICC-01/04-01/07-1179, Public redacted version of the Decision on the Protection of Prosecution Witnesse s, Trial Chamber II, 28 May 2009, para. 52; Rules 69, ICTY, ICTR and SCSL RPE.

41 Rules 79, ICTY, ICTR and SCSL RPE; Rule 87, ICC RPE.

42 Rule 87(3)(d), ICC RPE; Rules 75, ICTY, ICTR and SCSL RPE; *Prosecutor v Bemba*, ICC-01/05-01/08-3014, Decision on 'Prosecution Request for a Variance of Protective Measures of Trial Witnesses to Allow Access to Transcripts of Evidence in a Related Article 70 Proceeding', Trial Chamber III, 12 March 2014, para. 1.

43 Rule 87(3)(c), ICC RPE; *Prosecutor v Kordić*, IT-95-14/2-PT, Order for Video-Conference Link, 24 February 2000; *Prosecutor v Dokmanović*, IT-95-13a-T, Decision on Defence Motion for Video-Link Conference, 18 May 1998, p. 2; *Prosecutor v Dokmanović*, IT-95-13a-T, Decision on Defence Motion for Video Link Conference, 29 April 1998; *Prosecutor v Tadić*, IT-94-1-T, Decision on the Defence Motions to Summon and Protect Defence Witnesses, 25 June 1996, para. 19; *Prosecutor v Delalić*, IT-96-21, Decision on the Motion to Allow Witnesses K, L, and M to give their testimony by Means of Video-Link Conference, 28 May 1997, para. 17; *Prosecutor v Mrksić*, IT-95-13a, Decision on Defence Motions for Video-Conference Link, 29 April 1998.

44 Art 68(2) ICC Statute; Rule 88, ICC RPE.

45 Rules 70 and 71, ICC RPE; Rules 96, ICTY, ICTR and SCSL RPE.

protection programmes or lesser protective measures than anonymity.[46] The ICTR accepted the *Tadić* precedent in its own case-law,[47] although it never actually granted full anonymity to any witnesses. The ICC, in the pre-trial stage of the *Lubanga* case, granted anonymity to a number of witnesses.[48]

Relatedly, the tribunals have, over time, adopted a more flexible approach to the admissibility of witness statements in place of oral testimony, including where the witness is unavailable owing to intimidation.[49] We might question how this rather liberal admissibility regime might fit with the ECtHR's three-step test, outlined above. The ECtHR's standard on whether a conviction is based 'solely or decisive extent' on untested testimony is, of course, difficult to apply to admissibility decisions, where the decisive effect of a piece of evidence is difficult to predict. However, the *ad hoc* international criminal tribunals weigh the probative value of a piece of evidence against the accused's right to a fair trial and only exclude evidence where the probative value is 'substantially outweighed' by the need to ensure a fair trial.[50] This means that the more a piece of evidence is likely to be important to a final decision, the less likely it is to be 'substantially outweighed' by the rights of the accused. This seems to directly depart from the 'solely or to a decisive extent' principle in ECtHR case law.

One might question the extent to which the 'solely or decisive' rule could be applicable to international criminal trials, which tend to involve huge volumes of evidence and numerous witnesses,[51] and where a lot of the evidence is cir-

46 *Prosecutor v Tadić*, IT-94-1-T, Decision on the Prosecutor's Motion Requesting Protective Measures for Victims and Witnesses, 10 August 1995, paras 62–66. See also, *Prosecutor v Blaškić*, IT-95-14-T, Decision on the Application of the Prosecutor Dated 17 October 1996 Requesting Protective Measures for Victims and Witnesses, 5 November 1996.

47 *Prosecutor v Rutaganda*, ICTR-96-3-T, Decision on the Preliminary Motion Submitted by the Prosecutor for Protective Measures for Witnesses, 26 September 1996; see further, Joanna Pozen, 'Justice Obscured: The Non-Disclosure of Witnesses' Identities in ICTR Trials' (2005–2006) NYU Journal of International Law and Politics 281.

48 *Prosecutor v Gbagbo*, ICC-02/11-01/11, Decision on the "Prosecution's Request for Redactions Pursuant to Rule 81(2)", 10 January 2013; *Prosecutor v Lubanga*, ICC-01/04-01/06, Decision Concerning the Prosecution Proposed Summary Evidence, 4 October 2006.

49 Rule 92 *quinquies*, ICTY RPE; Rule 68, ICC RPE.

50 This is the general principle established in Rule 89(d), ICTY RPE; see further, *Prosecutor v Haradinaj*, IT-04-84*bis*-T, Decision on Joint Defence Oral Motion Pursuant to Rule 89(d), 28 September 2011.

51 For example, in the *Karadžić* case, the testimony of close to 600 witnesses was received by the Trial Chamber, and admitted more than 146,000 pages of exhibits: *Prosecutor v Radovan Karadžić*, IT-95-5/18-T, Transcript, p. 48098, 7 October 2014.

cumstantial but, 'when taken as a whole', leads the Trial Chamber to its ultimate conclusion.[52] However, the *Kenyatta* trial, where the trial collapsed after a small number of key witnesses were unwilling to testify or recanted their testimony owing to alleged interference,[53] highlights that convictions even for crimes of this magnitude can in fact hinge on a small amount of decisive testimony.

In 2013, the ICC Rules of Procedure and Evidence, which previously deemed that prior recorded testimony would only be admissible where it had been subjected to cross-examination during the recording of that evidence, were amended to allow prior recorded testimony to be admitted where the witness had been subjected to interference.[54] In *Ruto and Sang*, the prosecution requested the admission of untested witness statements pursuant to the amended Rule 68, where some of the witnesses in question had allegedly been subjected to improper interference.[55] Trial Chamber V(A) of the ICC admitted the prior recorded statements of five of the witnesses, considering 'that their *prima facie* probative value outweighs any prejudicial effect caused to the accused', but that the admissibility decision had no bearing on the weight that the Chamber would attach to the statements.[56] In February 2016, the Appeals Chamber overturned this decision, finding that the amended Rule 68 was applied retroactively to the detriment of the accused.[57]

IV From Exceptionalism to Selectivity

The *Tadić* witness anonymity decision, mentioned above, was the first case to discuss the applicability of international human rights law standards to international criminal tribunals at length. Quite remarkably, the ICTY Trial Chamber

52 See further, Yvonne McDermott, 'Inferential Reasoning and Proof in International Criminal Trials: The Potentials of Wigmorean Analysis' (2015) 13 Journal of International Criminal Justice 507, 508.

53 *Prosecutor v Kenyatta*, ICC-01/09-02/11-1005, Decision on the withdrawal of charges against Mr Kenyatta, 13 March 2015.

54 Rule 68(d), ICC RPE, as amended by ICC-ASP/12/Res.7, Amendments to the Rules of Procedure and Evidence, Adopted at the 12th plenary meeting, 27 November 2013, by consensus.

55 *Situation in Kenya: Prosecutor v Ruto*, Decision on Prosecution Request for Admission of Prior Recorded Testimony, Case No. ICC-01/09-01/11-1938-Corr-Red2, 28 August 2015.

56 ibid para. 151.

57 *Situation in the Republic of Kenya: Prosecutor v Ruto*, Judgment on the appeals of Mr William Samoei Ruto and Mr Joshua Arap Sang against the decision of Trial Chamber V(A) of 19 August 2015, ICC-01/09-01/11-2024, 12 February 2016, para. 95.

began by going to great lengths to distinguish the unique context of international criminal tribunals compared to the 'ordinary' nature of domestic criminal proceedings in ECHR member states, but it then went on to apply (albeit, as shall be seen, quite selectively) ECtHR precedent to the circumstances before it. This selective approach was not unique to the *Tadić* decision—as shall be seen, the tribunals have made use of key concepts of ECtHR jurisprudence, such as the 'fairness as a whole' approach, in inappropriate contexts, or selectively used quotes from ECtHR case law without giving the full picture, in order to justify their decisions. Therefore, we can derive that the international criminal tribunals take one of two approaches to the case law of the ECtHR in these decisions on balancing the rights of the accused, which can be dubbed 'exceptionalism' or 'selectivity', and that these approaches are not always mutually exclusive.

1 *Exceptionalism*

The *Tadić* anonymous witnesses decision referred extensively to the permissibility of derogation in times of emergency pursuant to Article 15 of the Convention.[58] According to the majority:

> The fact that some derogation is allowed in cases of national emergency shows that the rights of the accused guaranteed under the principle of the right to a fair trial are not wholly without qualification.[59]

The Chamber declined to elaborate on what kinds of derogations could be permitted in such states of emergency, but instead noted that guidelines on such derogations 'can be found in domestic law'.[60] From there, the judgment relied extensively and exclusively on an unreported decision of the Court of Appeal of England and Wales, *R v. Taylor and Crabb*,[61] which was an ordinary murder case and had absolutely nothing to do with derogation in times of emergency.

The Chamber also noted that ECtHR findings on the right to a fair trial 'are meant to apply to ordinary criminals',[62] whereas it likened itself more to a military tribunal. It noted that, in war crimes trials, 'much reliance has been placed ... on affidavits',[63] referring to the Nuremberg Tribunal, one of only

58 *Tadić* (n 46), para. 61.
59 ibid.
60 ibid.
61 Unreported, 22 July 1994, Court of Appeal Criminal Division.
62 *Tadić* (n 46), para. 21.
63 ibid. para. 28.

two trials held before international criminal tribunals before the *Tadić* case, in support of this generalisation.

This denigration of the persuasiveness of ECtHR jurisprudence is remarkable, given that the *Kostovski* judgment is cited no less than nine times in the decision. In justifying this apparent departure, the Chamber noted that it could garner persuasive precedent from the jurisprudence of the ECtHR, along with domestic courts, but the standards set down by human rights law 'must be interpreted within the context of the unique object and purpose of the International Tribunal, particularly recognizing its mandate to protect victims and witnesses.'[64] This distinction is stretched, perhaps, because domestic courts also have a mandate to protect their witnesses, although they do also have the support of domestic policing mechanisms to assist them in this regard.

Nevertheless, the 'exceptionalism' mantra was repeated in later case law. Judge Shahabuddeen, in the *Galić* case before the ICTY, noted that 'internationally recognised human rights instruments do not apply to the Tribunal lock, stock and barrel'.[65] In *Delalić*, the ICTY justified its previous regime of detention of suspects awaiting trial as the rule, rather than the exception (in contrast to human rights standards, which require release to be the rule, and detention to be the exception) with reference to the gravity of the crimes alleged:

> [B]oth the shifting of the burden to the accused and the requirement that he show exceptional circumstances to qualify for provisional release are justified by the extreme gravity of the offences with which persons accused before the International Tribunal are charged and the unique circumstances under which the International Tribunal operates.[66]

Exceptionalism has been rather less common in the practice of the ICC to date, presumably because Article 21(3) of the Court's Statute states that the application and interpretation of applicable law by the Court 'must be consistent with internationally recognized human rights'.[67]

---

64 ibid. para. 70.

65 *Prosecutor v Galić*, Case No. IT-98-29-A, 30 November 2006, Separate Opinion of Judge Shahabuddeen, para. 19.

66 *Prosecutor v Delalić*, IT-96-21-T, Decision on Motion for Provisional Release filed by the Accused Zejnil Delalić, 25 September 1996, para. 19.

67 ICC Statute, Article 21(3).

2 *Selectivity*

The emphasis on *Kostovski* as justification for the ultimate outcome in the *Tadić* anonymous witnesses decision provides an example of what could be termed 'selectivity'. As mentioned above, the ECtHR in that case took a very restrictive approach to the 'balancing' question, and indeed did not even toy with the notion of balancing the rights of witnesses with the rights of the accused, but stated explicitly that at some point in the proceedings, the accused must be given the opportunity to challenge witnesses against him/her.[68] The Chamber did not cite that particular excerpt of the *Kostovski* judgment, although defence counsel had expressly relied upon it in their submissions. According to the former President of the Tribunal, the late Antonio Cassese:

> The Majority Opinion of the Trial Chamber was, of necessity, selective in its reliance on the *Kostovski* case. Indeed, it must be borne in mind that the finding of the majority ... was that fair trial guarantees were not violated with anonymous witnesses, whereas the finding of the European Court in *Kostovski* was that such guarantees were violated.[69]

We might conclude that the Chamber's interpretation is in fact closer to the ECtHR's ruling in *Doorson*, but *Doorson* was not decided until the year following the *Tadić* protective measures decision.

The *Tadić* Trial Chamber attempted to draw a distinction between the circumstances in *Kostovski* and its own situation, where the witness would be present in court and the judges (but not the accused) would be able to assess his or her reliability and demeanour.[70] Of course, the right to test witnesses against you says nothing about the judge's ability to assess the witness's demeanour—that is an entirely different matter. Where the witness's identity is not revealed, nor can he or she inform the accused of how they obtained the incriminating information if that were likely to identify them,[71] it makes it very difficult to challenge that individual's version of events.

The *Tadić* anonymous witnesses decision is not unique in its selective use of ECtHR case law. In a 2008 motion for anonymity for participating victims, the Office of Public Counsel for Victims before the ICC submitted that the *Doorson* case held that courts must ensure that 'an appropriate balance is struck

68 See above, section I.

69 Antonio Cassese, 'The International Criminal Tribunal for the Former Yugoslavia and Human Rights' (1997) European Human Rights Law Review 329.

70 *Tadic* (n 35), para. 43.

71 ibid.

between the rights of the accused and those of the witnesses or victims.'[72] As we know, this was not the wording of the ECtHR in that case; rather, it was stated that where certain rights are protected elsewhere in the Convention and come into conflict with the rights of the accused, domestic criminal justice systems should endeavour to ensure that those rights are not 'unjustifiably imperilled'.[73] On the question of balance, the ECtHR had said that 'in appropriate cases[,] the interests of the defence [should be] ... balanced against those of witnesses or victims called upon to testify.'[74] This is not an explicit recognition of the need to balance the 'rights' of the competing parties; instead, the reference to 'interests' of these parties seems to be cognisant of the fact that sometimes, witnesses and victims will be interest-holders, as opposed to rights-holders, at trial.[75] Moreover, the 'called upon to testify' phrase is crucial—in *Lubanga*, victims had volunteered to present their views and concerns, as was their entitlement under Article 68(3) of the Statute, and so were not called upon by the Court to testify, as such. Nonetheless, the Trial Chamber (against the protestations of both prosecution and defence) rejected the argument that anonymous victims should never be allowed to participate in proceedings.[76]

Although the international criminal tribunals often refer to ECtHR decisions to justify their findings on absent witnesses, it is crucial to recall that a decisive factor in ECtHR decisions on this question, until recently, was whether the conviction was based solely or decisively on such untested evidence. Where that is the case, the decision will be subjected to 'the most searching scrutiny'. This fits in with the ECtHR's role as a final arbiter of fairness, where it can assess holistically to what extent a piece of evidence has influenced a decision. By contrast, the approach of the international criminal tribunals, where probative value of evidence is weighed against the right to a fair trial in assessing admissibility,[77] is quite distinct. The principle in assessing weight is that untested, uncorroborated witness testimony is of a lower probative value than other forms of evidence.[78]

---

72 *Prosecutor v Lubanga*, ICC-01/04-01/06-1219, Decision on Victims' Participation, 18 January 2008, para. 79.

73 See above, section I.

74 *Doorson* (n 10), para. 70.

75 See further McDermott (n 36) 117.

76 *Lubanga* (n 72), para. 130.

77 See e.g. Rule 89(d), ICTY RPE; *Prosecutor v Tadić*, Decision on the Defence Motion on Hearsay, Case No. IT-94-1-T, 5 August 1996.

78 See further, Yvonne McDermott, 'The Admissibility and Weight of Written Witness Testi-

The 'overall fairness' approach of the human rights tribunals, which assesses whether proceedings as a whole have been fair, is best suited to their particular mandate, given that they assess the fairness of proceedings long after their close. Nonetheless, the international criminal tribunals have embraced this notion of fairness as a whole, which of course do a very different job. To give an example, in one of the cases before the ICC in the *Situation in Darfur, Sudan*, defence counsel were denied access to the country by the Government of Sudan. They moved for a stay of proceedings, arguing that this hindrance rendered a fair trial impossible. In relying on the jurisprudence of the ECtHR, the Chamber, and particularly Judge Eboe-Osuji, declined to grant a stay of proceedings on the basis that it remained to be seen whether the proceedings as a whole would be rendered unfair by this imposition.[79] Of course, the ECtHR should be seen as a last resort, that an individual must have recourse to only when they feel that a trial has been unfair and they have exhausted all available domestic remedies. To impose this standard on decisions regarding stays of proceedings denigrates the intended purpose of stays of proceedings as a remedy—to stop the unfairness, and deprivation of the accused's liberty, before the damage becomes irreparable.

V Conclusion

This chapter has examined the use of ECtHR case law on the interplay between the rights of witnesses and the rights of accused persons by the international criminal tribunals. It started with an examination of the case law of the ECtHR and a critical reflection of whether, as is often presumed by other tribunals and by commentators, the ECtHR case law truly requires that a 'balance' be struck between both sets of rights. It showed that the notion of 'balance' only entered into ECtHR case law in later cases, and frequently the notion refers not to balancing the rights of the accused person against the rights of witnesses, but that the criminal justice system introduces some remedy to counter-balance any prejudice suffered by the accused.

The chapter then examined the scope of witness protection measures before international criminal tribunals, and the extent to which the tribunals draw

mony in International Criminal Law: A Socio-Legal Analysis' (2013) 27 Leiden Journal of International Law 971.

79 *Prosecutor v Banda*, ICC-02/05-03/09-410, Decision on the Defence Request for a Temporary Stay of Proceedings, 26 October 2012. See especially, Separate Opinion of Judge Chile Eboe-Osuji, para. 41.

on—and derogate from—ECtHR precedent in making their decisions. It showed two themes, which may be dubbed 'exceptionalism' and 'selectivity' in the tribunals' use of ECtHR case law. Exceptionalism notes the differences between the international criminal tribunals and domestic criminal justice systems that the ECtHR adjudges upon, and seeks to distinguish the international criminal tribunal from the 'ordinary' criminal trial. Selectivity, on the other hand, suggests that the international criminal tribunal's approach is well-founded in the precedent of the ECtHR and other human rights bodies, but either misapplies the standard derived from human rights law, or selectively quotes from the relevant case(s) in drawing quite different conclusions. These two approaches are not mutually exclusive, as highlighted by the *Tadić* protective measures decision, where both approaches can be witnessed.

Given that, broadly speaking, human rights standards are not binding on international criminal tribunals,[80] we might ask why these tribunals choose to apply the case law of the ECtHR and other human rights tribunals so readily. This is especially notable when creative interpretation is needed to make the decision appear to conform with the ECtHR precedent, as we witnessed in the *Tadić* protective measures decision's extensive use of *Kostovski*. Vasiliev has argued that human rights law plays a 'gap-filling' function where international criminal law does not have specific provisions on a particular issue.[81] The use of human rights case law in this manner also clearly has a function in legitimising the tribunals' decisions and making them appear in conformity with established international standards.[82] To this end, the ECtHR's influence on international criminal tribunals in this sphere is unlikely to wane any time soon.

80 Article 21(3) of the ICC Statute does, however, state that the application and interpretation of the law that the Court applies 'must be consistent with internationally recognized human rights'.

81 Sergey Vasiliev, *International Criminal Trials: A Normative Theory, Vol. 1*, available online at http://dare.uva.nl/document/2/138932 (last accessed 2 April 2016), 98–99.

82 McDermott (n 36) 19.

CHAPTER 13

The Special Court for Sierra Leone's Misapplication of the European Court of Human Rights Case Law on Hearsay Evidence and Corroboration: The *Taylor* Appeal Judgment and the *Al Khawaja and Tahery* Case

*Yael Vias Gvirsman**

Introduction

On 26 September 2013, the Special Court for Sierra Leone Appeals Chamber issued its last and, arguably, most important Judgment.[1] The legacy of the *Prosecutor v Taylor* case to international criminal law cannot be overestimated. The significance of this Appeal Judgment is threefold. Firstly, it was the first final conviction of an acting Head of State. Secondly, it set a precedent for convicting a Head of State responsible for actions that occurred in a third State.[2] Finally, it addressed legal questions of great importance to international criminal law, in particular questions about the 'specific direction' standard of conviction for aiding and abetting,[3] and the probative value of (uncorroborated) hearsay evi-

---

* The author served as a legal assistant on the Charles Taylor defence team throughout the appeal. The author wishes to thank the anonymous reviewer and the editors of this book for their useful and thoughtful review, as well as their indulgence and encouragement in view of publication. The author would also like to thank Nikki Lee for English editing, and Michael Herz and Yvonne McDermott for their very useful last minute input. The usual caveats apply.

1 *Prosecutor v Taylor*, SCSL-03-01-A-1389, Judgment, Appeals Chamber, 26 September 2013 ('*Taylor* Appeal Judgment').

2 It would not be surprising if the *Taylor* case were to be used as a precedent when prosecuting the forthcoming crime of aggression at the ICC.

3 See, aside from the SCSL case law, the legal 'debate' in the ICTY case law on 'specific direction' among other sources in *Prosecutor v Šainović*, IT-05-87-A, Judgment, Appeals Chamber, 23 January 2014, paras 1617–1651; *Prosecutor v Perišić*, IT-04-81-A, Judgment, Appeals Chamber, 28 February 2013; as opposed to *Prosecutor v Perišić*, IT-04-81-T, Judgment, Trial Chamber, 6 September 2011, as well as the ICTY's most recent say on the question of specific direction in *Prosecutor v Stanišić*, IT-03-69-A, Judgment, Appeals Chamber, 9 December 2015, paras 104–107.

 | DOI: 10.1163/9789004313750_015

dence in convicting an individual. This latter procedural question is at the core of this chapter.

This chapter raises arguments against the SCSL interpretation and application of the ECtHR judgment in the case of *Al Khawaja and Tahery v United Kingdom*.[4] It will examine existing international criminal standards and applicable rules relating to hearsay and the 'sole or decisive' rule derived from longstanding ECtHR case law. Then, looking at the reasoning of the SCSL Appeals Chamber when rejecting the Taylor Defence's arguments on uncorroborated hearsay, this chapter will demonstrate why, in the author's view, the SCSL misapplied relevant ECtHR case law, if not in its actual wording then at least in spirit. The key claim is that the SCSL deviated from the regular standard for conviction based on a misguided interpretation of ECtHR case law. The crux of the argument rests on the view that the ECtHR recognised a flexible application of the 'sole or decisive' prohibition to cases *originating from the UK legal system*, due to the particularly strong procedural safeguards provided for therein, as opposed to legal systems that adhere to inherently different rules of evidence.

I The Standard of Evidence for Conviction: Hearsay Evidence and Corroboration

The SCSL Appeals Chamber's interpretation of ECtHR case law, notably the Grand Chamber's Judgment in the *Al Khawaja and Tahery* case, is flawed. To explain this position, it is necessary to (1) understand the *sui generis* nature of international criminal procedure as applicable under the SCSL RPE;[5] (2) examine the implications of the *Al Khawaja and Tahery* case to international criminal procedure, namely in terms of procedural safeguards; and (3) explain why, under the circumstances of the *Taylor* case, the Appeals Chamber applied the *Al Khawaja and Tahery* case in wording (at best) but not in spirit.

a *The Discretionary Role of the Judge in Assessing Evidence in International Criminal Procedure—and 'Procedural Safeguards' under the SCSL RPE*

International criminal procedure is of a mixed nature resulting from compromises between the common law and the continental law systems.[6] The differ-

4 *Al Khawaja and Tahery v United Kingdom*, App no 26766/05 and 22228/06 (ECtHR, 15 December 2011).

5 *Taylor* Appeal Judgment (n 1), para. 70.

6 At times qualified as *sui generis*. See eg *Prosecutor v Delalić*, IT-96-21-T, Decision on the Motion

ence between the two legal cultures is particularly significant in respect of the question of evidence. On the one hand, international criminal procedure draws on a fundamentally adversarial system.[7] On the other hand, international criminal procedure also displays significant traits borrowed from continental legal systems, in particular with respect to the admissibility and probative value of evidence.[8] SCSL procedure under its RPE is no different.[9] Therefore, almost all evidence is admissible[10] and a different probative value can be assigned to different types of evidence.[11] The judge has a crucial role in using his or her discretion to determine the weight and significance of each piece of evidence

---

on Presentation of Evidence by the Accused, Esad Landzo, Trial Chamber, 1 May 1997, para. 15: an 'amalgam of both common law or civilian elements, so as to render it *sui generis*'. See also *Prosecutor v Tadić*, IT-94-1-T, Decision on Defence Motion on Hearsay, Trial Chamber, 5 August 1996, para. 14.

7 Kai Ambos, 'International Criminal Procedure: "Adversarial", "Inquisitorial" or Mixed?' (2003) 3 International Criminal Law Review 1; See also an updated version in Kai Ambos, 'The Structure of International Criminal Procedure: "Adversarial", "Inquisitorial" or Mixed?' in Michael Bohlander (ed), *International Criminal Justice. A Critical Analysis of Institutions and Procedures* (Cameron May 2007) 429. For the procedure at Post World War II 'Nuremburg Trials', see Richard May and Marieke Wierda, 'Trends in International Criminal Evidence: Nuremberg, Tokyo, The Hague, and Arusha' (1999) 37 Columbia Journal of Transnational Law 725; Evan J. Wallach, 'The Procedural and Evidentiary Rules of the Post-World War II War Crimes Trials' (1999) 37 Columbia Journal of Transnational Law 851.

8 ICTY Rules of Procedure and Evidence, IT/32/Rev. 49, as revised on 22 May 2013, Rule 89(C) and (D); at the ICC, see RPE, Rule 63(2); Rome Statute, Article 64(9): 'A Chamber shall have the authority [...] to assess freely all evidence submitted in order to determine its relevance and admissibility'. Notably, and as outlined by Ambos (n 7), the evolution of international criminal procedure is marked by the increase in the 'mixity' of the procedure from what was originally an adversarial system to an increasingly inquisitorial or continental system. Accordingly, RPE drafted later are marked by their continental character and more prominent role for the judge, where nearly all types of evidence are admissible and freely assessed by the judge in terms of their probative value.

9 SCSL RPE applied the ICTR RPE *mutatis mutandis* with SCSL judges having the ability to make necessary amendments. See Article 14 of the SCSL Statute.

10 Under Rule 89(C) of the SCSL RPE: 'a Chamber may admit any relevant evidence'. Rule 89(C) of the ICTY RPE applies a more restrictive language: 'a Chamber may admit any relevant evidence which it deems of probative value'. See eg *Prosecutor v Martić*, IT-95-11-T, Decision Adopting Guidelines on the Standards Governing the Admission of Evidence, Trial Chamber, 19 January 2006, para. 2 of the 'Guidelines' (henceforth '*Martić* Guidelines'): '*The practice will be, therefore, in favour of admissibility*' (emphasis added).

11 See *Martić* Guidelines (n 10): 'Parties should always bear in mind the basic distinction that exists between the admissibility of documentary evidence and the weight that documentary evidence is given under the principle of free evaluation of evidence'.

in reaching a conviction or an acquittal based on his/her *intimate conviction*.[12] At this crossroads between continental and common law legal systems, where nearly every piece of evidence is admissible and its probative value dependent on the judges' discretion, the few rules limiting this discretion are of crucial importance in safeguarding a fair trial. One such central rule is that 'evidence which has not been cross-examined and goes to the acts and conduct of the Accused or is pivotal to the Prosecution case will require corroboration if used to establish a conviction'.[13] This general rule is often referred to as 'the sole or decisive' rule or prohibition. The Defence in the *Taylor* case relied on the 'sole or decisive' rule in its appeal submissions (Ground 1).[14] The Appeals Chamber found that 'there is no prohibition against the use of uncorroborated hearsay evidence, even if such hearsay is the basis of the conviction, provided that the Trial Chamber has subjected the hearsay evidence to a fair and proper assessment of its reliability'.[15] This ruling constitutes a misinterpretation of the relevant ECtHR jurisprudence, which led the Appeals Chamber to accept reliance on hearsay evidence without applying the 'yardsticks'[16] introduced by the ECtHR.

b *The Definition of Hearsay Evidence and the 'Sole or Decisive' Rule*

In the past, both Defence and Prosecution[17] have relied on the 'sole or decisive' rule in relation to hearsay evidence before ICTs. Even when arguing about hearsay, parties rely on case law referring to the 'sole or decisive' rule as applied

12 For one example of the principle of free evaluation of evidence in national laws, see French Code of Criminal Procedure, Article 427.

13 *Prosecutor v Martić*, IT-95-11-AR73.2, Decision on Appeal Against the Trial Chamber's Decision on the Evidence of Witness Milan Babić, 14 September 2006, para. 20, where the Appeals Chamber validates the Trial Chamber's conclusion and reliance on ECtHR case law; see also *Prosecutor v Galić*, IT-98-29-AR73.2, Decision on Interlocutory Appeal Concerning Rule 92 bis, 7 June 2002, fn. 34, referring to judgments of the ECtHR.

14 *Prosecutor v Taylor*, SCSL-03-01-A-1326, Appellant's Submissions of Charles Ghankay Taylor ('Defence Appeal Brief'), 2 October 2012, paras 23–36.

15 *Taylor* Appeal Judgment (n 1), para. 91.

16 To use terminology used in Elmar Widder, The Right to Challenge Witnesses—An Application of Strasbourg's Flexible Sole and Decisive Rule to Other Human Rights (2014) 3 Cambridge Journal of International and Comparative Law 1084.

17 For the Prosecution arguments, see *Prosecutor v Popović*, IT-05-88, Decision on the Admissibility of the Borovčanin Interview and the Amendment of the Rule 65 ter Exhibit List, 25 October 2007 ('*Popović* Trial Chamber Decision'), para. 42 where the Trial Chamber refers to 'Prosecution Further Submission Regarding Admissibility of the Interviews of Ljubomir Borovčanin as Evidence Against the Co-Accused' of 20 July 2007 ('Prosecution

to untested written witness statements.[18] The question is whether this case law is relevant to hearsay. The fact of the matter is that hearsay and untested witness statements are often intertwined in the case law and legal reasoning, given that in both cases the Defence right to cross-examine the source of information is limited and the original or direct source is not available for examination.[19] Revealingly, in the *Taylor* case, the Appeals Chamber applied the *Al Khawaja and Tahery* case, which involved untested witness statements[20] when responding to the Defence argument on uncorroborated hearsay. The 'sole and decisive' rule means a conviction *cannot* be based solely and decisively on evidence where the direct source of information was not cross-examined.[21] Admittedly, in order to determine whether case law referring to untested written statements is justifiably applicable to hearsay, it is necessary to draw the similarities and differences between the two and to determine the hierarchy between them, if such hierarchy exists. Hearsay evidence is evidence of facts not within the testifying witness's direct knowledge.[22] Therefore, at most, the

---

Further Submission'), para. 10 and summarises the Prosecution arguments petitioning the Trial Chamber to admit the interviews into evidence stating that it would not violate the fairness of trial in light of safeguards such as the rule by which 'an accused may not be convicted solely on the basis of uncorroborated hearsay evidence'.

18 In *Popović* Prosecution Further Submission (n 17) the Prosecution relied on *Prosecutor v Galić*, IT-98-29-AR73.2, Decision on Interlocutory Appeal concerning Rule 92 bis(C), Appeals Chamber, 7 June 2002, fn. 34; *Prosecutor v Milutinović*, IT-05-87-T, Decision on Prosecution Motion for Admission of Evidence pursuant to Rule 92 quater, Trial Chamber, 16 February 2007, para. 13: 'the Trial Chamber will bear in mind the jurisprudence of the Tribunal, which has clearly stated that the admission of a written statement in lieu of oral testimony cannot support a conviction all by itself where the witness does not appear for cross-examination unless the written evidence is otherwise corroborated'; *Prosecutor v Milutinović*, IT-05-87-T, Decision on Second Prosecution Motion for Admission of Evidence pursuant to Rule 92 quater, Trial Chamaber, 5 March 2007, para. 11. All references relate to untested witness statements but are used to support an argument in favour of the 'sole or decisive rule' as applicable to hearsay.

19 See eg *Popović* Trial Chamber Decision (n 17), in which the untested co-accused's interviews given prior to his indictment and where the co-accused could not be forced to testify without violating his right not to self-incriminate, were finally admitted into evidence as hearsay. See also *Prosecutor v Popović*, IT-05-88-AR73.1, Decision on Appeals against Decision Admitting Material related to Borovčanin's Questioning, 14 December 2007.

20 *Taylor* Appeal Judgment (n 1), paras 85–91.

21 See (n 13) above.

22 *Prosecutor v Halilović*, IT-01-48, Judgment, Trial Chamber, 16 November 2005, para. 15; *Prosecutor v Blagojević*, IT-02-60, Judgment, Trial Chamber, 17 January 2005, para. 21; see also

testifying source (witness) can attest to what his source *told* him and to what his *impressions* are from what his source told him. By definition, hearsay is *indirect* evidence where witness X states that Y told him something. Therefore the 'actual' or direct source of information, first-hand, is not available for cross-examination. A statement by Y would be direct evidence. Notably, if the direct source of information (Y) is available for cross-examination, then the question of hearsay as a basis for incriminating findings becomes moot, since the source of information can be challenged by cross-examination. At most, what cross-examination of hearsay can confirm is the credibility of *the hearsay witness* (*X*), not that of his source (Y). Cross-examination of X, however, does not strengthen the credibility of information provided by Y to X. Therefore, if we were to draw a hierarchy between the two, on the scale of probative value and in relation to how prejudicial they are to the Defence right to challenge evidence, hearsay evidence is arguably more prejudicial to Defence and fair trial rights than untested witness statements.[23] In the author's view, this is the underlying ratio preventing a trial chamber from reasonably relying thereon solely or decisively when entering a conviction.

This is why the Taylor Defence contended that '*A fortiori*, the prohibition must apply with even greater force in respect of hearsay with much lesser guarantees of accuracy and reliability'.[24]

The *Taylor* Appeals Chamber underlined the particular importance of the Defence's first ground of appeal relating to the assessment of hearsay evidence, as follows:

> The Defence raises two issues of law which the Special Court *has not had occasion to discuss to any extent in any of its previous judgments:* [...] and second, whether triers of fact are precluded by law from relying solely or decisively on uncorroborated hearsay evidence as the basis for incriminating findings of fact.[25]

The starting point adopted by the Appeals Chamber was to review customary international law and general principles of domestic law.[26]

Prosecutor v Aleksovski, IT-95-14/1-AR73, Decision on Prosecutor's Appeal on Admissibility of Evidence, Appeals Chamber, 16 February 1999, para. 14.

23 *Al Khawaja and Tahery* (n 4), para. 139.

24 Defence Appeal Brief (n 14), para. 25.

25 *Taylor* Appeal Judgment (n 1), para. 52 (emphasis added).

26 *Prosecutor v Taylor*, SCSL-03-01-A-1355, Scheduling Order, Appeals Chamber, 30 November 2012.

c *Customary International Law and General Principles on Uncorroborated Hearsay as the Basis for Incriminating Findings of Fact*

The Appeals Chamber sought to identify the rule on uncorroborated hearsay and incriminating findings under customary international law. ICTY and ICTR case law were particularly relevant to the SCSL Appeals Chamber in this context.[27] As affirmed by the ICTY Appeals Chamber:

> [u]nacceptable infringements of the rights of the Defence, in this sense *occur when a conviction is based solely, or in a decisive manner*, on the depositions of a witness *whom the accused has had no opportunity to examine* or to have examined either during the investigation or at trial.[28]

ICTR case law states as follows:

> It is well established that, as a matter of law, it is permissible to base a conviction on hearsay evidence. A Trial Chamber has the discretion to cautiously consider hearsay evidence and has the discretion to rely on it. While the weight and probative value to be afforded to that evidence *will usually be less than that accorded to the evidence of a witness who has given it under oath and who has been cross-examined, it will depend upon "the infinitely variable circumstances which surround hearsay evidence"*. Thus, the fact that the evidence regarding a specific event is hearsay evidence does not in itself suffice to render it not credible or unreliable. The source of information, the precise character of the information, ***and the fact that*** *other evidence corroborates the hearsay evidence* are relevant criteria in assessing the weight or probative value of hearsay evidence.[29]

Therefore, hearsay evidence will have lesser probative value while corroboration is needed for an incriminating finding based thereon. This was the standard applied by the ICC Trial Chamber II in the *Ngudjolo* Acquittal Judgment,[30]

27 Article 20(3), SCSL Statute.

28 *Prosecutor v Prlić*, IT-04-74-AT73.6, Appeals Chamber, Decision on Appeals Against Decision Admitting Transcripts of Jadronko Prlić's Questioning into Evidence, 23 November 2007, para. 53.

29 *Prosecutor v Karera*, ICTR-01-74-A, Judgment, Appeals Chamber, 2 February 2009, para. 39 (internal footnotes omitted; emphasis added).

30 See *Prosecutor v Ngudjolo*, ICC-01/04-02/12-3-tENG, Judgment pursuant to Article 74 of the Statute, Trial Chamber, 18 December 2012 ('*Ngudjolo* Acquittal Judgment').

as upheld by the ICC Appeals Chamber.[31] While other factors relating to the circumstances of the case, such as the credibility of the witness, the lack of detail, and the witness's remoteness from the crime-scene admittedly played a role in the acquittal of *Ngudjolo*, the fact that crucial evidence was hearsay served as the tipping point in the Trial Chamber's Judgment. For instance, the Trial Chamber stressed that 'evidence, which is based on hearsay, must be considered with the greatest circumspection, especially as it relates to a crucial point in the Prosecution's case'.[32] The *Ngudjolo* Acquittal Judgment stated that anonymous hearsay was admissible but that its probative value would be evaluated with due consideration of 'the impossibility of cross-examining the information source'.[33] The Trial Chamber sought corroboration for hearsay on a case-by-case basis, and rejected facts because, among other reasons, they were based solely on hearsay evidence.[34] Notably, two non-hearsay elements of evidence were not enough to corroborate nine hearsay testimonies. Therefore, while hearsay was not the only factor that led the Trial Chamber to refuse to enter incriminating findings, there is no doubt that the fact that vital evidence was hearsay was significant in leading it to attach lower weight thereto. The

31 *Prosecutor v Ngudjolo*, ICC-01/04-02/12-271-Corr, Judgment on the Prosecutor's Appeal against the Decision of Trial Chamber II entitled 'Judgment pursuant to Article 74 of the Statute', Appeals Chamber, 7 April 2015, paras 112, 117–118, 204, whereby it found no unreasonableness in the Trial Chamber's view that hearsay evidence on which a crucial point in the Prosecution's case is based 'must be considered with the greatest circumspection'. See also ibid paras 42–44, whereby the Appeals Chamber provides a summary of the Prosecution's first ground of appeal on the standard of proof as to hearsay evidence. According to the Prosecutor, the *Ngudjolo* Trial Chamber applied a threshold too high for conviction of 'beyond *any* doubt' instead of 'beyond any *reasonable* doubt' based on evidence, logic or common sense. The Appeals Chamber rejected the Prosecution's arguments.

32 *Ngudjolo* Acquittal Judgement (n 30), para. 496. This is notwithstanding the fact that other reasons played a role (see ibid para. 496: 'for *all* these reasons' (emphasis added)).

33 *Ngudjolo* Acquittal Judgment (n 30), para. 56.

34 *Ngudjolo* Acquittal Judgment (n 30), paras 270–272. See also, on the need for corroboration of facts alleged in human rights reports, ibid paras 294–295; and although the Trial Chamber did not question Witness P-317's honesty, ibid para. 476. Another witness's anonymous hearsay evidence was rejected relating to Ngudjolo's functions during the Bogoro attack, see ibid paras 431–433. A credible witness's statement was rejected concerning Ngudjolo's role in the Bogoro attack because it was uncorroborated hearsay and was too vague on this point, ibid para. 434. At least nine other witnesses provided hearsay evidence confirming the Accused's leading role in Bogoro and Zumbe, these were either rejected or assigned lower probative value, see ibid paras 435–442.

Trial Chamber applied this high (and appropriate) standard of caution in relation to hearsay 'especially as it relates to a crucial point in the Prosecution's case'.[35] The Trial Chamber concluded by acquitting Mr Ngudjolo on this point and, subsequently, on all charges.[36]

The case law of the ECtHR is a particularly relevant authority to ICTs when interpreting fair trial rights and the applicable law on the assessment of hearsay when entering a conviction. Thus, the ICTY Appeals Chamber recognised that:

> [T]he right to cross-examination in Article 21(4)(e) of the Statute is in *pari materia* with Article 6(3)(d) of the [ECHR] and its importance has been repeatedly stressed and its violation sanctioned by the [ECtHR]. The Appeals Chamber considers that the jurisprudence of the ECHR provides a useful source of guidance for the interpretation of the right to cross-examination and the scope of its permissible limitations.[37]

ECtHR case law is paramount in recognising the principle of an adversarial system and the principle of equality of arms,[38] in demonstrating how the right to confront evidence can be restricted by hearsay,[39] and, finally, in establishing the 'sole or decisive' rule.[40] 'In the case of a deposition that has been made

---

35 *Ngudjolo* Acquittal Judgment (n 30), para. 496.

36 *Ngudjolo* Acquittal Judgment (n 30), para. 503.

37 *Prosecutor v. Martić*, IT-95-11-AR73.2, Decision on Appeal against the Trial Chamber's Decision on the Evidence of Witness Milan Babić, Appeals Chamber, 14 September 2006, para. 19. Article 21(4)(e) of ICTY Statute is identical to Article 17(4)(e) of SCSL Statute. Moreover in ibid para. 20, the Appeals Chamber upheld the Trial Chamber's assessment of ECtHR case law when it asserted that 'evidence which has not been cross-examined and goes to the acts and conduct of the Accused or is pivotal to the Prosecution case will require corroboration if used to establish a conviction, are consistent with the jurisprudence of the International Tribunal as well as that of national jurisdictions' (internal footnotes omitted); see also *Prlić* (n 28), para. 31.

38 *Rowe and Davis v the United Kingdom*, App no 28901/95 (ECtHR, 16 February 2000), para. 60; *Laukkanin and Manninen v Finland*, App no 50230/99 (ECtHR, 3 February 2004), para. 34.

39 Kai Ambos, *Treatise on International Criminal Law, Vol. III: International Criminal Procedure* (OUP 2016) 1739–1740 and references cited therein.

40 The 'sole or decisive' rule was first recognised by the ECtHR in *Unterpertinger v Austria*, App no 9120/80 (ECtHR, 24 November 1986), para. 33. Also refer to *Mild and Virtanen v Finland*, App no 39481/98 and 40227/98 (ECtHR, 26 July 2005), para. 42; *Doorsen v Netherlands*, App no 20524/92 (ECtHR, 26 March 1996), para. 76, where the ECtHR held that there was a violation of Article 6(3)(d) even where the absence of the witnesses

by a witness whom the accused had no opportunity to examine, the final assessment depends on the circumstances of the concrete case, in particular whether this deposition has been corroborated by other evidence and whether the court has relied exclusively on it'.[41]

The present examination of international case law on the 'sole or decisive' rule has thus revealed the importance of corroboration[42] and the circumstances of each case. The circumstances of reliance on hearsay evidence in the *Taylor* case by the Trial Chamber and its validation by the Appeals Chamber will be discussed in Section II below, after examining the *Al Khawaja and Tahery* case and its misguided application in *Taylor.*

II The SCSL Deviation from the 'Sole or Decisive' Rule and the Misapplication of the ECtHR Case Law

It is argued that, in the *Taylor* Appeal Judgment, the Appeals Chamber deviated from the 'sole or decisive' rule based on a misapplication of the ECtHR Grand Chamber Judgment in *Al Khawaja and Tahery.*[43] Notably, the Appeals Chamber applied the wording of the ECtHR, but misapplied the spirit of its Judgment. The pivotal point of departure is a misguided understanding of the 'procedural safeguards' as understood and applied in the *Al Khawaja and Tahery* case.

a *The Taylor Appeal Judgment on Uncorroborated Hearsay*

The Appeals Chamber rejected Ground 1 of the Defence's appeal by relying on the *Al Khawaja and Tahery* ECtHR Judgment, in particular on its paragraph 147, which it quoted only partially. The Appeals Chamber concluded that in light of the fair trial guarantees offered by the SCSL Statute and Regulations, it was satisfied that the Accused was offered a fair chance to challenge the evidence against him.[44] That evidence included uncorroborated hearsay as a decisive base for conviction.

---

was justified; *van Mechelen and others v Netherlands*, App no 21363/93, 21364/93, 21427/93 and 22056/93 (ECtHR, 23 April 1997), para. 55; *Lucà v Italy*, App no 33354/96 (ECtHR, 27 February 2001), para. 40; *A.M. v Italy*, App no 37019/97 (ECtHR, 14 December 1999), para. 25; *Saïdi v France*, App no 14647/89 (ECtHR, 20 September 1993), paras 43–44.

41 *Bracci v Italy*, App no 36822/02 (ECtHR, 13 October 2005), paras 54 ff.

42 As defined in *Prosecutor v Nahimana*, ICTR-99-52-A, Judgment, Appeals Chamber, para. 428 (emphasis added).

43 *Al Khawaja and Tahery* (n 4).

44 ibid para 91.

At paragraph 85 of its Judgment, the Appeals Chamber stated as follows:

> The Appeals Chamber considers that the issue in this case in regard to hearsay evidence *turns on* whether the Defence was right in its contention that reliance on uncorroborated hearsay evidence as the sole or decisive basis for incriminating findings of fact leading to a conviction amounted to an error in law. *It is, therefore, in this context relevant and instructive to note that the ECtHR in the case of Al Khawaja and Tahery*, decided on 15 December 2011, considered and expressly rejected a similar view as that put forward by the Defence in this case. In *Al Khawaja and Tahery*, the Grand Chamber of the ECtHR held that reliance on an uncorroborated hearsay statement as the sole or decisive basis for a conviction is not precluded as a matter of law and does not *per se* violate the Accused's right to a fair trial.[45]

The Appeals Chamber disregarded the ECtHR *ratio* assessing the counterbalancing measures in the context of the case.[46] It implicitly referred to the ECtHR's reasoning that in order for a conviction decisively based on uncorroborated hearsay *not* to be in breach of Article 6(3) of the ECHR, there must be 'counterbalancing factors, including the existence of *strong procedural safeguards*' (emphasis added). Whereas the ECtHR examined the counterbalancing measures in English law existing at the time of the decision, the Appeals Chamber made an 'intellectual leap' to state that: '*There exist in the laws applied by the Special Court safeguards designed to ensure the accused's rights of fair hearing and to ensure that evidence can be fairly challenged at trial*'.[47]

The Appeals Chamber did not question existing SCSL procedural safeguards in light of the ECtHR's specific examination of English law, as opposed to other legal systems,[48] and it overlooked the intrinsic difference between the two systems on rules of evidence. It is also argued that the Appeals Chamber did not sufficiently examine the Trial Chamber's assessment of evidence in the specific circumstances of the *Taylor* case. For if it had, it would, arguably, not have applied nascent ECtHR case law, which is still subject to debate several years after its pronouncement,[49] relating to procedural rules presumably not analogous to international criminal procedure on rules of evidence—and

45 Emphasis added.

46 *Al Khawaja and Tahery* (n 4), para. 147.

47 ibid para. 87 (internal footnotes omitted; emphasis added). See also ibid para. 91.

48 *Al Khawaja and Tahery* (n 4), paras 130 ff.

49 See eg Widder (n 16), where the author applies the 'ECtHR yardsticks' to other human

applied it to 'fourth-hand hearsay'.[50] Interpretation by analogy is particularly uncalled for in international criminal law, especially when it results in serious restrictions on an individual's personal liberty and considering the spirit underlying the principle of legality,[51] which requires adherence to strict interpretation. While there is a variety of opinions on the point,[52] it is submitted that the ECtHR delivered a nuanced and sophisticated judgement in *Al Khawaja and Tahery*. In contrast, the Appeals Chamber applied a 'one-size-fits-all' standard. Indeed, a cautious examination of procedural safeguards to ECtHR 'yardsticks' is warranted in light of the ECtHR's contextual examination of the counterbalancing measures in English law.[53] In that regard the Appeals Chamber overlooked a crucial element of law with serious implications.

b 'Strong Procedural Safeguards' in the UK System as Opposed to 'Safeguards of a Fair Trial' at SCSL

i The ECtHR *Al Khawaja and Tahery* Judgment of 2011

In the European context, the *Al Khawaja and Tahery* case offered 'fine-tuning' to existing ECtHR case law and admitted that the 'sole or decisive' rule could be applied flexibly *to the UK system*.[54] Thus, legal systems where a conviction is possible based 'solely or decisively' on uncorroborated hearsay would normally be in breach of Article 6(3) of the ECHR, whereas it would not be possible under the strict hearsay rule in the UK system.[55] However, the UK system deviated from its strict rule on the inadmissibility of hearsay in *Al Khawaja and Tahery*. Nevertheless, according to the ECtHR, 'these dilutions of the strict rule against hearsay have been accompanied by statutory safeguards and, accordingly, *the*

---

rights bodies to see how they would have ruled, taking into account the common law/continental law divide.

50 Defence Appeal Brief (n 14), para. 27.

51 See eg Antonio Cassese et al., *Cassese's International Criminal Law* (OUP 2013), Chapter 2. Although the principle of legality relates directly to the scope of crimes, it is argued that its rationale suggests a cautious interpretation of other areas of law that significantly impact on an accused's fundamental rights.

52 See eg above, chapter by Yvonne McDermott.

53 *Al Khawaja and Tahery* (n 4), paras 148 ff.

54 ibid para. 146. The ECtHR fine tuning in *Al Khawaja and Tahery* (n 4) is limited to absent witnesses and does not apply to anonymous witnesses where the strict 'sole or decisive' rule would apply also in the UK system, ibid para. 137.

55 ibid para. 130.

central question in the [Al Khawaja and Tahery] cases is whether the application of these safeguards was sufficient to secure the applicants' rights under Article 6 (1) and (3)(d)'.[56]

The ECtHR examined specific safeguards in the 1988[57] and 2003[58] UK Acts. It stated for example:

> Of particular significance is the requirement under the 2003 Act that the trial judge should stop the proceedings if satisfied at the close of the case for the prosecution that the case against the accused is based "wholly or partly" on a hearsay statement admitted under the 2003 Act, provided he or she is also satisfied that the statement in question is so unconvincing that, considering its importance to the case against the accused, a conviction would be unsafe.[59]

A close reading of the decision reveals that the ECtHR finds that basing a conviction on uncorroborated hearsay evidence no longer automatically violates the accused's rights, given the very specific safeguards *applicable in the common law system in the UK*.[60] A review of the ECtHR jurisprudence clearly demonstrates that *continental or civil law legal systems* do *not* generally offer the same safeguards.[61] In those systems, the prohibition of reliance on hearsay evidence as sole or decisive evidence for conviction should be applied strictly. This is a critical point. The ECtHR admits broadening its previous case law when relevant to common law systems and the safeguards therein, continuing to confirm as valid its previous case law, developed in relation to civil law systems, on the sole or decisive rule.[62] Hence what the SCSL Appeals Chamber did in *Taylor* was the equivalent of comparing apples and oranges.

Notably, and similar to the SCSL, all continental law systems have safeguards to ensure the fair trial of defendants, including his or her right to

---

56 ibid (emphasis added).

57 Sections 23 to 28 of the Criminal Justice Act 1988 ("the 1988 Act").

58 Part 11, Chapter 2 of the Criminal Justice Act 2003 ("the 2003 Act"), entered into force in April 2005.

59 ibid 149.

60 *Al Khawaja and Tahery* (n 4) paras 40, 133, and 148ff., as examples for ECtHR review of common law safeguards.

61 According to previous ECtHR case law (see (n 40) above), safeguards existing in The Netherlands, Germany, Austria, Italy, Finland and France would not be sufficiently strong to allow deviation from the sole or decisive rule without breach of Article6(3) of the ECHR.

62 See *Al Khawaja and Tahery* (n 4), paras 118, 142.

challenge evidence. However, UK procedural safeguards and ICTs' procedural safeguards, including those at the SCSL, ICTY and ICTR, are distinct.[63] The latter call for a strict application of the 'sole or decisive' rule, unless the inability to cross-examine evidence was somehow compensated for. In *Popović*, the ICTY Trial Chamber accepted the Prosecution's arguments on the difference between ICTY safeguards and UK safeguards and admitted into evidence the co-accused's interviews conducted prior to his indictment as hearsay.[64] The Prosecution stated:

> [U]nlike jury trials in common law jurisdictions, ICTY cases are heard by professional judges who are able to consider the reliability and probative value of evidence, consider the effect of absence of cross-examination, and assign the evidence whatever weight is deemed proper.[65]

This is the underlying premise for the admission of hearsay evidence in international criminal procedure, ie the trust in the judges' best judgement. This is why the 'sole or decisive' rule is relevant in international criminal procedure, as a rule restricting judges' freedom of assessing evidence in view of fair trial rights.

At the SCSL, judges would weigh the probative value of hearsay, which in the UK system would normally not be admitted into evidence. Also, what is an exception in the UK system—that is, admission of hearsay evidence—is the rule in ICTs' procedural regulations. That is why the two systems are incomparable; they result in two distinct legal cultures and, without adequate adaptation, the wording applied by one cannot be adopted by the other. Indeed, arguably, the same language in both legal systems would result in different outcomes.

---

63 In a later decision, the ECtHR stressed the 'counterbalancing measures of the common law': *Horncastle v United Kingdom*, App no 4184/10 (ECtHR, 16 December 2014), paras 102 and 115.

64 *Popović* Trial Chamber Decision (n 17), paras 56–59 where the co-accused interviews are analysed as hearsay against the other accused; ibid paras 77–80 where the Trial Chamber decides to admit the interviews into evidence.

65 Prosecution Further Submission (n 17), para. 10.

ii The Dialogue between the ECtHR and the UK Courts: Necessary Adaptation of ECtHR Case Law Seeing Inherent Procedural Safeguards in UK Law

In *Al Khawaja and Tahery*, the ECtHR took the effort to analyse relevant domestic law and practice,[66] including safeguards offered by the Criminal Justice Act 2003, the Coroners and Justice Act 2009 and the Human Rights Act 1998. When examining case law of the UK, the ECtHR focused on how UK courts have applied ECtHR case law. The first UK case examined, *R v Sellick and Sellick*, highlighted the need for UK courts to distance themselves from a strict application of ECtHR case law.[67] According to the UK Court, this distance is necessary considering that the UK system is jury-based, and the judge removes hearsay evidence at the admissibility stage. The UK court held that the existing ECtHR case law pertaining to the 'sole or decisive standard' is inadequate in light of the fact that, at the admissibility stage, it is impossible to determine whether one piece of evidence will be decisive or not at the judgment stage.

The ECtHR decision quoted Lord Philips, stating as follows:

> Indeed the rule seemed to have been created because, *in contrast to the common law, continental systems of criminal procedure* did not have a comparable body of jurisprudence or rules governing the admissibility of evidence.[68]

The second UK case examined by the ECtHR is *R. v Davis*. The ECtHR refers to Lord Bingham and holds as follows:

> [The UK Court] found that the witnesses' testimony was inconsistent with the long-established principle of the English common law that, subject to certain exceptions and statutory qualifications, the defendant in a criminal trial should be confronted by his accusers in order that he may cross-examine them and challenge their evidence, a principle which originated in ancient Rome (Lord Bingham at paragraph 5).
>
> Moreover, this Court had not set its face absolutely against the admission of anonymous evidence in all circumstances. *However, it had said that a conviction should not be based solely or to a decisive extent on anonymous statements*. In any event, *on the facts in Davis's case, this Court would*

66 See *Al Khawaja and Tahery* (n 4), paras 40–62. For a review of 'relevant [common law] comparative law' see ibid paras 65–87.

67 Namely, *Lucà* (n 40), para. 40.

68 *Al Khawaja and Tahery* (n 4), para. 58 (emphasis added).

> *have found a violation of Article 6: not only was the anonymous witnesses evidence the sole or decisive basis on which Davis had been convicted, but effective cross-examination had been hampered.*[69]

The UK system contains an internal 'sole or decisive' rule. The *Al Khawaja and Tahery* judgment reconfirmed previous ECtHR case law, stating that:

> *[If] effective cross-examination is hampered and anonymous witness evidence is the sole or decisive basis for conviction, there would still be a violation of Article 6 of the ECHR.* Moreover, at paragraph 142 of the *Al Khawaja and Tahery* judgment, the ECtHR confirmed that '[w]ith respect to the Government's final argument, the Court is of the view that the two reasons underpinning the sole or decisive rule that were set out in the *Doorson* judgment *remain valid*'.[70]

Finally, the Grand Chamber went to considerable lengths in examining *R. v Horncastle* and others.[71] It reports the conclusions of Lord Philips as follows:

> Lord Phillips instead concluded that the 2003 Act made such a rule *unnecessary in English criminal procedure* because, if the 2003 Act were observed, there would be no breach of Article 6(3)(d) even if a conviction were based solely or to a decisive extent on hearsay evidence. To demonstrate this point, Annex 4 to the judgment analysed a series of cases against other Contracting States where this Court had found a violation of Article 6(1) when taken with Article 6(3)(d). *In each case, had the trial taken place in England and Wales, the witness's testimony would not have been admissible under the 2003 Act either because the witness was anonymous and absent or because the trial court had not made sufficient enquiries to ensure there was good reason for the witness's absence. Alternatively, had the evidence been admitted,* ***any conviction would have been quashed*** *on appeal.*[72]

In the UK, the 'sole or decisive' rule is applicable and hearsay evidence is generally regarded as unreliable and inadmissible. The Judge also directs the jury not to rely on hearsay evidence. Only a few limited situations justify a

69 ibid para. 49 (emphasis added).

70 ibid para. 142. See also ibid paras 118–119.

71 ibid paras 51–62.

72 Emphasis added.

departure from this rule under UK law. One example is provided by Lord Philips in *R. v Horncastle and others*, where he argues against a strict application of the ECtHR 'sole or decisive' rule when evidence is verifiable such as an untested witness testimony reporting a car registration number, when the car is red and the owner has a beard;[73] all of which have been verified by police afterward.

This illustrates the limited extent to which hearsay evidence could be reliable—that is, when it is provided by the (deceased) victim who is a *direct* witness, and the information he provides is accurate and *testable*/tested. In practice, this would amount to a tested witness statement, perhaps by other tested testimony, ie corroboration. As the ECtHR stated:

> Experience shows that the reliability of evidence, including evidence which appears cogent and convincing, may look very different when subjected to a searching examination. The dangers inherent in allowing *untested hearsay evidence* to be adduced are all the greater if that evidence is the sole or decisive evidence against the defendant.[74]

iii The Post-*Al Khawaja and Tahery* Case Law—A Cautious Approach

Admittedly, more recent ECtHR case law stresses the *Al Khawaja and Tahery* 'yardsticks' result in case specific (and different) outcomes.[75] While pre-*Al Khawaja and Tahery* case law offered a clear-cut 'indiscriminate' 'sole or decisive' rule, post-*Al Khawaja and Tahery* case law calls for an assessment by the ECtHR of the overall fairness of the trial.[76] In every case, the ECtHR observes whether there was good reason for the absence of the witness (first step), whether admitted hearsay played a sole (or decisive) role in conviction (second step), and whether sufficient counterbalancing measures existed in each legal system (third step).[77] Subsequent cases confirm the *Al Khawaja and Tahery* judgment as an adaptation of existing case law to the UK's strong procedural safeguards.[78] The ECtHR declared a breach of Article 6(3) of the ECHR when

73 ibid para. 60.

74 ibid para. 142 (emphasis added).

75 *Schatschaschwili v Germany*, App no 9154/10 (ECtHR, 15 December 2015), para. 113.

76 ibid para. 112.

77 ibid paras 125–131 for a list of procedural safeguards sought in ECtHR case law; ibid paras 145–165 for available safeguards and how they were applied in the specific case.

78 The ECtHR reiterated its *Al Khawaja and Tahery* (n 4) findings in a recent case, see *Horncastle* (n 64). The ECtHR found that even assuming that the written statement of the victim had been 'decisive', there had been sufficient safeguards in UK law to protect their right to a fair trial. In relation to two other applicants, the Court concluded that the

hearsay was a sole or decisive base for conviction without sufficient safeguards in a traditionally continental law system (Russia) in *Sigbatullim v Russia*[79] and *Karpenko v Russia*.[80] In *Schatschaschwili*,[81] the ECtHR concluded that there was a breach of Article 6(3) of the ECHR, since German courts did not apply safeguards available in domestic law.[82] After close examination of the latter, it seems that the 'sole or decisive' rule is as relevant as always. Thus, the ECtHR found a violation of Article 6(3) of the ECHR considering that the evidence was decisive and, therefore, the Accused should have been given the chance to cross-examine the absent witnesses.[83]

iv *Al Khawaja and Tahery* as Applied by SCSL in the *Taylor* Case

The Appeals Chamber did not proceed as cautiously as the ECtHR when applying *Al Khawaja and Tahery* to the *Taylor* case. The casuistic factors, ie the ECtHR three step approach,[84] that should have been applied to the *Taylor* case and are relevant when determining the legality of reliance on hearsay would have necessitated the following analysis.

(1) First step—Existence of good reason for the absence of the direct source:

In the *Taylor* case, Sam Bockarie's words were reported through hearsay. Sam Bockarie is reportedly dead. Therefore the direct source was never available for cross-examination or for an untested recorded witness testimony by a stenographer. Even though eight different witnesses, regardless of their reliability, reported Bockarie's words, there is no testing of Bockarie's reliability.[85]

(2) Second step—How was hearsay used? Was it decisive to any incriminating finding?[86]

---

statement had been neither the sole nor decisive basis of their conviction and, accordingly, that there had been no violation of their defence rights. The ECtHR reconfirms the 'sole or decisive' rule at ibid para. 151.

79 *Sigbatullim v Russia*, App no 1413/05 (ECtHR, 24 April 2012), paras 50–59.

80 *Karpenko v Russia*, App no 5605/04 (ECtHR, 13 March 2012), paras 70–77, for conviction based on pre-trial depositions.

81 *Schatschaschwili* (n 76).

82 ibid paras 162–165.

83 ibid paras 163–164.

84 *Horncastle* (n 64), para. 139.

85 Defence Appeal Brief (n 14), para. 28.

86 ibid para. 134.

Uncorroborated hearsay evidence was decisively relied upon by the Trial Chamber in *Taylor* when entering the conviction of planning and aiding and abetting insofar as, 'coupled together, you would not have a *mens rea* finding for planning without those two pieces of hearsay'.[87] The two pieces of hearsay to which the Defence was referring in its oral pleading was Isaac Mongor's testimony (1) that he heard from Sam Bockarie (deceased) that the accused told him to make the operation fearful, and (2) that Sam Bockarie told him that the Revolutionary United Front should use all means to get to Freetown. So, in fact, there is hearsay from one witness (not two) from one source and on which the Trial Chamber found the accused had *mens rea* for planning.[88] The Defence Appeal Brief reported in Ground 1 that this 'error was committed repeatedly' and in one case an incriminating finding even relied on 'fourth-hand hearsay' where the witness overheard Mohamed Kabbah allegedly in a conversation via satellite in Buedu with Sam Bockarie who allegedly spoke with Yeaten who was allegedly told by the Accused to release the Pademba Road prisoners.[89] The Appeals Chamber did not make a finding as to whether or not the Trial Chamber relied on hearsay solely or decisively. Rather, it focused on the Trial Chamber's liberty to do so considering the procedural safeguards in the SCSL RPE.[90]

(3) Third step—Counterbalancing measures: enshrined in the SCSL RPE and applied by the Trial Chamber:

The Appeals Chamber did not conduct an in-depth review of how the Trial Chamber applied SCSL procedural safeguards. Admission of hearsay at the SCSL is the rule not the exception.[91] Existing counterbalancing measures are listed in the case law and are according to international standards of fair trial rights. In order to examine the legality of the Trial Chamber's assessment and reliance on hearsay evidence, it is necessary to look into the specific circumstances of the case. To follow the criteria applied by the ECtHR in the *Schatschaschwili* case,[92] the Trial Chamber at the beginning of the Judgement purported to instruct itself that it must approach hearsay evidence with 'cau-

87 Transcripts of 23 January 2013, p. 49994, lines 7–8 (Counsel for Taylor).

88 ibid, p. 49993, line 24 to p. 49994, line 8.

89 See Defence Appeal Brief (n 14), para. 27, based on *Taylor* Appeal Judgment (n 1), para. 3588.

90 *Taylor* Appeal Judgment (n 1), paras 85–91.

91 Rule 89(C) of the SCSL RPE.

92 *Schatschaschwili* (n 76), paras 132–165.

tion',[93] the accused was given a chance to provide his own version.[94] However, it is argued that the fact that the Taylor Defence never had a chance to cross-examine Sam Bockarie, directly or indirectly, at trial or pre-trial, would have led the ECtHR to find that the Taylor Trial Chamber judgement did not respect the accused's fair trial rights.[95] This is because the hearsay in *Taylor* is unverifiable and the safeguards in the SCSL procedural system are clearly insufficient, as demonstrated by their comparison to those in the UK system. Consequently, this evidence could not provide a sufficiently credible source for an incriminating finding.[96]

III Conclusion

The Trial Chamber based Taylor's conviction for planning on unverifiable uncorroborated hearsay evidence. It did so by misapplying nascent ECtHR case law based on the *Al Khawaja and Tahery* case. The ECtHR replaced the strict 'sole or decisive' rule by a flexible application to each legal system and the application of the procedural safeguards therein, to compensate for the accused's inability to test the direct source of information. Where the accused was not accorded the ability to test a direct source and where a court based a conviction on an indirect source's hearsay evidence, the ECtHR would find that the trial was, overall, unfair. Whereas in the UK system, as examined in the *Al Khawaja and Tahery* case, such evidence would not have been admitted into evidence and if it were to have been (for the sake of argument) and decisively relied upon by the UK court, the UK appellate chamber would have quashed the decision.

Admittedly, the *Al Khawaja and Tahery* case introduces a flexible approach where parties have less certainty as to the outcome of ECtHR review of fair trial rights. Nevertheless, a close observation of the ECtHR approach leads to the conclusion that it is still incorrect to base a conviction solely and decisively without an accused ever having had the chance to test the direct source of the information. The ECtHR reviews each procedural (domestic) system and its application by the respective court. The Appeals Chamber 'flattened' the nuances introduced by the *Al Khawaja and Tahery* judgment and applied it thoughtlessly to the *Taylor* case. The danger is that other ICTs would be tempted to rely on the *Taylor* case. Instead, the author calls for a cautious approach.

93 *Schatschaschwili* (n 76), para. 163.

94 ibid.

95 *Schatschaschwili* (n 76), paras 162, 164–165.

96 *Taylor* Appeal Judgement (n 1), paras 166–169, and Defence Appeal Brief (n 14), para. 29.

CHAPTER 14

The Interaction between the International Criminal Court and the European Court of Human Rights—The Right to the Truth for Victims of Serious Violations of Human Rights: The Importation of a New Right?

Paolo Caroli

1 Introduction

In the practice of the International Criminal Court (ICC), the reference to the case law of the European Court of Human Rights (ECtHR) is not limited to decisions regarding the notion, the role, the rights and the powers of victims.[1] Nevertheless, this represents one of the main points of interaction between the ICC and the ECtHR.[2] Since the concrete modalities of victims' participation at the ICC are still subject to a wide degree of legal and practical uncertainties and still raise a broad debate both within the ICC and among scholars,[3] the refer-

1 The ICC resorted to the ECtHR's jurisprudence with the specific purpose of reinforcing the rights of the accused, such as issues raised by retroactivity (see William A. Schabas, 'Synergy or Fragmentation? International Criminal Law and the European Convention on Human Rights' (2011) 9 Journal of International Criminal Justice 609, 613), or issues of procedure and fairness: length of proceedings (ibid 627), equality of arms (ibid 630), adversarial hearing (ibid 631). European human rights law sources have also been used to interpret provisions in the Rome Statute, such as the reference to 'reasonable grounds to believe' in Article 58 or the 'substantial grounds' standard for the confirmation hearing in Article 61(7) (ibid 627).

2 On several occasions the judges of the ICC have resorted to the case law of the ECtHR. See eg *Situation in the Democratic Republic of Congo*, ICC-01/04-101-tEN-Corr, Decision on the Applications for Participation in the Proceedings [...], Pre-Trial Chamber I, 17 January 2006, paras 50, 54; *Prosecutor v Kony*, ICC-02/04-01/05-356, Decision on Victims' Applications for Participation [...], Pre-Trial Chamber II, 10 August 2007, para. 7.

3 See Paolo Lobba, 'Le vittime nel sistema penale internazionale' in Enrico Amati and others (eds), *Introduzione al diritto penale internazionale* (3rd edn, Giappichelli 2016) 287; Carsten Stahn and others, 'Participation of Victims in Pre-Trial Proceedings of the ICC' (2006) 4 Journal of International Criminal Justice 219; Christine H. Chung, 'Victims' Participation at the International Criminal Court: Are Concessions of the Court Clouding the Promise?'

 | DOI: 10.1163/9789004313750_016

ence to the ECtHR's jurisprudence seems to be used as a source of legitimacy, persuasion and authority. In fact, close attention is also paid to the ECtHR's jurisprudence on victims outside the ICC by other international and national courts.[4]

However, the aim of this chapter is not to discuss victims' procedural powers before the ICC. On the contrary, it will concentrate on a particular decision among those related to victims' rights: specifically, a decision rendered by the Single Judge Sylvia Steiner. In this decision, for the first time in the case law of the ICC, Judge Steiner refers to the 'the right to the truth', a disputed right which belongs to a new generation of rights.

Generally speaking, the topic of the right to the truth is interesting *per se*, because of the relevance of the interactions between criminal law and history and of the role that trials can have with respect to building a narrative of those facts and to contributing to the search for historical truth. In this particular case, though, the reference to the right to the truth also represents an example of the circulation of principles from human rights bodies to international criminal tribunals and of the potential influence the former can have on the latter. The aim is not to question the legitimacy of the reference. In effect, this is methodologically correct and its use within the decision largely serves an argumentative function in rejecting the arguments of the Prosecution and Defence.

The point of this chapter is to highlight how resorting to a right developed in the case law of human rights courts in an international criminal decision can lead to potential modifications and have negative effects on the rights of the accused within the international criminal trial. This potential danger exists (and is probably significant) when the reference to a human right is superficial, which means that the judge does not investigate the content of that right, as the reference is only used to support the judge's argument. Even though the impact of the reference is meant to be minimal, the generic mention of that extraneous right (such as the right to the truth in this particular decision) represents a precedent, or a basis that can subsequently be used by others. In a sort of heterogony of ends, human rights jurisprudence can fertilise a system

---

(2008) 6 Northwestern Journal of International Human Rights 459; Chantal Meloni, 'Vittime e giustizia penale internazionale' in Luca Luparia (ed), *Lo statuto europeo delle vittime di reato. Modelli di tutela tra diritto dell'Unione e buone pratiche nazionali* (Cedam 2015) 45.

4 By way of example, the case law of the ECtHR on vulnerable victims is mentioned by the Italian Corte di Cassazione: eg Cassazione penale (II) no 13935 (18 February 2014). In the Inter-American system see eg a reference to European case law on victims' right to an identity and to the truth in *Contreras and others v El Salvador* (ICtHR, 31 August 2011).

of international criminal justice and principles can circulate from one system to another. This implies that the goal-directed activity of the Judge can result in consequences that modify the original motivational pattern.

2 Cross-fertilisation and the ICC

Both international criminal law and international humanitarian law in the end share the aim of protecting human rights; that is why an interaction between international criminal tribunals and human rights courts (in the form of a reference to each other's case law) is not a rare occurrence. This practice, which not only relates to the ICC, has been referred to as 'cross-fertilisation'.[5]

Cross-fertilisation[6] is a phenomenon related exclusively to the jurisprudence of the different courts and tribunals; it relates only to practice and does

---

5 On the one hand, references to the case law of human rights courts can be found in the jurisprudence of the ad hoc and hybrid tribunals. For examples of references to the ECtHR's case law from the Special Court for Sierra Leone and the Extraordinary Chambers in the Courts of Cambodia, see Emanuela Fronza, 'Derechos humanos y crímenes internacionales. Observaciones sobre el párrafo 3 del artículo 21 del Estatuto de Roma' in Kai Ambos and others, *Sistema interamericano de protección de los derechos humanos y derecho penal internacional,* vol 2 (Konrad Adenauer Stiftung 2011) 229, 235; Alicia Gil Gil, 'La fertilización cruzada entre las jurisprudencias de derechos humanos y de derecho penal international [...]' (2012) (special issue) Revista de derecho penal 111, 119; Schabas (n 1) 616. On the other hand, the ECtHR has growingly drawn inspiration from the ICTY's case law regarding sexual violence in order to inform the prohibition against torture, inhuman or degrading treatment and the positive obligations stemming therefrom. The ECtHR has also referred to the ICTY and, to a lesser extent, to the ICTR and ICC, when discussing and developing the principle of non-retroactivity of criminal offences and penalties as provided for by Article 7 of the ECHR. See *Jorgic v Germany,* App no 74613/01 (ECtHR, 12 July 2007), paras 42–44 and paras 49–51; *Scoppola v Italy (No 2),* App no 10249/03 (ECtHR, 17 September 2009), paras 40, 41, 105; *Kononov v Latvia,* App no 36376/04 (ECtHR, 17 May 2010), paras 211, 215; *Korbely v Hungary,* App no 9174/02 (ECtHR, 19 September 2008), paras 51, 81. Croquet noted that 'nevertheless, in cases where the ICC was referred to, the ECtHR only looked at the ICC Statute without borrowing any ruling from its jurisprudence'. Nicolas A.J. Croquet, 'The International Criminal Court and the Treatment of Defence Rights: A Mirror of the European Court of Human Rights' Jurisprudence?' (2011) 1 Human Rights Law Review 111, 112.

6 For a broader discussion on this phenomenon see Triestino Mariniello and Paolo Lobba (eds), 'Special Issue: The Cross-Fetilisation Rhetoric in Question: Use and Abuse of the European Court's Jurisprudence by International Criminal Tribunals' (2015) 84 Nordic Journal of International Law 363.

not involve their respective Statutes.[7] A partial explanation of this practice is the existence of a margin of appreciation (or even creativity) in the role of the judge in the application of law.[8] Cross-fertilisation is also part of a wider circulation among courts horizontally (for example between national supreme courts) or vertically (between national and regional courts). There is no specific norm at the core of this practice expressly imposing a duty upon a court to consider as binding a decision made by a different court. Indeed, no such rule exists (and the stare decisis doctrine cannot be applied among very different courts which are not part of a hierarchical structure). On the contrary, a decision circulates because of its *persuasive authority*, a quality which is attached not only to the content and the legal argumentation of the decision itself, but also to the court that issued it. *Persuasive authority* also requires the implicit basis of a shared system of human rights principles.

This is true also for the ICC, which is neither obliged to consult the precedents of other jurisdictions, nor to defer to their legal reasoning. Nonetheless, the ICC has its own peculiarities. While, on the basis of Article 38 of the Statute of the International Court of Justice, subjects of international law are bound by internationally recognised human rights law, to the extent that it belongs to customary international law or it consists in general principles of law (Article 38 of the ICJ Statute), the Rome Statute took an autonomous approach. Article 21 of the Rome Statute lays down the sources of law that are to be applied by the ICC and establishes their hierarchy. Article 21(3) of the ICC Statute states: 'The application and interpretation of law pursuant to this article must be consistent with internationally recognized human rights'. Article 21(3) is certainly the most innovative and problematic part of the article.[9] Opinions on its legal nature differ.

7 See Elena Maculan, 'Corte Penal Internacional y Tribunales de Derechos Humanos: ensayos de diálogo y de armonización' in Miguel Requena and Díez de Revenga (eds), *Seguridad y conflictos: una perspectiva multidisciplinar* (Instituto Universitario Gutiérrez Mellado 2012) 97, 100.

8 ibid.

9 For Kai Ambos 'the interpretation and importance of this article is by no means clear. The ICC itself has various times made recourse to it but has so far failed to establish any systematic or coherent approach [...] without, however, dealing with such fundamental questions as the legal nature and value of the source, its effect with respect to the Court's legal regime and its correct integration into Article 21'. Kai Ambos, *Treatise on International Criminal Law*, vol 1 (OUP 2013) 80. For its application by the ICC in the *Lubanga* case, see *Prosecutor v Lubanga*, ICC-01/04-01/06-772, Judgment on the Appeal of Mr Thomas Lubanga Dyilo against the Decision on the Defense Challenge to the Jurisdiction [...], Appeals Chamber, 14 December 2006, paras 36–37.

Notwithstanding the given interpretation of Article 21(3),[10] this norm officially legitimates, for the first time at a normative level, the importation of the case law of human rights courts. Article 21(3) does not give any definition of the expression 'internationally recognized human rights';[11] although generally it is not considered limited to the norms, but also including the case law of human rights bodies. In fact, the term 'internationally' (and not 'universally') can also include regional systems of protection of human rights.

The ICC has been more consistent and systematic than the ad hoc tribunals in its references to and analyses of the ECtHR system, often refraining from reviewing case law developments of other international human rights monitoring bodies. The ICC's judges have mostly regarded to the case law of the ECtHR as having *persuasive authority*. In addition, they have often relied upon Article 21(3) of the ICC Statute but, in several instances, they have simply taken the ECtHR's case law into account, without theorising as to the legal basis for its incorporation into its final reasoning.[12]

Less attention has been given by the ICC to the jurisprudence of the Inter-American Court of Human Rights, and no attention at all to the African Commission on Human and Peoples' Rights.[13] Different factors need to be considered: first of all, the number and the importance of the precedents issued by the ECtHR, some of which have been invoked by other international human rights bodies and national constitutional courts. The ECtHR has been described as a 'sort of world court of human rights',[14] also because the European Convention on Human Rights is a compromise between common law and civil law. The number of States subject to its compulsory jurisdiction is also greater than in the Inter-American system. The Strasbourg Court occupies a central role, and 'enjoys an element of 'universality-legitimacy' in the dissemination of its judicial practice across various legal and judicial systems worldwide'.[15]

---

10 For Sheppard it is a source of law in and of itself: Daniel Sheppard, 'The International Criminal Court and "Internationally Recognized Human Rights". Understanding Article 21(3) of the Rome Statute' (2010) 10 International Criminal Law Review 43, 60. Cf Fronza (n 5) 235.

11 On this issue see Sheppard (n 10) 63; Alain Pellet, 'Applicable Law' in Antonio Cassese, Paola Gaeta and John R.W.D. Jones (eds), *The Rome Statute of the International Criminal Court: A Commentary* (OUP 2002) vol 2 1051, Gilbert Bitti, 'Article 21 of the Statute of the International Criminal Court and the Treatment of Sources of Law in the Jurisprudence of the ICC' in Carsten Stahn and Göran Sluiter (eds), *The Emerging Practice of the International Criminal Court* (Brill 2009) 301.

12 For different examples, see Croquet (n 5) 109.

13 See ibid 125.

14 John B. Attanasio, 'Rapporteur's Overview and Conclusions: Of Sovereignty, Globalisation, and Courts' (1996) 28 NewYork University Journal of International Law and Politics 1, 1.

15 Croquet (n 5) 123.

3 When the Imported Human Rights are Victims' Human Rights

Behind the specific discussion surrounding Article 21(3) of the ICC Statute, there is a broader issue: the relationship between criminal trials as such and human rights. Defining this relationship is not as easy as it could appear. Moreover, this definition seems to have quickly evolved in recent years.[16]

There is no doubt that the primary role of human rights is to ensure protection from criminal law.[17] Human rights are basic individual entitlements against the abuse of public power. They have an intrinsic individualistic nature and stem from a self-centred (we could say 'egotistic') perspective, as they represent an empowerment of individuals, protecting their freedom to act in the world.[18] Human rights, nevertheless, 'are historically exposed to constant revisions. They are formulated in imprecise and semantically ambiguous terms, they have a heterogeneous nature and above all they show deontic antinomies, preventing any attempt to give them a coherent and united foundation'.[19]

For these reasons, it is not surprising to find an intrinsic ambiguity in the relationship between human rights and criminal law. Indeed, human rights can either promote (by demanding specific protection through criminal norms) or protect (if the human rights in question are those of the accused) from the intervention of criminal law. 'In short, human rights have both a defensive and an offensive role, a role of both neutralizing and triggering the criminal

---

16 See Gerhard Werle and Florian Jessberger, *Principles of International Criminal Law* (3rd edn, OUP 2014) 51; for a general overview Mireille Delmas-Marty, Emanuela Fronza and Elisabeth Lambert-Abdelgawad (eds), *Les sources du droit international pénal* (Société de Législation comparée 2004). On the impact of human rights on international criminal proceedings, see Robert Cryer and others, *An Introduction to International Criminal Law and Procedure* (3rd edn, OUP 2014) 435; Salvatore Zappalà, *Human Rights in International Criminal Proceedings* (OUP 2003). On the impact of international criminal law on the protection of human rights, see Fausto Pocar, 'The Rome Statute of the International Criminal Court and Human Rights' in Mauro Politi and Giuseppe Nesi (eds), *The Rome Statute of the International Criminal Court: A Challenge to Impunity. Proceedings of Trento Conference on the ICC (13–15 May 1999)* (Ashgate 2001) 67.

17 Françoise Tulkens, 'The Paradoxical Relationship Between Criminal Law and Human Rights' (2011) 9 Journal of International Criminal Justice 577, 579.

18 Danilo Zolo 'Fondamentalismo umanitario' in Michael Ignatieff, *Una ragionevole apologia dei diritti umani* (Feltrinelli 2003) 135, 139; Domenico Pulitanò, 'Diritti umani e diritto penale' in Massimo Meccarelli and others (eds), *Il lato oscuro dei diritti umani* (Universidad Carlos III de Madrid 2014) 81, 84; Norberto Bobbio, *The age of rights* (Polity 1996) 4.

19 Zolo (n 18) 139.

law'.[20] The paradox affecting this relationship has already been discussed by many scholars. According to Mireille Delmas-Marty, it lies in the fact that 'the criminal law appears to be both a protection and a threat for fundamental rights and freedoms' or, in other words, not only 'a law which protects' but 'a law from which protection is required'.[21] Others have expressed it by describing human rights as both the 'shield' and the 'sword' of criminal law.[22]

In criminal law, duties represent the originating deontic figure, rights do not.[23] As the first task of criminal law is to protect the life of each individual, it is not difficult to understand that, in early criminal law, evil has priority.[24] Original criminal law deals with evil and with the minimal conditions for a collective coexistence without abuses. In this scenario, the original practical translation of human rights within the criminal trial are the guarantees of due process, fair trial principles and rules. This means that human rights in the criminal trial first emerge as limits to criminal law, as negative liberties: the rights of the accused as the *Magna Carta* of the alleged offender.[25] A reference to human rights norms and to the jurisprudence of human rights courts in an international criminal decision can therefore be made in order to interpret other rules, to override hierarchically inferior ones or to derive power conferring norms,[26] with the aim of reinforcing the guarantees for the person subjected to the proceedings.

The paradox becomes visible when it comes to victims, as their human rights are clearly not meant to protect the rights of the accused. This does not mean

---

20 Tulkens (n 17) 579.

21 Mireille Delmas-Marty, 'Le paradoxe penal' in Mireille Delmas-Marty and Claude Lucas de Leyssac (eds), *Libertés et droits fondamentaux* (Seuil 1996) 368, 368. See also Mireille Delmas-Marty, 'Los procesos de interacción' in Mireille Delmas-Marty and others (eds) *Los caminos de la armonización penal* (Tirant lo Blanch 2009) 527, 539.

22 Tulkens (n 17) 578.

23 Pulitanò (n 18) 88.

24 ibid.

25 Franz von Liszt, 'Deterministische Gegner der Zweckstrafe' (1893) 13 Zeitschrift für die gesamte Strafrechtswissenschaft 325, 330.

26 For a case law analysis of the interplay between human rights norms and rules of international criminal procedure, see Lorenzo Gradoni, 'The Human Rights Dimension of International Criminal Procedure' in Göran Sluiter and others (eds), *International Criminal Procedure: Principles and Rules* (OUP 2013) 74. According to Gradoni, this relationship is complex and it 'may be aptly described as one between ends and means, where full respect of human rights norms are not strictly speaking rules of international criminal procedure, they have nonetheless a considerable impact on the way in which those rules are defined, interpreted and applied' (ibid 74).

that they are *per se* incompatible with a fair trial, but their relation to the fair trial principle is at least complicated, given the presence of a public prosecutor and the general reluctance towards the privatisation of criminal justice. The latter is clearly one of the main achievements of the Enlightenment. Indeed, in recent years, a new tendency of criminal and international criminal justice has emerged, especially in the Inter-American system: it consists not only in recognising new substantive and procedural rights for the victims, but also in endowing the criminal trial with new important goals (finding the truth, sending messages to the victims or to society as a whole, strengthening democracy, etc.) which are aimed at an implicit choice to satisfy victims' legitimate social claims (for punishment, truth, closure, memory, etc.) through (and only through) judicial proceedings.[27] This aim of protecting victims' rights through the criminal trial can be at odds with the protection of the rights of the accused within the criminal trial. The tendency to promote human rights through criminal trials shows a strongly individualistic perspective, while an important point remains in the shadows: the concept of a legal system goes beyond the claim for rights. A legal system is also related to a collective dimension, insofar as it also includes duties and limitations of rights. A legal system cannot be reduced to a sum of pretensions. On the contrary, the original individualism of rights must be integrated in a social dimension.[28]

These victim-centric tendencies do not seem to be a feature of the ECtHR's jurisprudence but, indeed, on these issues even the Strasbourg Court needs to balance the opposing interests of victims and accused persons. Depending on the results of this balance, the floodgates could be opened for those tendencies. Interesting examples can be found in the case law on the protection of vulnerable victims and vulnerable witnesses in the courtroom and the effects of this protection on the 'quality' and genuineness of evidence and the right afforded to the prosecution and defence to examine (or have examined) witnesses under the same conditions.[29] The ECtHR's case law about victims' right to the truth and right to an effective investigation is, at any rate, even more interesting for those seeking a more victim-centric justice.

---

27 Giovanni Fiandaca and Costantino Visconti 'I crimini internazionali tra punizione, riconciliazione e ricostruzione' in Giovanni Fiandaca and Costantino Visconti (eds) *Punire mediare riconciliare* (Giappichelli 2009) 13, 16; Franklin E. Zimring, *The Contradictions of American Capital Punishment* (OUP 2004), 59. For a general analysis of the new role of victims in criminal trials, see Caroline Eliacheff and Daniel Soulez-Larivière, *Le temps des victimes* (Albin Michel 2007).

28 Pulitanò (n 18) 112.

29 See eg *Lemasson and Achat v France*, App no 49849/99 (ECtHR, 14 January 2003); *S.N. v*

4 The Specificity of Judge Steiner's Reference to the Right to the Truth

In the above mentioned ICC case law about victims with references to the ECtHR,[30] an interesting example is Single Judge Sylvia Steiner's 'Decision on the Set of Procedural Rights Attached to Procedural Status of Victim at the Pre-Trial Stage of the Case'. This is a 2008 decision at the Pre-Trial Stage in the *Katanga and Ngudjolo* case (Situation in the Democratic Republic of the Congo). In this decision, the Single Judge refers to a 'well-established right to the truth for the victims of serious violations of human rights' as upheld by the case law of the Inter-American Courts of Human Rights and the ECtHR:

> 32. In this regard the Single Judge underlines that the victims' core interest in the determination of the facts, in the identification of those responsible and the declaration of their responsibility is at the root of the well-established right to the truth for the victims of serious violation of human rights.[39]
>
> Footnote 39 The victims' right to the truth understood as the determination of the facts, the identification of the responsible persons and the declaration of their responsibility, can be traced back to articles 32 and 33 of the 1977 Additional Protocol I to the Geneva Conventions, and has subsequently been developed by national and international case law, especially in cases of forced disappearance. In this regard particularly relevant has been the role played by the case law of the Inter-American Court of Human Rights [...] The case law of the European Court of Human Rights also developed the victim's right to the truth. See in this regard the case of Hugh Jordan vs. Uk, Judgment of 4 May 2001, Application No. 24746/1994 [2001] ECHR 327, para 93.[31]

At this stage, this is the only decision which expressly refers to victims' right to the truth. An implicit reference can be found in Judge Christine Van den Wyngaert's Dissenting Opinion in a different decision in the same case. Again,

---

Sweden, App no 34209/96 (ECtHR, 2 July 2002); *Accardi and others v Italy*, App no 30598/02 (ECtHR, 20 January 2005); *W.S. v Poland*, App no 21508/02 (ECtHR, 19 June 2007).

30 Reference is generally made to decisions such as *Ogur v Turkey*, App no 1594/93 (ECtHR, 2 May 1999); *Kelly and others v United Kingdom*, App no 30054/96 (ECtHR, 4 May 2001).

31 *Prosecutor v Katanga*, ICC-01/04-01/07-474, Decision on the Set of Procedural Rights Attached to Procedural Status of Victim at the Pre-Trial Stage of the Case, Pre-Trial Chamber I, 13 May 2008, para. 32.

this decision and the related Dissenting Opinion do not explicitly discuss the right to the truth. The object (the power of the re-characterisation of the facts) is neither the right to the truth, nor the same as Judge Steiner's decision. Nonetheless, what is relevant for the present discussion is that, in her argumentation, Judge Van den Wyngaert states:

> I am not persuaded that trial chambers have an unqualified truth seeking mission. There is no equivalent to the prosecution's duty under article 54(1)(a) of the Statute, and article 69(3) alone could not serve as a legal basis to entertain that proposition. In any event, I do not believe that this mission, should it exist, takes precedence over the Trial Chamber's core mission, which is to decide whether, upon evidence produced at trial, the charges against the accused have proven beyond a reasonable doubt.[32]

By referring to the right to the truth and to the IACtHR's and ECtHR's case law, Judge Steiner does not affirm that victims have a right to the truth that can (or must) be satisfied only through criminal proceedings. Moreover, she does not address the question of whether satisfying this right is a mission of the ICC. Had the Judge faced this question, she should also have explained where it is possible to find a norm that legitimates this conclusion in the Rome Statute. On the contrary, she explicitly tries to avoid this broad discussion about whether this right can be satisfied 'through mechanisms alternative to criminal proceedings'. She affirms that when there is an actual criminal trial taking place, this trial has to satisfy the victims' right to the truth. She explicitly calls this pretension a 'right' but, when she defines it, she calls it, cautiously, 'a central interest'. Judge Steiner's complete definition of the right to the truth is: 'a central interest in that the outcomes of such proceedings (i) bring clarity about what indeed happened; and (ii) close possible gaps between the factual findings resulting from the criminal proceedings and the actual truth'. She also

32 *Prosecutor v Katanga*, ICC-01/04-01/07-3319, Decision on the Implementation of Regulation 55 of the Regulations of the Court and Severing the Charges Against the Accused Persons, Trial Chamber II, 21 November 2012, Dissenting Opinion of Judge Christine Van den Wyngaert, para. 34; see also *Prosecutor v Ruto*, ICC-01/09-01/11, Decision on Victims' Representation and Participation, Trial Chamber V, 3 October 2012, para. 25. For a public position of Judge Van den Wyngaert, see Christine Van den Wyngaert, 'Victims before International Criminal Courts: Some Views and Concerns of an ICC Trial Judge' (2012) 44 Case Western Reserve Journal of International Law 475, where she affirms that 'victims may have a very different theory of the case, which may, or may not, be conductive to the truth-finding process' (ibid 488).

states that 'the issue of the guilt or innocence of persons prosecuted before this Court [...] affects the very core interests of those granted the procedural status of victim in any case before the Court insofar as this issue is inherently linked to the satisfaction of their right to the truth', which 'can only be satisfied if' those responsible 'are declared guilty; and those not responsible [...] are acquitted'.[33]

4.1 *Judge Steiner's Recourse to the ECtHR as Example of* Probative Importation

It is important to remember that the right to the truth in the context of this particular decision is not relevant *per se*. Judge Steiner refers to this right while explaining and justifying her decision to grant procedural rights to the victims. The Judge appears to be using the jurisprudence of human rights courts in order to reinforce (or possibly even legitimise) her choice of the interests or principles being discussed in an internal ICC dispute on the modalities of victims' participation. Would the Judge's decision be different without this reference? Does the ECtHR's case law affect the content of the decision? Reading the decision, it is easy to understand that its object is not related to the existence, or absence, and the content of the right to the truth, as the reference thereto is used by the Judge in an instrumental way, as a tool to support her point in response to the arguments by the Prosecutor and the Defence. These have little to do with the right to the truth *per se* and relate more to the procedural rights that should be accorded to victims and those that should not be part of their procedural status of 'non-party participants'.[34] The right to the truth is used as additional evidence of the increasing powers attached to victims in general and in different legal systems. Nevertheless, it does not have a direct link with the legal question that the Judge has to answer, which is a question of pure international criminal procedure within the ICC system. Rhetorically, the reference supports the argumentation, however legally it does not. There is not a causal connection between the right to the truth, as recognised by the ECtHR and the IACtHR, and the legal reasoning which brings the Judge to the resolution of the procedural question, which she must answer.

The present decision is a clear example of the use of cross-fertilisation in light of what has been called a *probative importation*,[35] where 'the use of *extra-systemic* parameters [...] has the function of adding rhetorical and evidentiary

33 *Prosecutor v Katanga* (n 31), paras 33–36.

34 See ibid para. 25.

35 Expression taken from Andrea Lollini, 'Legal Argumentation Based on Foreign Law. An Example from Case Law of the South African Constitutional Court' (2007) 3 Utrecht Law Review 60, 65.

force to the interpretation'.[36] The formula used by Judge Steiner appears to be similar to what Andrea Lollini calls the second pattern of probative importation, that:

> corresponds with the assertion: '*considering that they think this way abroad*' [...], then '*we also assign it with this same meaning*'. This formula differs from the previous one because it proceeds first with identifying the foreign interpretive model to which it subsequently links the interpretation.[37]

This technique has problematic consequences, because its application could mean that the interpretation of ICC rules and norms is derived 'directly and automatically from *extra*-systemic parameters'. This 'indirectly means, incorporating a *pseudo*-source',[38] which might lead to superficial comparisons and the use of extra-systemic parameters as part of an internal dialogue among the ICC judges.

4.2 *The Need for ECtHR's Legitimacy in the Inter-American Importation*

In the light of the probative method, the reference to the ECtHR's case law, next to that of the IACtHR, acquires a particular argumentative meaning. If the Judge had mentioned just the Inter-American court, the probative quality of the reference would have been lower. The IACtHR indeed is accused by its detractors of judicial activism, antidemocratic interventionism and creativity, particularly when it comes to victims.[39] On the contrary, as has already been said, the Strasbourg Court plays a central role and its case law is considered to be a high quality source. In this respect, resorting to two human rights courts

36 ibid 66.

37 ibid.

38 Ibid.

39 Ludovic Hennebel describes the Inter-American case law as an 'original, creative, avant-garde and even 'legally non-conformist' jurisprudence'. Ludovic Hennebel, 'The Inter-American Court of Human Rights: the Ambassador of Universalism' (2011) Quebec Journal of International Law 57, 60. Ezequiel Malarino writes that using the justification of the 'need to protect victims on the basis of the seriousness of the crime [...] the Court is judicially creating a law of exception for serious violations of human rights where the principles of ne bis in idem, of non-retroactivity of criminal law, and of the reasonable duration of the trial (speedy trial), are not contemplated and the statute of limitations and amnesty norms are abrogated'. Ezequiel Malarino, 'Judicial Activism, Punitivism and Supranationalization: Illiberal and Antidemocratic Tendencies of the Inter-American Court of Human Rights' (2012) 12 International Criminal Law Review 665, 683.

from two different continents, with different approaches, adds rhetorical and evidentiary force to the Judge's interpretation and is a stronger means of persuasion with regard to the efficacy of the choice made. Although the Judge is not explicitly importing the right to the truth into the ICC system, rather just mentioning its existence, the way the reference is constructed implicitly signifies a reference to a universally recognised right to the truth, since the Judge states that it has been recognised by the two major human rights courts.

What would that mean? There is no doubt that victims have a legitimate claim to the truth, but defining a claim as a universally recognised human right means (explicitly or implicitly) defining that claim as non-negotiable.[40] But does this universally recognised victims' right to the truth exist? Or, at least, is it correct to reference one single right to the truth as recognised by both human rights courts? Does it have the same content and meaning in both the European and in the Inter-American jurisprudence? In fact, the nature of this claim is still debated,[41] considering the potential consequences for the criminal trial;[42] it

---

40 Ignatieff (n 18) 25.

41 This right was first defined as an emerging principle in international law; today it has been mentioned in many legal systems, by the jurisprudence of national supreme or constitutional courts, (eg Argentina: *Hagelin* (Corte Suprema de la Nacion, 8 September 2003); Perù: *Genaro Villegas Namuche*, case no 2488–2002-HC/TC (Tribunal Constitucional del Perù, 18 March 2004); Colombia: C-370/06 (Corte Constitucional de Colombia, 18 May 2006); South Africa: *The Citizen 1978 (Pty) Ltd and Others v Mc Bride*, CCT 23/10 2011 ZACC 11 (Constitutional Court of South Africa, 8 April 2011)), by national legislations (eg Colombia: Ley de Justicia y Paz (975/2005); Bosnia and Herzegovina: Law on Missing Persons, 2004), UN resolutions (General Assembly Resolution 57/105 (2003), para. 12; General Assembly Resolution 57/161 (2003), para. 17; Security Council Resolution 1606 (2005), paras 2, 7; Security Council Resolution 1593 (2005), para. 5) and it is even possible to find an explicit statement of this right in an international treaty: Article 24 of the International Convention for the Protection of All Persons from Enforced Disappearance, signed in 2006. On the one hand today it is difficult to doubt its existence, on the other there are still lingering doubts about its normative content. See Yasmine Naqvi, 'The Right to Truth in International Law: Fact or Fiction?' (2006) 88 International Review of Red Cross 245, where she affirms: 'the truth about the right to the truth is still a matter to be agreed upon' (ibid 273); Elena Maculan and Daniel Pastor, *El derecho a la verdad y su ejercicio por medio del proceso penal* (Hammurabi 2013); Juan E. Méndez, 'Derecho a la verdad frente a las graves violaciones a los derechos humanos' in Martin Abregu and Christian Courtis (eds), *La aplicación de los tratados sobre derechos humanos por los tribunals locales* (Editores Del Puerto 1997) 517.

42 Daniel Pastor, '¿Procesos penales sólo para conocer la verdad? La experiencia argentina' in Pablo Eiroa and Juan Otero (eds), *Memoria y derecho penal* (Fabian di Placido 2008) 325, 373.

can be affirmed that 'the right to the truth stands somewhere on the threshold of a legal norm and a narrative device'.[43] In the Inter-American system, this right first emerged in 1988[44] with reference to enforced disappearance. At least from 2006,[45] the object of this right is an historical truth 'as complete as possible',[46] which has to be determined through a judicial proceeding. It is difficult to believe that this is the same right to the truth recognised and defined by the ECtHR as the right to an effective investigation, with the related quality requirements (transparency, diligence, etc.).[47] No 'historical truth' comes into question here and there is no specific goal attributed to the criminal trial to find and spread a truth as complete as possible.[48]

---

43 Naqvi (n 40) 273.

44 *Velázquez Rodríguez v Honduras* (IACtHR, 29 July 1988).

45 The decision which explains this evolution is *Almonacid-Arellano and others v Chile*, (IACtHR, 26 September 2006).

46 *Valle Jaramillo y otros v Colombia* (IACtHR, 27 November 2008), para. 102. 'It should include not only the facts, but also 'all the masterminds'' (*Gómez-Paquiyauri Brothers v Peru* (IACtHR, 8 July 2004), para. 231).

47 The ECtHR has inferred the right to the truth from the right to be free from torture, the right to an effective remedy and to an effective investigation. In *Cyprus v Turkey*, App no 25781/94 (ECtHR, 10 May 2001) the Court found that Turkey's persistent failure to account for the missing constituted a continuing violation of Article 2 and of Article 3 with respect to the relatives of the missing persons. See also *Hugh Jordan v United Kingdom*, App no 24746/94 (ECtHR, 4 May 2001), para. 160, where the Court states that: 'Article 13 requires [...] a thorough and effective investigation capable of leading to the identification and punishment of those responsible for the deprivation of life'. In *Association '21 December 1989' and others v Romania*, App no 33810/07 and 18817/08 (ECtHR, 23 May 2011), para. 144, the Court affirmed that the right to the truth amounts to 'the right to an accurate account of the suffering endured and the role of those responsible for that ordeal'. In the Joint Concurring Opinion of Judges Tulkens, Sicilianos and Keller, in the case *El Masri v The Former Yugoslav Republic of Macedonia*, App no 39630/09 (ECtHR, 13 December 2012), para. 6, the judges write: 'the search for the truth is the objective purpose of the obligation to carry out an investigation and the raison d'être of the related quality requirements (transparency, diligence, independence, access, disclosure of results and scrutiny)'.

48 A truth that, according to the Inter-American version, should satisfy the victims and strengthen society as a whole. See *Méndez* (n 39). Unlike the IACtHR, the ECtHR is traditionally cautious also when it comes to the duty to prosecute and the necessary use of criminal proceedings. In *Mc v Bulgaria*, App no 39272/98 (ECtHR, 4 December 2003), Judge Tulkens in her Concurring Opinion (para. 2) states that 'criminal proceedings should remain, both in theory and in practice a last resort or subsidiarity remedy and [...] their use, even in the context of positive obligations, calls for a certain degree of 'restraint''.

In Judge Steiner's reference, two very different concepts were combined and referred to as one. Referencing a single right to the truth could be seen as meaningless in the context of this decision, but what can the effect of this reference be on future decisions? Could it be stated that the ICC recognised the existence of a right to the truth as upheld by the case law of both the IACtHR and the ECtHR? Could it be stated that that the ICC recognised the existence of a right to the truth, upheld by the case law of the ECtHR, which has the same content of the one declared by the IACtHR? Could it be argued that the correct interpretation of a single universally recognised right to the truth is the one given by the IACtHR? Judge Steiner explicitly affirms nothing to this effect, but indeed her precedent could be used as argumentation for any of these statements. Should this happen, it would not be wrong to say that, with such a specific reference, the ECtHR's case law has been implicitly harnessed in order to legitimise the importation of a victims' right to the truth, as recognised by the IACtHR.

5 Judge Steiner's Decision in a Broader Context

This decision, as we have argued, follows a recent wider victim-centric tendency in criminal and international criminal justice, a tendency that seems to turn criminal law from the *Magna Carta* of the alleged perpetrator into the *Magna Carta* of the victim.[49] In any case, this does not seem to be the direction of recent ICC jurisprudence. In 2011 for instance, in the pre-trial phase of the *Muthaura* case (Situation in the Republic of Kenya), the Single Judge Ekaterina Trendafilova noted that:

> both Pre-Trial Chamber III and Trial Chamber III referred to the jurisprudence of the Inter-American Court of Human Rights in order to justify the participation of the successors on behalf of a deceased person. The Single Judge considers that the said case-law cannot be transposed to the present case, on the basis of the following considerations: (i) human rights institutions like the IACtHR, in contrast to criminal justice bodies, such as the Court, do not deal with individual criminal responsibility, but

In *Sejdic and Finci v Bosnia and Herzegovina*, App no 27996/06 and 34836/06 (ECtHR, 22 December 2009), Judge Bonello, in his Dissenting Opinion, warned of the consequences of a rigid application of human rights norms when the sensitive compromises of peace agreements are concerned. See Schabas (n 1) 622.

49 Jesús-Maria Silva Sanchez, *L'espansione del diritto penale* (Giuffré 2004) 24.

> with State responsibility for human rights violations; and (ii) the jurisprudence of the IACtHR relates to the right of the successors to receive reparation for the harm suffered by the deceased person, whilst in the system of the ICC there is a clear distinction between participation in the proceedings [...] on the one hand and reparation on the other hand, with the former not being a precondition for the latter.[50]

Trendafilova's decision is totally in contrast with a 2008 decision by Judge Hans-Peter Kaul in the *Bemba* case (Situation in the Central African Republic), in which the Single Judge incorporates the right of the successor to participate as a victim on behalf of a deceased person, on the basis of the case law of the IACtHR.[51]

In the same vein, Judge Steiner appears to be more open towards the Inter-American jurisprudence, which she combines with a reference to that of the ECtHR, to recognise victims' right to the truth. This gives us the opportunity to meditate on the growing impact of the case law of human rights courts on criminal law and on the possible role that these courts can play, in light of the above mentioned victim-centric tendency, which affects not only criminal law and criminal justice, but also international criminal justice.

Cross-fertilisation is the means by which this impact can be achieved, as it has an informal and discretionary nature. Indeed, there is no mechanism within the ICC to control the interpretation of 'internationally recognized human rights' given by the ICC and, consequently, there is no control over cross-fertilisation.[52] At the same time, if the reference is superficial or the reasoning for applying the human rights court's precedent in the context of the ICC is not sufficiently precise, there is a risk of a 'shotgun approach'.[53] This means an uncritical, tactical and instrumental use of the case law of human rights courts in order to justify or legitimate the interpretation given by the Judge, while avoiding consideration of the difference between international criminal and international humanitarian systems. The absolute freedom of the judges in cross-fertilising, could lead to manipulations or simply

50 *Prosecutor v Muthaura*, ICC-01/09-02/11, Decision on Victims' Participation at the Confirmation of Charges Hearing and in the Related Proceedings, Single Judge (Pre Trial Chamber II), 26 August 2011, para. 52.

51 See *Prosecutor v Bemba*, ICC-01/05-01/08-320, 4th Decision on Victims' Participation, Single Judge (Pre Trial Chamber III), 12 December 2008, para. 44.

52 See Fronza (n 5) 242; Maculan (n 7) 112.

53 Sheppard (n 10) 49.

mistakes in their application.[54] Article 21(3) of the ICC Statute represents the first normative framework for the judicial and spontaneous practice of cross-fertilisation, but it contains no criteria and limits for the choice and the selection of the precedent and it gives no real rational guidelines to the judge. While a stricter normative framework could regulate the phenomenon, in order to reduce the creative role of the judge, it could be also argued that a normative approach is an illusion, as judges will (and must) always have a natural margin.

As Sergey Vasiliev points out,[55] cross-fertilisation itself could be considered the result of an erroneous expectation towards international human rights law as a unified and coherent system. On the contrary, human rights law is a pluralistic system, construed upon autonomous conventions and regulations and driven by different institutional and cultural dynamics. From this perspective, cross-fertilisation is an attempt to 'normativise' international criminal justice, by keeping it in the shadows of human rights courts. It is a way to control international tribunals and to protect human rights against abuses. Nevertheless, the practice shows a different reality. In Judge Steiner's decision, for example, cross-fertilisation is used in order to support the Judge's argumentation in rejecting the submissions of the Prosecutor and the Defence. This begs the question as to whether the dynamic of cross-fertilisation is driven by convenience, in light of the results that the judges want to reach, in an outcome-based selection of human rights courts' jurisprudence. Reference seems to have little to do with the reasoning and the judicial rationale.

6 Final Remarks

Judge Steiner's decision is an example of how cross-fertilisation has less to do with the effective protection of human rights than it has to do with rhetoric. Nevertheless, with this reference, the Inter-American notion of victims' right to the truth is mentioned for the first time in an ICC decision and, in future, this could be seen as a first basis from which to develop the thesis of a universal recognition of this right, in its Inter-American interpretation. At least this could be a possibility, in light of what Tulkens calls the new role of human rights towards criminal law: no longer a bad conscience contributing to the

54 Gil Gil (n 5) 117.

55 Sergey Vasiliev, 'International Criminal Tribunals in the Shadow of Strasbourg and Politics of Cross-Fertilisation' (2015) 84 Nordic Journal of International Law 371, 393.

humanisation of criminal law, but rather a 'good conscience', in ensuring the protection of such rights. In her words:

> the affirmation of the role of the criminal law in protecting human rights generally appears to be accompanied by an overall weakening of its traditional function as a shield [...]; we should consider whether taking that other side into account does not frequently result nowadays in our forgetting that there are two sides to the balance and upsetting the necessary equilibrium between them, [...] especially in international criminal law. [...] On the basis of this new form of instrumentalism, where the legitimacy of the end pursued once again justifies the choice of means, [...] it will come as no surprise to see the different safeguards traditionally associated with criminal remedies collapse to such an extent that the very principle of subsidiarity of the criminal law will cease to have any relevance.[56]

This consideration goes back to the aforementioned concept of human rights as integrated in a social scenario. According to this conception, human rights are seen as political values, not merely individualistic. Political here is meant literally, as inherent to a group of individuals constituted as a community, as a polity. The individualistic perspective, on the contrary, explains what Tulkens calls 'the shift from collective feelings of communal or religious entities towards the individual and, as a corollary, the replacement of crimes 'against divinity' by crimes 'against humanity''. This is the theoretical background of the new relationship between victims and criminal law and therefore the logical background of the right to the truth; 'from the right to civil redress to the right to satisfaction in criminal proceedings', which 'has enabled victims to become involved in criminal trials by showing an 'interest in punishment' which coincides with a desire to obtain both practical redress and symbolic satisfaction'.[57]

From this point of view, beyond rhetoric, cross-fertilisation can have a potential influence on criminal law. This may not be a direct and immediate effect of the decision, but, as explained above, cross-fertilisation could plant a seed for future developments, in light of the above mentioned victim-centric tendency. When it comes to victims' rights, the reference to human rights jurisprudence cannot be considered a safeguard of international human rights law. On the

56 Tulkens (n 17) 593.

57 ibid 595.

contrary, it highlights the intrinsic contradiction of human rights which trigger criminalisation through an expansion of the judicial protection of the human rights of victims, thereby leading to weaker protections of the human rights of the accused.

CHAPTER 15

Self- or Cross-fertilisation? Referencing ECtHR Jurisprudence to Justify Victim Participation at the ICC

Kerstin Braun

I Introduction

The interconnectivity among different fields of international law, especially between international criminal law and human rights law, has become more apparent over the past decades.[1] Scholars have identified an emerging cross-referencing practice, particularly between the European Court of Human Rights and international criminal tribunals.[2] This is mostly based on ICTs referencing ECtHR cases,[3] and occurs despite the fact that ECtHR jurisprudence is not binding on ICTs.[4] Some refer to this practice as cross-fertilisation and associate mainly positive effects with it, including a more evenly evolved understanding of human rights and a fair procedural playing field in international criminal law.[5] Vasiliev explains that, in international criminal law, human rights jurisprudence is considered 'highly authoritative' and relying on said jurispru-

1 This chapter explores this issue in the context of one decision by Pre-Trial Chamber I of the ICC and its use of ECtHR legislation: *Situation in the Democratic Republic of Congo*, ICC-01/04, Decision on the Application in the Proceedings of VPRS 1, VPRS 2, VPRS 3, VPRS 3, VPRS 4, VPRS 5 and VPRS 6, Pre-Trial Chamber I, 17 January 2006 ('Situation in the DRC').

2 Reference to ICTs in this chapter also includes the ICC unless otherwise stated.

3 Sergey Vasiliev, 'International Criminal Tribunals in the Shadow of Strasbourg and Politics of Cross-Fertilization' (2015) 84 Nordic Journal of International Law 371, 374. For detailed analysis of this issue see generally William A. Schabas, 'Synergy or Fragmentation? International Criminal Law and the European Convention on Human Rights' (2011) 9 Journal of International Criminal Justice 609. See also Antonio Cassese, 'The Influence of the European Court of Human Rights on International Criminal Tribunals—Some Methodological Remarks' in Morten Bergsmo (ed), *Human Rights and Criminal Justice for the Downtrodden, Essays in Honour of Asbjørn Eide* (Martinus Nijhoff Publishers 2003) 19.

4 Julia Geneuss, 'Obstacles to Cross-fertilisation: The International Criminal Tribunals' "Unique Context" and the Flexibility of the European Court of Human Rights' Case Law' (2015) 84 Nordic Journal of International Law 404, 405.

5 Discussed in Triestino Mariniello and Paolo Lobba, 'Editorial: The Cross-fertilisation Rhetoric

 | DOI: 10.1163/9789004313750_017

dence constitutes 'an aspect of good judging'.[6] He points out that the 'mere fact of citation generally suffices' to prevent tribunals from criticism.[7]

However, not every referenced ECtHR case which ICTs deem relevant and persuasive necessarily supports their respective decision-making. This chapter explores this point by critically analysing the 2006 ICC Pre-Trial Chamber I's ('PTC I') interpretation of 'proceedings' as enshrined in Article 68(3) of the Rome Statute.[8] On 17 January 2006, PTC I found that, at the ICC, victims have the general right to participate during the investigation of a situation prior to the naming of a suspect.[9] To support its finding, PTC I used a teleological interpretation methodology for the term 'proceedings' and relied on, *inter alia*, ECtHR case law including *Berger v France* and *Perez v France*.[10] The Chamber argued that the two ECtHR decisions affirmed that victims should be able to exercise rights independently vis-à-vis the prosecution at the investigation stage. It furthermore opined that ECtHR jurisprudence applied Article 6(1) of the European Convention of Human Rights, the right to a fair trial, to victims at the investigation stage thus also supporting a general right to victim participation at the investigation stage at the ICC.[11]

The analysis in this chapter suggests that PTC I may not have relied on said cases to endorse the ECtHR's legal reasoning with the consequence of cross-fertilising their decision. Rather, the human rights jurisprudence may have been referenced in an attempt to add authority to its decision which calls into existence a victim's right that, at the ICC, is not explicitly provided by statute and has not been established at the ECtHR level as such. Referencing unpersuasive ECtHR jurisprudence in an attempt to add validity to a court decision and perhaps to avoid subsequent criticism may be better described as self-fertilisation rather than cross-fertilisation rhetoric.[12]

---

in Question: Use and Abuse of the European Court's Jurisprudence by International Criminal Tribunals' (2015) 84 Nordic Journal of International Law 363, 364.

6 Vasiliev (n 3) 373. See also Erik Voeten, 'Borrowing and Nonborrowing Among International Courts' (2010) 39 Journal of Legal Studies 547, 550.

7 Vasiliev (n 3).

8 Rome Statute of the International Criminal Court, UN Doc A/CONF.183/9 of 17 July 1998, entered into force 1 July 2002. All unspecified articles in this chapter are those of the ICC Statute.

9 Situation in the DRC (n 1), para. 41.

10 *Berger v France*, App no. 48221/99 (ECtHR, 3 December 2002); *Perez v France*, App no 47287/99 (ECtHR, 12 February 2004). Pre-Trial Chamber I also relied on case law from the Inter-American Court of Human Rights to support its interpretation, which is not subject to analysis in this chapter.

11 Situation in DRC (n 1), para. 51.

12 For further discussion of so-called strategic communication and strategic borrowing of

Firstly, this chapter provides general background to victim participation at the ICC (II). Subsequently, it deals with PTC I's decision from 17 January 2006 (III) and the question of cross- and self-fertilisation in light of the referenced ECtHR jurisprudence (IV). It discusses subsequent proceedings (V) before considering pragmatism in the use of ECtHR jurisprudence (VI). Lastly, it concludes that while cross-fertilisation on the international level may allow for the evenly oriented development of human rights and thus be a positive development, not every decision fits within these parameters and caution should be exercised to avoid turning cross-fertilisation into a meaningless exercise (VII).

II Victim Participation at the ICC

The ICC is a permanent international court and has jurisdiction over persons suspected of the serious international crimes of genocide, crimes against humanity and war crimes.[13] For the first time in the history of international criminal law, the establishment of the ICC and its statutes and regulations afforded victims participatory rights in proceedings.[14] The ICC Statute contains provisions specifically relating to victims' participatory rights intended to introduce an element of victim recognition into international proceedings.[15]

---

external sources including the argument that judges have certain goals in doing so, for example 'to see the law reflect their policy preferences' see Voeten (n 6) 553–554.

13 ICC Statute, Article 5.

14 Alexandra H. Guhr, 'Victim Participation During the Pre-Trial Stage at the International Criminal Court' (2008) 8 International Criminal Law Review 109, 110. No provisions for victim participation (apart from participation as witnesses) were introduced at the International Criminal Tribunals for Rwanda and the former Yugoslavia, see Hector Olasolo, 'Systematic and Casuistic Approaches to the Role of Victims in Criminal Proceedings Before the International Criminal Court' (2009) 12 New Criminal Law Review 513, 513–514. Victim participation has since been included at the Special Tribunal for Lebanon and the Extraordinary Chambers in the Courts of Cambodia. See in general Jérôme de Hemptinne, 'Challenges Raised by Victims' Participation in the Proceedings of the Special Tribunal for Lebanon' (2010) 8 Journal of International Criminal Justice 165; James Bair, 'From the Numbers Who Died to Those Who Survived: Victim Participation in the Extraordinary Chambers in the Courts of Cambodia' (2008) 31 University of Hawaii Law Review 508.

15 ICC Statute, Articles 15(3), 19(3), 68(3). For detailed analysis on international recognition of victims' rights see M. Cherif Bassiouni, 'International Recognition of Victims' Rights' (2006) 6 Human Rights Law Review 203.

The inclusion of victims at the ICC is based on the assumption that participation can have restorative benefits for victims.[16] In addition, SáCouto and Cleary point out that the drafters of the victim participation regime at the ICC were influenced by the perceived shortfalls of the International Criminal Tribunals for the former Yugoslavia and Rwanda. The Tribunals have generally been criticised for failing to establish a connection with the affected communities, creating an overall disconnect with their work, which may also be related to the lack of victim participation in their proceedings.[17] Victim participation at the ICC was therefore considered 'an essential tool for bringing the Court and its proceedings closer to the persons who have suffered atrocities'.[18]

The ICC Statute contains three provisions explicitly relating to victim participation.[19] As per Article 15(3), victims may make representations to the PTC where the Prosecutor, under his *proprio motu* powers, requests the authorisation of an investigation from the Chamber. In addition, Article 19(3) provides that victims are able to submit observations where the Court's jurisdiction or the admissibility of a case is challenged. Lastly, Article 68(3) broadly states that 'the Court shall permit [victims'] views and concerns to be presented and considered at stages of the proceedings determined to be appropriate by the Court' where their personal interests are affected and 'in a manner which is not prejudicial to or inconsistent with the rights of the accused'.[20]

---

16 Susana SáCouto and Katherine Cleary, 'Victims' Participation in the Investigations of the International Criminal Court' (2008) 17 Transnational Law and Contemporary Problems 73, 76–77; Guhr (n 14) 110. Moffett explains that the Court nevertheless upholds its core goal of prosecuting and punishing perpetrators of international crimes, see Luke Moffett, 'Meaningful and Effective? Considering Victims' Interests Through Participation at the International Criminal Court' (2015) 26 Criminal Law Forum 255, 260, 264. See also Christine van den Wyngaert 'Victims Before International Criminal Courts: Some Views and Concerns of An ICC Trial Judge' (2011) 44 Case Western Reserve Journal of International Law 475, 476.

17 SáCouto and Cleary, 'Investigations' (n 16) 79–81; see also van den Wyngaert (n 16) 477.

18 Gilbert Bitti and Håkan Friman, 'Participation of Victims in the Proceedings' in Lee Roy (eds), *The International Criminal Court: Elements of Crimes and Rules of Evidence* (Ardsley 2001) 456 as cited in SáCouto and Cleary, 'Investigations' (n 16) 82.

19 As per Rule 85(a) of the ICC RPE, 'victim' means natural persons who have suffered harm as a result of the commission of any crime within the jurisdiction of the Court; and 'may include organizations or institutions that have sustained direct harm to any of their property which is dedicated to religion, education, art or science or charitable purposes, and to their historic monuments, hospitals and other places and objects for humanitarian purposes'.

20 The wording of Article 68(3) of the Rome Statute was heavily influenced by Article 6(b) of

In light of Article 68(3), the ICC must determine the appropriate stages of proceedings during which victims' views and concerns can be presented. Different ICC chambers have concerned themselves with questions relating to the applicability of Article 68(3). McGonigle Leyh explains in this context that 'inconsistent approaches to Article 68(3) determinations as well as to the appropriate modalities of participation have plagued the Court throughout its operation'.[21]

The below examines the first decision relating to victim participation at the ICC handed down by PTC I; a decision whose key issue was to identify whether victims have a general participation right during the investigation stage of a situation in light of Article 68(3).[22] Ultimately, the analysis seeks to identify whether PTC I's reference to ECtHR jurisprudence in this context can be justified by the cross-fertilisation argument and represents inter-judicial dialogue or qualifies more as self-fertilisation in an attempt to enhance the validity of the decision made.

III The Decision of Pre-trial Chamber I, 17 January 2006

On 17 January 2006, PTC I handed down its decision on whether and to what extent six victims were able to participate in the investigation of the situation in the Democratic Republic of Congo ('DRC') prior to the identification and naming of an accused.[23] Object of the investigation were crimes committed

---

the 1985 UN Declaration of Basic Principles of Justice for Victims of Crime and Abuse of Power, GA Res, 40/34, UN GAOR 40th sess, 96th plen mtg, supp no 53, UN Doc A/RES/40/34 (29 November 1985) annex ('Declaration'). On Article 6(b) see Brianne M. Leyh, 'Victim-Oriented Measures at International Criminal Institutions: Participation and its Pitfalls' (2012) 12 International Criminal Law Review 375, 381.

21 Brianne M. Leyh, *Procedural Justice? Victim Participation in International Criminal Proceedings* (Intersentia 2011) 258.

22 Other pre-trial stages include the preliminary examination phase and the confirmation of charges phase. Victim participation during these phases is not subject to analysis in this chapter but has been undertaken by others elsewhere. See eg Leyh, 'Procedural Justice' (n 21) 261–267, 273–290.

23 The DRC referred the situation to the Prosecutor of the ICC in March 2004. On 23 June 2004 the Prosecutor officially decided to commence the first investigation of the ICC. The situation was assigned to PTC I. For detailed analysis of the decision see also Jérôme de Hemptinne and Francesco Rindi, 'ICC Pre-Trial Chamber Allows Victims to Participate in the Investigation Phase of Proceedings' (2006) 4 Journal of International Criminal Justice 342.

during the Second Congo War. The Office of the Prosecutor had elected to proceed with the investigation into the situation but no arrest warrant or summons against an individual had been issued yet at that stage. Proceedings were therefore in the investigation phase of the pre-trial stage.

One of the key questions the Chamber had to decide was whether victims have the general right to participate during the investigation phase prior to the naming of a suspect.[24] This would only be possible if the investigation stage falls under 'proceedings' in the sense of Article 68(3).[25] The term is vague and therefore requires interpretation. PTC I was the first chamber of the ICC called upon to interpret the term in the context of the victim participation regime. The Chamber ultimately affirmed that victims had a general participation right during the investigation of a situation and gave all six victims status to participate through their legal representative during this phase. None of the victims had made an application to participate in any particular pre-trial proceedings, which is why the Chamber did not decide the specifics of their participatory role.[26] Instead victims were provided with access to all public documents.[27] However, PTC I outlined that participation may be possible during specific proceedings as well as investigations in general.[28]

---

24 The other questions discussed by PTC I were whether the applying victims could receive victim status and how victim participation at the pre-trial stage should look. The general right to participation goes beyond those specific participation rights enshrined in the ICC Statute including Articles 15(3) and 19(3).

25 McDermott argues that the wording of Article 68(3) excludes victims from presenting views and concerns at the investigation stage of a situation, see Yvonne McDermott, 'Some Are More Equal than Others: Victim Participation in the ICC' (2008) 5 Eyes on the ICC 23, 33–34.

26 The decision was described as 'extremely vague' regarding the modalities of participation, see ibid 37.

27 Situation in the DRC (n 1), para. 76.

28 Situation in the DRC (n 1), 42 (explicitly excluding non-public documents). In practice, victim participation during the investigation stage in this case has been very limited. The Legal Representative of victims submitted arguments regarding the Prosecutor's application to appeal the decision (*Situation in the Democratic Republic of Congo*, ICC-01/04-105-tEN, Observations of the Legal Representative of VPRS 1–6 [...], Pre-Trial Chamber I, 27 January 2006) and unsuccessfully requested documents regarding the Prosecutor's decision to suspend their investigation concerning other possible charges against Thomas Lubanga Dyilo (*Situation in the Democratic Republic of Congo*, ICC-01/04-399, Decision on the Requests of the Legal Representative for Victims VPRS 1 to VPRS 6 Regarding 'Prosecutor's Information on Further Investigation', Pre-Trial Chamber I, 26 September 2007).

In assessing whether proceedings in light of Article 68(3) encompass the investigation of a situation stage, the Chamber applied a three-pronged interpretation approach: terminological, contextual and teleological.[29] In its interpretation the Chamber was bound by the ICC Statute according to which any interpretation must be in accordance with 'internationally recognized human rights'.[30]

The Chamber sought guidance on the interpretation of 'proceedings' and the question of whether victims should be able to participate early on during the investigation stage by relying on ECtHR case law in the context of its teleological argument—namely the object and purpose of the victim participation regime under the ICC Statute. It argued based on two ECtHR cases, *Berger v France* and *Perez v France*, that the ICC Statute grants victims the right to express views and concerns independently before the Prosecutor at the investigation stage given that

> the European Court has affirmed on several occasions, victims participating in criminal proceedings cannot be regarded as 'either the opponent—or for that matter necessarily the ally—of the prosecution, their roles and objectives being clearly different.'[31]

In addition, the Chamber supported its interpretation of Article 68(3) by noting that the ECtHR applied the right to a fair trial according to Article 6(1) of the ECHR to victims from the investigation stage prior to confirmation of charges and cited seven ECtHR cases.

The above interpretation was later described as 'endorsing the jurisprudence of the ECHR'.[32]

29 For analysis of the literal and contextual interpretations see de Hemptinne and Rindi (n 23) 344. For critical discussion of victim-focused teleological reasoning see Darryl Robinson, 'The Identity Crisis of International Criminal Law' (2008) 21 Leiden Journal of International Law 925, 933–938.

30 ICC Statute, Article 21(3). In addition any interpretation of an international treaty is governed by the Vienna Convention on the Law of Treaties, 1155 UNTS 331 of 23 May 1969, entered into force 27 January 1980.

31 Situation in the DRC (n 1), para. 51. This statement is only supported by two referenced ECtHR cases: Berger (n 10) and Perez (n 10).

32 *Prosecutor v Katanga*, ICC-01/04-01/07, Submissions of the Defence of Mr Mathieu Ngudjolo in the Context of the Confirmation Hearing, Pre-Trial Chamber I, 28 July 2008, para. 85.

IV Cross-fertilisation Rhetoric

In the past a cross-fertilisation practice between the ICC and the ECtHR, mostly by the ICC relying on ECtHR jurisprudence, has developed.[33] Many consider this a positive development essentially preventing the fragmentation of human rights and promoting holistic human rights standards.[34] Although no hierarchy between international courts exists in general and ECtHR judgments are not binding on the ICC,[35] the ICC has frequently applied ECtHR case law in its decisions often without 'theorising as to the legal basis for its incorporation'.[36]

The below discusses PTC I's use of ECtHR jurisprudence and seeks to determine whether the referenced decisions support a right to general victim participation at the investigation stage at the ICC.

1 Berger *and* Perez*: Support for Independent Victim Participation vis-à-vis the Prosecutor at the Investigation Stage?*

PTC I established that the object of the victim participation regime at the ICC is to grant victims an independent voice and role in proceedings before the Court. It argued that victims must therefore be able to act separately and independently from the Prosecutor at the investigation stage. In support, the Chamber relied on two ECtHR cases, *Berger* and *Perez*. The question arises whether the referenced cases establish and support an independent participation right for victims vis-à-vis the Prosecutor, as suggested by PTC I, which can be generalised as an 'internationally recognised human right' and transplanted into the ICC context.

When assessing this question it needs to be noted that ECtHR judgements are generally limited to the case on which proceedings are based and the specifics of the legal system in which the case arises.[37] Geneuss explains that the ECtHR is foremost 'a review court deciding individual cases arising from domestic jurisdictions'[38] and notes that ECtHR case law is not intended to

33 Mariniello and Lobba (n 5) 363; Voeten explains that the ECtHR seldom cites other courts in its judgments, see Voeten (n 6) 549.

34 Mariniello and Lobba (n 5) 364.

35 Nicolas Croquet, 'The International Criminal Court and the Treatment of Defence Rights: A Mirror of the European Court of Human Rights' Jurisprudence?' (2011) 11 Human Rights Law Review 91, 108.

36 ibid 109.

37 Geneuss (n 4) 418.

38 ibid 417.

develop 'clear-cut, visible, and generalisable procedural standards'[39] as possibly suggested by PTC I in the context of its decision.

The below provides a brief overview of the two decisions before analysing whether a general right to independent victim participation at the investigation stage of the ICC can be derived therefrom.

a *Berger v France*

As per the facts of *Berger v France*, the applicant Mrs Marie-Thérèse Berger, a French national, lodged a criminal complaint against a company for theft and fraudulent breach of trust under French criminal law. At the same time she sought leave to join the proceedings as a civil party seeking damages.[40] The investigating Judge discontinued proceedings, arguing that the actions by the company did not fall within the ambit of criminal law. The applicant appealed the decision to discontinue charges unsuccessfully to the Indictment Division of the Colmar Court of Appeal and the Court of Cassation[41] prior to lodging an application against the French Republic with the ECtHR on the basis of unfairness of criminal proceedings, especially before the Court of Cassation.

The Court of Cassation held that the applicant's appeal was invalid as it was not based on any of the limited grounds allowing civil parties to appeal under Article 575 of the French Code of Criminal Procedure. According to this provision, the civil party can only appeal the judgment of the investigation division where the prosecutor lodges an appeal, which did not occur here, or, in another seven narrowly tailored cases explicitly named in the provision, none of which, so the Court of Cassation argued, applied. The French Government, as the respondent to the ECtHR proceedings, explained that Article 575 of the French Code of Criminal Procedure limiting the cases in which a civil party can appeal did not violate the applicant's right to access to a court or the principle of equality-of-arms. It argued that the limitations are justified by the fact that the civil party cannot be regarded as the prosecution's opponent warranting separate and broad appeal rights and that even prosecutors are only able to appeal where the respective decision affected general rather than private interests.[42]

39 ibid 421.

40 In France, civil parties have ample participation rights, are recognised as a party to the proceedings and are able to claim compensation in this way, see Jacqueline Hodgson, 'Suspects, Defendants and Victims in the French Criminal Process: The Context of Recent Reform' (2002) 51 International and Comparative Law Quarterly 781, 792–793.

41 The Court of Cassation declared the appeal inadmissible, Berger (n 10), 2–3.

42 Berger (n 10), 6.

While assessing whether the right to a court in light of Article 6(1) of the ECHR was impaired, the ECtHR agreed with the French Government that civil parties should not have an unlimited right to appeal[43] and did not find that the applicant's right to a court was infringed by the conditions set out in the French law limiting the right to appeal. The ECtHR pointed out that 'a civil party cannot be regarded as either the opponent-or for that matter necessarily the ally-of the prosecution, their roles and objectives being clearly different'.[44] This is why the Court found that the principle of equality-of-arms between the rights of the prosecutor and the rights of the civil party was not violated by national legislation limiting the civil party's right to appeal in comparison to those of the prosecution.

b *Perez v France*

As per the facts of *Perez v France*, the applicant Mrs Paule Perez, a French national, lodged a criminal complaint of having been assaulted with an offensive weapon, namely a syringe containing traces of diazepam and benzoic acid, by her two children. During the investigation the applicant had been joined to the proceedings as a civil party. The investigating Judge ruled that there was no case to answer due to insufficient evidence. The applicant appealed the decision to the Indictment Division of the Court of Appeal of Saint-Denis-de-la-Reunion which ruled her appeal inadmissible due to missing the legal deadline and failing to sign the notice of appeal. The applicant subsequently unsuccessfully appealed on points of law to the Criminal Division of the Court of Cassation, which dismissed her appeal confirming that her original appeal had been out of time.

Her subsequent application to the ECtHR against the French Republic was based on the argument that the procedure before the Court of Cassation had not been fair. She especially enunciated that it was a violation of Article 6 of the ECHR that, in its judgment the Court of Cassation, had not re-quoted all the legislation the applicant had relied on and that the Court did not address all her grounds of appeal and thus failed to give sufficient reasons for its decision.

The ECtHR held that Article 6 of the ECHR was applicable to civil party proceedings in France. It characterised said proceedings as civil parties being able to enjoy 'the benefit of being a party to the criminal trial' being 'kept informed of the steps in the proceedings' being able to 'file requests for documents' and to lodge appeals as well as to obtain compensation from the criminal courts

43 ibid 7.

44 ibid 8.

for the harm suffered.[45] The ECtHR held that Article 6 of the ECHR is applicable even during preliminary investigations where a civil party complaint is involved but qualified that the decisive factor for the application of Article 6 of the ECHR is whether the criminal proceedings affect the civil component. The Court affirmed the statement made in *Berger v France* that 'a civil party could not be regarded as the opponent of the prosecution, nor necessarily as its ally, given that their roles and purposes were clearly distinct.'[46]

Ultimately, the ECtHR found that Article 6 of the ECHR, the right to a fair trial, which included submitting any party observations that the party considered relevant to their case, was not infringed in the case at hand and that the Court of Cassation had not failed in providing due consideration of the victim's arguments and sufficient reasons for its decision.

c An Independent Victim Participation Right Based on *Berger* and *Perez?*

The above shows that the only two cases cited by PTC I in support of independent victim participation at the investigation stage vis-à-vis the Prosecutor are not concerned with the question of whether victims should be able to present views and concerns at the investigation stage as such. Both decisions are based on a national criminal justice system, the French system, where victims have the right to participate as civil parties in order to seek remedies and the question of what rights victims can exercise as civil parties. Neither decision discusses the question of whether victims should generally have the right to victim participation in a party role at different stages of the proceedings.

It is also noteworthy that both decisions have dismissed claims by victims in regards to participation as civil parties in France and thus upheld laws and court decisions limiting victims' participation rights.[47] Neither case therefore appears to support the notion that for victim participation to be meaningful they must be afforded an independent voice and role.

While, as explicitly cited by PTC I in support of the interpretation of Article 68(3) of the Rome Statute, the ECtHR did agree with the French Government in *Berger* that participating victims and prosecutors have different roles

---

45 Perez (n 10), 17.

46 ibid 18.

47 A similar argument is made by Susana SáCouto and Katherine Cleary, 'Victim Participation at the Case Stage of Proceedings' International Criminal Court Legal Analysis and Education Project (War Crimes Research Office, Washington College of Law 2009) 53; Göran Sluiter and others, *International Criminal Procedure: Principles and Rules* (OUP 2013) 1338.

and objectives and requoted this in *Perez*, the context of this statement is important. The ECtHR found in *Berger* that because civil parties and prosecutors have different objectives the equality-of-arms principle is not violated where civil parties have more limited appeal rights than the prosecution.[48] The statement thus supports limited victims' rights vis-à-vis the prosecution and not, as suggested by PTC I, the necessity to create an independent victim participation regime.

In addition, the two ECtHR decisions do not refer to victims as having different roles and objectives in criminal trials but especially relate to 'civil parties'. It is therefore questionable whether this statement by the ECtHR explicitly relating to civil parties in two specific French cases can be generalised and transported into the ICC context in support of opening up a general participatory right in an entirely different context.[49]

2 *Article 6(1) of the ECHR: An Independent Victim Participation Right at the Pre-trial Stage?*

a Referenced Jurisprudence

In support of general victim participation at the investigation stage at the ICC, PTC I further referenced a number of ECtHR cases[50] as demonstrating a trend in international human rights law and explained that the ECtHR applied Article 6(1) of the ECHR to victims from the investigation stage prior to confirmation of charges, especially where the criminal proceedings are relevant for the determination of reparations. While PTC I cites seven ECtHR cases in total, none is discussed in detail in the decision and, overall, it remains unclear how the ECHR was used to support its interpretation of victim participation at the investigation stage.[51]

---

48 Berger (n 10), 8.

49 Safferling points out that the difference between the procedure to obtain reparations and the criminal trial itself makes clear that there is no intention to afford victims at the ICC party status during proceedings to determine the guilt or innocence of an accused, see Christoph Safferling, *International Criminal Procedure* (OUP 2012) 176.

50 PTC I also referenced decisions from the Inter-American Court of Human Rights, Situation in the DRC (n 1), para. 53, which are not subject to the analysis in this chapter. Manning argues, however, that the cited IACtHR decisions are inappropriate to support PTC I's interpretation, see Jason Manning, 'On Power, Participation and Authority: The International Criminal Court's Initial Appellate Jurisprudence' (2007) 38 Georgetown Journal of International Law 803, 823.

51 *Moreira de Azevedo v Portugal*, App no 11296/84 (ECtHR, 23 October 1990); *Tomasi v France*, App no 12850/87 (ECtHR, 27 August 1992); *Acquaviva v France*, App No 19248/91 (ECtHR,

In addition, none of the cited ECtHR cases articulates a human right to independent victim participation in general and to victim participation at the pretrial stage in particular based on Article 6(1) of the ECHR or any other article of the Convention. The majority of cited cases set out that in national criminal justice systems which allow for victim participation in order to receive civil reparations such as, for example, the civil party in France, participating parties have the right that criminal proceedings are carried out within a reasonable timeframe.[52] Delays in criminal proceedings can therefore constitute a violation of Article 6(1) of the ECHR. This, however, does not support the assumption apparently employed by PTC I that Article 6(1) of the ECHR creates an independent right to victim participation at the investigation stage.

The above analysis suggests that the ECtHR case law cited by PTC I does not support a right to victim participation at the investigation stage as such and is not persuasive for the interpretation of Article 68(3) of the Rome Statute. The below outlines that, even if such a right could be assumed from the cited ECtHR jurisprudence, significant differences between the domestic and the ICC criminal justice systems may prohibit a direct transplant of such a right into the ICC setting.

b Differences between the Domestic and ICC Setting

Walker points out that a translation of a principle from one system into another requires 'detailed hermeneutic understanding both of the context in which it was originally embedded and of the new context for which it is destined'.[53] In its decision, PTC I would have had to explore whether an independent victim participation right at the investigation stage can be abstracted from the national setting over which the ECtHR has jurisdiction and placed into the ICC context without modification.[54] PTC I, however, did not address whether victim

---

21 November 1995); *Selmouni v France*, App no 25803/94 (ECtHR, 28 July 1999); *Calvelli and Ciglio v Italy*, App no 32967/96 (ECtHR, 17 January 2002); *Perez v France*, App no 47287/99 (ECTHR, 12 February 2004); *Antunes Rocha v Portugal*, App no 64330/01 (ECtHR, 31 May 2005).

52 Manning (n 50) 824; Leyh, 'Procedural Justice' (n 21) 269.

53 Neil Walker, 'Postnational Constitutionalism and the Problem of Translation' in Joseph H.H. Weiler and Marlene Wind (eds) *European Constitutionalism Beyond the State* (CUP 2003) 27, 37; see also Geneuss (n 4) 406.

54 Guhr questions whether the referenced ECtHR decisions are transferable without modification as they originate on a national level where victim participation has a different purpose, see Guhr (n 14) 119.

participation regimes during the investigation stage in national criminal justice systems and at the ICC are actually comparable and whether the referenced ECtHR jurisprudence is therefore translatable.

The translatability is doubtful, however, given that the ICC operates in a different mode and context than the domestic courts whose human rights compliance is supervised by the ECtHR.[55] In comparison to victims at the domestic level who can participate as individual victims, mass victims at the ICC participate collectively regardless of any diverging interests.[56] Due to this difference, the objective of victim participation, namely achieving some form of restorative justice for victims, may not be reached at the ICC level in the same way as in national criminal justice systems.

In addition, victims at the ICC who have been afforded victim status at the investigation stage may lose said status again at the trial stage if the warrant against an individual accused specifies crimes which are not causal to the victims' injuries.[57] For example, all six victims who received victim status and the general right to participate during the investigation of the situation in the DRC lost victim status to participate in the trial against the arrested Thomas Lubanga Dyilo. The loss in status occurred as there was no nexus between the harm the victims suffered and the charges ultimately laid against the accused, namely the war crimes of child enlistment, child conscription and use of children in hostilities.[58] This loss of status may leave victims at the ICC unsatisfied and possibly traumatised due to being ineligible for reparations and stripped of the chance to tell their story at trial.[59] A loss of participation status is minimised at the national level given that most offenders will be investigated for offences against specific victims from the outset and the character of the offences is unlikely to change severely.

55 Leyh suggests that the transplantation of domestic procedures to the international level is uneasy due to the 'unique context in which international criminal courts operate', see Leyh, 'Procedural Justice' (n 21) 342.

56 Leyh, 'Victim-oriented Measures' (n 20) 404–405.

57 Rule 85(a) of the ICC RPE requires a causal link between the crime and the consequence(s) for the victim.

58 *Prosecutor v Lubanga*, ICC-01/04-01/06-2, Warrant of Arrest, Pre-Trial Chamber I, 10 February 2006, 4. The crimes reported by the victims included murder, looting, abduction and enslavement, torture and unlawful detention, see Situation in the DRC (n 1), paras 123, 134, 151, 166, 175, 185.

59 The risk of victim frustration is further discussed in de Hemptinne and Rindi (n 23) 349; Guhr (n 14) 120.

While all of these issues may denote the necessity to depart from ECtHR jurisprudence regarding victim participation at the investigation stage, PTC I's decision remains silent on potential differences between the domestic and the ICC settings and the translatability of potential human rights of victims under the ECHR.

In light of the above, PTC I's teleological interpretation of Article 68(3) appears to be insufficiently supported by the referenced ECtHR's jurisprudence.

V Subsequent Proceedings and Decisions

As the 2006 decision was an interlocutory matter, an appeal required leave to appeal by PTC I, which the Prosecutor unsuccessfully sought. A similar decision allowing victim participation at the investigation stage and citing PTC I's 2006 decision was subsequently issued by PTC II in 2007.[60] The decision, however, only referenced the approach taken by PTC I and abstained from quoting any ECtHR jurisprudence in this context. Again, the Prosecutor was not granted leave to appeal. Finally leave to appeal was obtained against a pre-trial decision based on a similar constellation in 2007.[61]

In its 2008 judgment, the Appeals Chamber reversed the PTC decision on which the appeal was based and found that the investigation stage as such is not a judicial proceeding but rather constitutes an inquiry by the Prosecutor and therefore does not fall within the scope of Article 68(3).[62] The Appeals Chamber outlined that granting victims a general right to participate during the investigation stage, as done by the PTCs, contravenes the ICC Statute by creating a right that it does not provide.[63] It is noteworthy that the Appeals Chamber did not reference the ECtHR jurisprudence relied upon by PTC I in regards to victim participation at the investigation stage anywhere in its

60 *Situation in Uganda*, ICC-02/04-101, Decision on Victims' Applications for Participation, Pre-Trial Chamber II, 10 August 2007, para. 7.

61 *Situation in the Democratic Republic of Congo*, ICC-01/04-417, Decision on the Requests of the OPCD on the Prosecution of Relevant Supporting Documentation Pursuant to Regulation 86(2)(e), Pre-Trial Chamber I, 7 December 2007.

62 *Situation in the Democratic Republic of the Congo*, ICC-01/04-556, Judgement on Victim Participation in the Investigation Stage of the Proceedings, Appeals Chamber, 19 December 2008, para. 45.

63 ibid para. 52.

decision. The finding of the Appeals Chamber, namely that there is no general right to victim participation at the pre-trial stage as such, has since been followed by other chambers including PTC II.[64]

VI Pragmatism in the Use of the ECtHR Jurisprudence

While an argument may well be made in favour of broad victim participation at the investigation stage at the ICC,[65] this right is neither explicitly set out in the ICC framework nor is it necessarily supported by the referenced ECtHR jurisprudence. The question therefore arises why PTC I cited numerous ECtHR cases in its decision whose overall persuasiveness for the interpretation of Article 68(3) appears questionable.

It can be imagined that by relying on ECtHR jurisprudence the Chamber sought to secure 'legitimacy and acceptance'[66] of their interpretation and decision. The decision was concerned with an entirely new issue, namely the extent of victim participation at the ICC, which had never before been decided by any ICC chamber and thus constituted muddy waters. Indeed, the International Federation of Human Rights has subsequently described the decision as an 'international legal first'.[67] Given the hybrid inquisitorial/adversarial procedural nature of the ICC, concerns may have existed at the time of deciding that the Chamber's interpretation of 'proceedings', essentially granting victims broad participation rights that are usually associated with inquisitorial systems, could subsequently be subject to heavy criticism.[68] Voeten notes that citing external sources 'signals that legal reasoning is shared by others and thus is not arbi-

64 *Prosecutor v Ruto*, ICC-01/09-01/11-371, Decision on the 'Request by the Victims' Representative for Authorisation to make a Further Written Submission on the Views and Concerns of the Victims', Pre-Trial Chamber II, 9 December 2011, paras 11–12.

65 See, for example, Moffett (n 16) 272 arguing that the Appeals Chamber rejecting the right 'may not have fully considered victims' interests in the investigation' and the importance of early victim participation.

66 Discussed as some of the reasons for borrowing from another court in Vasiliev (n 3) 376.

67 Press Release of 20 January 2006, Worldwide Movement for Human Rights, First Victim Recognised by the International Criminal Court (10 January 2006) https://www.fidh.org/en/region/Africa/democratic-republic-of-congo/First-victims-recognised-by-the accessed 14 March 2016.

68 For criticism that the decision expanded victims' participation rights beyond the foreseen definition by the drafters and the text of the Rome Statute, see Christine Chung, 'Victims' Participation at the International Criminal Court: Are Concessions of the Court Clouding the Promise?' (2008) 6 Northwestern Journal of International Human Rights 459, 467.

trary'.[69] As such, it seems possible that in the Chamber's view, reference to ECtHR case law and the assumption of an internationally recognised human right to victim participation at the pre-trial stage served to enhance the interpretation's validity. This could particularly be the case because, as some point out, the 'Strasbourg system of human rights protection enjoys an element of "universality-legitimacy"'.[70]

Sheppard contends that ICC judges sometimes apply a 'shotgun' method to support 'a given principle's status as an internationally recognised right' by identifying 'as many concurrent sources as possible for the proposition' and subsequent conclusion 'that the right is internationally recognized'.[71] This may also have occurred in this decision as PTC I, in addition to ECtHR jurisprudence, cited cases from the Inter-American Court of Human Rights whose applicability to the case of victim participation at the ICC has been considered questionable.[72]

It is especially noteworthy in this regard that in the aftermath of the decision, few authors overall addressed the Chamber's use of ECtHR and IACHR jurisprudence in the context of victim participation at the pre-trial stage.[73]

VII Conclusion

Without a doubt it is important that ICTs embrace and operate in accordance with international human rights principles and standards. While some decisions of ICTs may rely on cross-fertilisation with ECtHR jurisprudence to create such holistically applicable human rights standards across the national,

69 Voeten (n 6) 553.

70 Croquet (n 35) 123.

71 Daniel Sheppard, 'The International Criminal Court and "Internationally Recognized Human Rights": Understanding Article 21(3) of the Rome Statute' (2010) 10 International Criminal Law Review 43, 49.

72 See Manning (n 50) 824–826, Leyh, 'Procedural Justice' (n 21) 269.

73 For criticism on the use of ECtHR jurisprudence in the decision see Manning (n 50) 823–824 ('The Decision on the Application relies on inapposite jurisprudence from the European Court of Human Rights'). McDermott describes the interpretation based on the referenced decisions as 'erroneous' because the rights recognised in domestic legal systems cannot be transplanted into the ICC context, mainly due to the larger number of victims, McDermott (n 25) 35. On the other hand, de Hemptinne and Rindi describe the interpretation of PTC I as 'well argued and balanced' (n 23) 347. Moffett considers PTC I's reasoning with regard to victim participation at the pre-trial stage as 'in line with the jurisprudence established by the human rights courts', see Moffett (n 16) 270.

regional and international levels, not all decisions are exclusively motivated by this desire. In this context, this chapter explored PTC I's use of ECtHR jurisprudence in its 2006 decision on victim participation at the pre-trial stage.

It is doubtful that the cited ECtHR jurisprudence supports an independent right to victim participation at the pre-trial stage as proposed by PTC I in light of its teleological interpretation of the ICC Statute. PTC I's decision fails to explore how *Berger* and *Perez*, two cases revolving around the specifics of civil party rights in the French national criminal justice system, can give rise to an international human right to victim participation at the ICC. The additional ECtHR jurisprudence cited also does not appear to articulate a human right to independent victim participation in general and to victim participation at the pre-trial stage in particular based on Article 6(1) of the ECHR or any other article of the Convention.

This chapter therefore addressed the question as to why PTC I cited numerous ECtHR cases whose overall persuasiveness for the interpretation of Article 68(3) of the Rome Statute remains questionable. It suggested that perhaps PTC I relied on said cases in an attempt to add validity and authority to its decision and to avoid subsequent criticism by referencing Strasbourg jurisprudence, which enjoys universal legitimacy.

Where an international court relies on jurisprudence from the ECtHR or another human rights court in an attempt to add validity to its decision and perhaps to deflect subsequent criticism rather than to endorse the legal reasoning of said court, it may be more appropriate to speak of a self-fertilisation than of a cross-fertilisation practice. Ultimately, it is important to ensure that the cross-fertilisation approach does not turn into a meaningless exercise potentially masking other underlying considerations for decision-making rather than furthering inter-judicial dialogue. Such an approach could do more harm than good to international human rights law.

Index of Subjects

Printed in the United States
By Bookmasters